THE COMPLETE STORY

Sydney Herbert Allard, 1910–66

THE COMPLETE STORY

ALAN ALLARD AND LANCE COLE

THE CROWOOD PRESS

First published in 2020 by
The Crowood Press Ltd
Ramsbury, Marlborough
Wiltshire SN8 2HR

enquiries@crowood.com

www.crowood.com

British Library Cataloguing-in-Publication Data
A catalogue record for this book is available from the British Library.

ISBN 978 1 78500 559 6

Photographic Acknowledgements
Black and white period photographs are taken from the Allard family archives and former Allard Motor Company archives. Where possible relevant copyright has been researched and cited. Every effort has been made to source and credit the original photographer where possible. Other black and white and colour photographs have kindly been supplied by the Allard family, Allard Owners Club, Allard Register, AOC club members, and: L. Cole, S. Grant R. Gunn, M. Herman, A. Picariello, C. Warnes. Main colour photos on pages: front cover, 16, 18, 24, 67. 68, 73, 74, 75, 78, 79, 80, 85, 88, 93, 97, 197, 198, 199, 200, 203, 205, 208, 209, 210 and 212 are by co-author Lance Cole.

Typeset by Jean Cussons Typesetting, Diss, Norfolk
Cover design by Maggie Mellett
Printed and bound in India by Replika Press Pvt. Ltd.

CONTENTS

Acknowledgements 6

Preface 7

Introduction: An Unorthodox Orthodoxy 9

CHAPTER 1 THE EARLY DAYS OF ALLARD 19

CHAPTER 2 ALLARD SPECIALS AND EARLY IDEAS, 1930–39 29

CHAPTER 3 THE ALLARD MOTOR COMPANY, 1946–66:
MAKING THE CARS 47

CHAPTER 4 THE CARS: MODEL BY MODEL 67

CHAPTER 5 ALLARD IN MOTOR SPORT, 1946–66 107

CHAPTER 6 ALLARD AND DRAGSTERS 145

CHAPTER 7 ALLARD IN THE USA 161

CHAPTER 8 THE ALLARD OWNERS CLUB (AOC) 193

CHAPTER 9 ALLARD DIVERSIFIES 215

CHAPTER 10 ALLARD SPORTS CARS – RESTORATION AND REVIVAL 223

References and Bibliography 230

Appendix I The Allard Specials 1936–1946 231

Appendix II Allard JI (Competition) Racing Car Specials
1946–1948 232

Appendix III Allard JR Sports Racing Car Chassis
Numbers 3401–3408 233

Appendix IV Palm Beach Mk 2 235

Aooendix V Allard Car Production 236

Index 237

ACKNOWLEDGEMENTS

FIRSTLY, I WOULD LIKE TO GIVE my heartfelt thanks to my wife Lynda, for the endless hours spent typing my text, filing and saving on the computer, then having to make revisions to the draft on several occasions.

It goes without saying that a book of this nature, which covers such a wide range of motoring activities, spread over nearly a hundred years, needed much time and research from both Lance and I.

I thank the following people for the advice, information, text and photos supplied. If we have inadvertently missed out anyone, please accept my apologies.

Jesse Alexander; Darell Allard; Gavin Allard; Lloyd Allard; Nick Battersby; Bob Bull; Bob Francis; Walter Grodd; Mel Herman; Kerry Horan; Dave Hooper; Matt Howell; Dudley Hume; Mike Knapman; Rob Mackie; David Moseley; John Peskett; Andy Picariello; Chris Pring; Des Sowerby; Brian Taylor; Jim & Sheila Tiller; Ted Walker; Colin Warnes. Library pictures: Revs Institute; LAT Images.

Alan Allard

PREFACE

MY FATHER SYDNEY was never a nine-to-five worka-day man, nor was he to be seen getting involved with my mother in the daily household family chores. Mainly, during my early childhood years, I can recall him scribbling away making notes and sketches, with his briefcase alongside, seated in his armchair by the fireside. A mystifying memory of his habit of always blowing into his shoes before putting them on made my enquiring child's mind ask why: his reply was 'there might be a mouse in my shoe!'

Being sent to boarding school at around eight years old was challenging for me, only being reunited with my sisters and parents at the end of term time. It was during this period 1948–54 that my father's business and motor sport activities were at their most intense.

During these years he was unable to share holiday trips to the South of France, where we rented a villa for three

Sydney with Eleanor just after Sydney won the Monte Carlo Rally, 1952. Press coverage was huge.

Sydney and Eleanor with Alan, aged nine, in the paddock at Prescott hill climb, 1949. Sydney went on to win the British Hill Climb Championship that year in his Steyr Allard.

Sydney and Eleanor posing in front of their home 'Karibu', near Esher, Surrey, in 1951, with the 'M' Type Allards that they both drove in the Monte Carlo Rally.

weeks. My mother Eleanor (who we always called Mumma), with the support of her sister Hilda, had no problem driving five children 850 miles in the Allard Safari estate down to Cannes. Mumma, in fact, was a confident driver in her younger years and with Sydney's encouragement took part in many events: Brighton Speed Trials, various hill climbs and rallies, even competing twice in the Monte Carlo Rally with her sisters. In later years, however, she devoted herself to her lifelong interest in gardening, indeed a hobby that both my sisters and I enjoy today – all in our seventies!

From around 1955 onwards, when my father was doing far less motor sport, he drove us on a grand tour in the Allard Safari to Denmark, Sweden, Finland and Norway. He loved to go fishing, a complete contrast to his exhilarating racing days. He found remote spots and we often caught fish for our supper. The task of baiting the hook or gutting the fish fell to me: my fearless fast-driving father couldn't handle worms!

He had a strong, quite intense personality and spoke quickly. He was a generous, fair-minded man with a sense of humour and liked a bit of fun. I can remember my sisters and I, probably aged between six and ten, tussling with him, trying to bring the big man down.

He had many motor sport crashes through his racing career, some where he could have suffered serious injury and even death, but as far as I know, miraculously, he never once broke a bone! Perhaps the most serious non-racing incident occurred on holiday in Sweden. When working on the Allard Safari estate car exhaust, the car partially slipped off the jack and, although he had a wheel and tyre underneath for safety, the heavy car came down and pinned his head between the ground and chassis rail. I don't know to this day how I managed, but I was able to lift the car just enough to release his head and he only suffered a minor cut.

With the help of Ted Flint, the carpenter from the works, he built a model railway set that travelled all around the large attic at our house in Esher. I helped him build up the track. Another interest of his was stamp collecting (a far cry from racing) and later he became a committee member for the Railway Conversion League (the conversion of abandoned railway lines into roads).

During all the years spent with my father, I never once heard him swear or have a heated argument with anyone, including at home with the family. In later years, however, there was one occasion when we were doing a recce for the Monte Carlo Rally. I was a young lad, with special permission to have leave from school, sitting in the back seat, watching and listening. Tom Lush was navigating and got it all wrong. Poor Tom received a tongue lashing then, but still no swear words! I can imagine that long-suffering Tom must have gone through this scenario on other occasions during the many times he was navigating for my father.

In his approach to life he always conveyed a sense of optimism. I never saw him depressed or grumpy. He had an air of authority about him as the boss, so much so that he could motivate people to do a particular errand or job, including friends or family, without seemingly having given any specific instructions! Indeed, they might find themselves doing a task that they may not have wanted to do. His saying, 'why have a dog and bark yourself', comes to mind.

Every year from 1954 to 1959 we had a three-week touring holiday to the 'Continent' of Europe. Often it felt as if we were on a long-distance rally, often attempting to get to remote places along routes where others feared to go.

The May sisters, Edna, Hilda and Eleanor, with children (from left) Alan, Simon, John , Sally, Marion and Bill, about to set off on holiday to the south of France , the in the Allard Safari, April 1952.

The Queen Mother and Princess Margaret admiring the Allard Palm Beach on the Allard stand at the Earls Court Motor Show, 1956.

In 1957 and 1958 we had a Ford Thames van converted to a motorhome. Disappointed with the performance of the heavily laden vehicle the previous year, father decided that it had to have more hill-climbing performance, so he had a Shorrock supercharger and front wheel disc brakes specially fitted. Supercharging a Ford van just for holiday driving – who but my father would have done this in 1958!

Away from family life and the holiday escapades, he was a motor sport competitor at heart, taking part in an amazing range of motor sport events, mostly in cars carrying his own name – mud plugging trials, sand racing, Brooklands, sprints, hill climbs, autocross, rallying, circuit racing, drag racing – the list seemed endless.

Sadly, still with so much ambition, his life was cut short after losing a six-month battle with cancer. He died on 12 April 1966 at the relatively young age of fifty-six.

Such was his continued optimism and drive that, even when lying ill in bed, he insisted that Tom Lush put in his entry for the January 1966 Monte Carlo Rally.

Had he been fortunate to survive another twenty-five years, I wonder just how many more challenges he would have had a go at.

Compiling and writing this Allard story, together with Lance, has been a great experience as we revealed a treasure trove of memories concerning the motor sport activities of Allard cars and the man whose determination and tenacity were behind them all. His contribution to the motor sports arena will never be forgotten.

Alan Allard

INTRODUCTION:

Sydney with Jim Mac, his trusty mechanic, in J2X at the Le Mans 24 Hour Race.

AN UNORTHODOX ORTHODOXY

INTRODUCTION: AN UNORTHODOX ORTHODOXY

ALLARD OCCUPIES AN INTRIGUING PLACE in the history of British motoring and a vital ranking in motor sport's story. Today some remember Allard fondly as a brand from a time when single-minded entrepreneurs, garagistes and men in sheds created sporting cars for competitive use in motor sport specifics, such as hill climbs, trials, rallies and races. For others, Allard evokes a post-war era when powerful cars built in low numbers could be purchased directly from the factory to varying specifications and also used on a daily basis, as well as campaigned in the calendar of racing events. Allards were also set into a front-line competitive context in America, where the fame of the brand and its creator reached from Watkins Glen to high-society owners.

Let's not forget that it was one man, Sydney Allard, who built Britain's first true dragster and launched the American sport of drag racing in a British context. We might wonder then why so many people have never heard of Allard? Many have, of course, but there is a 'gap' even among motoring enthusiasts.

Allard means different things to different people, yet one thing is constant: Sydney Allard, his band of men and the cars that bore his name shone on the national and world stages to a degree that was significant in the tide of automotive affairs. Allard expert, restorer and serial Allard owner John Peskett sums it up very accurately: 'For a brief period, Allard really was the one of the top motor sport names in the world.'

This is no idle boast. It is a very real truth that might be hard to grasp more than sixty years since it was headline news, but it is true. Sydney Allard went from 'backyard built' trials specials to production cars and dragsters via the international stage and its winners' podiums.

At Le Mans in 1950 Allard was third overall and Sydney himself had led in a car bearing his own name. So Allard's name was splashed all over the newspapers for all the right reasons. Sydney, his exploits and latterly his cars had a national and overseas profile in big headlines. An Allard J2X model was featured in the famed *Eagle* magazine on 13 June 1952. It was Sydney Allard who beat Stirling Moss in the Monte Carlo Rally. It was Sydney who overtook Fangio (in a Cooper-Bristol) in the Chichester Cup at Goodwood – Fangio overtaken by a bespectacled gent in a tweed jacket and a tie!

As the respected writer and commentator Simon Taylor said in *Classic and Sports Car* in 1996: 'The Monte Carlo Rally caught the attention of the British public every year.

British winners became heroes and Allard in 1952 was the biggest hero of all.'

The unique Steyr Allard became the 1949 Hill Climb Champion with hill records and many wins. This factory publicity shot shows some of the employees gathered behind the trophies and the car.

Sydney attempted to drive his Allard Special CLK 5 to the top of Scotland's highest mountain, Ben Nevis, but failed when the car rolled off the track.

Surely the fact that Sydney was more of a 'normal' bloke than most upper-crust or well-heeled drivers of the era, who worked on and drove his own race cars, underlines the reason why Sydney was so loved by the British public and press alike. And who else but Sydney would supercharge a Ford Thames van back in 1958?

Simon Taylor also recently pointed out that those who modify their classic Allards are *not* committing sacrilege: 'After all, if it makes the car faster, do it – Sydney would have approved.'

There is of course a point to be made that, given how rare Allards are now and how valuable some have become, we should aim at preserving the original specification, keeping the cars on the road and maintaining the ownership. The days of wiping out absolutely everything in a stripped bare, new-for-old total classic car restoration must be over, since a new old car is not a true old car,

The basic fact, however, is that speed – competitive speed – was what Sydney was focused on from 1928. This remained the case, probably at the cost of much else.

The recent words of Sir Stirling Moss about Sydney to David Hooper, the chief draughtsman at the Allard Motor Company, frame Allard's achievement and the esteem in which he was held: 'I knew Sydney Allard quite well, and competed against him many times in rallies and races. He was a very fast and pretty fearless driver, and also a very nice man.'[1]

Tony Mason, a top rally navigator and a mud-plugger driver, reckoned that Sydney Allard was fearless and the only driver he had ever met who actually liked driving in fog.

Cyril Wick drove Sydney's modified, lightweight J2 and broke the 40 seconds barrier at Shelsley Walsh for the first time in the hill's history. He also beat Jaguar's famed driver Norman Dewis in an Allard versus Jaguar head-to-head at the Brighton Speed Trial. Further proof, then, that Sydney and his Allards were the stars of their day.

We should never perceive Sydney as an 'enthusiast', nor see Allard as a 'cottage-industry', 'kit-car' producer. Whatever the cars' 'parts bin' oddities, Allards were true low-volume production vehicles produced in a professional manner on a form of production line that was typical of its era and context, if not of today's perceptions.

The key fact in Allard's success was that the product defined the brand, not the other way around. It was an added ingredient that Allard the man defined his products. As *Autocar* stated back in the 1950s, the Allard J2 'might be described as the finest sports motorcycle on four wheels ever conceived!' While Donald Healey's marque achieved great success, it was Sydney Allard who beat Healey's Cadillac-powered Silverstone at Le Mans in 1953 and finished

third overall. This helped make him big news in the British motoring world in the 1950s.

In America in the early 1950s Allard was one of the 'big three' British sports car manufacturer names: Jaguar, MG and Allard. Few people know just how close Allard came to doing a vital 1950s US deal with Dodge, or with the Kaiser company to market a glass fibre-bodied Palm Beach Mk 2. American sports car enthusiasts really took Sydney and his cars to their hearts and Allard was so close to a new chapter, yet the company was to be the victim of several circumstances.

Dean Butler, the dedicated American Allardiste, recently summed up Sydney very neatly: 'Sydney Allard was a Californian hot-rodder who happened to live in England!'

After a period of great success on the track and on the road, Allard's star faded as times changed. The larger car manufacturers, notably Allard's rivals, moved into the new late 1950s world of mass production, economies of volume and scale, and expensive design research resources. Smaller British, European and American car brands, all once famous names, died out. In the early 1960s Allard also succumbed as a car maker, although the company and the family have remained involved in engineering and motor sport to the present day.

The era of specialist, hand-built, powerful, separate chassis cars with 'grunt' was passing, even though the likes of the AC Cobra and various American ideas survived for a time in a new automotive world: Carroll Shelby drove, raced and studied Allards long before he created the Anglo-American AC Cobra, a car of similar 'grunt' context. Elements of the Allard designs may also be found in the origins of the Corvette.

Sydney Allard's achievements at the 24 Hours of Le Mans, winning the Monte Carlo Rally and taking the British Hill Climb Championship, as well as selling nearly 2,000 cars to

Sydney Allard receives his Monte Carlo Rally winners trophy from Prince Rainier.

Fearless Sydney 'flying high' in the Steyr Allard at the top of the Rest and be Thankful hill climb, 1949.

customers all over the world, are not completely forgotten. Beyond the world of the Allard enthusiast and the classic car fan, however, such achievements have become obscured by time and are perhaps almost unknown by a younger generation of 'petrol heads' or 'gear heads', as they are termed in the USA.

The Allard cars of our story stem from an age before drive-by-wire digital authoritarianism intervened in our cars, which has largely separated man from the mechanical act of driving. Today the driver of a computerized supercar, enhanced by electronic intervention in its steering, gearbox, suspension, engine management and throttle response, perhaps even with 'fake' exhaust sound piped into the cabin, can park up at a classic car event at a historic venue, such as Prescott, Shelsley Walsh, Bo'ness, Goodwood, Le Mans, Pikes Peak, Pebble Beach, Sebring, Phillip Island, Geelong or Lime Rock, and then watch a real, oily 'car' – as once was defined by that word – being commanded by a man

or woman using physical and mental abilities in a true act of driving. Allard cars and Allard drivers have no place for digital systems and synthetic 'stuff'. They are about the mechanical act of driving.

Many exploits coloured Allard's rich American history across the decades, right from the day Erwin Goldschmidt won the Watkins Glen Grand Prix in an Allard J2 in 1950. Burrell, Carstens, Cole, Duntov, Fogg, Tiley, Shelby, Wacker and Warner are just a few of the illustrious names on the roll call, but how many people know that Cameron Argetsinger, who founded the original Watkins Glen races, owned a 1951 Allard J2? The 1950 Allard J2s were so dominant in America that Ferrari, beaten on the track and to the podium by Allard, had to increase its engine size and create a new more competitive model to fight back and regain its credibility. More recently the *Allard Register* has been at the centre of interest in the USA, and Allard enthusiasts have held a series of 'Gatherings' at race meetings where many have competed.

Wherever you look, Allards were there, then and now.

The Allard and its origins lies in a complex set of circumstances and design characteristics that created the Allard marque, a gestation and lifespan that ranged from about 1928 to 1959. From those years came not just a unique range of cars, but also a record of competition driving and victories that are legends in the annals of motor sport. A modern major car-maker who enjoyed such a record would be splashed across the media backed by a multi-million pound marketing budget. Back about 1950 Sydney Allard and his team just got on with it, earning their place in *Motor Sport* and across the motoring and national media by their results, not by paid placement. And this was against such famous drivers as Stirling Moss, Peter Collins, Carroll Shelby, Briggs Cunningham and Alberto Ascari, and so on down into the club men and the ranks of amateur enthusiasts.

Even after all this time Sydney Allard remains the only man to have competed in and won outright the Monte Carlo Rally in a car of his own design and manufacture. This was in 1952, when he won with Guy Warburton co-driving and navigator Tom Lush, beating Stirling Moss in a works Sunbeam Talbot. He also competed four times at the Le Mans 24 Hours doing the same thing, sometimes driving there in his race car. His best result, third overall in 1950. These were incredible feats for a team who did not boast the resources of major marques such as Ferrari, Alfa Romeo or Jaguar. All of this was achieved in a car of his own design and bearing his own name. When you add in his victories in the 1949 British Hill Climb Championship and many regional events,

Tony Hogg's description in *Road and Track* in July 1966 sums up Sydney Allard's legacy: 'An achievement unique in motor sport, and a tribute to his persistence, ingenuity and resourcefulness.'[2]

The pre-war 'Allard Specials' period saw Sydney on a hectic schedule of national events that included trials, circuit races, rallies, hill climbs and sprints, but this was little compared to the years from 1947 to 1953, when he would spend hours driving to compete at events, all while running the Allard Motor Company and a rapidly growing Ford dealership.

This is not a tale of smoke and mirrors, a brief puff of bold claims followed by bankruptcy after failing to produce more than a single car – a scenario so familiar to motoring observers when someone says that they are going to start making cars. Allard made a total of just under 2,000 cars and for a short period was a big British success. The death of the Allard brand by 1960 was not the result of profligacy or incompetence, but rather the result of difficult decisions amid changing circumstances in a developing marketplace. Yet for a period spanning less than two decades, one man and a band of brothers operating from several south London workshops not only took on the greats, they created a niche marque of unique cars that truly found a place in the nation's affections and wherever Allards competed across the European racing calendar. Allard in America remains a vital story and the marque's place in Australia and South America should not be forgotten.

An essential question must be: what is an Allard? How

Sydney in his new dragster chassis, without its clothes!

Sydney's wife Eleanor, seen here in a J2 at Prescott, was a great asset to Sydney, rallying and racing many of his Allard cars.

1929 – Sydney aged 19 on the start line at the famous pre-war Brooklands banked motor racing track. The three-wheel Morgan was classed as a motorbike. Starting last on handicap, Sydney went on to win, this his first circuit race.

and why did the cars become what they were? Ultimately, we might well ask, how did the once famous tale of Allard and his cars become confined to the world of classic car enthusiasm, consigning a massive public and PR profile of worldwide fame to distant memories? The remembrance of Allard faded in the years after it ceased making cars, but just sixty years ago Allard was a household icon, a great British brand and a major name. Members of the British Royal family were seen on the Allard stand at the Earls Court Motor Show and numerous celebrities owned Allards. Allard had a massive profile and so did Sydney, the driving force.

Both the name of Allard and its recognition as a car brand is now resurgent with the family's launch of cars that are not re-creations, but continuations of Sydney's thinking, through the activities of his son Alan and grandson Lloyd (with his brother Gavin curating the brand's archive). Darell Allard, the son of Sydney's brother Leslie, also figures in today's Allard scene and is a key contributor to maintaining the profile of the cars and the owners' club. Darell's late brother Terry followed in the family tradition as a motor sports man, motorcycles being his thing; he was best known for his scrambling exploits as a top national rider in his youth. All the Allard family, from sons and grandsons to cousins, remain Allardistes.

This, it seems, is a story full of questions. Everyone has heard of the Aston Martin series, Morgans, MGs, Triumphs, Austin Healeys or Jaguars, quintessentially British national icons that rank with the institutions of the Supermarine Spitfire, Hawker Hurricane, Avro Lancaster and the Concorde. And what of Americana and the Shelby AC Cobra, the Ford Mustang and other 'muscle car' delights? What of Italian exotica and racing Maseratis and Ferraris? Yet alongside these legends, there was once a car and a man of perhaps equal fame that captured an essential essence of British design and motor sport: Sydney Allard was that famous, and so were his cars.

Just under 2,000 cars sold on the global stage was a huge achievement for any small company, let alone a post-war 'start-up' brand whose competition success, and the public profile that it inspired, was mostly down to the founder himself.

Two decades ago about 700 Allards, from wrecks to restored cars, were known to survive, but recent research by ex-Allard employee David Hooper and the Allard Owners Club suggests that 507 Allards are known to remain in one piece, scattered across the globe in various states of splendour or disrepair. It is possible that the remains of another ten, twenty or perhaps fifty may exist worldwide. Two J2s, for example, were recently discovered under a bush in America as 'yard finds': there could be more.

The prices that some Allard models have achieved have been interesting, up to about £500,000, yet others can be had for well under £50,000. Overall many Allard prices have been rising and interest remains gratifyingly strong, at least among dedicated Allardistes. Even Wayne Carini, renowned classic car restorer and star of his own TV series *Chasing Classic Cars*, has purchased an Allard for his personal pleasure: Bill Bauder's J2X. Allards still race during the Monterey car week and at other annual gatherings, proving that interest in Allards in America continues to this day.

Allard's claim to be 'Britain's premier competition car'

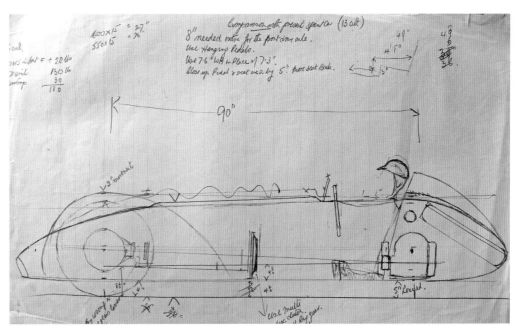

One of Sydney's unseen sketches for a 1950s sports car development. He was always sketching and planning new cars, exploring new variations using existing, proven and cost-effective parts.

The impressive engine in Chris Pring's J2.

was based on the output from a number of small works sites in south London, not the better-known locations such as Brooklands, Feltham, Malvern, Coventry or Bristol. But Allard's reputation was significant: we should not forget that by 1948 Allard was producing between eight and ten cars a week, a significant figure for a small-scale car manufacturer, let alone one in cash-strapped, ration-book Britain. In fact the largest number of Allards produced in one month was forty-five in July 1948: two cars a day.

In its heyday the Allard Motor Company was on its way to becoming a British icon with a celebrity client list that modern marketing would have loved. We can safely assume that nothing could have been further from Sydney's intentions: customers were customers, and racing was racing! And racing was Sydney's priority, probably at the expense of other elements in his life.

We should not forget that the likes of Carroll Shelby and Tom Cole raced Allards, and that Steve McQueen owned one. A gathering of assorted Allards at Watkins Glen became a regular event, such was the allure of Sydney Allard's cars. A 7-litre Chrysler 'Firepower' engine in an Allard J2 lightweight must have been a deeply moving sight and a great experience from the driving seat.

This iconic ex-Desmond Titterington J2 spent many years in India. It has been beautifully restored with Ardun OHV heads on the Ford V8 and is owned by AOC news magazine editor Chris Pring.

This classic eye-catching American Allard K2 belongs to Andy Picariello, Allard Owners Club Vice President, who has long been associated with the promotion of the Allard legend in the USA.

Several major commentators and writers on motor sport and the wider motoring world have been Allard fans, including Douglas Blain, Tony Dron and Simon Taylor. Today there is a healthy and growing worldwide interest in Allard, backed by an enthusiastic owners club, which was founded in 1951 with Sydney's personal support. The *Allard Register* has helped maintain Allard's reputation in the USA as something of an icon among those in the know, with a particular emphasis on the J2, J2X, K2, K3 and JR models. The resurgence of Allard at club level proves that true, race-winning design, performance and individuality never go out of fashion.

Allard enthusiasts, sometimes known as 'Allardistes', have strong opinions about which model is the best, or perhaps the 'purest' Allard car when it comes to reflecting its pro-genitor's ethos.

Chris Pring, owner of the ex-Titterington Allard J2 and current editor of the Allard Owners Club magazine, frames an essential issue:

The Allard Motor Company was a star that shone brightly for a handful of years in the late 1940s, early 1950s. It is fair to say the enthusiasts and motoring press couldn't get enough. But, like many others before and since, that star has faded and been eclipsed by better resourced operations, some of which survive as the giants of today. There is no doubt that Sydney Allard left a fantastic legacy but each generation of the Allard community has a challenge: how do we educate them in matters Allard? Simple: race them, drive them, show them, share them, write and talk about them. Do that often and the Allard star will keep its glow.

This book is the first major work on Allard for several decades and the only story co-written by a member of the Allard family. The rightly respected books by Tom Lush and David Kinsella are long out of print and there is a place for a new perspective on the Allard story. It is hoped that this book will help to draw in a wider and younger audience to the achievements and exploits of Sydney Allard. Times may have changed, but the passion for cars has not.

While the book will cover the main outline described in the earlier narratives of the Allard history, it will broaden out to encompass an even wider range of Allard designs and activities. Sydney's family have told it how it was. From the mid-1920s to the present day, which has brought a new Allard family-built car, the intention is to present a commentary of interest to the classic car world, enthusiasts, drivers and racers of Allard cars.

This new Allard book covers old themes from new angles, with previously unpublished content and a fresh perspective provided by Sydney's son Alan Allard, who has spent a lifetime engineering, driving, racing and fettling cars, and by Lance Cole, designer, motoring writer and Allard enthusiast. Together they offer not just an up-to-date commentary, but a new reference point for a new generation. The narrative is therefore in joint hands, with Alan's personal recollections adding another dimension to the tale. Sydney's grandsons, Lloyd and Gavin, have also added their thoughts, as have Mike Knapman and Andy

Picariello at the AOC and Colin Warnes at the *Allard Register* – all true Allardistes who deserve due credit and thanks.

The authors hope this text leaves a reference point for Allardistes, enthusiasts, 'mud-pluggers', 'tail waggers', 'slime stormers' and new converts or discoverers of the brand, and that all readers will find old and new themes, ranging from engineering and design to motor sport, and across every aspect of the inspiring story of Allard. How one man and a handful of helpers created a prominent British brand is the stuff of legend. It is a great British tale, a part of automotive history that should not be forgotten.

Sincere acknowledgement must go to the Allard Owners Club, the *Allard Register* and the many Allardistes who have allowed important material to be cited.

So here is the story of how Sydney went from overalls to overcoat, but always kept his head under the bonnet. The authors hope that, just like the cars, this tale reflects the fun to be had in an Allard and leaves you an admirer of the marque and the man who made it.

**Alan Allard and
Lance Cole**

**Alan and Lloyd Allard in the Palm Beach Mk 2 that they restored in 2016
as a step towards the revival of the Allard car marque.**

16 May 1936 – Sydney on the banking at Brooklands in his first Allard Special CLK5.

| CHAPTER 1 | # THE EARLY DAYS OF ALLARD |

SYDNEY HERBERT ALLARD was born on 10 June 1910 in Streatham, southwest London. He was the second of five children, his elder brother being John Arthur Francis, known as 'Jack'. After Sydney there came two twin brothers, Dennis and Leslie, followed by the youngest Allard, Mary, the only girl. All the boys were educated at Ardingly College in Sussex. The unusual name 'Allard' may have Dutch or Flemish origins: it can still be found in telephone directories in the Netherlands, Belgium and France as Allard or its variant, Allaert.

Their father, Arthur William Allard, was a director of Allard and Saunders Ltd, and a successful master builder and property owner, who was consulted by the architects during the building of Guildford Cathedral. The flats that Arthur built in the 1930s at Millbrooke Court on Keswick Road, Putney, however, were bombed by the Luftwaffe during the Second World War.

Unlike some of the aspiring British car manufacturers and racers of that era, the young Sydney did not come from a privileged family, as the Allard family were not from the

upper crust or old money. Instead they came from farming stock and for several generations had been agricultural workers based at Upper Deverill in the beautiful Wylye valley in Wiltshire, between Warminster and Mere. The decline in agriculture in the late Victorian era, following on from the effects of the war in the Crimea and social change, saw the Allard family move to London to seek more secure employment. Sydney's father had trained as a slate layer and general builder before he used his intellect to establish his own small business. So the Allards knew about hard graft, even if they would go on to live a comfortable post-Edwardian existence with a view over Wandsworth Common.

At the time of his birth the family lived at 25 West Side, Wandsworth Common, but Sydney was to grow up in a house named 'Uplands' in Leigham Court Road, Streatham. The 1911 Census shows that also living there were a cousin named Phillip, aged 16, and a domestic servant called Lizzie Cole. Arthur Allard's Allard's job was stated as 'Slate Trade'; in another entry he is given as a 'Surveyor'.

Sydney Herbert Allard was tall and sturdy. As well as wearing horn-rimmed spectacles, he had a damaged right eye as a result of a boyhood injury sustained by an airgun pellet fired in a mock fight by his brother Dennis. Yet the eye problem never seemed to affect his abilities and Sydney was undoubtedly a talented driver. This was the era of shirt-sleeved drivers and no seat belts. On several occasions in later years Sydney was even seen racing in a sports jacket and tie, but he was not a toff, a playboy or, in any sense, a man 'on the make'. He simply thought about cars, drew cars, chopped up cars and welded them back together again until one day he created a car of his own conception. From there came the brand.

Sydney's brothers were avid motorcycle enthusiasts who shared the family's wheeled obsession. William Boddy, Editor of *Motor Sport*, who was a big Allard fan, described Sydney and his brothers as 'pretty wild, even as youngsters go'. Dennis Allard, who had survived a major accident on his Brough Superior when he was just 21, was sadly killed in a cycling accident on his way to the Brighton Speed Trial in the 1950s. His twin, Leslie, would have an interest in both two- and four-wheeled devices.

Sydney's boyhood was surrounded by younger brothers who fettled and tweaked their motorcycles. Sydney learned to ride on a Francis-Barnett and moved on to a Douglas with a flat-twin engine. He learned to drive at the age of 16, soon after leaving Ardingly College. He decided not to join the family building business, and instead started work in a garage, F.W. Lucas. Evening courses in engineering at Battersea Polytechnic enabled him to become accredited with the Institute of Engineers. Beginning as a fitters mate, earning

In the early 1930s, just before building his first Allard Special CLK 5, Sydney campaigned a Ford TT in trials events. The TT had been part of a Ford-supported team effort prior to sale.

a few shillings a week, Sydney worked his way up through hands-on experience as a mechanical engineer. Admittedly there was family money and a good education behind him, but his father was not keen on his son's sporting aspirations in the risky new world of cars. Sydney was soon an active member of local car and motorcycle clubs.

All the members of the family enjoyed motorcycle trips and days out in the family Ford, frequently to Sussex. This was where Sydney's 'Clubman' and 'Trials' driving experiences began. Jack's belt-driven Douglas motorcycle was handed down to Sydney and this gave him his first taste of fiddling with greasy mechanical devices that needed servicing and repairing. A Morgan three-wheeler that had been tweaked in various ways by the brothers was also handed down by Jack.

Arthur Allard soon accepted that his second son was not going to join the family building firm, but it was clearly a father's duty to provide guidance and support. This was manifested when Arthur bought his way into a business and then encouraged the young Sydney as he turned it into a viable motor business. His son's developing love of things wheeled and noisy was funded and controlled by an older and wiser business partner, Alf Brisco (spelled without an 'e', according to the Adlards Motor Company letterhead). Hard graft was required, but Sydney also relied on his father's helping hand. The small garage that sowed the seed of Allardism was located in Keswick Road, Putney. By a strange coincidence, the trading name of the business purchased for Sydney was R. Adlard. This was soon rejigged as the trading entity Adlards Motors, and the unintended similarity of the owner and company name was to cause some later confusion. The Allard family eventually lived almost 'over the shop' in a block of flats with roof gardens and views over London that Arthur Allard had built on the site of the original Adlards premises, with its garage on the ground floor.

Sydney repaired, modified and sold cars from the Adlards garage under the tutelage of Mr Brisco. The new enterprise was a Limited Company and the named officials were Sydney, Alfred Brisco and, curiously, Sydney's mother Cecilia. The Adlards Motor Company was officially inaugurated on 5 April 1930. Two important events that took place by 1934 were the appointment of Reginald 'Reg' Canham to the company and the award of a dealership franchise by the Ford Motor Company of England. The financial security and personal confidence that this brought enabled Sydney to undertake a flourishing amateur career away from the garage, where he could store his various mechanical projects and hope that his father did not ask too many questions. Not yet twenty-five, the essential construct of Sydney's personality and direction was now set. His early interest in mechani-

cal devices had been concentrated on motocycles. When he was twelve years old, for example, he was interested in Francis-Barnett motorcycles and the family still has a scrapbook full of cuttings about them.

The Streatham and District Motorcycle Club was also important on the local scene. Cars were also popular in this part of south London and Sydney was immersed in a world of emerging wheeled opportunity in a new age of growing mass motoring.

Bill Boddy later claimed that it was he who persuaded Sydney to form the Ford Enthusiasts Club in 1938. After the war he was a passenger when an Allard driven by Sydney turned over, but fortunately he was thrown clear. Boddy lived until he was 98 and was much loved by the Allard Owners Club.

Sydney was not an egotistical extrovert, but he was a confident speaker who enjoyed social gatherings and often gave talks to motor clubs and other groups in later years. His sister Mary, who served as Company Secretary for his ventures, recently told the Allard Owners Club that she thought Sydney was the one of the brothers who 'tried to be in charge', and that he 'had a great deal of charm and people liked him, helped him'. Because of that he could 'get around anybody. Even if people did not like him in business, they thought he was a damn good bloke! Everything came easy to him. Everyone rushed to help Sydney.'

Mary's first husband was Eddie McDowell, who worked for Allards as purchasing manager. Three years after his untimely death she remarried Sydney's brother in-law Alan May in 1959. Prior to that Mary had been closely involved in running Allards, including organizing Sydney's vital trip to New York to set up the Allard Motor Company Inc., New York (USA).

Her nephew Darell described Mary as an outspoken character in his 2017 published tribute to her:

The first four-wheeled car was a one-off 'special' modified Morgan. It was emphatically not a fully fledged 'Allard Special'. Sydney carried out extensive work on his Morgan to convert it from three wheels to four in a vain attempt to make it more suitable for trialling.

ALLARD & CO

Intriguingly, Allard as we know it was the second British carmaker called Allard. The unrelated Allard & Co started production of motorized tricycles of a distinctly 'Benz' design in Coventry in 1899. The company also produced an air-cooled 3hp car. By 1902 this short-lived early 'Allard' company had merged with the Rex Company, which was itself extinct by 1914. There is no link between the Coventry company and Sydney's.

She did not always agree with anecdotes I heard from other members of the family, mainly my father Leslie. Even at the age of 94, when I showed her a photo of a P1, which Sydney was known to have driven, parked outside Dralda House in Putney, I was told in no uncertain terms that this was 'her car', which he used to 'borrow'!

Mary clearly contributed to the day-to-day running of Allard and dealt with payments, supplies, orders and all sorts of company affairs. It must have been interesting to see the interaction between Mary and Sydney, two strong characters. Sydney was a driven personality who inspired other people to work for him, backed by Allard family money.

Sydney's training in mechanical matters and formal engineering studies show he was not an amateur who stumbled upon his cars' form and function through step-by-step 'episodes', but we can say that he used his experiments to create a range of curiously diverse cars. Some of Allard's later issues, particularly the diverse model range in the 1950s, which was expensive to manufacture, and Sydney's inability to develop his car designs without being sidetracked, may have been down to this working method.

The roots of Sydney's production cars lay in his early 1930s 'Allard Specials' designed to compete in Trials events, which were a popular combination at that time of road, rally and off-road trialling exploits. Elements of these were combined with their predecessor, Sydney's Morgan three-wheeler, modified to take a fourth wheel and hand built with revised mechanicals and suspension. Based on his early experiment with the Morgan, Sydney built a Ford 'flat-head' side-valve V8-powered Special, giving a high power-to-weight ratio with consequent rapid acceleration, and swathed in an aluminium body. Allard's Trials cars were relatively low-geared, high-powered and rear-driven, resulting in the 'Tailwagger'

team sobriquet, since the oversteering rear ends were renowned for swinging out on mud and gravel, and being caught with armfuls of opposite lock.

During the Second World War Adlards Motors was turned over to repairing military vehicles, but within a year of the end of hostilities Sydney Allard was a carmaker, an option he had been thinking about for some time. Uniquely, Allard was ahead of the social curve since in many ways his thoughts and marketing were a decade ahead of the times. The imminent breaking down of social and class barriers was in one sense reflected by the motor industry in the rise of classless design and new money to pay for exotic or powerful cars, both 'Specials' and post-war sportsters.

Yet Allard's true, car-creating roots lay in the Specials he produced in the heady pre-war days. Eleven of these were built at that time, plus one after 1939. It was these designs that coalesced into the first Allard roadsters of 1946.

Allard's competition cars relied little on seat belts, roll cages, fire-eater systems or bodywork protection. Only the strength of the underpinning chassis and metal shell offered safety. The bespectacled Sydney, only sometimes wearing a hard hat and doing without a seat belt or roll-cage, would win event after event, while running his company at the same time. He darted about all over the place to compete in events on an almost inconceivable schedule. In a single month he would think nothing of competing in Italy, France, Jersey, the Isle of Man and Northern Ireland, often driving to and from the events in his race car. On other occasions the competition cars were transported in the Allard team transporter by Jim McCallan, Tom Lush or others. Week in and weekend out Sydney would compete in races at Goodwood, Silverstone, Shelsley Walsh, Prescott, Bo'ness and at various regional Trials. He kept overalls and personal cleaning kit in his office just in case he was needed down on the factory floor to do some manual labour. The works and competition schedule was hectic and fatiguing, and his workaholic behaviour and high stress levels may have contributed to the stomach cancer that eventually killed him at the early age of 56.

Allard was a brave man in an age when death was commonplace in motor sport. He survived a horrific, mass pile-up on the Isle of Man in the Empire Trophy in 1951, and it was only by chance that both Sydney and his wife Eleanor escaped a major roll-over crash. Many commentators remarked on Sydney's personal bravery and wondered how he had avoided being badly injured or killed in a series of off-road excursions, including several dramatic escapes in Europe. His co-driver Tom Lush was quite open about the nature of Sydney's driving style: determined, fast and, it seems, occasionally a bit furious.[3]

THE ETHOS OF ALLARD

Allard cars are unsung heroes of an age long gone. What was their magic ingredient? What, how and why did Allards develop an ethos and a style, a brand and a marque that was world famous for a few years before fading into a motoring footnote?

Sydney Allard was not a motor-industry boss somehow intent on mass production, neither was he looking for celebrity stardom. He was interested in opportunities to race, rally and make the most of any circumstance, rather than pursuing some grand plan to build and sell cars and carve a niche. This was carried out with a focused dedication lightened by a strong sense of humour that came to the fore in his relationships with his family and factory team members. While approachable, he was also 'the boss' and it seems he could be forceful and dominant, which should hardly be a surprise in one who achieved so much with so little.

In 1936 Sydney married Eleanor May, whose family's principal business was repairing and restoring Rolls-Royce cars from large premises in south London. Eleanor later drove Allard cars in competitive events. Eleanor's brothers, Norman and Alan May, owned Southern Motors in Park Hill, Clapham, which later became the head offices of the Allard Motor Company. Alan May drove a very powerful Vauxhall 30/98 in which he beat Stirling Moss at the Brighton Speed Trials in 1948 and in the following year he was Sydney's co-driver in the 1949 Monte Carlo Rally in an M Type.

The record shows that Sydney Allard was a competitive driver with a winning record in British championships and major events. He was rarely off the podium and was a pure enthusiast who knew about powerful and 'hairy' rear-driven cars, such as his very fast modified V8s. This required a determined streak, but he also needed to keep making money. Fortunes could be lost very quickly in car racing in the 1950s, let alone in low-volume design and production. In fact, seemingly a touch obsessed with competition driving, Sydney employed salesmen and engineers to get on with creating and marketing the cars, led in the 1950s by H.J.A. 'Dave' Davis.

The marketing driving force behind Alllard was co-director Reg Canham and a close-knit group that helped Sydney build and frame his brand. It was Tom Cole in America who first suggested, in March and April 1950, fitting the recently announced Cadillac V8 to an Allard, although a vital paper trail of evidence indicates that a customer, Frederick Gibbs, seems to have come up with the same idea almost simultaneously.

It took a long list of names to help develop Allard from its roots, based on the garage and premises of the confusingly named Adlards Motors. The many members of the Allard staff team whose deeds are described here included Reg Canham, Tom Lush, Jim McCallan, Eddie McDowell, Jimmy Minnion, Dave Davis, Jack Jackman, Sam Whittingham, Bill Tylee, David Hooper and Dudley Hume.

The notion that Sydney was not bothered by the need for publicity is disproved by his appointment of Jack. R. Bullen as a resident Allard Publicity Manager in 1949, based at the 24/28 Clapham High Street offices. Sydney outlined the company's intentions in a 1952 statement: 'The aims of the Allard Motor Company are, as they have always been, to produce high-performance cars and to sell them at the lowest possible price consistent with limited and specialist production.'

These cars were not exclusive exotica for the raffish boulevard poseur, but 'proper' sports cars cast entirely in their own mould. Many of the cars, however, were more tourer than two-seat racer. They employed both off-the-shelf parts, mostly of Ford provenance, and bespoke items, but everything was brought together to meet a formula defined by Sydney. This was well before the rise of Healey as a British sporting marque of distinct identity. Sydney Allard knew that a product defines a brand, not the other way around. His cars were therefore the measure by which he wished to be judged. Perhaps only the British Railton Company, which used Hudson-derived parts in their 1930s sports cars, could be cited as similar to the Allard approach. Other cars contemporary with Allard's early era included the supercharged Vauxhall Villiers, based on a 1920s TT chassis that was drastically modified by Raymond Mays and Amherst Villiers, just as Allard would do with his cars.

Sydney Allard said that his competition cars were 'tailored'. This was true, but it might also be a euphemism for every car being different according to what parts were on the shelf! This, to some degree, also applied to his road cars. The story of the Allard car began in somewhat curious circumstances. There were no known engineering or mechanical antecedents in Sydney's story, but Sydney and his brothers were born into an age that may be viewed as the late dawn of the motorcar and motor sport.

FIRST THOUGHTS, 1910–30

From early boyhood Sydney Allard was an engineering enthusiast. He was modifying cars to incorporate his own engineering ideas before his twenty-fifth birthday, and it was not long before he created new configurations using other manufacturers' parts.

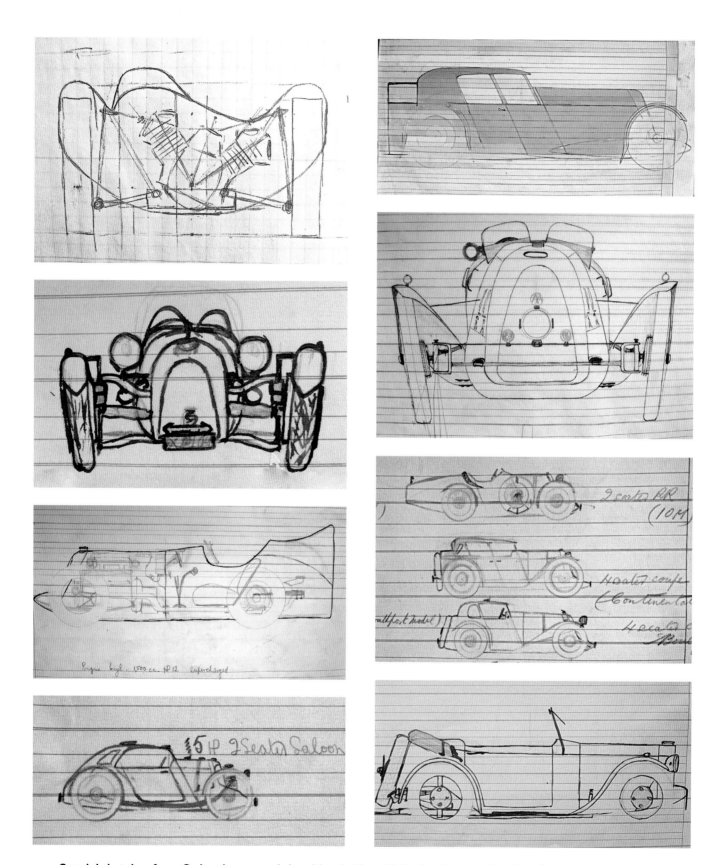

Special sketches from Sydney's personal sketchbook. Unpublished and unseen for decades, these design ideas from Sydney's pen show just how busy his brain was, always thinking of the next project. Styling, airflow and marketing are all obvious ingredients that challenge any ideas that Sydney was not interested in such matters.

He chronicled his early interest in a scrapbook of car reports, tests, brochures and information that spanned cycle cars, light cars and big beasts. This information fed his mind and his own car design ideas expressed in early sketches and specifications that showed he was thinking of cars in a serious vein, not just a hobby. These led to his first modifications to existing cars and then the true, home-built 'Specials' from 1936. We should not forget that Sydney won his first competitive entry on the banked outer circuit at Brooklands in 1929 in a Morgan.

Sydney Allard did not have an automotive inheritance and had access to few engineering, design, styling or testing resources, but he managed to break into a world that would soon be littered with names like AC, Aston Martin, Frazer Nash, Riley, MG and even the emergent Jaguar. The story of how a very determined man took on and defeated such established names with far greater resources is one of astounding achievement that can be followed in detail because he kept all his studies, and these have been preserved by the Allard family.

Sydney Allard did not dream of selling out to a major motor manufacturer or have any delusions about a 'celebrity' lifestyle. The family are certain that he knew who he was and that's the way he stayed. Indeed, as Sydney often stated, he choose his employees for their enthusiasm and loyalty. He did not have a Board stuffed with directors or need to satisfy the demands of shareholders relying on vast profits made at the workers' expense: 'As a family concern, we have no necessity to constantly aim at increased turnover and profits in order to satisfy shareholders whose natural interest is dividends rather than motorcars.'[4]

Sydney was instrumental in the development of British motor sport. He became Chairman of the British Automobile Racing Club (BARC) and was a key figure in the creation of the Thruxton circuit from its origins as an airfield: a bend there is named 'Allard' in recognition of his work. His fame at Prescott hill climb was also significant and is marked by a particular point on the hill being known as 'Allards Gap'. Sydney was 'the guvnor' to those that knew him well, but he built up a close-knit team of trusted people to run both the business and competitive activities. One who stands out from these is Tom Lush, who was alongside Sydney in many of his exploits. Lush seems to have been able to perform a variety of multi-disciplinary roles and served as Sydney's right-hand man from 1946 to 1966, providing a detailed diary of these events in his book *Allard: The Inside Story*.

Everyone has to start somewhere, however, and Sydney's achievements began with his 'Clubman' years.

THE CLUBMAN YEARS: THE GENESIS OF ALLARDISM

We are fortunate that Sydney recalled his start in competitive car racing at club level in his unpublished My Life as a Clubman:

> I suppose I can truthfully talk about life as a Clubman, as I joined my first club for motorcyclists in 1928, and entered my first trial that same year. I was a proud owner of a Morgan three-wheeler and I entered it in the Trial which was to be held in the West Country. Starting at midnight, on the way down I soon found that the combination of low ground clearance and plenty of wheel travel from the single rear wheel was not the right recipe for covering a motorcycle trials course on Dartmoor.
>
> However, I got a medal, my first motoring award. I am still a member of that Club, Streatham and District Motorcycle Club. Incidentally, one of the members used to bring his sisters with him and one of them was Eleanor, now my wife.
>
> I ran the Morgan for about four years, and most of my activities were centred around the various motorcycle clubs including the British Motorcycle Racing Club, whose headquarters were at Brooklands circuit.[5]

Sydney goes on to describe how, despite successes with the Morgan, notably at Brooklands, he was up against cars like Rileys, Salmsons and Amilcars, all nimble little lightweight things derived from 'cyclecar' or light car origins. Despite being capable of an 80mph lap at Brooklands in standard tune, and more than 90mph once he had tweaked it (records indicate a handicap lap time of more than 100mph in a fifteen-lap race), the three-wheeler Morgan was soon found to lack the stability at high-speed essential on the Brooklands banking and adequate ground clearance; good ground clearance was soon to be a key factor in Allard cars. According to Sydney, 'I eventually decided that the Morgan was not quite suitable for this sort of Trials event'.

This was the moment when the need for a four-wheeled car with higher ground clearance and better handling became defined in Sydney's mind. More power and torque was needed. Sydney could not ignore the hill-climb and racing success of the supercharged Villiers-tuned Vauxhall TT and the twin-supercharged, chain-drive Frazer Nash 'Shelsley' types. One of the Frazer Nash cars was actually campaigned by Margaret Allan, who achieved her 'Brooklands 120mph' badge in a Bentley. The early Anzani-engined Frazer Nash cars of 1928–30 gave way to a Meadows powerplant in the

1930s (supercharged to 18psi boost), which could provide hill-climb drivers with a massive wall of urgent and short-lived torque, but its reliability was bound to be problematic when exposed to long-distance, high-speed race running. By 1936 Frazer Nash would use straight-six BMW engines. As with other competition cars of these years, there was a trade-off between hill-climb power that would last for about five minutes or racing endurance to last several hours at lower revs. The key factor was engine weight versus component strength and reliability. Such issues were all relevant to Sydney Allard's thoughts on building his own 'Specials' to perform similar tasks.

During his early career the end-of-week and weekend racing scene required a frantic schedule and Sydney often worked through the night to straighten bent chassis rails and suspension components. His brother Dennis acted as support crew and the pair shared the driving of the Ford truck that towed the Morgan to events. In its later days the little JAP V-twin engined Morgan, known affectionately as 'Milly the Moocher', was modified to run on methanol with a 10:1 compression ratio. Dennis campaigned a highly tuned Brough Superior motorcycle and sidecar combination in which Sydney suffered his first really serious accident as passenger to Dennis.

Leslie would also suffer injuries due to his escapades. Just as Dennis was badly injured at Donington, Leslie managed to turn a car over on Wimbledon Common and suffered a skull fracture that would result in a legacy of disabling headaches. He was found to have suffered a broken neck, which was only revealed when another car crashed into him some years later. Leslie continued his motorcycle exploits and campaigned a blown J1; one of his greatest triumphs was beating the Bugattis in the Sports Car Class at Prescott. Leslie and Sydney also drove to Switzerland to compete in hill climb events. In the 1950s Sydney and Leslie would drive a 1904 Napier in the London-to-Brighton Veteran Run.

From late 1920s Leslie worked in his father's building company, but he later turned to farming, perhaps reflecting the Allard family's agrarian roots in Wiltshire. During the Second World War he assisted Sydney at the Allard works turning out military vehicles. After the war he competed three times in the Monte Carlo Rally, twice in a P1 and once in a 'works' Zephyr during a period with the Ford Rally Team. He was also a reserve J2X LM driver on Sydney's Le Mans team.

Sydney was not the only 'hot' driver in the Allard family. The brothers competed in differing classes so a comparison of driving talent would be unfair. Leslie later became interested in gliding, initially at Firle and then at Parham, where he became club Chairman and, in 1982, President.

Anthony 'Tony' Allard, the son of Sydney's cousin 'Bert' Allard, was another Allard with an interest in cars. He also worked in farming, but owned several Allards, including a K1, built a trials special and won several awards.

EMPTY ROADS

With little traffic and few police in the 1930s, drivers were able to race and pace themselves against fellow club members on public roads. Sydney wrote: 'On several occasions we went down to the New Forest, leaving Streatham Common at midnight. In the early hours of the morning we removed our silencers and, having marked off a section of road, held an impromptu speed trial over this distance.'

In 1934 Sydney made the move to four-wheeled, fully fledged Trials driving in a somewhat antediluvian 'sit up and beg' Ford 14hp four-seat tourer (soon fitted with a bigger 24hp engine). Even though Britain's road network was sparse and single carriageway, Sydney would think nothing of driving a competition car from London to Devon, competing in a Trials event, and then driving it back home to London. Such determination indicates the man's character, which was the expected practice for competitive driving in an era that cared little for health and safety.

Sydney joined the North West London Motor Club in 1933 and the Kentish Border Club in 1935. This was when his Ford V8 experiments had begun and he was starting to set down a formula. He always claimed that his decision to build his first real Allard Special came after winning the Knott Cup Trial:

Sydney, Ken Hutchinson and Guy Warburton with an early Allard Special in front of the Adlards Ford showroom in Keswick Road, Putney.

In the course of my Club life I have competed in almost all types of events: Reliability Trials, Brooklands, hill-climbs, grass track, road races, Aerodrome races and rallies, and regularly I meet old friends with whom I have competed in those days. To mention only two, I raced with Clive Lones at Brooklands and with Wally Waring (500cc Norton side-car) on a grass track at Waterloovile in 1929, and they form a direct link with my earliest days as a Clubman.

In these early years Sydney got his hands on a series of cars, from Morgan three-wheelers, to Ford saloons, to Austin Sevens. Turning to the British-built Ford side-valve flat-head V8 engine would soon be a big step for Allard and his future cars, yet its design was not without problems, whichever type of car or truck it was fitted to, and Sydney soon sourced the revised and improved American variants as they became available.

The early experiences set the landscape for Sydney's first thoughts about cars and car engineering, though perhaps not 'design' in the sense we now use the term. The result was an Allard ethos that was all about providing something unique that was notably about competitive performance, handling and sheer ability.

In order to save weight (and money) Allard did not paint

his cars: his focus was on the power-to-weight ratio. Add in traction, suspension design and a strong chassis to ensure that the handling remained consistent, and the ingredients were set for the Allard Specials formula, which was carried over to the Allard production series road cars. It was only after the process of devolment had brought competition success, and the interest of people who asked for a copy of his car, that the story evolved into car production.

The first ever attempt at an Allard sales brochure.

Sydney in CLK5 winning the hundred mile race on Southsport Sands in 1936. Note the sand deflector behind the front wheel on the driver's side.

All smiles, Sydney with Eleanor May, his wife to be, after a race on Southport Sands in 1936.

Norman May   Eleanor   Sydney   Jim Mac   Dennis Allard   Edna May

On 2 August 1937 Sydney attempted to drive to the top of **Ben Nevis**, the highest mountain in Scotland, in **CLK5**. The car is seen here just after leaving the track and rolling down the mountain side – members of the family and friends surround **Sydney**.

CHAPTER 2

ALLARD SPECIALS AND EARLY IDEAS, 1930–39

WHERE DID IT ALL BEGIN and what were the influences on Sydney's ideas? Did the 1930s Allard 'Specials' influence the design of the Allard car company's post-1946 products, or was this a separate process after the interruption of the Second World War? The distinct periods of the Allard story are the key to answering these vital questions. Several intriguing parallels can also be drawn between the American 'Specials' movement and Allard in the 1930s.

This was the decade during which the DNA of the Allard Specials, the core ingredients of the marque and its ethos, was set down. Although others contributed to the Specials, they were essentially the creation of one man. Their roots may perhaps be traced to the cause-and-effect process that began in 1927 when Sydney first started to express his ideas about motorcycles, cars and their engineering. At the time he had no intention of building his own cars: he just wanted to race and to find an effective car to do it in.

The fact that some Bugatti bits later found their way into the first true Allard Special is more likely to reflect the exploits of contemporaries like Amilcar, MG, Riley, Talbot and Bugatti, whose profile ensured that 'competition' parts for such cars were randomly available. It is unlikely that Sydney had a specific Bugatti-inspired plan in mind, but it is interesting to speculate whether the size, weight, shape and tractive ability of the Bugatti racing cars of the 1920s and 1930s had some influence over the same ingredients as demonstrated in Sydney's Specials. This is especially so since it mirrored Ettore Bugatti's own story of an individual setting the formula or ethos for his own cars.

During the mid- to late 1930s Bugatti spent some time in Great Britain competing in the major hill-climb events. The Bugatti company also developed twin-tyred, supercharged and four-wheel-drive cars to improve traction for trials, hill climbs and more traditional circuit races at the same time that Allard was making a mark in the same specialities.

Sydney, however, was not intent on aping a Bugatti 'boat-tailed' style. He used a Bugatti tail, scuttle panel and assorted mechanical parts in his first real Special (CLK 5) simply because it was available and would save the cost of commissioning a hand-built body. That several of the 'copies' of CLK 5 ordered in the 1930s mirrored such design should not be seen as suggesting a definitive design language or any styling preference. As Gavin Allard, Sydney's grandson, points out: 'A boat-tail was an unlikely Allard choice. It was likely to be simply an accident of the moment and of circumstance and should not be taken as an Allard design statement.'

That makes a valid point, but we should not say that Sydney was 'blind' to design or any benefits it might have on potential sales. An intriguing design sketchbook provides more clues that, from 1927 onwards, he had indeed been thinking beyond just the engineering and chassis to ideas about very stylized, aerodynamic car body designs.

SYDNEY'S SKETCHBOOK

The personal sketchbook that Sydney created in the 1920s and 1930s lies hidden away in the Allard family files. This A3-sized, hard-backed scrapbook folder contains the collection of press cuttings, brochures, advertisements and ephemera he had been gathering since he was a teenage boy. More intriguingly, however, it also contains a series of design concept sketches, doodles, detail drawings, styling ideas, calculations and future thoughts, all in his classic handwriting, that illuminate his ideas on car body design as well as under-the-skin engineering. These illustrate that he was studying everything of every shape, size and engine capacity that came to his attention, from Aston Martin, Chater Lea, Amilcar, Singer, Talbot, Riley, Edwardian and post-Edwardian era light cars, to Bentleys, the Marendaz Special, Fords and a wide range of 1920s carmakers. Handling, power and body design, including streamlining, are all portrayed and discussed. Sydney repeatedly sketched his own ideas for aerodynamically shaped cars and drew up detailed specifications. He also collected brochures and technical sheets for many of the cars mentioned.

From about 1930 he drew up ideas for a whole range of cars to his own design: from 'light car' to sportster, two-seaters, single-seat racers, hill climbers, and even big saloons and coupés. There are pages of his car designs, all unseen for decades and published here for the first time. Sydney, it seems, never stopped drawing cars and his ideas for cars, mostly in blue ink with additions in pencil and black ink.

Created through the late 1920s and into the 1930s, Sydney's combined scrapbook and design sketchbook is an incredible record that demonstrates his skill and how his thoughts about creating a series of cars, however 'imaginary', were being formulated at an early stage. He absorbed all the technical details that he could about all sorts of cars and then applied them to his own ideas. It is clear that Sydney had an eye for engineering and thought about design, if not 'styling' as it was then perceived. He must also have bought *Light Car and Cyclecar* magazine regularly as his folder is packed with its cuttings, along with examples from *Autocar*, *Motor* and other magazines.

Sydney's wonderful scrapbook categorically shows the evolution of the mental journey that would lead to his achievements. Family anecdotes reveal that his mind rarely stopped. He was always thinking of the next project, yet the sketches were aimed at resolving his needs, rather than suggesting any dreams of motor manufacturing or becoming famous. Speed and winning events may have been his main aim, but the sketchbook's contents reveal that cars and their design were his other passion, perhaps more than has previously been thought. Anyone who dismisses Sydney's cars as 'agricultural' or 'accidents of design' needs to consider how the sketchbook proves that far more thought went into his cars than perceived wisdom has sometimes suggested.

'SPECIALS'

Between 1920 and 1938 a widespread 'Specials' movement developed to supply cars suited to competitive use off-road in Trials or races. Such cars were derived from lithe, lightweight but low-powered early cars with their origins in the cyclecar, light car and *voiturette* models that formed the basis of early British and French motor sport. Early 'tuners' and builders of Specials were active shortly before the start of the First World War and soon their designs would form the basis of a popular American movement.

Specials were often based on chassis from well-known manufacturers. Many types were devised in the period before the Second World War, and some of those produced after 1945 may have been inspired by the Allards' earlier successes. An example that spanned both the pre- and post-war periods was the Freikaiserwagen, driven on the hill-climb scene by Joe Fry. Joe's cousin, David Fry, and Dick Caesar, who worked for the Bristol Aeroplane Company with Malcolm Sayer, were also responsible for the Gordano special from 1945. Alec Issigonis and George Dowson devised an 'elastic' suspension system based on aeronautical practice and incorporated this under a two-seater plywood and alloy special. Between 1949 and 1956 a number of specials were also produced by Dellow Motors. The huge range of specials made in the USA during the 1930s included a V8-engined Riley, tuned-up Chevrolets and Ford flat-head specials.

The period from the 1920s to the 1940s was marked by engineering and design development that took the light car from its early form to a 'proper' sporting single- or two-seater 'racing' car. Even Ettore Bugatti followed this route to success from the Type 12 to Type 35 and beyond. In time chassis designs would get bigger and heavier, and engine capacities larger. It can be argued that Sydney Allard contributed more to that movement than anyone else in Britain.

The range of specialist cars for hill-climbing, trials and race applications included the Wolseley 200 Mile 'George Miller' Special, the 1925 Bugatti Type 13-30 series, various GN, Frazer Nash and Amilcars (notably the Hispano-Amilcar Special), the MG J, L and PA-type series, Riley Sports

Lands End Trial, 10–11 April 1936. Sydney and Eleanor in CLK5, specially equipped with large headlights for this long, two-day event.

Tourers, Morris Specials (including the 1937 Ashley Cleave Morris Special designed with Shelsley and Brooklands in mind) and Singers. Such was the trend set by the 'special' scene that even the Austin Seven Chummy might be said to have had such traits at heart, if not its horsepower rating.

Sydney Allard raced at Brooklands in his tuned-up three-wheeler Morgan for the first time on 31 August 1929, aged just 19. The next year he took first place (with a top speed of 83mph) in the Light Car Club's July meeting at Brooklands, beating the well-known Morgan three-wheeler racer R.R. Jackson. Sydney's first attempt at building a modified car from an existing model was revealed in the late summer of 1931. He had failed to finish in several British Motocycle Racing Club (BMCRC) events, so now he set about modifying his Morgan three-wheeler and turning it into a four-wheeled car, selecting parts from cars by BSA, Morris, Chrysler and other makes. From the start Sydney was not immune to using existing components in his cars, which was certainly cheaper and quicker than designing and manufacturing his own. At the front, the Morgan engine, radiator and suspension were familiar in appearance, with the added allure of a rakish, angled vee-type split windscreen. Behind that came an elegant cut-away cockpit flowing back into a boat-tail.

The car he had been given by his brother Jack was, with modifications, an 8bhp JAP-engined three-wheeler Morgan. In 1931, after engine tuning by Baragwaneth of Brooklands Circuit, it competed at Brooklands and secured victory in the Morgan Cup at a heady average speed of 80mph. From this came the idea of a safer, more stable, four-wheeled competition car. The obvious solution was to convert the Morgan to a four-wheel configuration by grabbing whatever was most suitably and readily to hand at the least cost. That is how the axle, differential and drivetrain from the small BSA-built light car, which was produced in very low production numbers, became the basis of the first modified Allard (although it should not be described as a true 'Special' of the series that would soon follow).

The twin-tube chassis frame selected was carried below the wheel centres as suggested by an existing BSA design. Austin Seven universal propshaft joints also fitted nicely. The front suspension was via helical springs with Newton hydraulic shock absorbers, while the rear suspension was via eight (paired as four) quarter-elliptic springs with Hartford friction shock absorbers. This created an independently sprung rear suspension of unusual efficacy. Further thought was evident in the 'crabbed' narrower rear track (3ft 8in) compared to that at the front (4ft 8in). The JAP engine was fitted with a Lucas dynamotor of Morris origins, to which was added an extra drivetrain flywheel (at the rear end) and a Moss gearbox. Morgan brakes stopped the car at the front, but Chrysler brakes were used at the rear. In the cockpit the dashboard was a mass of ill-matched instrumentation.

From this it can be seen that the first Allard one-off had a bit of Morgan bloodline, but this was not just a 'Four-wheeled Morgan' conversion, despite the description in *Light Car and Cyclecar* on 30 December 1932, which called Sydney's car 'a very fine effort'. The publication also praised the car's stylish appearance. The first Allard-built car, however, lacked ground clearance, which was a vital factor in a trials

car of the day. Sydney's next step would need to allow for this. He was just 22 and his first 'car' was already in print.

Sydney's initial, heavily modified four-wheeled car was the beginning of a process that guided his designs. Much effort was put into re-engineering the rear suspension and creating its beneficial independent action, however crude. By blending all these elements together and making even this first attempted 'one-off' handle superbly, he set a trend of responsive performance and handling that characterized cars from the Allard factory. The Allard of Morgan lineage might have achieved wider recognition if it had not broken down at Fingle Bridge Hill on Dartmoor in its first major outing during the London–Exeter Trial of 1932. Nevertheless, this was the car that confirmed Sydney's belief that he could learn more and ultimately design and manufacture his own cars. The car again failed to finish in the 1933 Exeter Trial, but finally completed the course in the 1934 event. While accepting that the car was not 'successful' in the pure sense, it was to inspire further thoughts about modified cars in 1934 that would lead in turn to the actual Allard 'Special' of 1936.

It might be stretching the point to say that the bodywork of the first Allard-modded Morgan (registered JJ 761) was 'designed', yet it is coherent in its scaling, proportions and lines. The 'cycle' style mudguards were not flowing wings, but when that look was introduced it could be argued that such motifs reflected not just the first four-wheeled Morgans, but also the styles of cars from companies such as Squire, Triumph and MG, allied to some degree of influence from American Ford Model T racers. The reviewer in *Light Car and Cyclecar* said that it had 'distinctly imposing lines' and that Sydney had done a good job 'looks-wise'. One thing is for sure, if you parked it at Prescott today, it would cause quite a stir among the Vintage Sports-Car Club people and the Morgan aficionados.

Most Allardistes and the Allard family consider that Sydney's modified Morgan was not the first true 'Allard Special', since not enough alterations were made to be something else entirely. We should state categorically, however, that this was his first 'special' type car, even though it was not one of the more clearly defined and badged 'Allard Specials'.

FORD DEVELOPMENTS BEFORE THE SPECIALS

Twelve actual 'Allard Specials' were made, but the twelfth car, LMG 92, was not completed before the outbreak of war. It may therefore be more appropriate to say that there were eleven Specials up to May 1939, the last of these being

Another view of FGP 750, this time with Sydney awaiting the start of the Lewes Trial on the Sussex Downs. Note the solo 'Allard' badging in a pre-war setting.

FGP 750 being bashed back into shape after an 'off'. This rare shot shows Sydney (n left) at work with the May brothers, Alan and Norman.

FXP 469 (sometimes cited as EXP 469). Their sequence illustrates Allard's developing knowledge of engineering. Yet during the four years (1931–5) leading up to the first official Allard 'Number One' (CLK 5), there are a number of clues about earlier designs. Competition records show that an earlier iteration of a chassis described as an '1100cc Allard Special' was entered in events. In those years Sydney rashly had his hands on a Talbot 105 before buying a small open Ford saloon (registered as UU4922) and a Ford V8 TT (Tourist Trophy). It is clear that the route to CLK 5 was confusing. The Ford TT (CZ 5969) was widely used by Sydney before CLK 5 was available, and he tried it out over the Army tank-testing ground at Bovingdon.

The Ford 'TT' that Sydney Allard purchased had competed successfully in the Northern Irish TT event of 1934. Competition events were popular in Northern Ireland, where the Ards Tourist Trophy races took place on a glorious 13-mile circuit that could really test a car, an engine, and a driver. The Royal Automobile Club stipulated from 1934 that only 'production' specification engines without superchargers were to be used (the years from 1928 to 1933 had been dominated by a series of 'blown' supercharged, Jensen-bodied, Morris-based 'Specials').

Ford in the USA had kept an eye on its British operations and sent over three Ford Model 30 V8s for the 1934 TT. The cars were Ford US owned but were to be handed over to Ford GB after the races.

It appears that the three Belfast Ford dealers (Coulter, Wright and Hamilton) modified the standard cars by removing unnecessary items and fitting sports-style mudguards, which improved the power-to-weight ratio and the handling. Richard Jensen was responsible for modifying the bodywork of the three Fords: CZ 6054 driven by McCalla, CZ 5955 driven by Wright and CZ 5969 driven by Sullivan. All competed in the race schedule, but CZ 6054 was damaged (and repaired) after a crash at Craigantlet on 25 August.

Soon two of the cars were in England. Sydney bought CZ 5969 for £135 using money he had received as a birthday present. He then removed all the 'sporting' addenda, cutting away excess bodywork, as if to 'add lightness'. The car was further enhanced over its original 'TT' specification and immediately took class records at the Brighton Speed Trials and the Aston Clinton hill climb. This car introduced the early era of Sydney competing in off-road Trials, the muddy hill climbs that were a fast-growing British sport of the era. Sydney entered the Knott Trophy Trial in 1935, winning the Novice Cup. After further modifications the Ford was entered in other events including the Aldershot Trial, where he won the Premier Award. At the Gloucester Cup in December his times were close to that of R.A. MacDermid, an established name who was driving a supercharged MG PA. Sydney narrowly lost to MacDermid but the rash of results he achieved in the much-modified Ford V8 had led to media coverage. Still in his mid-twenties, Sydney was

Lawrence Cup Trial, 29 May 1936. Sydney wins the first class award and team award for the only successful climb of the new hill.

a recognized competition driver and class winner cited in the press.

As Sydney came to understand the characteristics of the Ford V8 engine, he soon realized that the converted Belfast TT car was not quite what he needed to develop his skills and win more events. Its engine, however, could provide the heart of such a car. CZ 5969 became the basis of his plans to put into action the ideas first mooted in his scrapbook sketches – absorbing, learning, updating and then creating his own car.

So was born the idea of Sydney's 'Specials', as they were later badged. The converted Morgan had been lightweight. The Talbot (BGT 407) was altogether more of a sports car, heavier in build and gauge, even if Sydney did saw the chassis in half to shorten it as he had decided it was far too long. He changed the small 14.9bhp engine in the Ford Tourer for a 24bhp unit from a Ford lorry, which gave the car real torque low down the rev range and more ground clearance, making it suitable for use at many trials events and outings. Ford engines became the power source of accessible choice. He took a further step with the TT car CZ 5969, which was re-registered as UU 4922. After a successful season with the TT Ford in 1935, winning seventeen major Trial awards, including four team wins with Ken Hutchison and S.L. Chappell, Sydney had established a firm association with Ford products, which were to become a recognized element in all Allard cars.

Sydney was now pursuing his dream of building one truly competitive car, and certainly not considering a car marque. It was the acquisition of a Ford Model 48 V8 coupé damaged in a crash that was to provide the basis of the first true 'Allard Special'. This became known as CLK 5.

CLK 5: THE ALLARD V8 SPECIAL – NUMBER ONE

CLK 5 went missing years ago, but there is always hope that it might turn up as an amazing 'barn find': the 1937 'Allard Special' AUK 795, known as the Gilson car, was rediscovered as a barn find in 2017 and is now owned by Marc Mears.

CLK 5 stands out as the first proper 'Allard Special' incorporating Sydney's developing ideas of how to make the machine competitive enough to win. His main requirements – and probably the only elements he had in mind at that time – were power-to-weight ratio and maximum traction, thus enabling him to beat the opposition and the Trials organizers' targets in climbing further than anyone else up a slippery, muddy hill. CLK 5 would take thirty-five awards in its short career.

By gaining a feel for the effectiveness of differing steering, suspension and drivetrain components, Sydney determined the key ingredients necessary: a good power-to-weight ratio, low rpm torque, sound suspension behaviour, enhanced

One of the original drawings for the four-seat 'Allard Special' series bodywork prior to 1939 as built by Coachcraft Ltd.

ground clearance and a strong chassis. Body design in terms of styling was not a consideration. These cars were not built using tooling, but were individually constructed.

A key design decision in CLK 5 was to move the engine 12in further back on the chassis towards the bulkhead. This yielded a dramatic improvement in handling by adding traction weight towards the rear-driven wheels. In fact it had the beneficial effect of shifting 3cwt rearwards.

CLK 5 was also fitted with a 'spare' Bugatti tail section, scuttle, steering box, alloy fuel tank (mounted vertically at the rear and as far back as possible), with one or two spare wheels behind it to place additional weight over the rear wheels for optimum traction. The engine was, of course, the Ford side-valve V8. The chassis was drilled for lightness, but reinforced for resistance to twist. After class placements in early competition, Sydney later modified the car by changing the front grille, which now displayed the name of an 'Allard Special' for the first time.

SOLVING A RIDDLE: THE BUGATTI BITS

Neither Sydney's Ford TT nor the modified Talbot had constituted anything other than modifications, even though these were significant. No major bodywork changes were involved. The more specific Allard Special registered as CLK 5, the Ford V8-powered car with Ford nose panels, was the first of his cars with self-build bodywork including real Bugatti parts: rear bodywork panels, scuttle/cockpit panel, fuel tank, chassis parts, steering box and column.

The Bugatti 'bits' are usually stated by commentators to have come off a Grand Prix Bugatti owned by Viscount Curzon, who became the 5th Earl Howe in 1929. This has been described as a Type 51 or, more rarely, a Type 43. The problem is that there has always been confusion over which Bugatti type and when this happened.

No one has ever conclusively explained how Sydney acquired a complete and apparently undamaged (or repaired) Bugatti tail body, scuttle section and assorted parts, such as steering gear and fuel tank, or determined their actual provenance. While most commentators, including David Kinsella, have accepted that the story about Earl Howe's Bugatti may be correct, Tom Lush wrote in his book that Sydney found unspecified Bugatti parts at a 'nearby coachbuilders' and that the tail was 'complete'. Some sources state that the mechanical and body parts used by Allard came from the Earl's Type 43, which he had recently 'damaged', but there is no published record of the Earl damaging his Type 43, although that does necessarily mean it is untrue. Other sources cite the Earl's Type 51 categorically as the source of CLK 5's Bugatti parts.

A less-discussed possibility is that the tail and scuttle (and parts) may have come from a Type 43 (chassis number 4317) owned by Malcolm Campbell, the British Bugatti concessionaire. This was partially burnt out after a fuel tank leak in the Ards trophy race in 1928 and was brought back to west London for storage. The tail section on that car, with its experimental, add-on fuel tank, was damaged and slightly different from the Bugatti tail that Sydney used seven years later on CLK 5. It remains possible, however, although unlikely, that Sydney acquired his parts from Campbell's earlier Bugatti, not his daily driver Type 35A.

Returning to speculation about Earl Howe, as early as 1930 he would sell off his Bugatti Type 43 and order a Type 51, which was delivered via the British Bugatti concessionaire in April 1931 with chassis number 51121. By 1934 the Type 51 had also become surplus to the Earl's requirements and he sold it to the British driver Arthur Dobson, who would later make his name as an ERA works driver. According to some records, after competing in several events Dobson sold the Bugatti to C. Mervyn White, a garage owner of Chalfont St Peter, Buckinghamshire. Early in 1937, which it should be noted is after Sydney had supposedly used ex-Howe Bugatti parts in early 1936 to build CLK 5, White won the Long Handicap race at the Brooklands Easter meeting and took third place in the Broadcast Trophy race. He also ran in the Brooklands Campbell Trophy and at Donington. During practice for the 1937 Cork Grand Prix, however, the Bugatti overturned and White suffered fatal head injuries.

The damage to the ex-Howe, Mervyn White Type 51 was to its front and rear axles and, significantly, the tail bodywork. The wreckage was reputedly purchased and rebuilt by Arthur Baron, owner of a Bugatti garage in Dorking, Surrey, with his business partner Norman Lewis. In 1939 it returned to Shelsley, Prescott and a new life. Today the car is a famous Bugatti that came to auction as recently as 2016, but the timeline shows that this cannot be Sydney's donor car. Something is not right in the story. It is said that an identifying feature of the Bugatti Type 51 was its twin filler caps (some oversized) on the tail. CLK 5 was fitted with caps of this type, but then many Type 35s and Type 41/43s were also retro-fitted with similar fillers, so the clue is a tenuous one. It is of interest, though, that CLK 5's Bugatti scuttle featured seemingly original twin aero screens and the Bugatti-type aerodynamically faired rear view mirror mounted at an angle.

Another circumstantial plot line features Earl Howe's Type 59 (chassis number 59123), which he raced with Noel Rees and alongside Charles Martin in Type 59 (59121). Martin's car went to the Duke of Grafton, but he was killed in it at Limerick in August 1936. Arthur Baron, who bought Mervyn White's Type 51, is then named as having similarly buying the wreck and rebuilding it: as a seller of Bugatti's Mr Baron may well have purchased two damaged Bugattis.

This, however, was a 2.8-litre (modified to 3.3-litre) Type 59. Even though the year of 1936 fits the Allard CLK 5 story, the month does not since August was long after Sydney had built CLK 5. Furthermore, the rear springs of the Type 59 protruded out of the tail bodywork at mid-height, whereas the Types 35, 43 and 51 did not, and CLK 5 showed no sign of such protuberances in its tail panels, nor repairs or modifications to suggest their former presence.

It is significant that in July 1937 *Motor Sport* categorically cited a '2.3 litre G.P. Bugatti' as the source of Sydney's parts for CLK 5. This was before the Type 51 or the Type 59 parts would have been available, and should further rule out the ex-Earl Howe 2.3-litre Type 51, which has so often been suggested. Errors or confusion may have crept into the established record over the decades, but the trail undoubtedly takes us back to Earl Howe's Type 43 (chassis number 51121), registered as YT 8241.

THE WANDSWORTH BUGATTI

It has not previously been revealed, however, that the Earl sold this Bugatti Type 43 in the early 1930s to a Mr D. Evans of the Bellevue Garage, Wandsworth Common, south Lon-

don, not far from the Adlards base and the Allard family properties. Dennis Evans, his racing driver brother Kenneth and the Bellevue name were well connected and supplied chassis, bodies and general sales. Bellevue's transporter was often seen parked close to Sydney Allard in the Prescott paddock.

It is interesting to speculate whether Sydney acquired the Bugatti Type 43 tail and parts from Bellevue, and whether Evans damaged the Bugatti after he had purchased it from the Earl: he certainly competed in the car in the mid-1930s, notably at Brooklands. The Evans Type 43 also disappeared, leaving another loose end in our story, but it is likely that this is the car from which Sydney took his parts.

The young Jean Bugatti, Ettore's son, spent many months on the British trials and hill-climb calendar in the late 1930s with his Type 53, notably at Prescott, where the Bugatti Owners Club has been based since 1938. His team of mechanics from the Bugatti factory was fully engaged on fettling and fiddling with mechanical parts and bodywork, and any parts left over were deposited at Bugatti's Brixton workshops, also very close to Sydney's base.

It seems that there were bits of damaged or modified Bugattis floating about all over London and the Home Counties in the mid-1930s. Colonel Godfrey Giles and his brother Eric, stylists and coach builders, for example, built many special-bodied Bugattis in the 1930s under the Corsica brand and may have been the 'nearby coachbuilders' mentioned by Tom Lush as a source of parts for CLK 5. Another London firm that may have had redundant Bugatti bodywork and parts lying about was the Bugatti body builders Vanden Plas.

Perhaps we will never be entirely certain about any details other than that a Bugatti tail and sundry mechanical parts, possibly linked to Earl Howe's ownership, were part of CLK 5. It is the authors' contention, however, that the circumstance that Earl Howe's Bugatti Type 43 ended up at a garage in Wandsworth in the early 1930s, so close to Sydney's home base, presents a reliable possible clue to the provenance of Sydney's Bugatti parts until other evidence is found.

As a final riddle, we should recall that the well-known 1930s motoring writer C.A.N. (Austen) May was a friend of Sydney's and regularly drove Allards supplied for road tests. In the 1940s Len Potter and May entered the postwar Alpine Rally in an Allard. May had been close professionally to Earl Howe and his Bugatti racing campaign in the 1930s. When Jean Bugatti arrived for the hill climb season, he stayed with Earl Howe in Buckinghamshire – and so did May. Howe, May and Bugatti were the keepers of the secret of the record-breaking time that Bugatti recorded at Shelsley Walsh. Sydney may have been aware of this and it is unlikely that May did not confer with Sydney over such mat-

Sydney at speed at Backwell, in sports jacket and tie and no helmet. Note the narrower, lighter mudguards used for tarmac surface events.

A very early Allard publicity shot for the company. Note the sporty lines of the hood and the twin rear spare wheel mounting behind the fuel tank.

ters. His later customer-commissioned Specials featured a 'clone' of the Bugatti tail design, including the vertical vents cut into the edges of the tail's pointed stern section. Altogether Bugatti had some influence on the early Allard narrative behind the scenes.

These may have been 'experimental' days, but it is clear that young Sydney really knew his stuff. His aim was always to create a high-performance car for competition use off-road, but this was not to be a neurotic racing-stable beast in need of daily servicing and repair. It could also be used on the road as a daily driver.

As an example of how much thought Sydney put into his first Special we can cite the friction clutch mechanism that he designed to enable the differential to be locked up for hill climbing. We can also cite his use of the L.M. Ballamy split-axle 'independent' front suspension designs, which divided the A-frame and pivoted in the centre of the chassis. This offered improved rebound and articulation abilities off-road, but on tarmac presented some directional stability issues: the 1950s reality was that Sydney was correct in favouring a swing axle type – 'divided axle' front suspension – and even Colin Chapman became a later exponent of the design.

FXP 470 – the new car built for V.S.A. Biggs, being 'tested' by Sydney. Windscreen folded flat, lightweight front wings and Reg Canham, the 'bouncing' passenger.

This 'Allard Special' publicity artwork depicts an overly large car and some curiously scaled occupants, but it certainly conveys that this is a real sports car.

Sydney added the Ballamy-type split front axle to CLK 5 in 1936 to increase its off-road articulation, thus eliminating the tendency for the front wheels to leave the ground in very rough Trials track conditions or when climbing and accelerating on steep hills.

Leslie Mark Ballamy went on to create the Ballamy-Ford LMB Special with split-axle suspension on parallel pivots and a shortened Ford Model 18 V8 chassis. There is a surprising personal connection in that Ballamy's cousin Doreen ('Dee') worked at the Allard factory for years and married Allard director Reg Canham in 1969. Today Mark Ballamy is well known in the club and sport scene and the Allard link is kept alive.

Although a low-line chassis would improve handling at high speed, such a chassis would restrict off-road capability in Trials events, so suspension travel and ground clearances were vital in this first true Allard Special chassis. The Specials had nearly 10in of ground clearance and an excess of the vital suspension and axle articulation; 17in wire spoked wheels completed the package.

Gil Jepson, Percy Stanfield and others assisted Sydney at the Upper Richmond Road site in building the early Specials. Stanfield would test-drive each one and subject it to a few runs over kerbs and humps to make sure the chassis was correct before the body was offered up.

EIGHTEEN DAYS, WINTER 1936

By 4 February 1936 Sydney had got his hands on a wrecked example of the newer V8-powered Ford Model 48 coupé. Like the Talbot 105 he had fettled, the car was cut down on the Allard garage floor and new dimensions chalked up. These were also set by the fact that Allard had bought the remains of the bodywork of something more exotic, an ex-racing Bugatti that he would fit to his new car. The pre-determined configuration of the new chassis-body combination followed the Bugatti body parts' dimensions, except that Sydney also cut it down to 'add lightness', which meant the bonnet did not line up with the radiator.

This determined the 100in wheelbase, the somewhat narrow 4ft rear track and the railway 'standard gauge' 4ft 8½in front track. A lighter front axle was deployed and the whole car was put together with some haste in less than twenty-one days in order to be ready for its first competitive outing with the North West London Motor Club for the Bridgewater Cup Trial in Somerset; with typical optimism, Sydney had previously put in an entry for the West London Motor Club's Coventry Cup Trial on 14 March. A registration was quickly allocated and the number plate 'CLK 5' was fitted to the car, which, it should be stressed, was not based on the ex-TT Ford and no Talbot 105 or TT parts were used.

FXP 470, built for V.S.A. Biggs in 1939, was arguably the precursor of the production Allards.

The start of the Trial at Bridgewater was a 140-mile journey from London and an early departure was made with passenger, spare wheel and a set of essential tools. CLK 5 arrived just in time for breakfast at the Clarence Hotel. More fortunate competitors had stayed in the hotel overnight but, as was to become a habit, Sydney drove to the event in the competing car. By this time Sydney had made a name for himself in the Trials world, so his appearance at the start with a new Trials Special after such a short build time was warmly welcomed. Teething troubles prevented CLK 5 taking a top position in its first event, but Sydney was awarded a 'Souvenir Award' for getting the car ready for competition.

One month later the Speed Trials on the sands at Southport resulted in even more publicity after CLK 5 won at 61.7mph in a duel with a Mercedes-Benz SSK played out over 50 miles in front of huge crowds. A local paper reported that Sydney's goggles had blown off in the race and on his final lap he had reached nearly 100mph while almost blinded by sand.

After more class wins in events and five further trials events in 1936, including the Land's End Trial, the Allard name was well established, even being mentioned in *Motor* on 6 July 1937. The first major 'Specials' press feature in *Motor Sport* in July 1937, however, had the misleading headline 'A Special Trials Ford'.

The trials scene was changing and amateurs with single-car, home-fettled entries were being moved aside by manufacturer-backed teams supposedly running as private entries. This was unfair, but so far Sydney was neither a singleton privateer nor a manufacturer.

In Sydney's hands up to 1937, and then with its next owner

Guy Warburton from 1938, CLK 5 entered more than 200 events and took awards for nineteen best performances, eleven runners-up, five special cups, fifteen first class awards and twenty-five team prizes. Sydney also achieved a 103mph lap in CLK 5 at Brooklands.

Sydney's exploits, together with Hutchison and Warburton as ad hoc drivers and later the young Len Potter, who then worked for Galiber Engineering Ltd of Farnham, brought enough publicity in journals and national newspapers to build a profile for the Specials. Even without consciously thinking about it, Sydney was building a future brand. Allard, Hutchison and Warburton in their respective Specials now formed the Tailwaggers competition team.

The Vintage Sports-Car Club (VSCC) was seemingly rather wary of the Allards and their creator, a snobbery that lasted for some time. Sydney was not really bending the rules, but he was interpreting them in an intelligent way. And of course he was not 'posh', which may have been an issue for some of the old guard in Britain's class-defined society. National media coverage of Allard and his Specials was considerable in the mainstream national newspapers and media, not just in *Motor Sport*, *Motor* and *Autocar*. From such success came the individual orders for more Specials. In old-fashioned terms, during the period from the mid-1930s to 1938 Allard was running an 'Equipe', a team of 'manufactured' cars that were not officially recognized. Entry into 'production' car events might therefore be questionable or argued over, but Sydney solved that problem with the rules by pointing out, not least to the Light Car Club (LCC), that the Allard Specials were under the provenance of the Adlards Motors Company and were included in its catalogue, so they were 'real' and listed items.

Sydney would later enter Ken Hutchison's Lincoln V12-powered Allard, with himself as co-driver, under the 'experimental' rules sanction in the LCC's three-hour sports car race. The V12 Allard ran up to third place before suffering a fan belt failure and finishing ninth. The race was won by a 3.5-litre Delahaye and a Frazer Nash was highly placed. Problems with the Ford V8 and later the Ford-Lincoln V12 continued into the post-war period. Hutchison was a well-heeled Old Harrovian and director of an engineering company, which made him an ideal customer and supporter.

One question that was raised from about 1936 to 1938 was whether it might be possible to replicate CLK 5 or at least build a handful of copies or variants. Some of the enquiries made to Sydney's London premises came from fellow competitors. In the Allard archives, for example, there is an interesting letter from Mr F. Allott, an established driver, asking if he could borrow an Allard Special for the Exeter trial of 6–7 January 1939. Sydney replied on 28 November 1938 that he would indeed lend Mr Allott the new Special, noting: 'The weather protection is rather on the skimpy side, but if you wrap up well it will be quite alright.'

So were born the Allard Specials, which were described in the Allard advertising material in the motoring press of the immediate pre-war years as the 'Cars that will go anywhere'. They were not cheap – Sydney would charge between £400 and £675 for one his Specials – and they appealed to what we might describe today as a 'niche' buyer. The beginnings of Allard car production was being enacted at Keswick Road, London. Adding a V12 engine to one of Sydney's Specials would really make a mark on the motoring scene.

THE TRUE SPECIALS

The following details represent an overview from numerous Allard sources and correct some errors that have have appeared in the previously published record. The allocation of registration numbers to chassis numbers and build dates has been a contentious area with these cars for some years.

Build dates indicate final completion as opposed to start of construction. It should be noted that the 'Car Number' is a chronological term: such numbers have sometimes been confused or errors have been compounded in the descriptions and in relation to the chassis numbers, build dates and 'Specials' numbers. Bill Boddy tried to define the Specials production record in *Motor Sport* in March 1952, but this brave effort was perhaps contaminated by the varying recollections of multiple contributors; loss of the company records did not help. A reply to Boddy at that time by David

L. Gandhi addressed some of the questions and Boddy took it on the chin with good grace. Peter Valentine later created a list with the Allard Owners Club in 1968, but this also raised questions, notably over registrations as applied to cars. Tom Lush provided a view in his book, but there were still issues over registration numbers and chassis numbers.

A correspondent to *The Automobile* in November 2016, writing as 'D'Arcy Lever', was alert to these past issues in a review of the pre-war Allards. C.A.N. May's son then wrote to the magazine with further clarification about FXP 470 and Des Sowerby, owner of FGP 750 for more than four decades, provided further details in the February 2017 issue. We here add the thoughts of members of the Allard Owners Club and arrive at a position.

The reader should note that, because the true Specials were built 'off the shelf' and the nearest parts to hand were used, the chassis and parts numbers can be out of sequence. And if no bolt could be found, Allards would make one up from a piece of metal to hand, so sizes were, shall we say, 'non-standard'. As David Kinsella, who owned an M-Type for more than four decades, pointed out in his book on Allard, CLK 5 was also subject to on-going modifications in 1936, with changes to its appearance including a proper nose-cone and a radiator screen. The script 'Allard Special' was also soon added, as were the Ballamy axle and numerous tweaks to the bodywork and fittings. CLK 5 was a true working prototype and always subject to modifications

Car No 1: CLK 5

Built February–March 1936. Chassis number as Ford-type, number 842. Contained various Ford, Bugatti and proprietary parts. Appeared on Land's End Trial and at Brooklands for the first time on 16 May 1936 and ran up to second place until timing wheel failed. Featured in *Motor Sport*. Rarely off the podium of class rankings, driven by Allard, Hutchison and Warburton. Attempt to ascend Ben Nevis in 1937. Taken over by Guy Warburton, who also drove the car to events. Occasionally suffered from the Ford V8 overheating issue, notably above 100mph at Brooklands, but remained highly competitive in Trials. Owned by J.P. Heatherington in the late 1940s and into the 1950s. CLK 5 was still an active Trials car in the 1950s, driven and navigated on occasion by a Mr Tony Rumfitt and Mrs Rumfitt. CLK 5 was also once owned by the artist Euan Uglow, who claimed to have achieved 100mph in the car over Waterloo Bridge in the 1950s, and he sold the car via Autosport in 1957.

Car No 2: AUK 59

Possibly later registered as OHA 695. Built June 1937. Chassis AM1 was the first production status Allard and had

BEN NEVIS, 1937

Sydney was looking around for another challenge for the new Trials season and decided to take the car to Scotland to attempt an extreme hill climb up Ben Nevis, the highest mountain in Scotland.

Jim Mac and a group of friends from the Streatham and District Motorcycle Club set off for Scotland, where they were soon joined by Sydney's brother Dennis, Eleanor May, who would soon become Sydney's wife, and her brothers Alan, Norman and Eddie.

The tracks to be traversed on the Ben Nevis attempt were narrow and unstable in places. Some attempt was made to improve them, but after climbing a considerable distance towards the summit, the side of the track gave way and CLK 5 rolled slowly over. Luckily the car came to rest upon its wheels, without serious damage to the car or to Sydney. The car was checked over and the attempt abandoned. CLK 5 was then driven all the way back to London. Sydney wanted to try to climb Ben Nevis again one day, but never found the opportunity to do so.

Sydney in the 1937–8 'Tailwaggers' team, with CLK 5 piloted by Warburton and ELX 50 by Hutchison. Beat the Bugatti at the opening Prescott event in 1938 with a time of 54.35s. Original owner J.F. Guest, later owned by B. Hankins of Preston, Lancashire (or Hawkins, according to C.A.N. May in *More Wheelspin*), then by R.M. Bateman.

Car No 4: ELX 50
Built December 1937 for Ken Hutchison. The first Allard Special to deviate from the Ford V8, being quickly fitted with a 4.4-litre Lincoln V12 (with a claimed 110bhp at 3,900rpm); converted to a rear-engined Mercury V8-Special specification in the 1940s by Len Parker. The V12 car was featured by Gordon Wilkins in *Motor* on 22 March 1938. ELX 50 competed at the first-ever Prescott event in 1938 with a time of 53.32s for the hill. Hutchison drove it at Brooklands using wire wheels. The Ballamy split front-axle suspension gave it strong hill-climbing ability. Ford three-speed gearbox and an Allard-modified narrower track. Top speed was 90mph and the car came within almost one second of the Brooklands test-hill record (8.8s versus 7.45s). Destroyed about 1950.

Car No. 5: EXH 455
Built March 1938 for Sydney's father, with full weather equip-

many similarities with CLK 5. The car was ordered by David Gilson and had a four-seat cabin.

It was fitted with a normal Ford V8 engine but with Scintilla Vertex magneto and twin-branch exhaust, a three-speed gearbox with overdrive, and Ranalah-built wood-frame, aluminium-clad coachwork finished in cream/yellow and black with the name 'Whirlwind' painted on the bonnet. The car featured in *Motorsport* in July 1937. The rear axle incorporated Sydney's own differential lock mechanism; the key cutdown items were the shorted propshaft and rear axle assembly. Re-registered in 1955 and heavily modified by Ken Wharton, it was lost for years but rediscovered in 2017 as a so-called 'Ford' barn find – and purchased by Marc Mears, to be restored.

Car No 3: ELL 300
Built November 1937. Close-coupled four-seater, painted black. Sometimes driven by

1938 and the famous Brooklands test hill; part of the pre-war track can be seen in the background. Sydney, seen here just leaving the start line, made one of the fastest climbs.

ment and a canvas top. Purchased in 1968 by Peter Valentine and then bought by Ken Nelson who did a 'cheque book restoration' in 1970–73. In 1973 Ken took the car back to his home in the USA. It was raced by John E. Aibel in New Jersey and by Pete McManus in Thornton Pennsylvania in 1988; it then returned in 1992 to England and was re-fettled. Now owned by Tony Piper and is in excellent condition.

Car No. 6: EYO 750

Built July 1938 and rakishly styled as a two-seater. Often seen badged as an Allard, not an Allard Special., it took part in the Southend on Sea Carnival Rally in 1938 and was driven by R. Tongue in the 1938 Intervarsity Trial. It was converted into a short-chassis car and in 1949 was re-registered as a Mercotto. More recently it was purchased by Josh Sadler (the AOC Chairman) and is being restored to the original Allard specification.

Car No. 7: FGF 290

One of the 'tailwagger' team cars, it was built in September 1938 for Ken Hutchison, with a V12 engine and boat-tailed body. Re-registered after 1945, with Ford front axle, as HPX 57, then purchased and re-bodied by V.S.A. Biggs in 1948. Recreated in 1996 with V8 engine, it is now in Basel, Switzerland and owned by Nicolas Joerin.

Car No 8: FGP 750

Built October 1938 (not late 1937). Original owner was Sydney Allard. This car achieved several pre-war course records, notably at Prescott (3-litre Unsupercharged Class). 'Allards Gap' at Prescott was named from this car going over the edge of the track. Confusingly, the car is chassis number 11, yet was the eighth Special: out-of-sequence builds and registrations were not uncommon at Allard. First driven by Martin Soames in the 1938 London–Gloucester Trial alongside Warburton in CLK 5. Driven by Sydney with Eleanor in the 1938 Wye Cup Trial. Competed in eleven events in 1938–9 with seven class premiers, two cups, one first in class award, one second place, and ten team awards. Featured drilled, lightweight chassis and suspension components, and a Bugatti tail. Engine heavily modified in 1939 with changes to carburation and exhausts and block bored out to 48mm. Enlarged to 4.4 litres capacity and modified crank, lower radiator mounts, new front panel design. Flywheel lightened by 13lb. Fitted with two twin-choke Stromberg carburettors.

Made the fastest sports car time at Prescott in 1939. Sold in 1940 to Clarkson of the Scottish Sports Car Club, then bought in 1946 by Ken Hutchison (navigator Brunell). Sprayed bright blue by Abbots of Farnham and 'dressed' with extra bodywork and trims. Purchased by Lady Mary Grosvenor in 1946, then sold to Harry D. Pritchard of Anglesey. Currently in original condition in pale blue. It has been owned by Des Sowerby for more than forty years and remains in competitive use with Jonathan Rose as mechanical fettler and supporter. FGP 750 returned to Prescott

Sydney on the sands at the Southport Race of 1936 in CLK 5. Looking on, friends Reg Canham in cap (years later to become Allard's managing director) and his wife Tilly on the right.

Prescott Hillclimb, 30 July 1939. Sydney shoots under the bridge in FGP 750, seconds before skidding off the course at Orchard Bend.

after fifty years in 2012. Described in the article 'Detroit Magic', *Motor Sport* (April 1944).

Car No. 9: FLX 650

Built March 1939 for Commander Derek Silcock as a three-seater fast tourer. The Lincoln V12 engine was supplied by Lincoln Cars of Brentford. Competed in Europe and at Brooklands (100mph), driven by Ken McAlpine. Changes were made to the bodywork design and the rear third seat was set transversely. Originally a 12-cylinder car, it was run during the fuel-rationed war years as a 6-cylinder car with pistons removed and inlet ports blanked off on one side of the block. Featured in Autocar on 5 November 1943, it was written off by Len Potter in the 1959 Alpine Rally.

Car No. 10: FXP 469

Built May 1939, this car was a short-chassis, close-coupled design. The original purchaser not known, but it was then owned by Tom Osborne. Lost for years, then found by Peter Redman and rebuilt for trialling in the 1970s, the car was purchased by Peter Bland in the USA in the 1980's and was owned by him until 2019.

Car No.11: FXP 470

Built May 1939 for V.S.A. Biggs. Very similar in style to FLX 650. V8-engined and effectively a final precursor to the first

'production' type Allards delayed by the Second World War. Used by Ken McAlpine. (This was definitely not the car used by C.A.N. May and Len Potter in the 1948 Alpine Cup, and totally destroyed by Potter and Arthur Gill in a crash during the 1950 Alpine Rally.) Also cited as being part of the inventory of Continental Cars, a sales outfit run by Potter and Rodney Clarke in the late 1940s.

Car No. 12: LMG 192

Build laid down in September 1939, but delayed and stored during the war and finally completed/modified in 1946. Essentially a 'replica' of FXP 470. Used 1938-style bodywork, but evidence of an 1937-type grille previously fitted. First post-war outing was a Sprint event driven by Sydney on 28 October 1946 at Filton Aerodrome, Bristol, achieving third place. Sold to Maurice Wick within the Allard Company.

SPECIALS SURVIVORS

AUK59	Now found and being restored
EXH 455	Restored
EYO 750	Being converted back to original spec
FGF 290	Re-created using later Allard parts
FGP 750	Original condition

NB: CLK 5 may still be out there.

DEFINING MOMENTS

In the issue of *Autocar* on 28 December 1948 Dennis May stated that, with the first 1936 'Allard Special', 'the cult of the prehensile [sic] automobile took a bound forward'. May also quoted 'Jabberwocky' by saying that Sydney Allard had 'added much to his renown as a conqueror of slithy toves'. These words were printed a decade after the first Specials in a 'Sportrait' of Sydney to mark the debut of a series production run of Allard cars – no longer Specials, but properly turned-out and finished 'showroom' vehicles. If we consider that between 1928 and 1936 Sydney Allard went from entering his first trial as an amateur driver to creating his own 'Allard Special' branded cars and gaining a national profile as a driver, then *Autocar*'s praise should not be underestimated, for it means that this respected publication was including Allard in the history of the British motor car.

Without the intervention of the Second World War there would have been no gap between the Specials and the Allard production cars. From 1948, however, Allard continued the theme of Ford V8 powerplants and drivetrains to create road-going cars that were also able to hunker down, gather their torque and grind their way up any incline, even without a tarmacked surface. Sydney was a national figure in his sport, winning podium places in the national hill climb championship in both 1947 and 1949. He went from nothing but sketches in a notebook to a national profile and his own brand of cars in a very short time, once the enforced interruption of the war years has been deleted from the time frame.

The Allard Specials of 1936–9 were accompanied by a move away from the Adlards garage as a trading entity towards new Allard car-dedicated premises. The old premises at 3 Keswick Road were developed, and a workshop and small showroom were opened at 51 Upper Richmond Road, Putney, just up the road from Keswick Road. The expanding business that came from orders for replica Specials made 1938 a defining year for Allard as a company within the Adlards Motors Limited operating base. Here we can cite Reg Canham's work as de facto marketing manager for the Specials, and all that went with them, in addition to his duties as sales and admin manager. Canham also drove the acquisition of premises to become a new Ford dealership. The experience, profile and cash flow generated between 1936 and 1939 was down to Sydney, the Specials, his team and Canham, and it was from these foundations that the Allard company would later rise. For now, however, domestic car and sporting car design stagnated while conventional industrial concerns churned out the weapons of war.

The Allard Specials comprised both hardcore hill-climb trials cars and types that could double up as a daily car, tourer or rally stage car. They had hand-fabricated steel coachbuilt bodies mounted over tough Allard chassis and ashwood frames, and featured wide use of Ford parts and easily available accessories. Between the two premises Allard was establishing what was almost a limited production run. The bodies were ordered from three separate specialist coachbuilders: Coachcraft, Ranalah and Whittingham & Mitchell. There remains a mystery, however, as to why Special No. 6 (EYO 750) was badged as an 'Allard' and not an 'Allard Special'.

Perhaps the most influential of the Specials were two specific orders received in late 1938: V.S.A. Biggs required a four-seat, 'milder' version, a car to compete with but also to use as a daily driver (registered FXP 40), while Commander Derek Silcock wanted a three-seat performance Special with added comfort for use as a touring car (FLX 650). The latter was a step away from the hill-climb ethos. It was very good looking and had the beginnings of enclosed one-piece bodywork, albeit still with separate front wings. The engine was not a Ford side-valve V8, but a Ford-derived Lincoln 12-cylinder. The car had an elegant grille, a fully trimmed facia and cabin with the third seat aligned transversely across the car.

It was these two cars, rather than the two Allard Specials (even though one was an Allard 'show' car), that marked a major moment in Allard's evolution. Indeed we might speculate that it was the decision to accept the orders from Mr Biggs and Commander Silcock for one-off 'softer' versions that pointed Allard towards series production cars for daily, sporting driving.

The badged Allard Specials were not just one-offs, they were the start of it all. *Motor* featured an Allard Special on 22 March 1938 after a test run at Brooklands of Ken Hutchison's V12 ELX 50, seen airborne. If four-speed gearboxes had been more widely available it is probable the Allard Specials would have been more easily topped the magic 100mph. In 1939 Derek Silcock's elegant Allard Special FLX 650 was fitted with a higher final drive ratio and did indeed top 100mph at Brooklands.

Motor road-tested the 'Allard Special V12' but continued calling it an 'Allard' in its coverage. *Motor* also realized that FLX 650 was a stepping stone for Allard and pointed out that the car was a different type of vehicle from the last Allard car it had tested (which was indeed a mud-plugger), yet FLX 650 still had 9in of ground clearance and mechanical and electric fuel pumps with separate lines. Communicative and light steering, responsive engine torque and a 100mph top speed all marked the car out as having stemmed from what the

Sydney and Eleanor in the Lawrence Cup Trial, 23 May 1936, climbing the very tricky Red Roads Hill, the first car to make it to the top.

magazine framed as 'expert' design and engineering. Priced at £625, the car was not cheap, but it was versatile and distinct. Few cars, said the editorial, could perform the dual role that made the Allard a consummate performer both on the road as a 'daily driver' and, without modification, on the racetrack or off-road. So was the Allard unique?

FGP 750 and FLX 650 are the two Specials that may define the critical moment when Allard was taken very seriously indeed. *Motor* found that the V12 Allard of 1939 had made the quickest standing start ever recorded in the quarter-mile sprint: 16.6s. Even in the midst of war, *Motor Sport* road-tested FGP 750 in 1944, with Harold Biggs suggesting that the Allard design formula was not just stunningly quick and of fine handling, a car that steered with precision, but also one of the most versatile cars on the market. Biggs thought that there were very few cars that could compete without modification.[6] Biggs's article failed to mention that he had a close relationship with Allards and with Sydney going back to the Streatham Motor Club days; in 1946 he would openly go to work for the Allard company, contributing design ideas with L. Hill.

In June 1938 *Motor Sport* labelled the Allard V8 Specials as being 'universally recognised as amongst the most potent trials and sprint motor cars of the present era'. The next month it carried a story that Allard were to begin actual 'manufacture' of the 'Allard-Special', as it was labelled. So perhaps we could recast the record to say that Sydney announced such plans for production in 1938, even if the true Allard production cars were delayed by war until *Motor*

announced a new Allard 3.6-litre range on 6 February 1946 and that the new company of Allard Motor Co. Ltd, Hugon Road, Fulham, London, was being formed to make and market the Allard sports car.

From the individualistic beginnings of a car to suit his own needs, the Allard car in 1939 was now probably the most successful example of all the 1930s Ford-based 'Specials' that were scattered across the automotive landscape. Suddenly Allard was a, perhaps unintended, 'motor manufacturer', even if small in size, resources and volume output.

The intervention of the Second World War, however, was to delay Sydney's course to that eventual reality. He and his men would spend the war years working on War Office or War Department contracts to rebuild military transport vehicles and special projects, such as making thousands of headlamp blinds, converting vans to gas power, and adapting chassis and bodies for transport use.

1939 AND AN ALLARD FOUR-WHEEL-DRIVE CAR?

Sydney and Reg Canham had approached the War Office in 1939 to discuss their ideas for applying their talents to the war effort. This was before the American Jeep was to prove so vital to the US Army and the British Army in the coming years. In fact the first British suggestion of a simple, four-wheel drive, light-bodied, high-ground clearance, all-terrain mud-plugger Army transport vehicle came, not from Austin

Sydney working on Hutchison's 'Tailwagger' Team Allard Special. Looking on (right), Ken Hutchison and behind (right to left), Norman May, Reg Canham and Eddie May (Sydney's brother-in-law, the youngest of the three May brothers).

or Land Rover, but from Sydney Allard in a submission to the War Office in 1939–40. He had even planned to demonstrate an adapted Allard trials-type military light car to the military top brass at the Chobham testing ground, but it did not happen. We can only speculate what might have happened if more intelligent minds at the War Office had commissioned Sydney to design and build a nimble Ford-based, four-wheel drive, military light vehicle that would have pre-dated the Land Rover by a decade. It is worth noting, though, that he often tested his cars on the Aldershot heathland owned by the Ministry of Defence and in the 1940s he tested a Jeep against an Allard Special to demonstrate his idea.

The 1939 Allard all-wheel-drive wartime vehicle was another example of Sydney's genius and vision overtaken by events. The mechanical transport-based wartime contracts forced the expansion of Sydney's small business into the larger premises at Hugon Road.

From repairing, servicing and modifying just about any make of vehicle sent to him, Sydney sought official permission to concentrate on his known expertise of Ford-based mechanicals and ideas. Soon the company was overrun with damaged Ford military vehicles. Together with his two brothers, Leslie and Dennis, Sydney created a stock

and vehicle control system with a repair and paint line that effectively amounted to a production line. Perhaps Sydney's knowledge of the functioning of Ford's Dagenham factory helped him devise this new set-up – a conveyor belt or line process of 'just in time' parts supply that is now standard motor industry practice. Sydney devised new methods and means of moving all the component parts around the large factory floor area. He also got his hands on a supply of brand new Mercury-specification Ford V8 engines imported under Lease-Lend.

Many military and official vehicles were dealt with in this way by Allards, which provided good experience for post-war car production. The Adlard Army Auxiliary Workshop became a finely tuned, seven days a week plus night shifts operation, among the most efficient of its type and making a significant contribution to the war effort.

During the war all the Allard team would work long hours and then take on extra duties, such as Home Guard service, fire watching and training Home Guard men to ride motorcycles. Sydney, however, would soon be planning the post-war Allard cars that may have been at the back of his mind since they were first outlined in his personal sketchbook. By mid-1945 he also happened to have a factory full of left-over Ford parts and engines.

THE ALLARD MOTOR COMPANY, 1946–66: MAKING THE CARS

Early post war J, K and L chassis assembly at the Park Hill Works 1947–48.

CHAPTER 3

THE ALLARD MOTOR COMPANY 1946–66: MAKING THE CARS

IN JANUARY 1946 Sydney and Reg Canham announced to the motoring press that the recently formed Allard Motor Company would be going into production with a range of Allard cars. The J Type (as a J-1) was to be the definitive first model of the new car range. Two early J-Type devices emerged from the works and were registered as HLF 601 and JGP 473, respectively. Even though the first chassis was not yet complete, *Autocar* wanted to do a feature on the new Allard and produce a drawing of the chassis. Photographs could not be taken, as they would reveal the missing parts, so the artist's imagination had to be used to some extent when drawing in the missing components. According to *Autocar*'s article on 1 February 1946:

> *Allard enters a new field. The first Allard was produced ten years ago as a trials special and it was so outstandingly successful that it was later put into limited production. The new Allard has changed its sporting tweeds for a lounge suit and has been designed for the driver who wants a high performance road car rather than an out and out competition machine. Much lower and with streamlined bodywork, the new car has a Continental appearance, but beneath all its refinements it still retains the flashing performance.*

The Allard Motor Company was fully incorporated in early 1946. It was first cited in a memorandum of association on 14 February 1945 with the meagre capital of £100. A Mr D. Griffiths was the second name (after Sydney's) cited on the paperwork. Things gathered speed from this point on, and the Allard car, badged and marketed as such, was a reality by 1947.

At this time Reg Canham was general manager. He had been with Sydney, effectively as his business partner at Adlards Motors in Keswick Road, Putney, since 1934. Canham ran the works on a day to day basis. Other key members of the team at the time were the pattern maker Jim Saunders, Fritz Skatula, who was an experienced welder, fettler and engineer, and Bob Arthur, a young apprentice straight from school.

As the war ended, Allard were looking for suitable premises for the production of Allard cars in London. Norman and Alan May, Sydney's brothers-in-law, had recently moved out of their works in Park Hill Road, near Clapham Common. Sydney gladly accepted their offer and moved into the workshops in March 1946; all the spares and equipment at the Hugon Road wartime premises were transferred to Park Hill, about 5 miles across London. A small Allard workshop was also secured for a short time at Ryfold Road, just down the road in Wimbledon, and this was where early chassis ideas for the first post-war 'special chassis' were put together. Sydney's own one-off 1946 trials special registered as HLF 601 was built at the Wimbledon workshop.

The main move to Park Hill was completed in a week and

Inside the assembly shop for K, L and M models in 1948.

The 'M' Type ash wood frames being clad with the outer metal skin.

many of the staff from Hugon Road also moved over. The stores were laid out in the way they had been at Hugon Road. Setting up the main workshop was much more time consuming, as a new set of jigs and fixtures had to be designed and made to produce the various chassis on a production line, together with numerous other components such as radius rods, track rods, suspension and body parts.

As was common practice at that time for a relatively small business, and when the availability of many components off the shelf was very limited, much of the fabrication – the bending and shaping – was done in the works by hand or with hand-operated machinery. Even a type of blacksmith's forge was transferred from the Hugon Road workshop. Apart from a lathe, presses and pillar drills, there were no other machine tools: all other machining was outsourced, some of it locally.

The factory at 72–74 Park Hill Road, Clapham, became the main workshop. Space for manufacturing and assembly was somewhat restricted: numbers 72 and 73 were originally houses converted to provide offices, a canteen, parts storage and an engine test bay. There was a separate staff flat on the top floor of number 74. For the most part, all the chassis for the P, L and M models were manufactured on jigs in this workshop from 1946 to 1952.

The pressed steel chassis side members arrived from Thompsons Ltd, who manufactured them in Wolverhampton. The chassis were completed on jigs in the works. Major components such as the V8 side-valve engines, gearboxes and axles were supplied by the Ford Motor Company, as well as other smaller components. Encon Motors, an Allard associated company, produced the petrol tanks. Steering boxes were supplied by the Marles Company and the steel wheels were manufactured by Rubery Owen.

The supply of materials, notably aluminium, steel and rubber, was extremely difficult just after the war and was strictly controlled by a quota system. Petrol rationing still applied. All this made starting up a new car production facility very difficult. Tom Lush recorded that the Allard team were working 24-hour shifts and that he was having to make collections in the middle of the night to keep things going. Two companies that assisted Sydney realize his dream were the coachbuilders Ranalah, who had produced aircraft parts during the war, and the Renown Metal Works Company, which was located close to the Adlards base. Renown, owned by Robert Leaman, would become Allard's supplier of fuel tanks, bulkheads and assorted steel items.

An early difficulty Allard encountered was finding a supplier for the new cars' chassis rails at an acceptable low-volume tooling cost. Thompsons secured the contract for the chassis rails and cross members for the J1, K1, L and M Type models that followed. It is difficult to understand how the body style evolved, as no one person was employed as the 'designer'. Godfrey 'Goff' Imhof, with his flair for style, often gets credit for providing some ideas, but as discussed earlier, this remains an area of much debate.

Godfrey Imhof, who was financially secure in his own right, had time to follow his passion for cars, engineering and design. He became a key contributor to Allard car design and also served as an early form of brand ambassador to the marque. Another important name in the small team was Robin Day, who was one of Britain's leading industrial designers in the 1940s and 1950s, responsible for the interior of BOAC airliners, lounges, plastic chairs and Sydney Allard's post-war brochures. Reg Canham, Harold Biggs, Jimmy Ingram, Sam Whittingham and Imhof all contributed to Allard's bodywork. Together with other members of the team they devised the profile and the alluring crimson enamelled badge, inscribed in silvered script with the one word: ALLARD.

Once a chassis was on its wheels it was moved around the workshop as other components were installed. There was never a moving 'production line' as such, since the limited space did not allow for it, but a *de facto* 'line' of cars in-build was possible. The fact that Allards never had a purpose-designed factory seriously slowed the build time for each car. This increased costs and led to the cancellation or loss of orders following late delivery of vehicles to customers. As an example, it took around 200 hours of labour to complete the build process of one P1 saloon – and this was from a rolling chassis to complete the build. Up to ten people might work on each individual car during its build process.

This was one of the main factors why the Allard Motor Company was not able to compete after 1953 with production-line car manufacturers such as Triumph, MG, Austin Healey and Jaguar.

Sydney's head office was at the rear of 24–28 Clapham High Street, above a small workshop called SI, where he did much of his racing and rally car preparation. At the front of the building, facing the street, was the Allard showroom. Another Allard premises was the spares and stores shop at 43 Acre Lane, later to become part of the growing Adlards Ford dealership, originally only at Keswick Road from 1937.

Around the corner at 51 Upper Richmond Road, Sydney had a machine shop where some parts for the cars were produced. It also acted later as a spares and service department for Allard cars. This building, comprising a block of flats with a showroom on the ground floor and a workshop at the rear, had originally been built by Sydney's father. Sydney took control of the ground floor showroom and the workshop in 1937 as part of Adlards Motors, the Ford commercial workshop for the Adlards Ford dealership.

Some of the people Sydney had met at the Streatham and District Motorcycle Club, such as Reg Canham, Jim 'Mac' McCallan, Ted Friend, Herbert Addy, Alan May, Harold Biggs, Eddie Worth and Eddie McDowell, were taken on by the emerging Allard Company. Reg Canham joined Adlards as the sales and marketing manager as early as 1933. Eddie McDowell, who married Sydney's sister Mary, was a post-war purchasing manager for Allard. Jim McCallan, a leading light in the club, became Sydney's chief mechanic in 1930 and stayed with Sydney right through to 1960. Tom Lush was with Sydney right from the start of the early Trials days and acted as his right-hand man, competition event organizer

and co-driver on many occasions after the war. It seems he could turn his hand to anything as an in-house troubleshooter, project manager, fixer and general ambassador. It was natural that he should write a defining Allard book – from his perspective.

Other significant names within the Allard Motor Company era from 1946 included the designer, engineer and draughtsman Dudley Hume, who worked on the design and development of several Allard models, notably the 1953 JR. David Hooper served a five-year apprenticeship at Allard, starting in January 1949, and was with the company as an engineer and draughtsman until 1964. He was later responsible for the design of many of the Allard components used in the creation or modification of Allard cars, the Steyr and the dragsters, and recommended that the split-axle front suspension should be abandoned.

One employee who has not received sufficient credit was John Farthing, who joined Allard in 1949 as a quality control man and stayed with the company until late 1954. He was a keen photographer and took many of the official Allard publicity/brochure photographs. He was also an Allard Owners Club member for over thirty years.

Dave Davis was Allard's sales manager from 1948 to 1954. Jack Jackman was a skilled coachwork craftsman and responsible for major components of the hand-rolled bodies in the last batch of Palm Beach type cars. Bill Tylee joined the Allard Motor Company from Bentley Motors in 1948 as service manager and was later manager of the Upper Richmond Road works. Gil Jepson was the engineer responsible for development work on the J2X, Le Mans cars, the JR and, later, the ill-fated 'Clipper'. Gerry Belton, public relations and marketing manager for tuning equipment and for the marketing of Shorrock superchargers, later became responsible for organizing and promoting the drag racing festivals. John Hume, an engineer from the Cooper Car Company, joined Allard's to build all the dragsters.

Another Allard workshop and part of the rather scattered Allard business premises was Encon Motors at 9 Estcourt Road, Ful-

The first Allard 'production' chassis built in 1937 for David Gilson, with divided front axle, transverse leaf springs and many Ford components, including Ford V8 engine and gearbox. From 1946 this design was on all the early Allard J1, K1 and L models.

ham. It was here that the aluminium body panels were rolled on hand rollers and shaped by a small group of expert craftsmen. All the panels for the J models were produced and assembled onto the rolling chassis, painted and finally prepared for the road. This was a process that could take up to six weeks in some cases (most of these cars were going for export), since often the specification was tailored to individual customer requirements. These factors created another delay in building the vehicles, which was to have consequences for Allard's reputation. Sydney had hoped to develop the Encon sub-company into a design and development concern, but funding was limited and the Allard family decided not to fund Encon further.

The SMMT (Society of Motor Manufacturers and Traders) 1946 cavalcade in City of London. Godfrey Imhof driving his white J1 (Allard chassis number 106) and Ken Hutchinson in the four seater 'L' Type (chassis number 101).

START UP

Allard car production started to evolve in the summer and autumn of 1946 with the J1 and the first of the K1, L and M models. A production line for K, L and M Type Allards was fully operational by 1947, with approximately 200 cars leaving the factory that year. To think that just two years earlier Allard had been rebuilding War Office Standard transport vehicles and struggling to find parts. Godfrey Imhof's all-white J1 (HLP 5), with its original multi-bar narrow fluke grille, looked like an undreamed of future when it appeared in the 1946 Society of Motor Manufacturers and Traders (SMMT) Jubilee Cavalcade of new vehicles in London. As well as the four-seater type J1 body, photographs of this event show the L Type (HLB 424), proving the L-Type's existence before 1947 and that it was not a separate development. Sydney added his pre-war tourer as the third Allard in the parade. This was the first appearance of the 'Allard' badge, rather than the earlier 'Allard Special' badge.

Godfrey Imhof and his wife Nina soon took the white J1 on what was in effect an Allard-supported, pan-European demonstration tour. By 1947, equipped with a supercharged engine, modified body venting and competition tweaks that included huge, knobbly tyres, HLP 5 was racing in Europe and the UK. An important win was the 1947 Lisbon Grand

Rally, a 1,600-mile rally around Portugal. Next up came the high-altitude Maloja race cup hill climb in Switzerland, which HLP 5 took in 8 minutes 57.2 seconds, a sports car record for the climb. Allard and its J1 had truly arrived.

The year 1947 was to feature Allard's first true 'production series' cars, while 1948 quickly became the best year for Allard car sales with 441 cars being sold (65 per cent of these were M Type coupés). The P Type saloon was not in production until near the end of 1949, but then more than 500 were sold in 1950: 75 per cent of sales were in the UK, but some were exported to Uruguay and Venezuela, while thirty-five went to Australia and New Zealand. The P1 saloon became the best-selling model with 556 units manufactured over a three-year period from late 1949 to September 1952.

Although the P Type saloon remained in production, the L and M models were discontinued after sales of these models in 1950 were already considerably down compared to the previous year. This reflected the sales total of all models, which had dropped from a high of more than 440 units produced in 1948 to 265 in 1949.

Readers who disagree that there was in any sense a 'design' or 'styling' aspect to Allard may be interested in a comment in The Times that, among the other cars in the Cavalcade, the new Allards looked 'streamlined'. Let's not forget that in 1946 even the motoring writer Bill Boddy stated that the new cars were of 'ultra modern' and 'almost futuristic form'.

The first two new J2 sports cars were developed towards the end of 1949. Sydney kept the first one, chassis number 888, for his racing programme. The second J2 was raced by Leslie Allard before being shipped to the Ardun Company in the USA, which was developing overhead valve cylinder heads for the under-powered side-valve Ford V8. Sydney supplied the J2 for testing and development of the ohv engine and received in return prototype heads for his own car.

The announcement of the J2 to the motoring press in September 1949 generated much interest in the new high performance sports car and a flood of orders. Unfortunately the company could not manufacture these new hand-built cars with an aluminium body shell quickly enough, and there was soon a growing backlog of orders. The figure claimed for the most Allards manufactured in one month – forty-five in July 1948, according to the records – has sometimes been questioned. The monthly Allard build figures certainly varied depending on orders and parts availability. Thirty-six P1 Saloons were manufactured in November 1950, for example, but anything between ten and twenty cars a month might be a more accurate average across the peaks and troughs of sales and deliveries. According to David Hooper, there were twenty-three individual Allard delivery dates 'missing' from Tom Lush's published record, more likely related to reasons such as missing records than to Lush's abilities. The high monthly delivery totals do tend to reinforce the 'production' status of the Allard output against some observers' claims of an *ad hoc* output.

By 1949 the venerable Ford 3.6- and 3.9-litre side-valve V8 engine was considered underpowered and out of date. J2 customers, particularly in the USA, wanted more perform-ance, at least for the sports models. Perhaps a larger Ford-Mercury 4375 engine option should be considered.

Even though the J2 was still under development, the first issue of *Autosport* (25 August 1950) carried the Mercury-powered Allard J2 as the lead feature test car and recorded times of 0–60mph in a stunning 8.3s. At this time a 'works' J2 retailed for £1,277, but soon Americans would throw money at their Allard specifications.

Sydney was looking for a suitable engine, but could not find what he was looking for in the UK or Europe. It would have to come from the USA, but the continuing wartime import restrictions and the prohibitive price of importing engines into the UK made the situation very difficult.

It was Allard's sales and export manager, H.J.A. Davis, who carved a niche in the North American market as early as 1950 when Sydney visited the other side of the Atlantic. Allard's West Coast distributor was E. Alan Moss, who ordered a maroon K Type and then a black J Type and a silver grey 'Tourer', according to a letter from Moss to Davis on 4 February 1950. Moss went on to found Moss Motors and became the leading supplier of British car parts in America.

TOM COLE STEPS IN

The Anglo-American Tom Cole, who was then racing a Jaguar XK120, had heard about the proposed Allard J2 and that Sydney knew a more powerful uprated V8 engine, rather than the outdated Ardun-headed 3917cc Ford Mercury V8 unit, was essential if he was going to have a successful racing year.

Allard rolling chassis production line in the Park Hill Works.

The Cadillac division of General Motors had just released details of a new 5420cc V8 engine producing 150bhp in standard form. It was quoted as being smaller, lighter and more powerful than the other contemporary V8 engines. Cole came to see Sydney and said that he wanted to race a J2 in the USA with a Cadillac engine. Tom agreed to purchase the first J2 and export it to the USA minus an engine. At the same time, he said he would try to find a way of getting a Cadillac V8 into the UK for 'experimental' use so that Sydney could fit it into his own J2.

Sydney was as busy as ever. He had become the British hill climb champion with the Steyr Allard in 1949 and competition success with his own Ardun Mercury-engined J2 had generated great sales interest in the J2. To satisfy the demand Sydney was forced to announce to the motoring press that the J2 for the UK market would be equipped with an Ardun Mercury V8, but cars for the USA would be shipped without engine and gearbox, so that customers there could fit their own choice of V8.

Tom Cole arranged for a Cadillac engine to be shipped to England 'for development purposes' and so circumvent normal import tariffs. The engine duly arrived at Southampton docks in January and was eagerly collected the same day by Tom Lush, who was on hand in the Customs shed to see the case being opened, inspected and cleared by Customs.

Once back at the works, an adaptor plate was quickly made to mate the new Cadillac V8 to the original Ford gearbox. It was then installed in a J2 (KXC 170) and taken to the Motor Industry Research Association (MIRA) test track.

Tom Cole was having great success with his Cadillac-engined J2, the El Morocco Blue Zebra liveried car, which was the first J2 exported to America, but without its engine or transmission. Tom won the sports car race at Westhampton, moving onto another win and a lap record at Bridgehampton. Sports car racing was then in its infancy in the USA and Tom's successes brought Allard great publicity. There is no doubt that many Allard J2s sold in the USA were due to the efforts of this true Allard ambassador.

An updated K1, to be known as the K2, with coil spring front suspension replacing the transverse leaf spring arrangement, was in preparation alongside a J2 for the forthcoming New York Motor Show in March 1950. Sydney would be at the show to meet prospective Allard dealers and to find ways to get the Cadillac engines into the UK.

There was much interest in the new K2 at the show and thirty orders were taken, but unfortunately the works did not have the production capability to fulfil these orders with the sort of delivery time expected by some of the customers. The inevitable result was that some orders were cancelled.

The M Type production line.

Each Allard model has its dedicated band of followers. When it comes to landmarks, however, we should consider that the J1 was a defining advance on what had come before, but the J2 laid down the marker for a rawer Allardism. The later Palm Beach model and its derivative, the GT or Grand Tourer of 1959, with its hard-topped coupé styling, similarly symbolize the greatness that Allard could have achieved but was lost. The Allard GT had the potential to challenge Jaguar, Ferrari or Aston. Sydney's GT design was a contemporary, upmarket, sporting coupé with massive marketing potential, but sadly it failed to reach production and only two were built. His own GT, registered as UXB 793, marked the end of the company's own series production creations. The models built were all different yet had the Allard touch and acquired a competition history that few other marques could match.

Allards had pace, if not exactly grace, and a certain panache presented in a wonderfully British way that developed into a style all of its own. Using American engines was not unusual; it would also be good enough for Bristol, Jensen and cars of exotic Latin origins. Not everything went well for Allard and the cars came in for increasing criticism for their poor fuel economy, somewhat raw design and, it has to be said, some underdeveloped fittings that did not reflect the progress of the car market from re-warmed 1930s products to more finessed affairs. Yet Sydney's nascent deal with Jaguar (via 'Lofty' England) to secure that company's engines for new Allards could have been a stepping stone to success – if only further design development of the Allard manufacturing process had been possible.

One advantage Allard had was the agreement with Ford to sell and service Allards in the British regions with Ford main dealer support. Up to twenty Ford dealers could direct a customer towards Allard and the Fulham office and then despatch a demonstrator upon request via the Ford dealer.

Allards were seen in Argentina and elsewhere in Central and South America. As late as 2010 a J2X owned by FIVA committee member and Allard collector Thomas Steur from Bogatá, Colombia, remained in the family. Three further Allards were known in Colombia, and a mystery still exists over the entry of Antonio Izquierdo Dávila's K2 in the 1953 Coupe des Alpes in Europe. Several Allards were delivered new to Mexico, Panama, Uruguay, Venezuela, Guatemala and Brazil. The 1951 Allard J-Type chassis number 2089, for example, was originally exported to Cuba. There may have been speculation that it had disappeared, awaiting rediscovery, but in 2011 the car was sold by RM to a Florida-based buyer, complete with both a Cadillac 429cu in (7 litre) engine and a period-correct 331cu in (5.4 litre) one.

The P1 Type saloon continued its run until September 1953, with the last car (chassis number 3102) being shipped to Sweden. David Hooper designed and produced the drawings for a tubular chassis to replace the P1 saloon for the P2, K2 and J2/J2X, as the pressed steel side rails were coming to the end of production and a new tubular chassis was required.

The last few P1 Type saloons had the new 'X' type front suspension and steering arrangement, so they should really have been designated as PX models. The 'X' arrangement, which allowed the engine to be moved forward, was principally designed to answer complaints about the lack of driver space in the J2.

Sales slumped from the 372 cars made in 1951 to 162

in 1952, despite competition success with Sydney's win in the 1952 Monte Carlo Rally. By the middle of 1953 the P saloon was past its sell-by-date, outclassed and undercut on price by the new Jaguars. Despite this, a further forty-three P Type saloons were sold in 1952, including five being exported to New Zealand.

THE J2X FACTOR

The new J2X was introduced towards the end of 1951 and fifty cars were sold in the USA during 1952. The J2X, like the earlier J2, was principally a car to use in competition, although it could be a road-going machine under favourable weather conditions. Even in 1952 the J Type ('Caddy') Allards were starting to lose their racing supremacy. It is easier to see with hindsight that this was the point when Allards should have elevated the smaller-engined Palm Beach model to compete with sports cars such as the Austin Healey 100, Triumph TR2, MG and Jaguar XK140. Unfortunately the Allard Motor Company did not have the resources to build and equip a new factory unit, nor the engineering team to design and build such a car in sufficient volume to be competitive.

Sydney flew over to New York in July 1952 to meet Larry Richards and set up the Allard Motor Company Inc., with an office in New York. Richards became the Managing Director, although the actual formation of the company was not completed until February 1953.

The J2 sports car rolling chassis exposed, showing the traditional Allard pressed steel deep section chassis side members. Engine is a Ford V8 with Ardun OHV heads. Classic Allard divided front axle and now with coil springs and de-Dion layout at the rear.

The K2 was replaced by the K3 from early 1953. The K3 was essentially a 'stretched' Palm Beach Mk I with similar tubular chassis. In the UK the cars had the old Ford side-valve 3.6- or 3.9-litre V8. Most of the K3 cars were exported to the USA minus the engine, where various Cadillac and Chrysler engines were installed.

Once again, Allard's lacked the engineering capacity to compete with the new cost-effective, production-line manufactured cars coming onto the market from the major car marques. Sixty-two K3s were produced in 1953 and into early 1954. Yet the writing was on the wall at this critical point. Adlards Motors, the associated Ford main dealership, now under the control of Reg Canham, was proving more profitable and growing steadily. A number of Allard Motor Company employees had moved over to Adlards. Others, such as the charismatic Sales Manager Dave Davis, left the company towards the end of 1953.

In an attempt to produce a smaller, lighter sports model to compete with the likes of the new Triumph TR2 and Healey 100, Allard introduced the Palm Beach Mk I in the later months of 1952. A total of eighty-three cars were built before Allard decided to cease production in 1955. Again this was because the company did not have the resources or manpower to build an individually hand-assembled car at a price to compete with the new models from other manufacturers, which were built on a production line and at a volume that brought costs down.

In 1953 car production had fallen to only 138 cars, most of the total being made up of 57 K3s and 45 Palm Beach Mk Is.

In that year a new racing sports car was needed to replace the J2X Le Mans. Dudley Hume, who had earlier fitted the 'X' arrangement suspension and steering to the J2, was employed to design a more compact car based on a new chassis. Similar in some respects to the Palm Beach, but with heavier gauge material and a substantial central cruciform assembly, this car was the J2R, later to be correctly known as the JR. Four JRs were built in 1953. The first car, less engine and transmission, was sent to Erwin Goldschmidt in the USA. Two of the other three cars were built for the 1953 Le Mans race; the third car was completed later. These three cars went to the USA later in the year. One other JR rolling chassis was supplied to the Tommy Sopwith racing team in early 1954 and then fitted, by arrangement with Allard at Fulham, with an Armstrong Siddeley 6-cylinder engine and new body became known as the Sphinx.

Robert Forsyth, who had joined Allard Inc. as sales manager in New York, suggested fitting a Dodge 'Red Ram' V8 engine to the Palm Beach to boost sales and sent over an example to be fitted and put on test. Among the companies Forsyth contacted was the Dodge Division of Chrysler, who

The last JR and the only left hand drive example built. Most of the bodywork had been done at Encon Motors, but as this shop was about to close, the JR was driven on trade plates to the new workshop at Southside, Clapham Common, occupied as the bodyshop for Allard builds from November 1956.

responded positively to his idea of appointing Dodge dealers to market the Allard Palm Beach 'Red Ram' V8 in the USA. Only one Red Ram Allard, however, was made at the time: it made its way to Argentina and was then housed in a Wiltshire motor museum prior to its current home in Germany.

Among Sydney's many ideas was for a racing version of the Palm Beach to run in the 1½-litre class and a J3 to be developed from the JR. Sales of the P2 saloon, K3 and Palm Beach Mk I had been poor during 1953, however, and the company did not have the resources to build new models.

Larry Richards and Robert Forsyth were becoming increasingly worried about the lack of sales in the USA and the limited response to the development of the Palm Beach 'Red Ram' car. It can be seen with hindsight that this was a critical time for the Allard Motor Company: should it attempt to continue expanding sales or wither and die? The choice would require much internal debate and difficult decision-making, and it was apparent that the 'wish list' could not always be achieved.

Sydney knew that the essential problem was the lack of finance to build up a new sports car with a production-line assembly system. Perhaps he was too dependent on the racing scene to promote car sales, and it should be remembered that he had one eye diverted to his successful and expanding Ford dealership, Adlards Motors, which was a vital source of income to the overall group.

The P2 Monte Carlo Saloon and Safari Estate, which were partly built at the King's Road works, had come to the end of the line, as had the J2X. With sales dwindling to only eleven vehicles built in 1956, the King's Road premises was closed and all spares and stock moved to the Keswick Road workshop and all car building to the Encon Motor Works.

The Allard Motor Company still occupied the offices in Clapham High Street, a spares and S1 competition area at the rear of the Adlards Ford showroom, and the Keswick Road premises shared with Adlards Motors.

Allard Motor Company also now used the showroom, offices and workshop at 51 Upper Richmond Road, Putney, previously the Adlards Commercial workshop. The Encon Motors workshop was still working with a skeleton staff on JR chassis number 3406 for export to Norman Moffat in Canada. It was the only left-hand-drive JR chassis built and took months to complete; it was finally shipped in March 1956. The JR with the last chassis number was built specially for Rupert de Larrinaga to replace his J2. Unlike all the other JRs, it had a Palm Beach chassis and it was completed in time to be raced at Prescott and Shelsley. Larrinaga agreed for Sydney to drive the car at Prescott and the Brighton Speed Trials.

After a poor year for car sales the company was now in a bad situation financially. Allard was already only building cars to order and was struggling to continue car manufacture. The order for the JR and the car that had been earmarked for display on the stand at the 1955 Earl's Court Motor Show was cancelled. Instead the Larrinaga JR had to be borrowed, steam cleaned and pressed into service for display in its place as a 'new' JR in order to prevent an empty space on the stand alongside a P2 saloon and Safari Estate. The order for the Safari was also cancelled due to its late delivery to the customer in Hong Kong. No orders were taken at the show.

The Encon works was run by the Hilton brothers and was commonly known as 'Hiltons'. With the Allard work coming to an end they needed to take on other fabrication and panel work. At the end of 1956 they decided to move out to Egham, so the Encon works was closed and the remaining stock moved over to Keswick Road, along with most of the jigs and chassis material for the failed Clipper project, which were sold or disposed of as scrap.

'Jack' Jackman and his remaining Allard staff moved over to join with Adlards in new premises in Clapham Common South Side, acquired in November/December 1955. The buildings at the rear of Southside, as it was known, were converted from two rows of lock-up garages into a sizeable workshop and the large house at the front was converted into offices with a car sales area. The Adlards Motors Ford dealership was thriving and expanding with a new showroom and extensive workshop facilities being built in Acre Lane, Brixton. It was decided that all used car sales and body repairs would move to Southside.

Although production of the Palm Beach Mk I had ceased by March 1955, orders and enquiries were still being received, so it was decided to restart production of a new Mk II Palm Beach, based on a slightly modified Mk I chassis with a new front suspension, designed by Sydney, that replaced, at last, the outdated split-axle arrangement seen on all previous Allards. The all-aluminium body was designed from the sketches originally received from Robert Forsyth. It was decided to produce a batch of the new Mk II Palm Beaches and to take a stand at the London Motor Show at Earl's Court in October 1956.

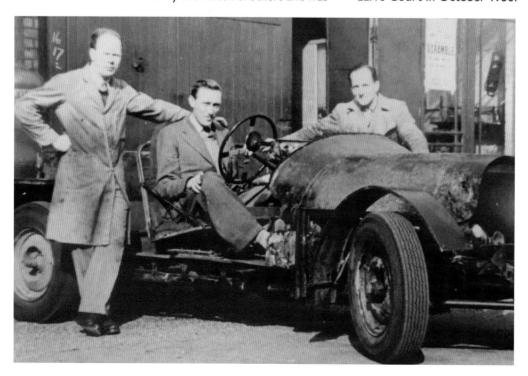

Gil Jepson, engineer on left, Dudley Hume in drivers seat of the prototype P2 saloon chassis, which he designed and with Jimmy Minion, road tester on right.

With the closure of the Encon Motors premises, the new Allards were to be built at the Southside works, amid the Adlards Motors body repair area. This was not an ideal situation and inevitably it was a struggle to get one new rolling chassis and one car ready in time for the show. In fact, the first new Mk II body was built on a Mk I chassis with minor modifications and with the old Mk I split front axle arrangement. The new Mk II chassis was the first Allard to be fitted with a Jaguar engine, by special arrangement with Jaguar in Coventry, from where the engine and gearbox was collected by Jim Mac.

Very little stand space remained by the time the decision was taken to exhibit at the Motor Show, so the company only had space for one Palm Beach Mk II and one rolling chassis. The Palm Beach, however, was effectively killed off by sports cars such as the Triumph TR 2 series and Austin Healey 100, which were more developed cars with money behind them.

Apart from lack of suitable space to build the cars, the Allard company was about to be hit, as was the motor trade in general, by the news that petrol rationing was to start on 17 December following the Suez Crisis. Two orders for the Mk II were immediately cancelled, as was the Monte Carlo Rally and other motor sport events. The prospect of any further sales was gloomy indeed. It is not surprising therefore that the build of the last few cars took several months, as the cars lingered uncompleted in the dusty workshop. The Allard Motor Company as a car manufacturer had sadly died. The remaining equipment and the handful of staff were absorbed into Adlards Motors without a murmur.

FAMOUS ENDORSEMENTS

The first true Allard Special, CLK 5, was owned in the 1950s by the artist Euan Uglow, who claimed to have reached 100mph driving over Waterloo Bridge. The broadcaster Richard Dimbleby purchased the M Type works demonstrator JLK 957 as chassis number M-331 in January 1949.

He used the car extensively, including taking Brian Johnson as co-driver and co-commentator to the south of France in pursuit of the 1951 Monte Carlo Rally. Deep snow forced the pair to abandon all hope of doing so and they retired to a hotel near Digne. Dimbleby sold his well-used M Type in April 1951 and it ended up in the hands of W. Bowden, who kept it for years.

Steve McQueen owned an Allard J2 at one time, and it is said that his son crashed the car with his father on board. Film director John Paddy Carstairs owned two Allards from new, one of which was a K3. Other media types, both real

Richard Dimbleby with his personal M Type.

Dirk Bogarde in an M Type.

and fictional, also ran Allards during the brand's heyday. The BBC radio announcer and actor Randal Herley owned an Allard (GGB 331). *Dick Barton – Special Agent*, played on the radio by Noel Johnson, Duncan Carse and Gordon Davies (1946–51), and on film by Don Stannard (1948–50), also drove an Allard. Other famous Allard owner/drivers included Kay Petrie, Dirk Bogarde, General Curtis LeMay, General Francis Griswold, Bill Marriott (of the hotel group), Tommy Sopwith (then of Armstrong Siddeley Motors) and Phillip Schwartz, Vice President of the Colt Firearms Company. George Putnam, a Los Angeles TV news anchor and talk show host, owned a J2X.

Other famous M Type owners of the time included the cycling champion Reg Harris, Nicolai Poliakoff (Coco the Clown), the model Barbara Goalen, the composer Eric Coates and Donald Campbell's wife, whose M Type was painted blue to match the colour of her husband's record-breaking hydroplanes. The L Type JGX 651 belonged to the wrestler Li'l Abner Osborne before being owned by Fred Damodaran and then Robert Robinson-Collins; it now has a new owner.

Sir Alan Ayckbourn's father Horace Ayckbourn, who was deputy leader of the London Symphony Orchestra, purchased one of the last J2s (ONK 21). This car had a J2X nose-cone and found its way to the USA and the ownership of Jim Weddle. J.C. Armstrong, a test pilot with the Douglas Aircraft Company in Long Beach, California, owned a J2 in the 1950s.

It is reputed that the infamous Kray Brothers were rather keen on Allards too. Perhaps an Allard would not have been suave enough for Ian Fleming's James Bond, but it has been suggested that Fleming toyed with the idea. Imagine Bond, the real, tough killer, in a J2! In Fleming's original novels Bond drove a Bentley, not an Aston Martin, which was a later, Hollywood-inspired idea. There is also a link from the former Naval intelligence officer Fleming to a real-life Second World War spy who owned an Allard, since he knew the famous double (or triple) agent Dusko Popov, whose M Type, KLP 821, featured in contemporary portraits of this colourful 'James Bond' type character.

More recently, the author Clive Cussler owned an Allard. Several recent media figures have liked Allard too, notably classic and vintage car guru and *Classic and Sports Car* magazine's editor-at-large Simon Taylor, who is a dedicated Allard enthusiast. Josh Sadler, the founder of the Porsche specialist Autofarm, is also President of the Allard Owners Club. The Cobra designer Carroll Shelby drove an Allard J2. Allard may have influenced the design of the Chevrolet Corvette through Zora Arkus-Duntov.

During the post-war years Allard published a bulletin-like news magazine for its customers and even three editions of the *Allard Official Year Book*, featuring Allard drivers such as Len Potter, Jean Kent and Giuseppe Farina.

INTO THE FIFTIES

The elegant (and now rare) Allard P2 Monte Carlo coupé, a fastback (styled by Ingham) imposing four-seat grand tourer with a walnut-face facia, leather trim and a Lagonda-esque style, should have been a top-selling example of the best of 1950s British fashion and driving. It should have been a natural alternative to a Jaguar, a Bristol, an Aston Martin, maybe even a large Mercedes-Benz or a big American coupé, but its details missed the ever-moving market and design targets. The grandiose P2 Monte Carlo was also more than twice the price of a Jaguar XK150, and so heavy and overburdened that is was hardly economically viable in fuel-rationed Britain. To some, however, the P2 Monte Carlo remains an intriguing jewel of what an 'alternative' and more developed version of Allard might have become, however obscure. The first one was sold to Dr David Reid Tweedie, who lived in Malaya.

As the 1950s progressed Allard's model line-up consisted of new ideas, old ideas and various amalgams of both that were vastly expensive in both development and manufacturing terms. The superb styling of the lighter-weight Palm Beach Mk II with new Ford or Jaguar engines should have saved Allard, but it was underdeveloped at launch and did not launch the company into the 1960s, even though Jaguar's XK150 was several hundred kilograms heavier and older in style. Then came Malcolm Sayer's aerodynamic design for the Jaguar E-Type and there was no hope for the likes of the Palm Beach Mk II or Daimler SP250. Only two examples of the Allard in its GT coupé variation were built.

A new, design-led 'free market' that allowed car customers to choose what they wanted from any marque's offerings was not obvious in the early years from 1945. Post-war carmakers used what they could get their hands on, and supine customers simply accepted what they were told was available in a society reeling from war and rationing.

Big companies turned out cars that were essentially prewar technology and standards, all wrapped up in old styling. But by the mid- to late 1950s a new age of style-oriented motoring was dawning based on new technology. The likes of Ford and General Motors were throwing millions at new ideas and developments. 'Design' was truly born, bringing a new era of body monocoque construction and 4- and 6-cylinder engine efficiency. Allard, however, was slow to adopt this expensive new process of car design and manufacturing, just like any small company operating with limited financial and staffing resources. Therein lay the seeds of decline. Sydney knew what was wrong, and took steps to protect his marque and employees and produce his way out of trouble, but time was against him. He took a big leap in terms of design, sales and risk going from the elegant J1 roadsters to the vital and truly dedicated sports car that was the J2 series.

The big manufacturers were faster to change their model ranges and model cycles, using their massive resources to keep their costs down and secure market advantage. The days of the 'one man band' were numbered. Sydney was a product of his era and his socially orthodox British environment, but his achievements show that he was a man of talent and vision, a free-thinking entrepreneur, a risk taker and design maverick who became a major national name in motor sport.

British society in the 1950s was framed by obedience to known knowns, so it is remarkable that Sydney should have stepped outside its boundaries with such personally driven success, yet never have been perceived or portrayed as a maverick or eccentric. Sydney was, simply, hugely respected. That his efforts were well received in America, where cultural and design obedience was less dominant, rather proves the point.

The British and American public had read about Sydney's driving exploits in their daily papers, not just in *Autocar*. Although it would have made him somewhat embarrassed, Sydney was a bit of a national hero. As such he was unorthodox. Perhaps it is these diverse ingredients that made the man and his cars unique. Sydney's enthusiasm and work ethic meant he was able to achieve so much. Finance and facilities were always limited, yet at one stage Allard was making more than twenty cars a month.

ALLARD AND GM?

In December 1953 Larry Richards visited London. There are no records of what was agreed at his meeting with Sydney, but it seems likely that he was told that Allards were unable to build the cars he needed. He resigned from the company shortly after his return to New York.

Robert Forsyth, who had taken over Allard Motor Company Inc. after Richards's departure, proposed a new more stylish body design for the Palm Beach (for the full story *see* Chapter 7). His sketches for the new body were sent over to Sydney and he continued to press for some action on the 'Red Ram' V8 Palm Beach and building a few cars to be sent out to Dodge dealers as demonstrators. He was convinced that the General Motors Dodge division was poised to give its backing to the Allard, in a similar way to Donald Healey's arrangement with the Austin Company in the UK.

The American Generals Le May and Griswold, were already Allard owners when they visited the Park Hill works. In 1953 Le May purchased a JR and supported the Allard racing team at Le Mans. Here they are seen with Reg Canham and Dave Davis, Allard Sales Manager.

Only thirty-eight cars had been built in 1954, mostly of the Palm Beach type, plus a few of the last J2Xs. All these cars were still assembled at the Encon Motors works in Fulham. With falling sales, the company was looking for other business to take their place. So when approached by David Gottlieb of Powerdrive Ltd, who had plans to build a three-wheeled mini-economy car to take advantage of the fuel price increases, Allard took on the partly designed project, agreeing after lengthy discussions to build two prototypes. The resultant 'economy' car as the Allard Clipper was a failure.

Others have speculated that if the J2X, JR or Palm Beach had still been in production, with some updates, when Carroll Shelby came along several years later, an arrangement similar to that which Shelby sorted out between AC and Ford could have been done with Allard.

GT, THE LOST HOPE

Just before this new era, Jack Jackman's team at Southside was completing the last batch of three Palm Beach Mk IIs during 1957: the chassis numbers were 7102, 7103 and 7104.

Chassis number 7102 was the first hard-topped, Jaguar-engined GT Coupé. It was built for Sydney and displayed on the Allards Motor Show stand along with chassis 7103. The GT was road tested by *Autocar* and made an appearance at the Goodwood test day for the Guild of Motoring Writers in 1958, where it was driven at high speed by the racing driver-turned-journalist Paul Frère.

Autocar criticized the very hard front suspension. This Palm Beach GT car, in common with all others except for the first prototype, had the suspension designed by Sydney with David Hooper, which incorporated laminated torsion springs mounted in-parallel with the chassis side members. Another two examples of the Mk II were under construction at Southside, including the second GT, which was fitted with a 'tuned' Chrysler Firepower V8, mated to a push-button Torqueflight automatic transmission. This car was built for export to the wealthy American Dupont family, who sent over the modified engine to be fitted.

The modified engine was not suited to automatic transmission, because power came in with a bang at about 1,800rpm, but with little response below that engine speed. This made manoeuvring in traffic somewhat hazardous. After driving the GT down to Southampton docks for special shipment on the *Queen Mary*, Jim Mac said that he had never been so nervous in all his long motoring career with Allards as he was during the two-hour drive.

The last two Palm Beach Mk IIs (7106 and 7107) built by the company at Southside in 1958 had Jaguar XK140 engines. They took several months to complete, surrounded by all the other Ford bodyshop work, and marked the true end of Allard car production by the Allard Motor Company. One car was run by the secretary of the Allard Owners Club, Ray May, for more than ten years before being shipped to the USA. The last car was converted to front wheel disc brakes and won the *Concours d'Elégance* at the Brighton Speed Trial, before being similarly shipped to the USA in 1959.

Reg Canham seen here with his cigar and customary cup of tea, was an essential part of the Allard story. 'Reg' became MD of Adlards Motors in 1950, Sydney's associated Ford Main Dealership.

A QUESTION OF DESIGN

In terms of design, we can see big differences between the later cars, such as the J2, and the K, L, M and Palm Beach series. Perhaps we should note from the outset that Allard did not employ a car designer or 'stylist' and did not spend vast sums commissioning Italian *carrozzeria* to dream up pretty bodies, as other British marques would do. One or two external body proposals, however, notably from the coachbuilders Abbott of Farnham, were made and built by Allard.

The 1930s early Allard Specials were functional in design and just built for purpose. While there was a need to create a car that was acceptable in terms of appearance, no actual 'styling' process was evident. However, it is clear that in the final Allard Specials the company had begun to make some attempt at creating a body design motif or 'look'.

The first stage of this trend, about 1937–8, seems to have been the creation of a very elegant front grille design, set at a rakish angle and leading back into a neatly proportioned body. Informed observers have suggested that the 1930s BMWs and Rileys may have been subconscious influences.

The last two pre-war Allard Specials, created as the 'Silcock' two-seater and 'Biggs' four-seater cars, provide the first evidence for a deliberate and defined Allard style. Commander Derek Silcock's V12-engined, two-seater was registered as FLX 650, while FXP 470, supplied to V.S.A. Biggs, was the final pre-war four-seater Allard car design. Dare it be said that FXP 470's razor-edge front and rear wings have a hint of style matched by the swept-back tail? The vee-shaped and faired-in central panel between the wings' front valance and grille surround was a notable departure that perhaps showed a touch of Riley Sprite-inspired elegance.

Allard purists might be horrified at such 'design' thoughts, but careful study reveals that the shape of these last Allard Specials clearly includes some suggestion of new 'styling', for want of a better word, perhaps reflecting the output of the British-designed but exotically named Corsica coachworks, as well as BMW or Riley. Bodies created by Eric Giles were applied to several other marques at this time, including Bugattis. The Giles brothers and their creations had a strong presence on the 1930s motoring scene, from smart West London streets to the Prescott hill climb and the Bugatti Owners Club events.

The two later Allard Specials were never intended to be 'pretty' as such – that's not the way Sydney thought – but someone clearly decided to try to inject some sense of design into the body styling. To emphasize that point, Tom Lush called them 'the new look cars'.

We do not know if one man penned these cars, or if their

features were an amalgamation of ideas, but hidden in the Allard archives are sketches by Sydney himself that contain hints of the styling elements seen in these cars. However, it is reputed that Derek Silcock and Martin Soames collaborated on the suggested body style of the car registered as FLX 650.

We can surely opine that the bodies of these two very good looking and modernistic cars, despite being categorized as Allard Specials of the 1930s, marked the beginning of an acceptable Allard design. They were built by the coachbuilders Whittingham & Mitchell in London; after the war the company supplied further bodies for the new Allard production series cars. Samuel Whittingham may well have been a key player in achieving the Allard 'look'. Sydney Allard himself, Reg Canham, Goff Imhof, Dudley Hume and David Hooper may also be cited as influencing various aspects of the design and engineering of the post-1946 Allards. David Hooper, Allard's resident engineer, inherited the title of Chief Draughtsman after Hume left the company. Various internal notes confirm that the company pursued the low front that would reduce frontal area and benefit drag reduction – 'always worth a few horse power', according to Sydney.

Before his death in 2019, Dudley Hume recalled his busy times working for Sydney with affection and a dose of reality. He recalled that he worked on entry airflow and under-bonnet cooling airflow as vital factors in the body designs. Allard money was spent on the research and development of an aerodynamically effective venturi-effect nose-cone and radiator airflow feed that could be fitted across the Allard models. It seems that despite such work, the special-flow nose-cone was not applied to all the cars as it took time and labour to install the panels.

Dudley made it very clear that the engineering and design process at Allard was a complex and close-knit affair between Sydney and his small team of men. There were many issues and constraints and, as Dudley said, 'I never criticized any decision he made because I knew he had a hell a lot of on his plate'.

Through such words, we can perhaps gather just how difficult and stressful low-volume car production on a limited budget can be. Hume recalls that finances were always tight and that Sydney had many worries. Investing in twin-tube chassis development, throwing off the old 'girder' chassis construction and avoiding one-off thinking in design and production terms brought many demands.

Another influence on the look of Allard cars, principally those built to his personal tastes and notably his long, low, sleek, low-drag, fixed-head two-door coupé, was Alfred Godfrey 'Goff' Imhof.

It was all very well for Sydney to lay out his ideas for chassis and components on the factory floor and arrange their configuration to suit, but who designed the aluminium or steel bodies that clothed the cars, or were they too an organic outcome of a non-process? The answer seems to lie in a bit of Sydney's typical free-thinking intuition, Dudley Hume's thoughts, David Hooper's ideas and the actual sketches and suggestions of Godfrey Imhof. Yet Jimmy Ingram drew up the later frontal styling and themes seen in the K3 and Safari. Harold Biggs and L. Hill have also been cited as part of the Allard in-house 'design' team.

Godfrey Imhof was financially secure as the heir to a radio and gramophone business. He owned the His Master's Voice record shop in central London and the Imhof's store on New Oxford Street for gramophones and hi-fi. He was a part-time inventor, refrigerator manufacturer and patented a device for sharpening gramophone needles. Imhof ordered several Allard cars, including one to his own design, and was someone who mixed with and employed known designers of the day. He gave the emerging architects Herbert Tayler and David Green an early opportunity to design the Imhof's shop on New Oxford Street. The pair also designed Imhof's own home in west London: Tayler and Green went on to great things in British architecture. Imhof may have been keen to claim authorship of certain Allard body designs, but others, notably Tom Lush, have eschewed actually citing a defining design or style influence.

Was there a hidden hand in Allard design who created the Allard logo and badge? It is known that Robin Day, the top industrial designer and graphics artist of his era, who was responsible for the interiors of the new London Heathrow Airport terminal and BOAC's aircraft, designed the 'professional' Allard brochures and sales material of the late 1940s. He also knew Imhof very well indeed. Imhof has been categorically referred to by Lush as having had an 'art department'. Since Day's name actually appears on the new, upmarket Allard brochures, it can only have been Day who was, with Imhof, a force behind the professionalization of Allard's imagery and brand materials – Sydney would have been far too busy to deal with it. Allard's crimson and silver badge simply reeks of Robin Day's industrial and interior design portfolio.

In Imhof's 1950s design for an extended-chassis coupé, the angled, split-vee windscreen and front wing line, the cabin turret and sweeping, low-angle rear deck and tail lines all look 'Continental'. Even *Autocar* noticed this about Allard styling in February 1946. The JIs were sculpted, stylish and displayed, as some have suggested, a touch of French design in their grand sweeping shape and scale. Maurice Chevalier apparently greeted Goff and Nina Imhof's white JI with the comment, '*Quelle jolie voiture*'.

Authorship of Allard body design remains a mystery. Chris Pring, current editor of the Allard Owners Club's newsletter agrees: 'The question of who designed those bodies has always fascinated me. Look at the pre-war specials and the post-war production cars and it is very hard to detect a lineage. Under the surface? Yes absolutely. But fully clothed? A different league.'[7]

Dudley Hume contributed knowledge of body engineering and an early appreciation of aerodynamic 'frontal area' concerns. Yet Allard's never had a single retained designer or stylist figure. Everything was in-house with contributions from 'regulars' such as Whittingham, Imhof, Ingram and Biggs. Fritz Skatula is cited in David Kinsella's book as being one of Sydney's regulars at the Fulham premises where Sydney and his men would sit down and sketch out their designs. Skatula, however, was an engineer and welder-fabricator, not a stylist. Tom Lush, on the other hand, cites Reg Canham.

COACHBUILD CONSULTANTS

So, what of Allard's various body builders? The small companies that Sydney commissioned for body panels and, perhaps, body shape were Coachcraft, Ranalah, Whittingham & Mitchell, Southern and Hilton. Did the Ranalah concern or Allard's other body suppliers, Whittingham & Mitchell, which were both expert panel builders with wartime aircraft experience, offer any advice? Several Allard experts cite Sam Whittingham's hand as an early influence on the two, stylish Allard Specials of 1938 and the post-war Allard shapes. It should also be remembered that Sam Whittingham would become manager of the Allard body shop after the war.

The late Brian Sewell, art critic and car design enthusiast, privately stated that Allard's post-1946 car design was a 'very intriguing story', because in his view: 'No British coachbuilding antecedents of obvious influence can be seen in the Allard. The slab-side cars might look American, but the sweeping lines of the J and L Types are redolent of France – Delahaye and Delage.'

Writing in 2010, Mel Herman wondered if Sydney, having used the back end of a Bugatti in 1936, might have been inspired by the front styling of the Bugatti Type 57C cabriolet with its unique bodywork by Voll & Ruhrbeck, which the 'standard' post-1947 Allard front design appears to reflect to some degree.

Certainly there is a step-change in styling between the wheeled 'bathtub' look of the Specials and the somewhat exotic, be-spatted body 'shell' of the truly post-war K2. From the K2, through the L and M Types, the same basic outer panels were used, but with differing cabins and A-pillar designs. In the P1 a smoother 1950s look was achieved. In the much more aerodynamic, fully bodied (that is, without separate wings or fenders) Palm Beach series and the Abbott-bodied low-drag coupé, Imhof and Allard began to flirt with enclosed lamps, podded features and smart, swept, rear-end styling themes.

David Hooper, whose ideas included the revised suspension design used on the Allard 'works' specification P series Safari, threw light on the origin of some of Allard's diverse ideas, many of which were non-starters or stalled at the development stage. The Allard quick-change differential drawings were by Hooper. As he explained, 'Sydney used to attract a wide range of projects to the company, some with potential, other required considerable investment, which was never forthcoming'.[8]

Such clues provide a hint as to how Sydney ended up looking at numerous schemes from the Atom to the Clipper, and beyond. Despite such projects, we can say that Sydney Allard ran a lean operation and relied on a close, trusted team, who were involved in more aspects of production than their job titles suggested.

Styled on the lines of a pre-war 'Doctor's Coupé', this one-off body on an Allard chassis was certainly unusual.

ENGINE AND GEARBOX PROBLEMS

The key issue for the true Allard production cars post-1946 was the use of the Ford V8 side-valve engine. As will be discussed later, the issue was addressed by various tweaks and major mechanical changes to the Ford engine until the switch to Cadillac power. The Ford gearbox was tough, but the later power ratings it was made to handle (up to more than 200bhp) could cause issues that the box was never originally designed to encounter.

The Ford three-speed gearbox was also built down to a price by Ford, so making it do things never envisaged for it was not easy without major and expensive casting and machining changes. One thing Allard did do, however, was upgrade the metal used in the gearbox for testing in a one-off racing gearbox. This gained a 30 per cent increase in strength, according to Dudley Hume.[9] David Hooper thought that it would have been much better to design and build an in-house gearbox to enhanced Allard standards.

After talks with Howard Hobbs, the designer of the Hobbs automatic gearbox, a one-off gearbox was constructed and installed in Sydney's personal P2 Safari with a Mercury engine. Hobbs is said to have wanted the gearbox back to show to Jaguar, but when they tested it they reputedly did not use enough oil.

The Clerk-type electromagnetic gearbox was designed for the Steyr Allard, but had been initially tested in a standard Allard chassis with an 85bhp Ford V8 flat-head engine. Despite many efforts by the team at Allard, not least the hours put in by Bob Arthur, the company's experimental and prototype mechanic, the Clerk box could not be made to function reliably and suffered from overheating. The design was abandoned. Bizarrely it has recently been discovered that the standard 1960s Volvo gearbox bell housing was almost identical to the 1950s Ford unit and can be modified to fit an Allard under restoration and requiring a gearbox.

The prototype body for the Palm Beach Mk.I was rejected because of its bug-eyed styling.

Apart from a small number of M and P Types, all of the Allard J1 and J2, L, K1 and K2 types were fitted with the angled (26-degree) axle beam and modified radius rod pivot design, while the Mk I Palm Beach, J2X, JR, K3 and P2 all had parallel axle pivots. The parallel design (X type) has a much improved steering geometry allowing the engine to be moved forward, and as a result increasing cockpit legroom on the J2X.

While many people voiced concerns on Sydney's insistence that the divided axle should be retained, his justification was that it was a simple, independent system that was extremely robust and cost-effective to produce; it was also competition-proven. As David Hooper explained to the Allard Owners Club: 'Sydney was well aware of the limitations of the divided axle but was concerned about the potential development costs to replace it. Also he probably always drove cars which were kept at a high level of maintenance, avoiding the inherent long-term problems which could happen with worn suspension components.'

One early Allard design issue was weather-sealing the soft-top roofs for winter. One way of solving this was to fit a wintertime hardtop to the car without making any structural alterations.

In 1947, however, Col John Dolphin, who had worked for the Special Operations Executive during the war, devising such innovations as a one-man submarine and a folding motorcycle for parachutists, designed an ingenious folding roof section using counterpoise springs to lift, rotate and slide down a hinged, two-piece hard roof, the boot lid opening up like a clamshell to let the descending roof into the boot space. The idea was for the roof to be fitted to Allard and Healey cars and it was featured in *Motor* on 5 May 1948.

The concept was not new, however, and seemed remarkably similar to the metal folding roof mechanism produced by the French designer Jean Andreau for Peugeot in the mid-1930s. Fitted to a modified Allard M Type body (registered KKE 59), *Autocar* also ran photos of the conversion in May 1948. Two Dolphin-Allard cars of this type were built.

Another nugget of unusual Allard history revealed by David Hooper in the AOC *Newsletter* was an outline drawing of the Allard Motor Company's truck from 1948. Unfortunately no photographic records are known to exist, but we do know that the design was built from the remains of an Allard P1 or M Type damaged in an accident. The truck was never taxed and was run on trade registration plates.

Its relatively light weight and V8 engine gave it the reputation of being perhaps the fastest truck in South London, easily capable of surprising unsuspecting car drivers as it sped away from traffic lights. David recalls that this was perhaps the reason why the truck met its doom: it is rumoured that shortly after a heated battle against a Jaguar when getting away from traffic lights, the works truck got a little too close while the Jaguar braked, and the two made contact.

FURTHER THOUGHTS, 1954–9

After a very good year in 1952, by 1954 production of cars was falling rapidly in response to a downturn in sales. As early as mid-1953 Sydney Allard needed to sell more cars, create new cars or diversify. Failure to achieve one or more of these outcomes could have serious consequences for the business.

The King's Road works closed and the manufacturing part of the Allard company was focused on the Encon works in

The same body, as demonstrated here, would accommodate three abreast. In the car from left, Eddie McDowel Parts Manager, Dudley Hume Chief Engineer and Reg Canham Managing Director.

Fulham. It was at this time that the ill-fated Clipper project encountered problems and delays, notably in its glassfibre construction moulding.

During 1953 the workforce turned to producing Allard spares and items such as grilles and trims. The grilles were manufactured in-house using a mechanism by which the copper slats or ribs (triangulated section) were drawn or extruded via an ingenious electrically powered device of great power. Aluminium grilles for the K and J Type cars were made using a press tool for the slats or ribs, which were then attached to their frames with low-temperature brazing. Indeed, Allard had become adept, early practitioners of the difficult skill task of welding aluminium, which was previously the preserve of racing car engineers, naval architects and the aviation world.

One customer for the engineering side of the Allard existence was Hersham and Walton Motors (HWM), to which Allard supplied axle tubes. Allard also repaired damaged tubes for HWM. According to David Hooper's AOC-published notes, some of these axles were articulated in their centre section and were impossible to repair without a very expensive jig, which HWM was not keen to fund.

The Allard version of the 'quick-change' differential axle was designed in 1953 by Robert Clerk and supplied to HWM and Cooper Cars. Clerk's original design had called for a steel insert to be cast into an aluminium collar or case (via the process). This was a difficult and expensive technique and British capacity to create such an item was rare. The resulting steel-alloy construction was fraught with complex issues and the alloy casing was likely to be brittle, leading to failure. (It would be another decade before the temperature-controlled 'chill' casting of aluminium gearbox casings would be truly mastered in the industry.)

In an explosion of ideas, Sydney began to think of new ideas and sketched many of them in his notebooks. They ranged from a new lightweight, aerodynamic racing car with a low centre of gravity to the later thoughts of a tuned-up and tweaked Ford Anglia that became the Allardette. Dragsters would later populate his fertile mind.

Long before that happened, the Allard company explored aluminium welding and panel fabrication, even investigating a proposal to manufacture an alloy-constructed sausage-making machine. This made it as far as Patent Office research, but was dropped before too much money was spent. Other potential manufacturing ideas were a device to empty cash from car parking meters and a device to straighten damaged alloy tubular structures, such a poles, posts and mounting tubes.

In between these projects there lay work on new engines, new steering mechanisms and, intriguingly, a new suspension design. David Hooper clearly recalls suggesting improvements to the Allard-standard swing axle front suspension:

On the Allard car side I managed to persuade Reg Canham that we needed to evaluate a revised front system to replace the swing axle. While the swing axle may have been simple and robust, it did have inherent problems, which were unacceptable to many buyers.

Contrary to the Tom Lush book, I, rather than solely Sydney, designed a MacPherson type suspension – which was fitted to the works Safari. It was based on the concept that it might have been possible to convert existing coil sprung suspension cars retaining the coil spring, shock absorber and steering arms in their existing positions. The strut loads were taken

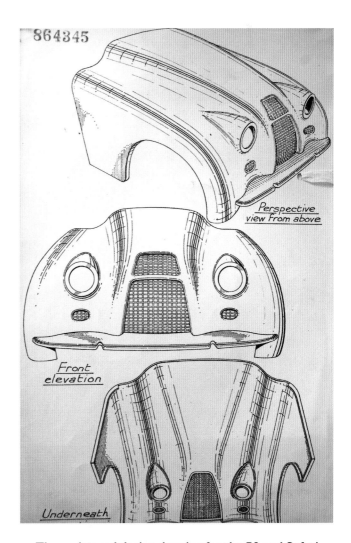

The registered design drawing for the P2 and Safari models, with one piece front end, which lifted at the rear. Normally manufactured in aluminium.

via a replaceable treaded trunnion and the upper loads via a self-lubricating bush. As a prototype it was acknowledged that upper sliding bush operation was not satisfactory in the long term, however there were numerous solutions available. Of course it would have been far simpler to have constructed a conventional wishbone set-up. However, Sydney did not share that view (but only because of the tooling costs).[10]

Hooper also drew up some ideas in the mid-1960s for a 'new' car with the Allard ethos. He built a prototype using a twin-tube chassis, de Dion rear suspension and a wishbone front suspension. The car was called the 'Manta Jaguar' but, says Hooper, 'could well have been an Allard for the future'.

Tom Lush had also built a Ford-powered trials Special for Sydney during the Second World War as an unofficial project for Sydney.

The French designer Jean Danninos had co-engineered the revolutionary monocoque body of the 1934 Citroen Traction Avant and went on to found the premier French luxury car marque FACEL (and the Vega series). During the 1950s he was in close negotiations with Sydney Allard

about a joint project to develop a chassis for a smaller, Hotchkiss-powered 2.0-litre FACEL model. The joint project failed to proceed, yet one Allard-built chassis (no. 5150) was supplied to FACEL; its whereabouts is now unknown. Allard was also in contact with the French transmission company Cotal and provided some gearbox tooling on a 'one-off' project. This episode was proof of how Sydney was looking around for new income streams. Setting up an Allard engineering consultancy was a real possibility.

From 1958 to 1965 Adlards Motors Ltd grew rapidly to become one of the largest Ford main dealers in the UK, selling up to 650 units, cars and commercials (new and used) per month. The Ford Motor Company put those with a main dealer contract under pressure to maintain high levels of stocks of their complete range of models.

Reg Canham ran the business as Managing Director, supported by four directors, but Sydney as Chairman was increasingly involved with finance, planning and stocking levels. The other directors were Arnold Scott (finance), Eddie Little (sales), Jack Jackman (workshops) and Alan Whillier (parts).

The early type front axle and steering arrangement, with the steering arms pointing backwards from the divided front axle and the radius rods running from the chassis forward to the axle.

THE CARS: MODEL BY MODEL

The elegance of the early J1 Type seen with spats fitted.

CHAPTER 4

THE CARS: MODEL BY MODEL

THE ALLARD MOTOR COMPANY did not exist at the end of hostilities in 1945. The eleven pre-war Specials (and the one wartime build Special, which lay in the back of the workshop throughout the war) had been made by Sydney and his Adlards Motors garage business, with the latter cars actually badged as 'Allard Specials' and then just as 'Allard'.

During the war, however, when Allard had focused on military maintenance and mechanical contracts for the army's transport needs, Sydney had been as busy as ever, making notes, plans and sketches. This was what he had always done, now developed to working on the idea of making Allard cars after the war, based on experience gained from his pre-war Specials and using many surplus parts from the Ford army vehicles that his company repaired and serviced during the war years.

By 1950, just five years after the war's end, Sydney had built more tahn 600 cars of the K, L and M series. But it was the early J Type and then its J2 and J2X progeny that were the height of the sporting Allard line and today form the core of Allard's rise in values.

ALLARD J1

As early as 1946 Bill Boddy drove the early Allard J Type prototype, but this was not the true beginning of cars available for delivery. That first J1 chassis was given the random chassis number 103 and was built in the spring of 1946. Six

J1s were built in 1946, four with alloy bodies. Five were sold to eager 'competition' drivers to be entered in the then still popular trials series, mostly in the British West Country and the Midlands. Chassis number 106 was registered as HLP 5 and became well known in the hands of Godfrey Imhof, competing in the UK and on the Continent (as Europe was then known to the British). Imhof became a close friend of Sydney and ambassador and supporter of Allard.

The handful of 'pre-J1' cars were devoid of the bulbous front wings that were later used across the Allard cars, except for the J2 series. In these early post-war days Sydney had envisaged a short run of twelve competition-use cars with engineering and characteristics reflecting his 1930s 'Specials' experience. Effectively the J1 was initially produced for selected competitors at that time: Jim Appleton, Ken Burgess, G.N. Mansell, Len Potter and Cyril Wick. An 'extra' competition-type J1 was built for Sydney's friend Ted Frost. Cyril Wick would later take the sports car record at Shelsley Walsh in his J2 Special (ex-Sydney Allard), which had a lightened chassis and very expensive aluminium hubs. With a time of 39.94 seconds, this was the first time the 40-second barrier had been broken at Shelsley Walsh. Subsequently at the Brighton Speed Trial, driving this Allard, Wick beat Jaguar's test driver Norman Lewis in his works car.

These early Allard cars were to be Mercury-Ford engined (bored out to 4.3 litres); several were to be supercharged (Marshall-Nordec type), converted to ohv configuration, or re-engined with General Motors engines (an Oldsmobile Rocket unit would later feature in one such car). The J1

Classic interior of the restored J1. The driver was close up and personal to the controls and the wheel.

chassis would also be used for Sydney's own car (JGP 473) and be adapted for the later Steyr Allard.

When the J1 Imhof supercharged trials car, KLD 5, first appeared it was clad with what became known as the 'joke body'.[11] The body had been specifically constructed like that by Imhof to highlight a loophole in a change to the rules governing the construction of trials cars introduced by the British Trial Drivers Association (BTDA) in the summer of 1948. Imhof had spotted that, while a new rule specified that passengers had to sit further back than the driver, there was no limit to how far back they could be. In KLD 5's case Tom Lush sat so far back the front wheels of the car were hardly ever on the road. After making his point in its first trial, the Colmore Trophy Trial in December 1948, the rear extension was removed as the car was so difficult to control on the road. The car was then given more 'conventional' bodywork, which it still more or less wears today.

We can say that in 1946 the J1 looked quite different and 'modern' alongside many of the square-styled vehicles that were still the norm. The great post-war step-change in car design had not really manifested by 1946. With its rounded nose, 'waterfall'-style slatted grille and large, bulbous front wings, J1 was actually quite imposing.

This first J1 development chassis bore the trade registration plate number of 078 YX. J1 could also be quickly modified to a competition or trials car by easily removing

Jim Appleton, another successful competition driver, at speed hanging the tail out!

the bolt-on wings to save weight. The windscreen could be folded flat or the entire fitting and frame quickly removed.

On the competition scene, the Ford V8-engined J1s, which had torque, traction and tractability, were soon the cars to beat. Imhof, Burgess and Appleton formed a team of Allard J1 drivers named the Candidi Provocatores ('White Challengers') and were all highly successful in a range of competition events from 1947, using enlarged and uprated 4375cc (4.3-litre) Ford Mercury V8s fitted with a Marshall-Nordec 'Roots' type supercharger. The Ford V8 had a natural tendency to run hot and further overheating resulted from

1946 at Prescott – Sydney in his J1 Special. HLF 601.

ALLARD J1: TECHNICAL SPECIFICATION

Body/chassis
Stylish aluminium bodied, two-seat two-door open competition car, which could quickly be converted for sports use. Shortened chassis, with reinforced channel section side rails. Ash wood frame supporting aluminium body.

Engine
Ford V8 side-valve 3622cc (3.6 litre), 85bhp at 3,800rpm
Iron block and heads
Bore/stroke   77.79 × 95.25mm
Compression ratio   6.1:1

Transmission
Ford 3-speed gearbox with heavy-duty centrifugally assisted clutch and enclosed (torque tube) propshaft. Final drive 4.1:1

Axles/suspension
Front: divided swing axle with transverse leaf spring. 26 degree angled radius rods, running outside chassis rail to front axle
Rear: rigid (live) Ford axle with Girling lever-arm type shock absorbers, transverse leaf spring

Steering
Marles worm and roller steering box

Brakes
Front/rear   Lockheed 12 × 1¾in drums

Wheels/tyres
Wheels steel   6.25 × 16in
Tyres   650 × 16in

Dimensions
Wheelbase   8ft 4in
Track   (front)   4ft 8in
               (rear)   4ft 4in
Overall length   13ft
Width   5ft 8in
Ground clearance   9in

Weight   19½cwt (2,175lb)
Weight distribution,
front/rear   50/50

Performance
0–60mph   13.0s
Top speed   80mph
Fuel tank   17 gallons
Fuel consumption   17–20mpg overall

Principal variations
Ford Mercury 4.3-litre V8, some fitted with Marshall-Nordec 'Roots' type supercharger

poor exhaust gas flow, especially when trying to extract more power and rpm out of the engine. This was a common problem and many experiments were carried out to cure it, including the overhead valve modifications.

The personal petrol ration of 7 gallons a month in 1945 was increased to 15 gallons per month in August 1946, which enabled the J1 competition drivers to enter more events. The reader might care to bear in mind that the J1 had a 16-gallon fuel tank and driven competitively would achieve less than 15mpg. Even bettering 25mpg on the open road was not easy.

Despite all the rationing and shortages, despite the difficulties of supply, 1946 was a defining and fast-moving year for the new Allard Company. Seven cars were sold and more were ordered, establishing the early beginnings of a true production series base. A further five J1s were constructed in 1947. Chassis number 114, registered as JGP 473, was campaigned by Sydney and he had many successful competition results. Len Potter had by now become one of the most successful J1 drivers: he had three special bodies built on J1 chassis as No. 152, 273 and 275.

Len Potter was categoric about Sydney's achievements when he discussed them in the 1980s: 'He achieved great things with very little. A remarkable story. But early on, some people were a bit sniffy about his modified cars – they were probably just jealous.'[12] It was Potter and Arthur Gill who somehow survived when their Allard plunged 500ft down a precipice in the 1950 Alpine Rally. The car was destroyed but the occupants thankfully survived.

ALLARD K1

This was a sporty two-seater for long-distance touring. According to the records, the first K1 was chassis number 104. This car was subsequently exported to Belgium on 22 October 1946. A total of 151 K1 cars were manufactured from 1946 to 1949. Most were for UK customers. At least eight went to countries in South America – Allard's name had spread that far.

The aluminium bodies for the very first four K1s were mounted via an ash wood frame and were manufactured for

Allard by the coachbuilders Abbott of Farnham, Surrey. The chassis was built at the Park Hill works in Clapham, London. The 6in extra length of the K1 over the J1 allowed a larger tail end and an increase in luggage space. The spare wheel was housed under a cover on the body rear panel.

The K1 was described as a tourer with two seats. It was based on the typical Allard chassis, with stamped-out channel section side rails and with a wheelbase increased by 6in as compared to the J1 'Competition' model (from 100 to 106in). The chassis featured transversely mounted semi-elliptic leaf springs at the front; at the rear there was a Ford-type live axle with torque tube and forward running radius arm at a 26-degree angle onto the axle beam. Hydraulic Girling-Luvax lever arm-type shock absorbers were mounted on the chassis side rails front and rear.

As a two-seater, the K1 had a more attractive close-coupled curved body line around the cabin and rear end than the four-seat L Type. However, we might see it as a developed J1.

With the torquey 3622cc Ford V8 producing 85bhp at 3,800rpm, a final drive ratio of 4.7:1 and weighing only 22cwt on the road, the through-the-gears performance with such a power to weight ratio is outstandingly good for a car of its time. A comprehensive road test in 1948 reported that the engine could even be throttled down to just 6mph in top gear and then accelerate away smoothly.

In common with all Allard models, the K1 had a 9in ground clearance, independent front suspension with a divided axle, and the engine was set well back in the chassis, providing the driver with excellent old-fashioned power-steer handling and traction, which was particularly noticeable in the wet.

Other features of a car with a sporting pedigree were the fold-flat windscreen, an extra hand-operated engine speed control, a fly-off handbrake, a 2-gallon reserve fuel supply and the floor-mounted gear lever with its remote extension.

Unlike the J1, the line of the rear edge of the door was vertical rather than following the line of the rear wing. Later modifications included a shorter grille. Some cars specifically used for competition had additional engine side panel louvres and ventilated steel wheels, which were made by Rubery Owen.

ALLARD K1: TECHNICAL SPECIFICATIONS

Body/chassis
Two-seat open tourer with hood and aluminium and steel body supported by ash wood frame.
Chassis: channel section pressed steel side rails with box section and fabricated cross members.

Engine
Ford V8 side-valve 3622cc (3.6 litre), 85bhp at 3,800rpm (option of 3.9 litre, 95bhp)
Iron block and heads
Bore/stroke 77.79 × 95.25mm
Compression ratio 6.1:1

Transmission
Ford centrifugally assisted single-plate clutch with Ford three-speed gearbox. Enclosed propshaft. Final drive: 4.11:1

Axle/suspension
Front: transverse leaf spring with divided swing axle. Hydraulic shock absorbers (arm type)
Rear: Ford live-rear axle with torque tube over propshaft

Steering
Marles, worm and roller type steering box

Wheels/tyres
Ford steel wheels 6.25 × 16in
Tyres 650 × 16in

Brakes
Front/rear Lockheed 12 × 1¾in drums

Dimensions
Wheelbase		8ft 10in
Track	(front)	4ft 8in
	(rear)	4ft 4½in
Overall length		14ft
Width		5ft 9in
Ground clearance		9in
Weight		22½cwt

Performance
0–60mph	16s
Top speed	84mph
Fuel consumption	17–20mpg overall

ALLARD K2 1950–51 (DIFFERENCES FROM THE K1)

Coil springs and telescopic shock absorbers replaced the transverse leaf springs (front only).

Revised front end body and bumper arrangement with J2 type grille and 'port' holes.

Engine options: higher compression 3.9- or 4.3-litre engine option with 140bhp, providing rapid acceleration up to 90mph. Cars exported to the USA less engine.

ABOVE: **Len Potter in his Allard K1 car with his co-driver Peter Smith. Potter was one of the most successful trials and rally drivers, seen here in the south of France after the 1949 Alpine Rally.**

LEFT: **Owned by Nick and Eleanor Jubert, this K1 was winner of the AOC 'Best Open Allard' award at the annual Concours d'Elegance in 1979.**

Allard aluminium higher compression heads and twin carburettor inlet manifolds improved performance. Overall the K1 feels like a much higher-powered car, with the ability for fast cross-country driving. It would go on to sporting prowess and a distinct following.

A little-known Allard special-bodied car was one with a lightweight body created by Whiteladies Garage of Whiteladies Road, Bristol. Under the pen of Jim Bosisto, a lightweight body for the K Type chassis, consisting of a tubular framework using the *superleggera* ('super light') system, was draped with a simple aluminium body skin, achieving a weight saving of nearly 100lb over the standard K Type. Bosisto built 500cc 'micro-specials' and entered Formula 500 races, so he knew a thing or two about reducing weight and frontal area. Sydney Allard did not support this project financially but he did encourage it and passed all enquiries on to Whiteladies Garage. It is said that up to twelve such rebodied K Types were constructed, although none are known today.

The K1 would lead to the K2 and ultimately the K3 (with a three-seat front bench), which had a stylish look that might lead to transatlantic success, but sadly it was a bit of a rush job, lacking the finesse of the development to its fittings.

Allard L Type

The L Type was very similar to the M Type in its general technical specification, but the bodywork, although still only two-door, was designed to accommodate four passenger seats, with the front seats folding forward to give access to the rear seats. The L Type came first, as early as late 1946, but did not really enter monthly production until the following year, when at least between three and five L Types were made each month. Unusually for Allard, the prototype chassis (101) was dismantled and not sold off as a 'new' car.

This overhead view of the four-seater **L Type** shows off the extended cabin design.

The wheelbase was 112in: 12in longer than the J1 and 6in longer than the K1. The car had an overall length of 15ft 2in. The extended cabin with its four-seat configuration (rear bench) and straight-lined extension behind the two front seats was a simple yet effective solution to the problem of creating space, though it was of its era, not elegant but functional in a straight-lined sort of way. An extended ash frame

An unusual special-bodied L Type estate; the builder is unknown.

**L Type interior displays how good an Allard
interior can look when correctly restored.**

lurked underneath and the lack of cross-bracing at the B-post at the trailing edge of each side door would later give rise to flexibility in the cabin 'tub'. The back seat was wide but low, with little protection for the passengers, but a snug-fitting hood with side screens kept in the heat-soak from the engine and provided warmth to the occupants. The windscreen could be folded flat.

The first production L Type was manufactured in 1946 with chassis number 102. This car was later registered HLB 424 on 18 March 1947. It was prepared for the Jubilee Cavalcade organized by the Society of Motor Manufacturers and Traders (SMMT) to celebrate the fiftieth year of the British Motor Industry. Three Allards took part in the Cavalcade.

Over the next two years 191 L Types were manufactured by Allard Motor Company at the Park Hill Works in Clapham.

The early-build cars had quarter bumpers front and rear, with rear wheel spats. Later cars had full-width bumpers and a shorter grille. The standard specification included a Bluemels 17in steering wheel, a steering column with telescopic adjustment and a column-mounted gear change.

**Despite being an add-on to the chassis, the longer cabin with rear bench seat still looks
right. This 1949 L Type was owned by Blair Shenstone for more than five decades.**

A 24-stud head suitably Edelbrook-modified. Classic Allard power.

ALLARD L TYPE: TECHNICAL SPECIFICATION

Body/chassis

Four-seat, two-door open tourer with folding canvas hood. Steel body on ash wood frame. Steel chassis with channel section side members, braced with tubular and fabricated cross members.

Engine

Ford V8 side-valve 3622cc (3.6 litre), 85bhp at 3,800rpm
Iron block and heads

Bore/stroke	77.79 × 95.25mm
Compression ratio	6.1:1

Transmission

Ford three-speed gearbox with column change. Heavy-duty single plate clutch with centrifugal assistance. Propshaft enclosed by torque tube

Axle/suspension

Front: divided axle with transverse leaf spring telescopic shock absorbers
Rear: rigid (live) Ford axle with transverse leaf spring, Panhard rod, lever arm shock absorbers

Steering

Marles type steering box

Brakes

Front/rear	Lockheed 12 × 1¾in drums

Wheels/tyres

Ford steel five stud	6.25 × 16in
Tyres	600 × 16in

Dimensions

Wheelbase		9ft 4in (112in)
Track	(front)	4ft 8in
	(rear)	4ft 2in
Overall length		14ft 6in
Width		5ft 8in
Ground clearance		9in
Weight		22½cwt (2520lb)
Weight distribution front/rear		40/60

Performance

0–60mph	15.7s
Top speed	85mph
Fuel consumption	17–20mpg overall

Variations

M Type four-seat drophead with hood. Redesigned body at rear, rolling chassis, similar to the L Type, but rear track 6in wider (4ft 10in). Improved build and trim quality over L Type.

The M Type has rigid windscreen and frame: L Type has fold-down windscreen.

ABOVE: **The M Type owned by Mel Herman looks very upmarket and quite unlike a J2.**

Leather- and wood-lined, the M Type had a traditional and classic British 1950s interior.

M Type seen from above with its well-designed convertible folding roof, sometimes called a cabriolet.

ALLARD M TYPE

'A modern high-performance car, with exceptional road holding qualities' – so said Allard's advertising. Writers in 1947 noted its 'strikingly modern lines', and how its 9in ground clearance gave it more rough-road ability than any other British production car. Another comment at the time noted that:

> road holding and traction is exceptional with 60 per cent of the weight on the rear wheels inspiring confidence in handling in all conditions. The low speed pulling power is remarkable – the acceleration in top gear from very low r.p.m., means there is rarely a need to change down for hill climbing.

Sydney Allard chose this model for his first Monte Carlo Rally, as did four other Allard owner teams in 1949. All the Allards were among the top fifty finishers.

The M Type was more of a cabriolet design than the convertible L Type. It was more luxurious and had a differing cabin/scuttle structure, rigid windscreen and frame, with better weatherproofing. The Park Hill works built the M Type as a drophead coupé alongside the L models. The M is built on the same 112in wheelbase chassis as the L Type, but has fixed windscreen pillars or A-posts (ash beamed), updated scuttle and dashboard, and a differing boot line, with more room and greater comfort in the rear seats, which are better shaped and individually padded. The rear track is 6in wider than the L Type.

The M Type is a car of some elegance and found fame with celebrity owners. Apart from the body style, seating and trim, the technical specification is as for the L model.

One M Type, original registration number JYH 496, was fitted with twin spare wheels mounted on each front wing. Apart from the Izquierdo K2, which had a similar fitting, this was a very rare Allard specification indeed. Another M Type was the 'thatched car', registration OVW 625. During the 1960s its owner, John Potter of Pebmarsh, Essex, could not afford a new roof for the car. Being a master thatcher, he really did thatch a new roof for his car: it cost him £15.

The two non-standard 'Safari'-type Allard estate cars, based on the M Type chassis and hand-built by the Sentinel Waggon Works of Shrewsbury, are little known. Sentinel was the English offshoot of a Scottish company originally known as Alley & MacLellan. Since 1875 the company had manufactured railway stock, locomotives, ships and small boats, steam-powered road vehicles and, after 1945, diesel lorries. According to research by John Peskett and Simon Richards, it is likely that M Type chassis numbers 781 and 779

Various L Types would later provide the basis for modified bodies and sporting 'Specials' created by individual owners. An early reference to a similar-looking modified L Type as an L1 comes in Tom Lush's book. There is photographic evidence of chassis number 771, an L Type minus front wings and built as a two-seater, dating back to the 1950s to show that it was from the early days a lighter, modified L Type, and that it always had a unique nose-cone and grille design. So there may have been a few ex-works factory L1 specials.

An example of what can be done to an L Type is chassis 191, registration VHX 555. Bought as a barn find for £50 in 1977 by Aubrey Howard, the car stood for two decades until an early 1990s restoration by Rick Newman for the owner. Sadly Aubrey died before the car was completed, but it was finished and given a new valve train with an Iskendarian 77 camshaft, twin Strombergs (97s), an Offenhauser dual-phase inlet manifold, a lightened flywheel and high-compression alloy cylinder heads. This car has won several Allard Owners Club Concours Awards in recent years as a true testament to a ten-year restoration and the essential correctness of the L Type idea.

Hans-Albert Oppenborn's immaculate red M Type is a German resident that appears at many classic car events.

formed the basis of these two 'woody' chassis/body conversions, constructed in October and November 1948. The two cars were created for the director of Sentinel and his friend E. Rogers, the owner of Rogers Haulage. Registered as EAW 813 and EAW 673 respectively, it is likely that these M Type-based estate cars (or shooting brakes) were built for typical use and to avoid purchase tax, since they were effectively cited as vans due to having no rear side windows – an Allard van!

M Type chassis 81M745 was delivered to Derby on 22 October 1948. It was for sale in Germany in 2012 fitted with a very rare Opel-built version of the Ford V8 3.9-litre side-valve, which has the distributor mounted vertically at the rear above the oil pump. Opel took over the German Ford factory in 1939 and these engines were constructed for military transport use. About 45,000 were manufactured, mostly for the Russian front. It is an unsolved riddle how such an engine was fitted to a post-war M Type.

A total of seven coachbuilt M Type special-bodied cars with a Ford V8 were constructed, but today only three remain extant. An M Type coupé, registered 359 XUJ, was built in 1948 by Gould of Regent Street, London: it was displayed in all its Ford Baltic Blue glory on the cover of the Winter 2010 issue of the Allard Owners Club *Tailwagger* magazine.

The very rare Gould of Regent Street special-bodied Allard M Type coupé. This example, formerly owned by John Turnbull, is one of only three known to survive.

An Offenhauser head fitted to Dave Lovey's K Type – an engine that breathes properly.

A Lea-Francis bodied M Type and the Gould-bodied M Type were two rarities. Even rarer was the one-off Shirman fixed-head M Type coupé built in 1949. It featured a hardtop, rear side windows and curved rear end sweeping down to the bumper. Constructed by J. Shirman of Charlwood Street, Victoria, London, this was the rarest of the privately built M Type coachbuilt oddities of the era.

ALLARD P TYPE

Manufacture of the P Type saloon followed on from the J1, K1, L and M Type models. The first saloon, chassis number 1041, was completed in early 1949 after about a year in development. It was related to the same base chassis frame as the L and M Types, with the same wheelbase of 112in. The body and wood frame development work had been handed over to the Hilton Brothers works in the King's Road, Fulham, and they were struggling to get the first car ready for display on the Allard stand at the Earl's Court Motor Show in October. The main problem had been in mating the jig-built alloy body, with its ash frame, to the chassis. Mating ash pillars and struts to alloy body panels, notably around the scuttle and doors, was a time-consuming and expensive hand-built technique that many manufacturers would quickly abandon. There was a frantic rush to get the four Allards onto the stand before press day. The new saloon attracted much attention, actually arriving on the morning of the press day.

This was the first post-war Motor Show and the crowds were huge. The Allard stand was placed just in from the main entrance and was swamped within minutes. It continued this way throughout the show. All four cars sustained body damage from the massed crowds attending the show, who trampled down all the protecting barriers.

Orders for the new saloon were taken, but the earliest deliveries were quoted for June the following year, some eight months ahead. Due to material and labour shortages, it was nearly a year before the first cars were delivered. Many new car-hungry customers were prepared to wait this long, but unsurprisingly some were not and inevitably orders were lost.

The Allard Company, with a full order book for the M Type already, simply could not build up the manufacturing capacity to capitalize on a seller's market. Another cause for delay was the new coil-spring front suspension that was incorporated to replace the transverse leaf spring. With more cars in use on the roads, weaknesses in this arrangement had begun to be highlighted, so Reg Canham as sales manager quite naturally wanted the new car to have the new

'improved' suspension. The saloon was also fitted with a higher 3.78:1 final drive ratio; these gear sets were made by the David Brown Company, one-time owners of the Aston Martin marque. Such a final-drive ratio gave 'relaxed' 70mph cruising at just over 3,250rpm, which is high by today's standards from five-speed gearboxes, but quite unstressed for 1949. A top speed of 85mph was not particularly fast, but was 'adequate' for the application, as Rolls-Royce might have said. The torque and good gear ratios mean that the 40mph to 70mph overtaking performance was excellent, however, and minimal gear changing was required across country. A fourth gear ratio, though, might have improved the mpg.

The Ford V8 still provided real thrust despite the car's increased weight over other Allard applications. Yet this saloon was designed and built in such a way that it required far too many, often hand-made, components requiring many man-hours to complete the build. It was inevitable, with hindsight, that the continued production of a saloon could not have been cost-effective without a complete redesign of the body and its materials, and the development of a faster production line.

Nevertheless, here was a full four-seater with rear-seat access and egress facilitated by folding front seats and two large doors. There were many 'developed' design touches: heating with demisting facility, an instrument cluster, a windscreen that, most unusually, could be cranked open vintage-style. Dunlopillo foam seats clad in British high-grade leather were an expensive fitting. This Allard also had door pockets and storage shelf. Lockheed hydraulic brakes provided ample anchors.

Light steering, low-roll handling and real 'oomph' created a saloon that drove well with high limits of adhesion. Sydney soon proved that point in France by winning the Monte Carlo Rally in a P Type.

A total of 28 saloons were manufactured in 1949, with 241 in 1950 and 245 in 1951. There were a further forty in 1952 and the final two in 1953, when production of this model ceased after 559 were built.

The Monte Carlo-winning Allard P1 saloon had remarkably few changes from the normal 'production' saloon. The engine was increased in capacity from 3.9 to 4.3 litres with an increase in bore and stroke, but the single Solex carburettor remained. Marginally higher 7.0:1 compression aluminium heads were fitted and the Dunlop Trakgrip tyres were grooved with specially cut 'V' angled slots, facing in opposite directions on front and rear wheels. Inside the car a fold-flat navigator seat allowed the occupant a chance to get some rest and on the facia they mounted a Halda Speed Pilot meter. There was also a vital tools and spares panel

The P Type fixed-head saloon was not exactly elegant, but an imposing, large and comfortable Allard, and a type that won the Monte Carlo Rally in Sydney's hands. R. GUNN

Darell Allard's bright blue P Type received a thorough restoration and brought many miles of enjoyment.

behind the rear seat. Two spanners, in the most commonly used sizes, were taped to the steering column for emergency use – every second counting on this major rally.

Installed under the bonnet was an inspection lamp with a very long lead that could reach all around the car for wheel changing or repairs in the dark. There was a collection of spares such as coil, spark plugs, distributor cap with leads, fan belts and hoses. There were additional Hella spot lamps and special snow deflectors below each headlamp.

Although not a particularly fast car, the V8 engine gave it the necessary low-speed punch out of corners and, with 57 per cent of its weight on the rear wheels, the P Type Allard had the grip on snow and ice to make it a winner.

Sydney won the Monte in 1952, but he had also finished eighth in 1950 and was in line to win that year. In 1953, too, he finished eighth out of 253 finishers. The P Type had proved its worth.

The original Allard publicity shot of the Safari in bronze, with beige vinyl roof and half-timbered style.

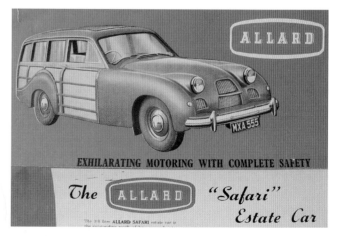

The company's 1950s advertisements, such as this for the Safari, featured a bright red treatment.

ALLARD P1 SALOON: TECHNICAL SPECIFICATION

Body/chassis

Four-seat, two-door saloon body at front, mostly of steel construction, mounted on ash wood frame. Steel chassis with full-length channel section side members, from bulkhead rearwards, all aluminium. Reinforced by central cruciform and cross members, with front and rear bulkhead support hoops.

Engine

Ford V8 side-valve 4375cc, 85bhp at 3,800rpm (option 3917cc)
Iron block and heads

Bore/stroke	77.79 × 95.25mm
Compression ratio	6.0:1

Also available with Ford Mercury 4375cc V8

Transmission

Ford single-plate heavy-duty clutch with Ford three-speed manual gearbox with column gear shift

Final drive ratio	3.7:1

Axle/suspension

Front: Allard divided front axle, with coil springs and telescopic shock absorbers. Radius arms running forward from the outside of the chassis rail to the front axle

Rear: Ford live rear axle with transverse leaf spring and telescopic shock absorbers

Steering

Marles steering box

Brakes

Front and rear	Lockheed 12 × 1¾in drums

Wheels/tyres

Ford steel wheels	4.50 × 16in
Tyres	6.25 × 16in

Dimensions

Wheelbase		9ft 4in (112in)
Track	(front)	4ft 8in
	(rear)	4ft 10½in
Overall length		15ft 6in
Width		5ft 9in
Ground clearance		9in
Weight		27cwt
Weight distribution		50/50

Performance

0–60mph	18.0s
Top speed	85mph
Fuel consumption	18–20mpg overall

Principal variations

High-compression Ford Mercury 4.3-litre V8 with 100bhp 'Monte Carlo' specification

Derivative

M2X: based on P Type rolling chassis and running gear. P Type body fitted with convertible soft top. Canvas hood assembly folds into rear seat well. Revised grille and frontal styling
At front, X Type suspension and steering arrangement

Today the P Type remains remarkably popular and only the need to renew the ash wood cabin frame and windscreen pillars poses serious work for the restorer. Everything else is pure cast iron Allard.

ALLARD M2X

The M2X was effectively a P Type saloon with the roof removed and a soft-top roof (a canvas hood that was neatly hidden from view when folded). It was a 'Drophead Coupé' of classic type, but more classic than sporting in appearance. The car had less 'show', but as with all Allards it did have go! Somewhat crude perhaps, but highly effective, durable and quite upmarket, the Allard M2X – a P-Type convertible if you like – was different and interesting, standing out in its marketplace.

Of note, the M2X development car ended up sold in Malaysia and a chassis marked as M2X under a P-Type body reputedly lurks in New Zealand.

The first two M2X drophead cars were built with the one-piece lift-up by hydraulic pump; the pivoting front bonnet and wings assembly were similar to the Safari estate. The remaining cars had the conventional P Type saloon bonnet. All twenty-five M2X cars were built between May 1951 and September 1952.

The chassis had coil springs, radius rods and the ubiquitous split axle at the front and the steering linkage had forward-facing steering arms as for the J2X, hence the (M2) 'X' symbol. The 3.6-litre Ford V8 flat-head was the obvious engine fitting. With the hood up, all-weather protection was good, and the rear (perspex) window could be opened or removed to allow ventilation. Like the P Type and the Safari, the wide torque curve of the engine mated to well-chosen

**The M2X, a convertible version of the
P Type that sold in low numbers.**

gear ratios provided easy and powerful driving in the key 40–70mph performance and cruising range. The 20-gallon fuel tank and final-drive ratio of 3.78:1 allowed long-distance touring if a light throttle was applied.

There were some further modifications to the ash under-body framework to stiffen the assembly (scuttle shake was an inevitable problem) and to accommodate the foldaway hood and frame. The front grille was a slightly modified 'A' type similar to the one on the Safari estate. In all other respects the chassis was a 'P' saloon chassis.

ALLARD SAFARI

The Allard Safari was essentially a P2 Type chassis developed into a capable and versatile large estate-type car having a wide passenger compartment, with a bench seat providing three-abreast seating front and rear for six passengers and with provision for two more seats facing to the rear – a true 'shooting brake' type estate car. These seats could be folded away under the floor – an advanced feature, although in practice, these were rarely fitted. The car was ideal for country and outback use and must surely have been targeted at the American and overseas 'colonial' export markets.

This capacious car offered six regular seats in the main cabin and 45 cubic feet of luggage space, or three seats on the front bench and nearly 100 cubic feet of flat cargo space in the rear deck area. You could even sleep in the car. This rugged estate car with decent traction and high ground clearance really should have been a big export earner for Allard. Priced at £1,250 ($3.500), the Safari had huge abil-ity, yet seemed to have lacked adequate marketing in the

'colonial' markets. The price rose to £1,771 and only eleven were sold.

The estate body was designed by Jimmy Ingram and the ash framing work and body were built in the Encon Motors workshop in Fulham. The body was mounted on a P Type saloon with an extended tubular chassis.

The suspension was by coil springs all round, with heavy-duty coil springs at the rear with separate shock absorbers, aided by a Panhard rod and twin radius rods controlling rear axle movement. A de Dion-style arrangement was fitted with dead axle de Dion tube and Ford 3.78:1 differential, combined with inboard 12 × 2in drum brakes.

At the front was the usual Allard/Ballamy split axle arrangement, with forward running radius rods, connecting and pivoting centrally onto the chassis front cross member.

Steering was by Marles cam and roller steering box. Under the huge bonnet, which was lifted at the rear by a

THE SAFARI GOES TO CANNES

After Sydney's win in the 1952 Monte Carlo rally, it was discovered that the prize money, being in French francs, could not be taken out of France as wartime currency restrictions still applied. Sydney therefore, used the money to pay for a family holiday in the south of France:

My mother Eleanor and her sister Hilda, drove the faithful Allard Safari the 850 or so miles down to the south of France. We rented a villa in Nice. There were eight of us in the Safari with all our holiday gear, so that demonstrated the huge carrying capacity, which very few other cars could match at that time.
On one occasion we had to stop and were surrounded by a huge flock of goats. My sister Marion started feeding them with the door open – a big mistake! The goats soon filled the front of the car. Luckily they did not stay long because, with an almost flat floor, a bench seat and column gear change, they were able to go in one door and out the other, with nothing in their way!
At another time, we took a cine film of the family stepping out of the car. When it got to person number 12 or so, it was obvious that there must be some trickery going on and of course there was – members of the family going around and through the car several times – but the trick showed the space capacity, and it was fun.

ALLARD P2 SALOON: TECHNICAL SPECIFICATION

Body/chassis
Four seat, two door saloon body, constructed in aluminium, mounted on a newly designed tubular chassis, but retaining the same wheelbase as the P1 saloon. Complete front-end body section, lifts from the rear operated by an hydraulic pump.

Engine
Cadillac 331ci V8, 150bhp at 4,00 rpm
Iron block and heads
Compression ratio 8.0:1

Transmission
3-speed Cadillac Lasalle or Cadillac automatic
Final drive ratio 3.78

Axle/suspension
Front: Allard divided front axle with coil springs and telescopic shock absorbers. Radius rods running forward to the front axle
Rear: Coil spring and dampers with de Dion axle arrangements, with Panhard rod and inboard drum brakes

Steering
Marles steering box

Brakes
Front and rear   Lockheed 12 × 2.25in drums

Wheels/tyres

Ford steel wheels	6.25 × 16in
Tyres	6.25 × 16in

Dimensions

Wheelbase		9ft 4in (112in)
Track	(front)	4ft 8in
	(rear)	4ft 10½in
Overall length		15ft 6in
Width		5ft 9in
Ground clearance		9in
Weight		27cwt
Weight distribution		60/40

Performance

0–60 mph	14.5sec
Top speed	100mph
Fuel consumption	15–18mpg

Principle variations
Various V8 engine and transmission options

hand-operated hydraulic pump from the passenger area, there could be the venerable Ford 3.9-litre V8, the Mercury 4372cc V8 or even a Cadillac 331cu in V8, as requested. The chassis had mounting points that could accept any of these. The spare wheel was housed in the cavernous engine bay area. The two rear doors opened out from the centre, although the first prototype built for Dennis Allard had a single lift-up door, making it an early hatchback! Standard equipment included heating, cool-air ventilation, radio, in-built aerial, fog lamps, leather seat trim and a laminated windscreen.

Eleven P2 Safaris were built: four are known today, and a fifth may lurk 'lost' in East Africa, as last seen by one of the authors. Of interest, Safari chassis 4009 (OUE 79) with a 3.9-litre German-spec Ford engine was extensively rebuilt and restored in the 1990s, including body restoration by Tamar Valley MG and major engine work by Nordian Garages. The car had originally been a very rare shade of Allard-applied metallic bronze (perhaps a Ford hue) but has been finished in a more traditional white (not least as the other British Safari survivor had been repainted in the bronze that had been original to OUE 79). Captain David Wixon RN saved the car and discovered that it had originally been sold via a Ford main dealer in Birmingham to a lady requiring transport for her goats. The car had subsequently lain at a Manchester garage for more than fifteen years until David purchased it in 1988. The vital structural woodwork was restored by a master wood craftsman, Tony Speare. The then Allard Owners Club's 'Captain', Jim Tiller, officiated at a Royal Navy-style 'commissioning' of the car at the historic Devonport naval dockyard.

ALLARD P2 MONTE CARLO

The Monte Carlo body of 1953 was a completely new design but mounted on the chassis of the Safari. It was not as might be thought a direct P1-to-Safari chassis derivative, having many differing structural and engineering components taken from the Allard parts shelf. Alluding to Sydney's Monte win was simply a marketing ploy. The P1 provided the basis of this 'developed' model cycle. Sydney, Reg Canham, the Hiltons and others in the bodyshop were involved in its design and engineering. The styling was led by Jimmy Ingram, who had by this time been hired on a consultancy basis to shape the body. Ingram had worked for major carmakers and turned

559 P1 Type saloons were sold, but only eleven P2 saloons were manufactured. The P2 had a completely new tubular chassis. It was marketed to make the most of Allard's Monte Carlo Rally win in 1952.

out a shape that was large and de luxe, but somewhat constrained by being forced to use a proprietary windscreen and some existing P Type Allard components. It was, however, a large, sleek and imposing car of a style we might suggest was later seen in cars from the Bristol Company and, perhaps, from Jaguar. We might also suggest that this Allard had an impression of grand tourer panache.

Ingram worked on the design of the P2 body to be ready for the Motor Show in November. He had previously worked on the body design for the Palm Beach Mk I and K3, so was a known professional to Allards. The front end was somewhat unusual for a large car, with inset frog-eyed headlights, but from a side and rear view the look was an improvement on the previous P1 model, being less bulbous and sleeker. The handcrafted aluminium body was mounted on a substantial ash wood frame manufactured by Encon Motors.

The chassis, built of reinforced twin longerons and steel side members with outriggers, was certainly of heavy duty construction; it was designed by Dudley Hume, following Sydney and Reg Canham's overall instructions, and was very similar to the P Type-derived Safari estate car chassis. The divided front axle was complemented by coil springs with dampers and forward-angled torque arms. The rear was a

de Dion arrangement with coil springs, twin radius rods and Panhard rod. The chassis was designed to accept a Ford, Cadillac or Chrysler V8 engine, with three-speed manual gearbox, or Cadillac automatic (Hydramatic) transmission. The same 112in wheelbase was retained, but lengthening the chassis at the rear provided much more space for the passenger compartment and increasing rear legroom. The overall length of the P2 was now 16 feet.

Like other large Allards, the fuel tank was safely located inboard, above the rear axle and away from the vulnerable rearmost boot floor-mounted position so inexcusably chosen in subsequent decades by some carmakers.

The one-piece front end had hydraulic lifts to actuate its lifting via manual actuation from a pump accessed in the driver's footwell; manual reversion was possible in case of failure. A right-hand gear stick location was also somewhat unusual, linked by steel rods to the transmission and easily switchable for left-hand-drive specification. The car could also be optioned with the hydraulic jacking system to aid wheel-changing. Allard also offered such luxuries as reversing lights, a built-in radio aerial, a trickle-charge plug and a heater (made by Clayton Dewandre).

Only eleven Monte Carlo saloons were sold and only four are known to survive. One owned by Mike Knapman, an Allard Owners Club stalwart and long-time editor of the *Tailwagger*, has an intriguing history. The car, OXE 475, was purchased new by a senior British businessman who then exported it to Port Moresby, Papua New Guinea (one wonders what the humidity did to the wood frame construction). Shortly afterwards, it found its way to Queensland, Australia, and after falling into decline it spent many years sweating away in a scrapyard in Brisbane. It now resides in

Mike Knapman's garage awaiting a phoenix-like return to the roads of south London.

ALLARD K2

The step-change for Allard came in 1950 with new cars, new designs and engineering, and new model names, existing side-by-side with developments of existing models.

The K2, very much like its predecessor, the K1, was a car for drivers who like to feel its sporty character. According to the records, the Allard Motor Company manu-factured 119 K2s in 1950, 1951 and 1952.

The chassis was similar to all the earlier L, M and P types, but with a 106in wheelbase, the same as the K1. The front suspension now had coil springs: at the rear, the live rear axle with transverse leaf springs was replaced by a de Dion system with in-board drum brakes.

About 80 per cent of the cars were shipped without engines to the USA, where they were fitted with various types, but

The essential K2. Note the bonnet side vents and changes to the front grille and inlet vents. A different windscreen frame and shorter bonnet panel also updated the K1 design and appearance.

mostly Cadillac V8. In the UK the cars were produced with the 3.6-litre Ford V8 or the 3.9-litre Ford Mercury, fitted with Ardun ohv cylinder heads and twin Solex carburettors, which raised power output to 140bhp at 4,000rpm, giving the K2 an impressive performance.

In common with all Allard models of the time, the engine was set well back in the chassis, with a weight bias to the rear to improve traction and handling.

The K2's distinctive appearance was enhanced by a smaller grille aperture, the six front side-panel portholes on the bodysides, two or four air vent holes across the front valance panel, and a bonnet strap. Twin quarter-bumpers were fitted front and rear. The canvas hood with its frame stowed neatly behind the seats, which had individual seat cushion 'air bags', in which the air pressure can be raised or lowered to adjust the seat position. The spare wheel was housed below a panel on the boot floor, leaving a good stowage area.

In the road test by *Autocar* in 1952, the experienced tester remarked, 'this is the fastest thing that I can remember up to 90 mph'. The car on test was running on Castrol R, which contributed to the atmosphere of the test and the individual nature of this car. The K2 was indeed a car for the driver who liked his or her motoring in the raw and who wanted a car that must be really driven to appreciate its impressive performance and road-holding potential. Lazy driving with few gear changes and mild steering control did not fit well with the K2's character – it needed to be driven, as did all Allards.

K2s in the USA had various types of V8 engines installed and owners carried out their own individual modifications over the years. The comprehensive ash wood frames carrying the aluminium body were eventually consumed by rot, which was often only found when the owner decided that the car needed some restoration. The K2 continued in production until November 1952, by when a total of 119 K2s had been made. The last car, chassis 3133, was exported to the USA.

What of the K2 that was a K1? In 1950 an American customer ordered a new-style K2 (coil sprung), yet the buyer cancelled the order and demanded a superseded K1 instead. Having already built the K2 chassis, Sydney was not going to waste it, so he built the K1 on the K2 chassis with the coil spring suspension and improved chassis. The car was delivered direct to the USA via the Allard Boston outlet of John Forbes. After a quiet life, it was restored after 2003.

ALLARD K3

The K3 was more modern and stylish, and a practical development of all that Allard had to hand. It certainly had a more modern and clearly designed 'style' and presence, and continues to have its admirers. Intriguingly, the K3 offered room for three side-by-side in its broad-shouldered cabin. Of the 62 cars manufactured between January 1953 and October 1954, all but one K3 of this variant were sold overseas: 56 K3 cars went to customers in the USA. The first UK customer was John Paddy Carstairs: registration number BEE 888, a right-hand drive car, chassis number 3286 with Cadillac V8 engine.

The very different K3 looked more like a bigger Palm Beach and had a wide front bench seat – hence the 3-seater tag. This is the London Motor Show car on the Allard stand.

K3 seen where it sold well – America. This one is on the California coast.
C. WARNES

ALLARD K3: TECHNICAL SPECIFICATION

Body/chassis
Open two/three seater with bench seat. Wide aluminium body with split windscreen. Strengthened Palm Beach type tubular chassis.

Engine
UK market: Ford V8 side-valve 3.9 litre. Nearly all K3 cars were exported to the USA less engine
Engine most commonly fitted was the Chrysler 5.4 litre (331cu in) V8, 180bhp at 4,000rpm
Iron block and heads
Bore/stroke   3.81 × 3.62in
Compression ratio   7.50:1

Transmission
Ford three-speed with gear shift on left of driver on left-hand-drive cars and on right of driver on right-hand-drive cars
Final drive 3.9:1

Axle/suspension
Front: divided front axle with coil springs over dampers
Rear: independent rear suspension with coil springs and telescopic dampers, de Dion axle with inboard drum brakes and Panhard rod

Steering
Marles steering box

Brakes
Front/rear   Lockheed type 12 ×1¾in drums
Wheels/tyres   600 × 16in

Dimensions
Wheelbase   100in
Track   (front)   56.5in
                      (rear)   58.5in
Overall length   150in
Width   70in
Ground clearance   7in

Weight   3,150lb
Weight distribution   50/50

Performance
0–60 mph   8.6s
Top speed   115mph
Fuel consumption   17–21mpg overall

Principal variations
Most of the 62 cars manufactured were shipped to the USA less engine. A Chrysler or Cadillac 5.4-litre engine could be fitted in the USA. A few other V8 engine types were also adopted. Produced 1952–3

From the records, it seems that most were exported with Ford three-speed transmission, all left-hand drive, but without their engines – with the engine then being fitted by the dealer or customer in the USA. The cars could take almost any V8, but most were fitted with Chrysler or Cadillac 331 cu in (5.4 litre) V8 engines. With up to 180bhp and 300lb ft of torque, acceleration of 0–60mph in around 8.0s and 0–100mph in under 30 seconds was quite rapid for a vehicle of that time, even with a big V8 fitted. Weight distribution was an ideal 50/50 front to rear.

All the cars had a bench-type front seat with a flat floor and no transmission tunnel. This made for a comfortable seating position for the central passenger, but the floor being raised over the transmission led to complaints from taller drivers who found themselves looking over the top of the split screen. The gear shift was also moved to the left, between the door and the seat on the left-hand drive cars, and there was a dash-mounted handbrake.

Top speed with the final drive ratio of 3.54:1 was limited to around 105mph. This could be improved with a higher 3.27:1 gear. From road tests of the time, the lack of a good turning circle was noted. The K3 twin tube chassis was a strengthened development of the chassis used in the P2 and Palm Beach. The first K3 chassis (3030) was shown at the 1952 Motor Show.

The stylish aluminium body was designed by Jimmy Ingram and built at Encon Motors, as a subsidiary of Allard Motor Company. The K3 had the traditional divided front axle, with coil spring-over-dampers and forward-running torque arms and a Marles steering box, all similar to the J2X or Palm Beach Mk 1, with 2.8 turns lock to lock.

At the rear there was a de Dion type arrangement with inboard drum brakes, with separate coil springs and hydraulic shock absorbers and axle location by twin trailing arms and Panhard rod. Fuel tank capacity was only 12 gallons with twin fuel tanks, one mounted in each rear wing. This does, however, allow a large boot area. A great-looking car, the K3 was underdeveloped in certain areas relating to trim and fittings and these counted against it in the hot competition of the American marketplace. Build quality was sadly missing.

ALLARD J2: A TRUE SPORTS AND RACING CAR

Work started in 1948 on the development of a new sports car that was to become the J2. Sydney knew that he needed a new sports car if the Allards were to remain one of the frontrunners in the post-war motor sport revival. His experience with the Steyr hill climb race car made him decide to

The first J2 was built in 1949. Most were exported to the USA – many without engine or transmission. The Cadillac V8 was the most popular engine. Ninety cars were produced up to the end of 1951, when the J2X model was introduced.

adopt some features of the one-off Steyr-powered Allard in the new J2 sports car, in particular the de Dion rear axle design. A small team in the Park Hill workshop carried out the development and assembly of the first J2, following Sydney's ideas and instructions, through the winter of 1948–9.

The desire to build the new sports car came after the competition successes and development of the J1 specials in the UK and from Reg Canham's enthusiasm after his return from a three-month marketing trip to the USA, which showed him the market potential for just such a sports racing Allard.

Sydney and Reg were meeting to discuss the building of the new sports car, later to be called the J2, and invited Godfrey Imhof to the discussion. Out would go elegant roadster style design as seen in the J1, in would come a 'real' sports car that was intended to appeal to a wider market. J2 might be seen as a retrograde step in pure body design terms, but in aspects of its engine, performance, handling, competition ability and a wider sales appeal – far away from the 'deluxe' Imhof effect – the J2 was the correct answer to the market and to current trends of the day.

Imhof was very much an ambassador for Allard. In 1948 he was looking for a new and improved special for his 1949 competition season. Discussion centred on the fact that the works were under pressure to produce the number of P1, L, M and K models to meet demand and so would not be able to complete the build of the J2 until July at the earliest.

Imhof, impatient to get his car built, suggested that he would get someone to build the car if Allard would supply the components. This was agreed as it would also help with development and testing of the new model. Thornes Garage in Leatherhead, Surrey, was chosen. Thornes was run by the experienced special builder and tuner Robin Jackson. A chassis and the main components were supplied to Jackson, who then built up the first J2 over the following two or three months.

Much of the design and development of the J2 sports (racing) car came from experience gained with the Steyr and with Sydney's J1 Specials. The J2 chassis was a development of the earlier J1 model, with the same wheelbase (100in) and front and rear track (56in and 52in, respectively). Shortened channel section side rails were used. Sydney developed the idea from his notebook sketches of the new J2 model. He retained the traditional Allard Ballamy divided front-axle arrangement, but now with coil springs and separate hydraulic shock absorbers, as opposed to the earlier layout with transverse leaf spring. At the rear there was a completely new set-up incorporating a de Dion rear axle assembly with 5in diameter coil springs over shock absorbers vertically mounted on the 'dead' axle tube.

The rear axle was located with long radius rods running forward to a central mount on a chassis cross member, just to the rear of the gearbox. The differential was supported on two substantial carriers attached to the two rear cross members and the axle carried 12in diameter inboard Lockheed brakes with Al-Fin drums. This de Dion rear axle design was developed from the layout used on the Allard Steyr 1949 hill climb championship-winning race car, built in the winter of 1946–7.

The first two J2s were built at Encon Motors in Fulham in early 1949, under the instructions of Sydney and Reg Canham. Announced in 1949, just 99 cars were built over the next two years, before it became the J2X with revised steering geometry and modifications to accommodate this change. After final road testing the new J2, which was to be Sydney's (chassis number J888 and registered KXC 170), raced its first event at the Prescott hill climb on 17 July; Sydney drove it to the Prescott venue and won the sports car class. Sydney's brother Leslie drove the J2 prototype chassis (no 1515) in the One Hour Production Car Race at Silverstone in 1949 as one of a three-car Allard team entry headed by Sydney himself, driving chassis 888 (later owned by John Peskett), and Len Potter driving a K1.

The following weekend the J2 was taken over to Jersey in the Channel Islands for the Bouley Bay hill climb, where both Sydney and Eleanor made Fastest Time of the Day (FTD) in their respective classes. It was Eleanor's first experience of competing in one of Sydney's sports cars and as she said afterwards, 'It was easy to win the ladies award as I was the only lady driver'.

By the time of the next event, the 1950 Silverstone Inter-

Robert Nellemann with his Danish championship-winning Allard J2.

national Trophy Production Sports Car Race, the second J2 was ready for Leslie to drive. As the new 331cu in Cadillac V8 was not yet available in the UK, the cars were still running with the now rather outdated and underpowered Ford Mercury V8, with no more than 115bhp. By finishing in eighth and ninth positions – Leslie in front of Sydney on this occasion – they put up a respectable performance in front of the large and enthusiastic crowd.

During the summer, the two cars had the bodywork at the front restyled to cover the coil springs, which had originally been exposed.

Tom Cole, the young Anglo-American racing in the UK and Europe, made contact with Sydney at this time, having seen the need for a more powerful V8 engine and the potential performance when fitted to the new J2. Cole purchased a J2 without an engine and had it shipped to the USA, where he intended to fit the recently announced new 150bhp Cadillac ohv V8. A comparatively light engine at that time with a capacity of 5.4 litres (331cu in), it had the potential to be developed to give well over 200bhp with huge torque. After discussion with Sydney, Tom was determined that he would find a way to get one of these engines over to Sydney 'for experimental' use. Allard Motor Company then issued a press release stating that the J2 would be racing in the USA, and that J2s would be shipped less engine to the USA, where an engine to the customer's specification would be fitted on arrival, frequently a Cadillac or another American V8 engine. Many J2s have had large capacity engines fitted by their owners.

Following the abandonment of Allards' development of their own ohv engine conversion for the Mercury V8, there was lengthy correspondence with the Ardun Corporation,

Peter Collins began his motor racing career
in an Allard J2. Aston Martin noticed him,
and just a few years later he became a
famous Formula One driver for Ferrari.

which had already developed an ohv cylinder head conversion kit for the Ford Mercury V8. It was arranged for a J2 to be shipped to them and a Mercury 3.9-litre V8 engine with ohv cylinder heads to come to Allards in the UK for development purposes. This arrangement was made after final agreement with the UK Import Control Department.

By the time of the delivery of the first ohv engine from America, late in 1949, a backlog of firm orders had built up, some with deposits for the J2. The usual cause of problems resulting in delivery delays was that materials and components were in short supply, particularly the de Dion rear axle assembly.

Tom Cole had started to make a name for himself and the Cadillac Allard in the USA, setting lap records and winning races at Westhampton and Bridgehampton. Cole and his 'Cad Allard' did much to spark interest in the growing sports car racing scene.

The J2 Cad Allards, as they were known, either won outright or were well placed in numerous events in the USA and other countries from 1949 to 1952. Several drivers who became internationally famous later in their racing careers had their 'baptism of fire' racing the Cad Allards, notably Carroll Shelby of Shelby Cobra fame in the USA and Peter Collins in the UK, who later became a Formula One driver alongside Mike Hawthorn in the Ferrari team. Peter Collins drove JWP 800 to victories at two national events held at Gamston and at least one more at Croft, where he set an outright lap record. From early exposure at Allard, Collins drove for Aston Martin and then Ferrari.

Sports car racing grew rapidly in popularity from 1950 and attracted other manufacturers who had the financial backing of substantial businesses, which allowed them to develop their cars to their full potential. Inevitably, by 1954 Allard were being eclipsed by other sports car manufacturers, such as Cunningham in USA and Ferrari, Jaguar, Mercedes, Aston Martin and others in Europe.

Sydney already had a long-held ambition of racing in the Le Mans 24 Hours, so he had no hesitation in putting in an entry when Tom Cole asked if he would race with him

On the limit, Bob
Francis, lifting a
wheel in his J2 at the
Goodwood chicane.

in the 1950 race, and started making plans for the race in June with the J2 Allard with a Cadillac 331cu in (5.4 litre) engine.

One well-known J2 was chassis 1570, registered as MWE 254, which was the tenth car off the production line and was sold to Maurice Wilde in 1950. Wilde was an enthusiastic racer and installed the then difficult-to-obtain Cadillac 331 cu in (5.4 litre) ohv V8 engine. In August 1950 Wilde finished third behind Frank Curtis at the Croft Circuit. Wilde sold the car and it passed through the hands of a series of owners who all competed with it on the national scene. The car ended up in the USA but was re-imported back to the UK in 1987 to become part of Nick Mason's Ten Tenths collection. Fellow Pink Floyd veteran David Gilmour is said to have raced this car. The car was then owned by BMW dealer and racing driver Frank Sytner. A subsequent owner was Allard Owners Club member Malcolm Verey, who prepared the car for international historic racing.

The Danish driver Robert Nellemann had great success in his J2 named C'est si bon – in 1951 he won the Danish speedway and hill climb championships. Jaguar XK120s were scattered in his wake. In May 1951 two J2s were shipped into Helsinki by Suomen Autoteollisuus Oy for Helge Hallman and Asser Wallenius to race in the Finnish Grand Prix. Wallenius would finish second in his J2 in the Helsinki street circuit race in 1952.

Four J2s were initially imported into Finland by Finnish Ford dealer Kuovolan Keskus-Auto Oy, who had taken over as official Allard distributor in Finland, together with three P1s (followed later by an M Type and a Palm Beach Mk 1). All the J2s and P1s saw race and rally action: one of the P1s competed against Sydney's own P Type in the Monte Carlo Rally and is now in the collection of Clas Palmberg, who is a big Allard fan.

The 'Ultimate' Allard might well be a Cobra-engined J2. Originally built in August 1951 and registered as FBA 685, this chassis originally had an Ardun-Mercury engine. After an early blow-up, it was re-engined with a Ford pilot V8 of a mere 85bhp. After having several owners earlier in the 1960s, it was purchased by Gerry Belton, who had been the marketing manager for Allard. By 1968 the car was under the ownership of American Bob Judd, who had the engine replaced with a new Ford 289, apparently a 'Cobra' specification of 225bhp rather than the 270bhp (HiPo) version, mated to a four-speed gearbox. The motoring journalist Simon Taylor road tested the car and labelled it the 'ultimate' Allard. Judd sold the car in 1969 to Otto Bowden, based in Florida. By 2008 the car was owned by Martin Stickley, who fettled the car back to its 1968 'Cobra' specification, as tested by Simon Taylor. Stickley then fitted the

relevant 1965 Ford HiPo 271bhp engine. The car was fully restored by 2011.

ALLARD J2X

There had been some criticism from drivers that more space was needed between the steering wheel and the seat and a certain amount of unpredictable handling was apparent when driven hard. These changes required extensive modifications to the chassis and steering linkage, so the J2 model was designated as the J2(X).

Dudley Hume was part of the J2 development process and recalled that:

> Sydney and Reg came to me and asked what I would do to facelift the J2. I had thought about that quite a bit as I did not like the J2, which looked as though it had been laid out by a designer of 'mud-pluggers'. I proposed moving the engine forward by seven inches, increasing the cockpit size by three inches, fitting the X-suspension and re-arranged steering linkage, and leaving the rear body panel as it was. Within a week Sydney had the prototype built up; it was an immediate sales success and Sydney was very happy about it.

The team agreed that the engine needed to be moved forward, but this could not initially be done due to the small clearance for the centre steering-arm, which pointed back towards the front of the sump. To achieve the necessary modifications, and to move the engine 7½in forwards, the chassis side rails had to be extended forward and the radius rods, which had previously run forward on each side from the chassis to the front axle, were now mounted at a central anchorage point on the front cross member, pointing backwards to connect to the axle.

As it was essential that the axle central hinge point was in line with the forward radius rod anchorage point, a new axle forging was required to maintain the optimum alignment.

With this new J2X layout, the steering arms now faced forward, allowing the engine to be moved forward at the same time as providing more driver legroom. The weight distribution front-to-rear was altered, with the weight on the front end increased by approximately 10 per cent, leading to more driver 'feel' through the steering: handling was improved as the car was less 'tail-happy'.

At the same time as the chassis was lengthened, the aluminium body was lengthened at the rear, which allowed a larger long-range fuel tank to be fitted. At the front the body was extended forward of the wheels by some

ALLARD J2/J2X: TECHNICAL SPECIFICATION

Body/chassis

Two-seat open (racing) sports car. All aluminium, two-door body with cycle-type front wings. Steel chassis with channel section side members, braced with cross members.

Engine

Ford V8 side-valve. Capacity options 3.9 litre or 4.3 litre
Ford Mercury 4.3 litre. Bore/stroke 84.13 × 98.42mm

Maximum power	140bhp at 4,000rpm
Compression ratio	8.0:1

Transmission

Ford heavy duty 3-speed gearbox and clutch

Suspension/axles

Front: Ford-derived split beam front axle with coil springs, telescopic shock absorbers with radius rods, running forward on J2X to pivot at centre of front cross member; on J2 radius rods running back from axle to chassis rail

Rear: de Dion arrangement with coil springs and telescopic shock absorbers

Steering

Adamant (Marles) worm and roller

Brakes

Front	12 × 2¼in 2LS Al-Fin drums
Rear	12 × 2¼in Al-Fin drums. Inboard mounted

Wheels/tyres

Bolt-on steel wheels or centre lock wires, 6.0 × 16in	
Tyres	Dunlop 600 × 16in or 650 × 16in

Dimensions

Wheelbase		8ft 6in (100in)
Track	(front)	4ft 8in
	(rear)	4ft 4in
Overall length		12ft 4in
Width		5ft 8in
Weight		21cwt (2,350lb)

Performance

	Ford 150bhp	Cadillac 285bhp
0–60 mph	8.5s	5.3s
Top speed	105mph	145mph
Overall fuel consumption	17–20mpg	14–17mpg

Main variations (options)

Aluminium engine heads with twin carburettor manifolds. Ardun ohv conversion

J2X series derivative

J2X Le Mans as J2X with fully enveloping bodywork

Engine options

Cadillac 5.4-litre (331cu in) V8. Tuned to 285bhp with four quad-choke Carter carburettors. Le Salle 3-speed gearbox. Many other one-off gearbox and V8 engine options

---

8–9in and the radiator moved forward. The Ford three-speed box was retained, despite experiments with the French Cotal gearbox. The heavier, stronger Ford four-speed commercial gearbox was often used in the true 'competition' J2Xs.

A total of 83 J2X cars were manufactured from 1951 to 1954, of which 77 went to the USA. The last car, chassis number 3214, was shipped to there in November 1954.

It is an interesting thought that if the Allard Motor Company had been able to update the J2X in 1954, or adapt and update either the JR or Palm Beach Mk II, the Allard production line could have continued, possibly becoming the Allard-Cobra. Twelve or thirteen (according to the records) of the eighty-three J2X cars listed were J2X Le Mans models with the fully enveloping aluminium body.

A typical J2X story can be found in the J2X chassis number 2222, which was built in late 1951 in Clapham with an alloy hand-formed body, divided front axle and de Dion rear suspension. It was set up for a Cadillac engine to be installed in New York after shipping. This car was initially purchased by

Russ Sceli, a well-known dealer and sports car racer from Hartford, Connecticut. In 1954 the car was bought by the Aldeborough brothers of Poughkeepsie, New York State, who raced the car at the Cumberland, Mt Equinox, Thompson, Beverly and Montgomery circuits. It was sold in 1969 to Dick Phillips, who intended to restore the car, but after years in storage it was sold again in 2000. This time it was restored and went on to achieve many show awards and competed in events including the historic Hershey hill climb. After winning a Barrett Jackson Choice Award, the car was put up for sale at $295,000, which is cheap by today's J2X prices.

ALLARD J2X LE MANS

The records indicate that thirteen J2X Le Mans cars were made. Under the new fully enveloping aerodynamic aluminium body, the car was in fact a J2X. The first two cars were built specifically for the 1952 Le Mans 24 Hour race. The new

Tom Walker, AOC member, has raced his J2X with Chrysler V8 power for many years. Driving with skill and speed.

BELOW: The 300bhp Chrysler V8 'Firepower' engine fitted to the J2X LM in 1952.

FIA regulations stipulated that full bodies were required for all entrants – motor cycle-type wings were out.

The new bodies were constructed at Encon Motors, a subsidiary of Allard Motor Company. Both cars had Chrysler 331cu in hemi-head V8 engines producing an estimated 300bhp. Ford four-speed commercial gearboxes with a set of closer ratio gears were fitted in both these cars, the gearbox being specially built at Allards. The 5.4-litre Cadillac engine was modified to deliver 270bhp.

Of the other ten cars built between 1952 and 1954, some were supplied complete but less the engine and gearbox; others had the Cadillac 331cu in V8 mated to a Cadillac three-speed box.

The new more streamlined, one-piece body shape, with inset headlamps, significantly reduced aerodynamic drag and increased top speed at Le Mans. Lift figures were unknown. The J2X Le Mans was timed at 148mph on the long Mulsanne straight during the 1952 race. Some years later this car was fitted with a new lower and more aerodynamic body and became known as the Hinton Special. Curtis also owned OBB 377, a J2.

The J2X Le Mans registered as JM7 942, now owned and raced by Tom Walker, is one of only two known to be in the UK. Others are in the USA, but the whereabouts of the remainder are not presently known or how many still exist. The J2X Le Mans chassis numbers were not listed separately from the J2X in the records.

ALLARD JR

Sydney needed a new car with a new chassis for the 1953 racing season and racers such as Erwin Goldschmidt and others in the USA were looking for a replacement for their now ageing J2/J2X cars to compete against the rising tide of competition from Jaguar, Ferrari and others.

Dudley Hume was asked to design and provide engineering drawings for the new car to be designated J2R (the 'R' standing for Race), and later to be known as the JR. He designed the JR chassis along the lines of the P2 chassis, with twin 1¾in diameter tubular side rails, joined by flitch plates and tubular cross members. Sydney oversaw the process and directed Dudley to include certain features as the design took shape. As so often, there was a rush to get the car ready for racing and the inclusion of a new type of front suspension design, which would have been significant, was cast aside. The traditional divided front axle was retained, although a modified MacPherson strut set-up was considered. It had been intended to use this on the proposed J3R, but that model was never made. At the rear there was a

de Dion system with twin 'A' frame arrangement with coil springs, an Allard quick ratio change differential and inboard 12in Al-Fin type drum brakes.

The wheelbase of the JR was 96in, compared to 100in on the J2 and J2X, and the track was reduced by 4½in at the front and 1in at the rear. Sydney wanted a wider cockpit, so Dudley introduced what he termed a 'kick-out' in the chassis side rails to achieve this. The JR had the same track as the Palm Beach, but its 16in wheels would have resulted in much higher rotational mass effects than the 13in wheels of the Palm Beach.

As mentioned earlier, it was suggested that a completely new double lateral link suspension or a wishbone arrangement should be fitted at the front, although this would have been expensive. Hume suggested a scheme using standard bushes, ball joints and basic geometry, but Sydney stayed with the anachronistic, but tried and tested, swing axle at the front.

Dudley Hume gave a detailed description of the JR's development:

> Sydney perked up a lot during this period. The K3 and the Palm Beach had been well received (in the USA) and Sydney's next plan was for the JR – the last major job I did for him. This was to be an entirely new sports racing car with no connection or similarity with the previous 'J'-Type models. After lengthy discussion one evening with Sydney and Reg after everyone else had gone home, Sydney outlined the specification with much reduced frontal area and drag, the 5.4 litre Cadillac engine, revised de Dion rear suspension and hubs, wheelbase and track similar to Palm Beach (with the 4ft 4in track), and lower weight than the J2X – Sydney saying that he wanted a truly competitive car for all the club events and Le Mans. I went away to produce initial sketches and details of components to be used. At another meeting two weeks later, Sydney was quite happy with my schemes and instructed me to go ahead with all the necessary working drawings.
>
> My input among several other aspects was the frontal area comparison with my proposed body design. Sydney looked at this first. The new area was about 25 per cent less than previously, which he opined was worth quite a lot of horsepower. The meeting went on for three hours and we established a clear programme of progress. Sydney was satisfied.
>
> As there were always problems with persuading our body builders to standardise, commonise, and generally speaking make parts identically, it was

decided that the body buck and the first two JR bodies were to be made by a separate panel-beating company who had made our steel wings for us. They worked closely to my buck and produced bodies as we wanted. These first two cars were sold to General Curtis LeMay and his aide-de-camp Colonel Reade Tilley. LeMay was Commander of the United States Strategic Air Command during the 'Cold War' and was a self-confessed 'English sports car nut' who visited our works quite often.

When the buck was moved to Encon Ltd in Fulham, where the 'J' models were built, Sam Whittington, who was proprietor when [Encon] was Whittington & Mitchell, said he did not like it and changed the back end and the doors – in my opinion completely ruining the look of the car. Reg Canham blew a gasket and went storming back to Sydney demanding that Whittington be 'dealt with'. Sydney came to Encon to view this 'modified' JR, walked all around it and then asked, 'What's different?' Reg blew another gasket and walked out in disgust and I followed him, I needed a lift back to the office!

There was another aspect of the JR design that I was not happy about. The track was to be the same as the Palm Beach so that we could use the Palm Beach axle beams and reduce the width of the car, but it was to be fitted with 16in wire wheels. This concerned me considerably as this meant that we would have the worst possible condition for the effect of gyroscopic processional torque interfering with the steering. I wanted to fit a double lateral link or 'wishbone' system, but Sydney was dead against. It was

the appallingly bad geometric layout of the average British cars of this time that had set him against using such a system. The usual layout of the period promoted excessive understeer to such an extent that it was quite easy to get on full lock and still go straight ahead – the cause of many accidents. I had studied the subject in-depth and I was aware of the best linkage arrangement to avoid this condition. I wrote an article on the subject which was published in the Automobile Engineer in 1956.

For the JR, I proposed therefore that we use the Borani wire wheels, which had a light alloy rim and which consequently would have less effect as far as the processional torque effect was concerned if it would be feasible to fit them to every car. In the event we only ever acquired one pair of Borani wheels and they were fitted to a JR for test purposes only; such was the financial stringency.

Seven cars were made, as chassis numbers 3401–3407, and one rolling chassis (3405) was supplied to Tommy Sopwith, a well-known name in motor sport and other sporting activities, who used an Armstrong Siddeley engine fitted by Allard's! The main run of JRs were of course Cadillac V8 331cu in (5.4 litre) engined.[13]

The first JR, chassis number 3401, was supplied to Erwin Goldschmidt less engine and transmission, and was exported to the USA early in 1953 so that he could compete in the 1953 racing programme. This JR later came within 0.5 second of the winning time of a Ferrari 4.5-litre at the Giant's Despair hill climb event.

A fully trimmed production specification JR with road-going windscreen and frame fitted. Note the chrome-rimmed radiator intake.

Sydney was very keen to run two JRs at Le Mans. The American team run by Briggs Cunningham attracted considerable interest on the other side of the Atlantic by finishing in fourth place in the Le Mans race in their CR-4 Cunningham with a Chrysler 5.5-litre V8 in 1952.

General Francis Griswold, a motor sport enthusiast and already the owner of an Allard K3, was one of those whose interest was aroused. He contacted Sydney sometime after the 1952 24 Hour race with the idea of entering an Allard in the event. A meeting was arranged between Griswold and other senior USAF officers, which resulted in an agreement to purchase three JRs and run a two-car team at Le Mans, with the third car as a backup. This third JR, chassis number 3404, was purchased by General Curtis LeMay.

General Griswold and the engineer who looked after his cars had a good contact in the engineering department at Cadillac and arranged for specially prepared Cadillac engines and transmissions. The gearbox was a three-speed manual, specially prepared from the Cadillac Le Salle saloon model. Chassis numbers 3402 and 3403 were to be the two Allard team cars for the Le Mans 24 Hour race in June (3402 had been ordered by Colonel Dave Schilling).

The two cars were completed by May, leaving only six weeks or so for testing before the race. The main problem with the engine was fuel surge in the carburettors, causing the engine to cut out on fast bends. Two Carter four-choke carburettors were fitted in an attempt to cure the problem and testing was done on the main runways at two US air bases, Heyford and Fairford, after receiving permission from the USAF.

As a shake-down test, prior to the main event, Sydney raced the car at the Ibsley, Silverstone and Thruxton circuits. He finished in two races at Ibsley, while at Silverstone he held third place for much of the race, before spinning into the hay bales, dropping him to eleventh place at the finish. Both JRs were entered in the first race at Thruxton: Sydney retired on lap 6 when the gear selector jammed, while Ray Merrick in the second JR finished tenth. Sydney took over Merrick's JR for the second race, but when the flag dropped a backfire through the carburettors caused an under-bonnet fire. Even after a lengthy delay, Sydney managed to climb back up to sixth position.

The build of JR chassis number 3404 was not completed for General LeMay until a couple of months later and then

ALLARD JR: TECHNICAL SPECIFICATION

Body/chassis
Sports racing car. Two-seat with single door. Aluminium body. Tubular steel chassis with twin side tubes, strengthened by flitch plates and braced with central cruciform assembly and additional tubular and fabricated cross members. Front and rear bulkhead hoops.

Engine
Cadillac V8 331cu in (5.4 litre) ohv race prepared, 285bhp at 5,000rpm
Iron block and cylinder head
Compression ratio 10.0:1

Transmission
Cadillac Lesalle three-speed; single-plate 11in clutch
Final drive ratio 3.29:1

Axle/suspension
Front: divided front axle with coil springs over dampers. Parallel axis, forward running radius rods
Rear: de Dion IRS arrangement with inboard drum brakes, located by a twin 'A' frame. Twin parallel radius rods, coil springs and dampers
Quick ratio change differential

Steering
Marles steering box (worm and roller)

Brakes

Front	12 × 2¼in Al-Fin type drums
Rear	12 × 2¼in Al-Fin type drums

Wheels/tyres

Wire type with centre locking	600 × 16in
Tyres	650 × 16in

Dimensions

Wheelbase		8ft (96in)
Track	(front)	4ft 3in
	(rear)	4ft 3in
Overall length		12ft 6in
Width		4ft 11in
Weight		2200lb
Weight distribution, front/rear		55/45

Performance

0–60mph	5.3s
Top speed	145mph

Options/variations
Long-range fuel tank; single driver's aero screen; alternative final drive ratios; magneto ignition

shipped to the USA. At this time JR chassis number 3405 was being built for Tommy Sopwith, the Managing Director of Armstrong Siddeley Motors.

Chassis number 3406 was built at the tail end of 1954 and shipped to Canada in March 1955. This JR was the only one with left-hand drive. It was fully trimmed and fitted with a full tonneau cover and some weather protection for touring.

The last JR built, chassis number 3407, was ordered by Rupert de Larrinaga to replace his J2 Le Mans. He took delivery of it in May 1955. Sydney made an arrangement with Larrinaga to race the car (registered OVT 983) at one or two events throughout the summer.

All JRs had the de Dion arrangement at the rear with 12 × 2¼in inboard Al-Fin style drum brakes and the Allard quick ratio change differential, coil springs, separately mounted telescopic dampers and a twin 'A' frame arrangement for axle location with twin radius rods.

Interestingly, it has been found that the last JR, chassis number 3407, has a Palm Beach Mk II chassis without the 'kick-out' in the chassis side rails. Presumably this chassis was readily available as Allard were then making a batch of MkII Palm Beach sports cars. Like all JRs, however, the Allard divided front axle was installed. Most, if not all, the original JR aluminium bodies were manufactured by a small independent firm, Ball & Friend. According to Dudley Hume, the JR chassis and body designer, they misinterpreted his drawings and made the air inlet duct smaller by 2½in width and 1½in in depth.

Larrinaga's JR was the only one to have a fairing on the body behind the driver's head. When he had the car, he had a polished aluminium frame fitted round the air-inlet mouth. Several JR owners fitted enlarged front air scoops and other modifications, including additional oil coolers for the engine and the differential; rack and pinion steering was also installed. This car is now owned by Vijay Mallya, the former boss of the Force India Formula One team, and has recently been restored by Lloyd Allard at Allard Sports Cars.

PALM BEACH MK I

The first Palm Beach Mk I was manufactured in early 1952 and shipped to a customer in the USA on 29 March 1952. A total of seventy-three Mk 1s were produced between 1952 and 1955. Eight had the Ford 4-cylinder Consul engine (model 21c) and sixty-five had the Ford Zephyr 6-cylinder engine (model 21Z). Those with the Consul engine were considered to be underpowered, even in 1952.

Allard cars were exported to many countries, but it had long been obvious that the prime market would be the USA, so some fifty Mk 1 cars went to that country. In 1951 the American auto manufacturers were starting to get back on their feet after the lean war years. A wider range of cars was also coming onto the market in the UK and Europe. With the increasing cost of fuel, car buyers had more models to choose from but they were more conscious of fuel economy.

The overall sales of Allard cars had shown a considerable fall in 1952 as compared to 1951. Sydney and Reg Canham realized that they needed a new smaller and more economical Allard. Reg, ever with an eye on the USA, suggested 'Palm Beach' as the model name, as this seemed appropriate for the American market, where there was thought to be a

David Moseley's (AOC Hon. Sec) Mk.I Palm Beach NY06, not to be confused with NY066, an Allard 1950's press demo car, now in Australia.

ALLARD PALM BEACH MK I TYPE 21: TECHNICAL SPECIFICATION

Body/chassis
Handcrafted aluminium body on two-seater sports tourer, with foldaway canvas hood. Tubular steel chassis with twin 1¾in diameter side rails with tubular and fabricated cross members and with bracing 'hoops' for body and bulkheads.

Engine
C-spec: Ford Consul 4-cylinder 1508cc ohv with 47bhp at 4,400rpm
Z-spec: Ford Zodiac 6-cylinder 2667cc ohv with 68bhp at 4,000rpm (could be uprated to produce 110bhp at 5,750rpm)
Iron head and block

Transmission
Ford three-speed
Final drive ratio   4.4:1 or 4.1:1

Suspension
Front: divided axle with radius rods running forward to central pivot points on front cross member; combined coil spring telescopic dampers
Rear: live rear axle with Panhard twin trailing arms and separated coil springs and dampers

Steering
Marles steering box

Brakes
Front	Girling with 9 × 1¾in drums
	Two leading shoe
Rear	Girling 9 × 1¾in drums

Wheels
Steel wheels   6.40 × 13in

Dimensions
Wheelbase		8ft (96in)
Track	(front)	4ft 3in
	(rear)	4ft 3in
Overall length		13ft
Width		4ft 10in
Ground clearance		6in

Weight
C-spec   1,850lb; distribution front/rear 55/45
Z-spec   1,950lb; distribution front/rear 58/42

Performance
0–60mph	C-spec 16.0s	Z-spec 11.89s
Top speed	C-spec 84mph	Z-spec 96mph

Fuel consumption (overall)
C-spec   26–28mpg
Z-spec   21–24mpg

great potential for a small sports car. Unfortunately, other manufacturers with cars such as the Triumph TR2, MGA and Austin Healey could also see the market potential, and they were able to dedicate their facilities and design and development departments, together with financial backing from larger motor manufacturers, to producing very cost-effective and attractive models.

Allard had to produce something new with high performance and eye-catching design. The Palm Beach Mk 1 was conceived before any of the competing models had been announced to the public and unfortunately it just did not have the necessary performance specification or appeal to achieve the level of sales needed to meet the market potential and compete with the rising tide of competition.

The prototype was designed and built during 1952. Larry Richards, an Englishman living in New York, had already corresponded with Sydney about the need to manufacture and market a new smaller-engined 'sports car'. Richards was convinced that there was a big potential for just such a car in the USA. Chassis 5003, with a Consul engine, was exported in September as the company's demonstrator.

The third car (chassis 5005) with a Zephyr engine was built for Major Grant Fisher, an aide to General Francis Griswold, an Allard enthusiast stationed in the UK. Two further chassis were built to have special bodies fitted (chassis 5200 and 5201 & 5201c). A racing version of the Palm Beach was proposed and an entry was actually sent for the Le Mans 24 Hour Race in 1952, but this was turned down by the organizers (presumably because it was considered a prototype, not a listed model). Sydney wanted to run an Allard in the small capacity class of up to 1.5 litres. The Ford 4-cylinder Consul engine could have been used if sleeved-down from its original capacity of 1508cc. It had been intended to name the car the 'Bridgehampton', after the American racing circuit, but the project was abandoned after the Le Mans entry was rejected.

With Palm Beach sales dwindling, something had to be done to revive flagging sales figures. The Allard Motor Company in New York, under the control of Larry Richards and Robert Forsyth, had suggested fitting an American V8 and negotiating a tie-up with one of the major US manufacturers.

Initially the prototype Mk I (chassis number 5000), which was sent over to New York, had a body designed by Ingram at Allard Motor Company, with the headlamps inset to create a 'frog eyed' look that most people did not like, particularly Forsyth and Richards. Over a period of a few weeks they had the styling changed before presenting it to dealers in the USA.

PALM BEACH MK II

A year later, Allard in UK adopted the new design, leading to some debate from Forsyth as to whether he received adequate credit for his authorship of the Palm Beach Mk II.

Recently uncovered paperwork shows that the design concept for the new Mk II body styling indeed came from the engineer and designer Richard Forsyth, who was a manager at the Allard sales office that had been set up in New York in 1951 to handle and promote Allard car sales in the USA. Forsyth was not satisfied with the rather bland and slab-sided appearance of the Mk I and proposed a more curvaceous design. He had been also continuing to promote the idea of fitting the more powerful Dodge Hemi V8 engine.

An article appeared in *Road & Track* in February 1956 with the title 'Sports Car Design No. 24. The Allard-Dodge car that never was'. This contained outline drawings showing the body's flowing style and a caption 'The Allard Dodge, designed by Mr. Forsyth'. If only the Allard Palm Beach had looked like this and used this engine! The article goes on to show the Palm Beach 'Red Ram', which was the sole Mk I Palm Beach fitted with a Dodge 'Red Ram' V8, as a prototype for the new model.

Some time later Forsyth sent over to Sydney sketches of the new body style that he proposed for the Palm Beach. The company were impressed by Forsyth's enthusiasm and his sketches, as well as the enquiries they were still receiving, so it was decided to build a small batch of Palm Beach Mk IIs.

Forsyth's outline design was largely adopted by Allards for the Mk II and the first car was built in 1956. This car, an open two-seat sports tourer (chassis number 72/7000Z), was displayed on the Allard Motor Company Motor Show stand in 1956; it was restored by Lloyd and Alan Allard in 2013–14.

It is powered by a mildly modified Ford Zodiac 2553cc 6-cylinder engine, sporting triple 1¼in SU carburettors and a free-flow six-branch exhaust manifold, and produced an estimated 110bhp.

The twin-tube steel chassis frame, with fabricated and tubular cross members, also has a cruciform-style central member. This chassis is very similar to the Mk I Palm Beach chassis, but is beefed up and has additional flitch plates. This first car has the traditional Allard divided swing front axle and suspension layout, together with Marles steering box, but all the other cars that followed have a front suspension system designed by Sydney. It was based on the MacPherson strut principle as used by Ford. The vertically mounted, oil-lubricated strut pivoted at the bottom with a Zephyr ball joint and at the top in a nylon bush assembly, connected to a chassis mounting post.

The GT Coupé with a Chrysler or Jaguar engine could have been Allard's big GT for the 1960s.

A single wide-based tubular wishbone was connected to the lower ball joint. Suspension was by a nearly vertical shock absorber mounted between the front arm of the wishbone and chassis post and a lengthways-mounted laminated torsion spring. In common with all six of the open (drophead) Mk IIs built, it has a 'live' Salisbury rear axle with coil springs, located by one upper tubular and one lower fabricated radius arm and transversely by a Panhard rod. Only eight Mk IIs were built, two of these being closed GT models. All had aluminium hand-formed and rolled bodies and were fabricated and assembled at the Clapham Common Southside works. Jack Jackman, the manager, was responsible for much of this work. He was a skilled panel beater and later to become a director of Adlards Motors.

The first GT Palm Beach fitted with a Jaguar 3.4-litre 212bhp engine was displayed on the Allard London Motor Show stand in 1957 and attracted the attention of the Queen Mother and Princess Margaret. This car had the de Dion rear suspension arrangement and front wheel disc brakes, as did the second GT and the last of the open cars. Of the six open cars, two had the Ford Zephyr engine and four the Jaguar 3.4-litre engine.

The six Palm Beach Mk II sports tourer dropheads and the

A LUCKY ESCAPE

I remember going with my father to road test the GT with Jaguar engine, somewhere on the A3 west of London, near Esher. The bonnet, which opened at the front, flew open and wrapped itself (being a relatively thin aluminium panel) around the top edge of the windscreen and pushed the roof panel down to within a few millimetres of my father's head – another lucky escape from injury!

PALM BEACH MK II, 1956–9: TECHNICAL SPECIFICATION

Body/chassis
Two-seat, two-door open sports tourer. All aluminium body with folding hood. Tubular steel chassis with twin side tubes (uprated version of Palm Beach Mk I chassis).

Engine
Jaguar XK140 3.4-litre 6-cylinder. DOHC aluminium cylinder head with iron cylinder block. 210bhp at 5,500rpm.

Bore/stroke	83 × 106mm
Compression ratio	8.0:1

Transmission
Moss/Jaguar four-speed manual gearbox (optional overdrive)

Suspension/rear axle
Front: Allard/MacPherson type sliding pillar arrangement with lower wishbone, telescopic damper and laminated torsion spring
Rear: Ford live rear axle with Panhard rod, twin trailing radius arms, coil springs and dampers.

Final drive ratio	3.7:1

Steering
Marles type steering box

Brakes

Front/rear	Lockheed 12 × 2¼in drums

Wheels/tyres

Wire wheels	15 × 6in
Tyres	600 × 15in

Dimensions

Track	(front)	4ft 4in
	(rear)	4ft 3in
Wheelbase		96 in
Overall length		13ft 6in
Width		5ft 3in
Weight		2,750lb

Performance

0–60mph	9.6s
Top speed	120mph
Fuel consumption	20–22mpg overall

Options/variations
The first Mk II of the seven built retained the Mk I style split-front axle arrangement. Girling front wheel disc brakes
Overdrive and Borg Warner automatic transmission
Two cars were fitted with Ford Zodiac 6-cylinder engine

Variant: Palm Beach Mk II GT
All aluminium closed GT body, two-door, two-seat
Girling front wheel disc brakes. Rear axle converted to de Dion arrangement with inboard-drum brakes, Panhard rod and twin trailing-arms
Two Palm Beach GT cars manufactured 1956 and 1958. The 1958 car was fitted with a Chrysler 5.4-litre V8, with a Torque-flite automatic transmission in place of the Jaguar unit

The very attractive Palm Beach Mk 2 – this is the car restored by Lloyd and Alan Allard, and road-tested by *Octane* magazine.

two closed GT Coupé examples were the last cars manufactured by the Allard Motor Company. The last two, a white drophead with Jaguar 3.4-litre twin overhead cam and a closed GT Coupé with Chrysler 5.7-litre V8 Hemi coupled to a Torqueflite automatic transmission, were both shipped to the USA in 1959. The GT went to the Dupont family, who were previous Allard owners.

The last car to be built by the Allard Motor Company, finally completed in 1959, was fitted with front wheel disc brakes. It was a white Mk II open two-seat drophead, chassis number 72/7107XK. It won a Concours d'Elégance at Brighton in 1959 and was then shipped to the USA.

Allards moved upmarket with the interior of the last Palm Beach.

In order to cut the cost of manufacture, a 'live' modified Ford Zephyr axle was installed at the rear in place of the more expensive independent de Dion system. Girling drum brakes offered retardation.

The last cars took months to complete during 1958 at the Allard workshops at Clapham Common Southside, which had largely been taken over by work for the growing associated Ford dealership, Adlards Motors, and turned into a Ford body repair workshop.

In 1957 the motor trade in general suffered a slump in sales as the Suez crisis worsened and the government announced that fuel rationing was to be imposed: 200 miles per vehicle per month, and the amount varying according to the engine size. Any motor sport activity was severely restricted. Two home market orders for the Palm Beach were immediately cancelled as a consequence. This series of events really sealed the end of Allard car manufacture in the latter half of 1959, but the writing had been on the wall as far back as 1952.

If the P Type formed nearly a third of the total Allard production run, despite its somewhat curious styling, and no doubt egged on by its Monte Carlo profile and genuine usefulness as a car, then the Palm Beach Mk II must surely be seen as influential as it preceded the cars of the later 1950s and 1960s cars that aped its styling. With Ford 4- or 6-cylinder engines, and ultimately with a Jaguar 3.4-litre engine, Palm Beach Mk II was a superb car that came so close to being a 'designed' full-status production car to take on the best the competitors could offer, yet it sadly missed its target.

BEHIND THE SCENES

Dudley Hume on working for Sydney Allard

Sydney was a big, tall chap and weighed sixteen stone. People thought he always looked cheerful but those were his natural features. In fact, he was very worried most of the time, as he confided in me more than once. Making motor cars can be a worrying business, particularly when you have six smallish and relatively inefficient works plants scattered around south-west London being run by the original proprietors, who went bust and were rescued by Sydney. One of the biggest problems was persuading them to get in to the twentieth century and forget the 'one-off' methods of their past. Sydney and Reg Canham spent hours discussing ways and means of getting round the very negative outlook of these dinosaurs of the horse and carriage era.

One example of how much Sydney was concerned with costs occurred when the P1 Saloon was about to go into production. Sydney had lent the first P1 made (chassis number 1500) to a London dealer for assessment. He came back after a few days and said his only criticism was that the front wings 'flapped' on certain poor road surfaces. Reg Canham and I took the car out for a test drive to see what the dealer meant.

I felt sure that the problem was a lack of stiffness in the chassis, but Sydney, who had tried the car earlier, felt it was the wing support arms that lacked stiffness and that we should stiffen these up first. This was worth doing because the new ones I designed came out at less than half the cost, were much stiffer and slightly lighter. However, as I rather thought they would, they emphasized the fact that the lack of chassis stiffness was the problem. Sydney was rather worried about this and asked me what we could do to stiffen up the chassis. I proposed adding reinforcements to the underside of the side rails and showed him sketches of what I had in mind. I had sketched out three schemes of varying 'effectiveness' and Sydney said we should try all three on different cars to see what we could 'get away with' – as he put it.

In the currency of the day, the cheapest schemes worked out at two shillings-per-chassis and the most expensive at four shillings. The most expensive one worked pretty well, one was conscious of a much stiffer chassis. The cheapest did the job 'most of the time' so Sydney decided we should use that. When I pointed out that we had saved four shillings on the wing arms, he countered with the comment that, as the body was costing more than originally thought, we ought to save every penny.

As a matter of interest, the problem had been brought about by the increased weight of the P1 body, which caused over an inch and a half of sag in the chassis and consequently lowered the natural torsional frequency of the the frame so that it readily hit resonance with the front suspension. The tramlines and cobbles along Balham High Road were ideal for exposing this weakness.

Because of financial stringency, Sydney had to abandon one of his 'pet' projects (the Clerk electric car), which involved expensive new technology. Fortunately business perked up with the advent of the twin-tube chassis models. The chassis were much cheaper to make, were much stiffer and lighter. Also they were made entirely 'in house' with only the materials having to be purchased – instead of side rails sourced from John Thompson and cross members from Ford, as in the case of the earlier models.[14]

Gil Jepson – more than a mechanic

Gil Jepson started out with Archie Frazer-Nash's outfit in 1935 and joined the Adlards Motor Company in 1939. Dur-

ing the Second World War he was an instrument maker for Rotax Ltd. By late 1949, however, he was on his way back to the recently formed Allard Motor Company as an experimental and development mechanic. This included working closely with Sydney on the design and prototype building of the Clerk-designed hill climb car, which used electro-mechanical signalling in its four-wheel-drive system (later used in the conversion of the Steyr Allard).

In 1953 Jepson helped build the special-bodied JR chassis as the Sphinx. Jepson worked on the 'Red Ram' Dodge-engined Palm Beach (UK registered as OGY 456), which was sold to Bernardo Wolfenson who toured Europe in the car before returning with it to his home in Argentina. Jepson worked on the chassis of the Atom 500c and even the small Allard Clipper, which Jepson liked for its conceptual purity and approach to minimalist post-war motoring. The Curtis Arkus-Duntov Allard J2X Le Mans was also fettled by Jepson.

According to Gil Jepson, Sydney disliked Rovers and would always overtake one, even when towing a loaded trailer behind him. Gil also 'borrowed' one of Sydney's 1952 Le Mans cars to drive in an event in London, causing quite a stir. Gil left Allard's in 1958, before the demise of the brand, but remained an active supporter of the Allard Owners Club until his death in 2005.

ONE-OFF ALLARD SPECIALS OF THE 1950s

Allards were often modified after they left the factory. Private 'Specials' of the era included a streamlined J2X known as the Clark-Davies Special and several very interesting Allard-based single-vehicle variations on the Allard ethos.

The Abbott-bodied coupé based on a Palm Beach chassis of 1954 was a clever attempt at an aluminium body with added style.

Imhof's one-off long-bodied aerodynamic grand tourer, **LXN 5**, seen as a prototype model and then in the metal. Its performance – 0–60mph in 8 seconds and top speed of 102mph – was helped by the low (if large) frontal aspect. Imhof, who penned the 'Continental' bodywork himself, believed that by replacing the Ford engine with a larger Chrysler unit the car could have reached 130mph.

LXN 5: Godfrey Imhof's Special Allard Coupé

Imhof was not just an Allard customer and regular supporter, but he was a major figure in the Allard story, not least through employing Robin Day's design skills. Imhof took delivery of the first Allard production car in 1946 and then purchased a Mercury-engined car too. He purchased an Allard for his mother, then an extended-chassis J1 for Trials and a sports special with the de Dion rear axle. In 1951 he ordered a Cadillac-powered J2, with which he won the International Round Britain RAC Rally.

Imhof also indulged himself in a sleek, aerodynamic, long-tailed special streamliner built upon an extended Allard J2 chassis (featuring Imhof's usual '5' numerical registration). According to Tom Lush, who was there at the time, the body for this bright red car was designed by Imhof himself, with the involvement of Reg Canham, but we cannot help but wonder how much assistance he had from Robin Day. With a two-piece vee-windscreen and smooth flanks, the car seemed to incorporate certain German styling themes, particularly at the front with shades of Veritas and Mercedes Benz.

Featuring twin 10-gallon long-distance fuel tanks, low drag, relaxed gearing and a long wheelbase, this was a true pan-European long-distance cruiser specified to one man's taste. A very clever, cranked windscreen wiper pantograph-type arm allowed extra coverage of the glass and predated by decades the use of similar ideas by other carmakers. The facia and controls were designed to aviation standards with everything within close reach of the driver. Even the head-lamps could be switched (very quickly by a control knob) to left-hand-drive setting. Inboard brakes, de Dion rear suspension, 16in wheels and 4.5 litres of Ford engine under the bonnet, all contributed to this unique car.

At just over 16 feet long, less than 4 feet high, long-tailed and long-nosed, with a small, swept cabin turret, the car had real elegance and road presence. The very long nose meant a high cross-sectional drag figure of the frontal area, but the low overall height, curved profile and swept roof-to-tail ensured a predicted low overall coefficient of drag. An intended fit of the Cadillac engine did not materialize due to cooling issues, perhaps related to aerodynamics, but this did not stop Imhof using the car on long hauls across Europe and in London. The top speed was 102mph and the 0–60mph time was 7.9 seconds. The car was, however, a personal one-off, soon abandoned due to too much flex in the extended chassis. Seen outside of its personal context, it was in some sense a failure, but a glorious one.

Sphinx

The Sphinx was commissioned by Tommy Sopwith and his Endeavour Equipe, who purchased Allard JR rolling-chassis 3403, and then asked them to fit a less-than-ideal Armstrong Siddeley Sapphire engine, which he supplied. It had a wind tunnel-developed body of somewhat Aston Martin DB3S style on the Allard chassis. Some years later Sopwith sold the car to a highly competitive driver named Brian Croot,

The Sphinx, based on an Allard JR rolling chassis, fitted with an Armstrong engine and special one-off body by Tommy Sopwith.

who fitted a Jaguar D-Type engine and even raced at Crystal Palace in the Griffiths Formula events. Croot damaged the Sphinx on a run at Shelsley Walsh, hitting several other cars off the track. During repairs to the Sphinx, Croot seems to have shortened the body (perhaps so it would fit into his new Commer Superpoise race transporter). In the 1960s the Sphinx was sold through a series of owners including David Cottingham and John Harper, and on to Paul Weldon. In a typical piece of Allard 'improvement', the Sphinx, which was now light blue, had 'gained' a 3.8-litre Jaguar engine along the way, having 'lost' its D-Type engine to Cottingham, and, it is bizarrely claimed, a Citroën Traction Avant steering box. The Sphinx was off the scene for years and reappeared in France.

In 2017 the Sphinx was restored to its long-nosed and tailed Armstrong Siddeley Sapphire engine configuration. The car failed to sell at a major auction and was then advertised in the AOC *Newsletter* for £600,000. The new owner is having the car further restored in the UK.

Farrallac

In the late 1950s the J2 registered as JWP 800 ended up in the hands of cycle manufacturer Don Farrell, who used the car to compete in hill climbs and sprints with his wife Stella, a champion cyclist. In order to improve the stability and straight-line speed of the cycle-winged J2, Don created an all-enveloping body with rising front wing lines. The car

was also fitted with a wishbone front suspension, with the unofficial aid of Allard's David Hooper.

In fact Hooper lay behind much of the Farrallac's development – with Sydney's approval. Changes to suspension, chassis, engine and carburation were brought together to form the special-bodied Farrallac. Hooper explored two options with Don: the twin-tube chassis design as used by Allard on Palm Beach and JR models, or a simple ladder-type chassis. Don opted for the simpler ladder type, which was easier to construct and almost certainly lighter and, more impor-

The Farrallac was developed from an Allard J2 by Don Farrell. The car is now owned and raced by Tony Bianchi.

The Essex Aero magnesium alloy-bodied lightweight coupé was rare in its day, but has recently been restored. The body in 16-gauge magnesium alloy (DTD 118A) may have been a world first in such construction. The bare shell weighed less than 150lb. Even the fuel tank was magnesium alloy. Argon welding was used in the construction. A Chevrolet V8 was later substituted for the original Mercury V8 engine.

tantly, torsionally stiffer. Tube size was 4in diameter and 12 SWG seamless cold drawn mild steel. The chassis rebuild was carried out by Don Farrell in his workshop in Edgware Road, Hendon, and was completed in early March 1958.

The Farrallac Mk I was used by the Farrells for two years until October 1959, when a track rod broke as it crossed the finishing line on a hill climb near Marlow, having set Fastest Time of the Day. This sent the car over a barbed-wire fence, rendering JWP 800 almost beyond repair and sending Don Farrell to hospital.

The remains were stored in various locations before Tony Bianchi secured the car and spent seven years bringing the car back to reality, including finding a Cadillac engine and fitting it with Offenhauser cylinder heads. A terminal velocity of 160mph has been recorded along Silverstone's Hangar Straight. Today the car remains in regular historic competition use at the hands of Tony Bianchi.

Essex Aero Allard

An interesting J2X derivative car was JW 7942, the Essex Aero two-plus-two coupé. Funded by the owner of the Essex Aero Company, A.E. 'Ernie' Freezer, this 'one-off' used a lengthened J2X chassis and was built in expensive, lightweight magnesium alloy. The curvaceously styled car was constructed by Essex Aero Ltd of Gravesend Airport, Kent, in the early months of 1952 and completed by November. German companies had used magnesium alloy in aircraft manufacture in the late 1920s and British manufacturers gained experience of the alloy in the 1930s and 1940s.

The Essex Aero used 16-gauge panels of magnesium DTD 118A and weighed only 140lb as a bare, untrimmed shell. The trimmed, road-spec 'wet' car weighed less than the standard

'bare' J2X. Even the petrol tank weighed 50 per cent less than a steel equivalent. Argon arc welding kept the shell together. The chassis was conjoined to the alloy body via six high-tensile steel bolts in a special Silentbloc mounting using rubber bushes. Originally powered by a 3.9-litre Mercury V8 engine with Ardun heads and driven through the rare Cotal gearbox, the car was reconfigured as a Chevrolet V8 with GM automatic transmission.

The body of the Essex Aero has been located and is under restoration. The plan is to reunite it with its chassis and resurrect a very rare Allard.

Hinton

The Hinton Special Allard started life as a heavily modified J2X Le Mans, raced by its owner Peter Woozley. As the Chrysler Firepower-engined, re-bodied, Hinton Special, it was campaigned by Woozley, Peter Farquharson and Todd Richards. MXF 974, the J2X chassis owned by Frank Curtis, had raced at Le Mans in 1952 and crashed through the barriers onto a public road with Zora Arkus-Duntov at the wheel. The damaged car was later sold by HWM in Walton-on-Thames to Woozley. Led by Fred Hinton, the original body was removed and a 'faux' cycle-winged Allard J2-type created. The car was painted yellow: Woozley was a Caterpillar tractor user and must have had lots of that company's yellow paint spare! The Chrysler engine was lowered in its mounts after being converted to dry-sump specification. Local USAF airbases are reputed to have been a source of Chrysler parts, including a Hillborn fuel injection system, which was briefly fitted and deemed unsuitable for British hill climbing. The car was refitted with its earlier Carter-type carburettors.

Hinton–Allard Special developed from the J2X Le Mans car, driven by Zora Duntov and Frank Curtis in the 1952 Le Mans race.

The Hinton truly became a special when the car's third body was fitted. The design credit for this new one-piece, faired-in body goes to Jim Keeble. It boasted outrageous vertical empenage-type fairings over each wheel in a Campbell-Bluebird style. A regular at the Brighton Speed Trial, it is claimed that Sydney Allard drove the car once at Brighton.

Fairley

Apparently inspired by the 1949 hill climb championship success of the Steyr Allard, the Fairley Mercury Special was built by Reg Phillips of Fairley Steels in 1950 around a 4.2-litre Allard Mercury unit, a Ford three-speed gearbox and Austin 8 front and rear axles. The car was campaigned on various occasions by ex-RAF Spitfire pilot and BBC Grand Prix commentator Raymond Baxter, who shared the car with its constructor: at the July 1955 Prescott hill climb event Baxter finished second to Doug Wilcocks in the Steyr Allard in the unlimited racing car class, ahead of Sydney Allard in third place, driving Rupert de Larrinaga's Allard JR.

Lotest

The 'Lotest Special' was an American backyard-built example of home-built hot-rodding. It used a J2X Le Mans chassis (3153) shortened by 6in and with a Buick engine. It was built by Scott Beckett.

HOT FORDS?

As Keith Baker, who restored a much modified and much improved Palm Beach (4655H, purchased in 1960), wrote in the Allard Owners Club *Newsletter* in March 2007: 'A large number of Allard models used the side-valve Ford V8 engine. It is well known that if it had the water capacity of a tanker, it would still overheat, the output of the dynamo was sad, the life of the twin-water pumps sadder.'

The basic, cheap-to-manufacture Ford V8 flat-head engine reached wider British fame in the Ford Pilot, but was available in American, British, German and French-built cars. Sydney Allard, however, had deployed the engine (in its early 21-stud version) before the debut of the British Ford Pilot. A 3.9-litre 100bhp 24-stud version would be launched in America in 1939 via the Mercury marque, a Ford sub-brand, and Allard quickly 'borrowed' versions of that too. In various iterations, notably aftermarket modified variants, the Ford flat-head was used across a range of vehicles from the 1930s to the 1960s. Widely successful, it provided the basis for many chapters in motoring history, including the development of the hot-rodding scene. But the Ford V8 flat-head engine had issues: its weight, lack of fuel economy and hot running. Engine mis-firing was a notable flat-head habit. Rotors, HT leads, points and plugs all require attention, as does the carbon bush in the ignition system's distributor cap. In the late 1930s even Lucas, with its DK distributor, had tried to address the last of these problems.

Allard tried numerous ruses to increase the cooling of the engine, including multiple water pumps that impelled flow rather than offering Ford's original 'suction' effect in the head's water jacket, close attention to radiator airflow, and special baffles to lower under-bonnet temperatures. Keeping the dynamo in good order was also a sensible idea. Radiator flow and under-bonnet aerodynamics were also vital in Allard Ford V8 installations. Not all Allard attempts to cool the Ford V8 were successful: how many water pumps could you fit to it?

Other expertise applied to the Ford included Ron Hogan's 1950s range of aluminium-cast, finned alloy heads, known as 'Hogan heads'. Hogan also adapted a 1930s twin-spark cylinder head and used an ignition system from the Nash straight-eight engine to good effect.

Sydney at the peak of his many competition activities, with his many trophies
celebrates his achievements in motorsport with family and staff members.
On the far right is Sydney's mother, with Eleanor behind. From the left
top is Sid Hilton, Dennis Allard, Reg Canham, Dave Davis. Further to the
right the group includes Sam Whittingham, Bill Tylee and Geof Imhof.

CHAPTER 5

ALLARD IN MOTOR SPORT, 1946–66

FAMOUS ON THE WORLD'S STAGE and revered across America, Allard's motor sport record is stunning. The record of events and results reveal the success and the energy of our highly driven hero, but Sydney's roots and motor sport beginnings are in British venues such as Brooklands, Bouley Bay, Dundrod, Shelsley, Prescott, Bo'ness, Goodwood and Silverstone.

Sydney's early three- and four-wheeled exploits were undertaken at Brooklands, although we cannot ignore the initial input of the Streatham and District Motorcycle Club. Even older than Brooklands was the Shelsley Walsh hill climb in Worcestershire: the first event on its original course was held on 12 August 1905. The 1,000-yard hill with its 1:9 gradient was the scene of many of Sydney's exploits and he took his Specials there in the 1930s. In 1948 an Allard held both the course record for its class and the unsupercharged record. As late as 1958 the lightweight Steyr Allard two-seater sports car VUL 543 won its class at Shelsley. The members of the Allard Owners Club have had a long affair with Shelsley Walsh and past Club Captain Jim Tiller caused quite a stir with his J2 'Old Fella' at Shelsley in the 1960s.

Over at the Prescott hill climb, Sydney's Tailwaggers team ran riot in their Specials in the period up to the outbreak of war. Sydney himself held more than a dozen British records including fastest sports car at Prescott. He would take further Prescott records in 1948–9 with the Steyr Allard, including a new course record of 44.26s with the original Steyr on 11 September 1949. He also clinched the 1949 British Hill Climb Championship and took the team award with Eleanor. The rivals he defeated, with a rash of first places and one second place between June and September 1949, included Peter Stubberfield in his Bugatti, Dennis Poore in an Alfa-Romeo, R. Dutt in a Maserati and Archie Butterworth in his own AJB Special, all high-performance racing cars in Class 3. In Class 8 he beat a Jaguar, an Invicta, and even Guy Warburton in another Allard, whose time of 48.16s was the only other sub-50-second run. Today, Allards roar again at the wonderful Prescott days that feature on the annual calendar of events at the home of the Bugatti Owners Club. Current Allards can also be seen burbling around the track at the annual Goodwood Members Day and at the Revival.

An example of what an ordinary man could achieve in an Allard was Freddy Mort, a dentist from Stranraer, who purchased a J2 new and took two class wins at Bo'ness (and at Rest and Be Thankful) in the early 1950s. Bo'ness, starting in 1947, became Scotland's premier hill climb track, attracting all the major names, including Allard, Moss, Clark and a very young Jackie Stewart.

During the heady years from 1947 to 1950 Allard's old friend Ken Hutchison was driving an Alfa Romeo 2.9-litre

and he linked up with Dennis Poore to form their own team in ex-Formula One racing cars. Other famous names that Allard and his Steyr competed against included Tony Rolt in an Alpine, Ken McAlpine in a Maserati 3-litre and Raymond Mays in an ERA.

Sydney's Steyr could be seen in the paddock at Bo'ness hill climb in 1949 beside his brother Leslie's Allard Special JYP 473. In fact seven Allards attended the Bo'ness of 1949, with six in the Sports Cars Class and Sydney's Steyr in the Racing Class. The 1949 Bo'ness Allard entrants were:

No. 71	S.H. Allard
No. 39	R. Allan
No. 38	H.B. Semple
No. 37	J.P. Hetherington
No. 36	G. Warburton (new Class Record)
No. 35	J.L. Fraser
No. 34	E.N.R. Hewit

Sydney's hectic schedule of Allard entries from January to September 1950 included: Monte Carlo Rally; Tour of Sicily; Goodwood Races; Prescott hill climb; Blandford hill climb; Craigantlet hill climb; Le Mans 24 Hours; Rest and Be Thankful in Scotland; Leinster Trophy Race in Ireland; Prescott; Blandford; Bouley Bay; Ulster Trophy Race; Tourist Trophy Silverstone; Brighton Speed Trial; Tourist Trophy Dundrod road race, Ireland; and Shelsley Walsh hill climb. Sydney's cars in these events were the M Type, J2 (Cadillac engine), the Steyr and J2 (Ardun-Ford engine). This 1950 schedule was no fluke either: 1949 and 1951 were equally as busy and Sydney was the main driver.

Allard was banned from the Motor Industry Research Association (MIRA) test proving ground for three months in 1952 after driving J2 (registered as MGF 850) rather too fast on the high-speed banking in company with the *Eagle* magazine.

Few people were hurt in Allards on the road or circuit, although sadly Ian Struthers died in an Allard J2 (owned by Hartley Whyte) at Bo'ness in 1952.

Hugh Braithwaite, who stood in for Sydney's regular navigator Tom Fisk at several events about 1960, somehow survived the violent gyrations and skids of a big Ford Zephyr caused by Sydney's manipulation of handbrake, throttle and opposite-lock: 'Navigating for Sydney was a memorable, exhilarating, exciting, rewarding and totally unique experience … Nobody, absolutely nobody I am sure ever drove as Sydney did and he did it so well. I am just so very glad to have had the opportunity of those experiences.'

Typical of Sydney's dedication to motor sport was his regular commitment to the Classic Brighton Speed Trial,

Sydney in his Steyr Allard setting a new record for the Prescott Hill Climb in 1948. Note the tie, but no sports jacket!

Sydney in his Steyr at Shelsley Walsh. This time he has his sports jacket on. The young man looking on is Mike Hawthorn.

an event run annually since 1908 and in which Sydney had already been competing every year since 1936. In 1949 he competed at Brighton in the J2 and was just beaten into second place; Eleanor won the ladies class. The following weekend Sydney, driving his Steyr Allard, made Fastest Time of the Day (FTD) at Prescott, setting a new hill record in the process, with a time of 44.26s, just beating Dennis Poore and Stirling Moss. Following this success he jumped into his J2 and proceeded to claim FTD in the Sports Car Classes. Finally, to cap a very successful Allard day, probably one of the highlights of Sydney's racing career, he won the team prize with Eleanor in the J2, backed up by Guy Warburton, the third Allard team member, in his J1.

THE STEYR ALLARD

Today, we are immersed in wind-tunnel, computer-evaluated, racing car body design and, in a wider motor sport context, the attributes of four-wheel drive and its power-handling capabilities. We also now appreciate the effects of engine location and chassis or body rigidity on suspension performance.

Back in the 1950s single-seat racing cars changed their configurations as the engine was moved from the front to the rear. Soon this became the norm. Drivers no longer sat upright and instead were almost recumbent, which allowed aerodynamic considerations to be incorporated, such as having as small a frontal area as possible and effectively positioned aerodynamic devices. Racing car manufacturers such as Cooper and Lotus dared to be different and set a trend in motion with rear-engined designs; Ferrari and others soon followed.

Sydney on the limit at speed setting the Steyr up for the hairpin corner at Prescott.

We are now used to electronics for the control of almost everything. Air-cooled engines have come and gone, as have old-fashioned mechanical twin-engined concepts, which are now returning as the electro-mechanical hybrid type of 'green car'.

Back in 1946 Sydney Allard decided he wanted to have a go at the sport of hill climbing on a surfaced road, which was rather different to the muddy hills tackled in his pre-war trialling days. Over the next few years hill climbing was to be dominated in the racing car classes by established circuit racing and ex-Grand Prix cars, nearly all supercharged, such as ERA, Alfa Romeo and Bugatti.

The Steyr Allard evolved in an entirely different way, not least as it was the brain child of Sydney alone and built by him personally, together with a small trusted team – Tom Lush, Bob Arthur, Gil Jepson and Jim McCallan – in Sydney's small private S1 workshop below his office in Clapham High Street.

Surely it is a mark of the man that Sydney went outside what today we would call 'the box' and took a fresh look at what he could design to be a winning machine, incorporating the two main design features that ran through all of his racing cars: power-to-weight ratio and the function of traction. In order to compete with his supercharged competition, these two features were a very high priority for his unsupercharged race car. Typically he did it on a very tight budget, using an undeveloped (for racing) war surplus engine, with secondhand and off-the-shelf bits. Here was evidence that he brought free thinking into his design ideas and then quickly turned them into a unique and winning combination.

The Steyr Allard's classic mono-posto body was hand-rolled and shaped by Charles Woodward & Co., a nearby bodyshop specializing in one-off bodies. There was no particular design ethos in the aluminium body. It was a minimalist low-weight body, unpainted to reduce weight, shaped to cover just the features that needed covering and protecting the driver only just as much as was essential. Aerodynamic drag was not considered critical as there were no long straights or really high speeds to contend with. However a low, curved front was deliberately created for the Steyr.

Sydney left the Steyr in its natural metal finish but had it polished up by the Welland Company, based close to his home in Esher. When it was towed to the Allard house nearby, a young Welland's apprentice sat in the Steyr's cockpit and steered. Welland's would later paint Sydney's first dragster in 'Allard Blue'.

As with his first 1936 Allard Special, the usual Sydney 'design' process was followed to determine the overall layout of the car. This meant that the various components would be laid out on the floor, with the engine and gearbox perched on wooden blocks, likewise the axles front and rear, chassis members and other components. The driver's seat would be placed somewhere in the middle and then Sydney, or one of the team, would sit in it, as if driving, and adjust the position of the various components to match the driving position. Sydney made some layout sketches with a few dimensions and from this would emerge the hill climb racer a few weeks later. Bob Arthur (assisted by Sydney, Tom Lush and Jim Mac) was responsible for the hands-on building work.

According to Tom Lush, the shape of the single-seater's scuttle cowling, which looked like an expertly sculp-

Jim Mac works on the Steyr in the paddock at Shelsley. Sydney stands with one of the drivers and Alan May, his brother-in-law on the right.

tured aerodynamic fairing, had simply stemmed from the natural curve of the works dustbin! The aluminium scuttle panel and chassis 'hoop' were placed over the bin and shaped to it. This was true 'men in shed' stuff – very simple and very quick, right up Sydney's street. As a result of this approach, it is claimed that this first version of the Steyr was complete in less than six weeks from December 1946 to January 1947.

It seems incredible now, in this computerized age, that a competitive car could come from such a hit-and-miss process and two years later it would be a championship-winning hill climb special. Perhaps only Joe Fry's Freikaiserwagen could match the audacity of the Steyr Allard. Fry and Allard were competitors in the same classes at the same tracks, and we should remember that Fry broke the outright hill record at Shelsley Walsh in 1949 in his rear-engined Vee-twin 'blue bathtub' special. Sadly Fry would die during practice at the Blandford hill climb in 1950. But the Steyr Allard and the Fry Freikaiserwagen epitomize the two different strains of hill climbing thought, two differing iterations of a formula. Both were stunning in their applied thinking.

The Steyr engine

At the heart of any successful racing car is the engine, but how did Sydney come to use a lightweight, air-cooled Austro-German engine instead of a Highland Park Detroit Ford lump?

Sometime in 1946 an acquaintance of Sydney named Robert Baird, a racing driver based in Northern Ireland, heard that he was searching for an engine for a new race car. Baird, who knew Sydney liked V8s, told him that he had found a number of war-surplus overhead valve light V8 Steyr-Daimler-Puch engines. Sydney needed to find another engine to replace the heavy side-valve Ford V8, with its somewhat unreliable overhead valve conversion. The engines were in southern England and Baird was going to encounter considerable expense getting them to Northern Ireland. Would Sydney be interested in at least looking at them?

Sydney jumped at Baird's offer and arranged transport to the Allard S1 workshop, then at Park Hill Works in Brixton. A few days later, two very strangely shaped containers, plastered with German markings, appeared.

The Steyr engine that reputedly found its way into Sydney's car came from a batch seized from a 'German vessel' intercepted by the Royal Navy en route to North Africa at the height of Rommel's desert campaign. The original hand-painted German script identification mark of '14PZ' very possibly indicated that it had been allocated to the Panzer

The Steyr engine, a 4.5-litre air-cooled V8 with eight Amal carburettors, enabled Sydney to win the British Hill Climb Championship in 1949, setting several hill records on the way.

Division, where it would normally have been fitted in an armoured vehicle, tracked carrier, lorry or support device. The Steyr-Daimler engines had been shipped back to Britain and analysed, before being sold off as war surplus material at a bargain price.

Perhaps in the months after the war's end it was felt necessary to obscure the engines' origins, stemming as they did from the Bohemian design brilliance that had benefited Porsche, NSU, Austro-Daimler and Tatra, to name just a few of the recipients of these exquisite engines and engineering in the period before the rise of Adolf Hitler. They were scooped up as 'war prize' material that went on to benefit American, British and Russian industry. The intercepted Austrian Steyr engines were alloy-headed and air-cooled, with an overhead valve configuration. They may well have reflected the thoughts of no less than Ferdinand Porsche, who had worked for Steyr until 1928. Porsche's rival Hans Ledwinka had also worked for Steyr and both men conceived radical engines (a large, air-cooled, ducted 2970cc V8 was found in the 1930s Tatra 77 and 87) and air-cooling was their chosen rationale.

Each cylinder in the Steyr unit had its own finned aluminium head, an ingenious engineering solution that Sydney relied upon once he had removed the ram-air ducting and cooling fans from the engine. It was cleverly engineered for the job it was designed for, namely working under hot conditions and running on paraffin or similar low grade fuel. This was the reason for its low 5.0:1 compression ratio and its application as a stationary engine driving a generator set. This unusual lightweight air-cooled aluminium-headed V8 engine, with eight individual deeply finned heads and cylinder barrel assemblies, immediately offered more than 100lb of weight saving compared to the other V8 engines then available, aided by its air-cooled design, which eliminated the need for a water radiator and a pipework thermal system.

Tom Lush collected the two Steyr engines, each packed in a strangely shaped wooden pallet 5ft tall and 3ft square, from the docks in Portsmouth, rushing them to the Park Hill works. The reason for the shape was soon evident on breaking open the boxes covering each engine: mounted on top of the engines was a huge twin-fan and air-ducting arrangement, together with two large oil coolers. Under close inspection, eight separate aluminium finned cylinders heads could just about be made out below the fans and all the ducting assembly.

At this point no one knew if the engines would even run, so after one was drained, refilled with new oil and connected to a petrol supply and throttle cable, the engine was set up on a rig in the Park Hill works.

After cranking over, the engine spluttered with pops and bangs, then with a shattering roar it burst into life. It had been estimated from the approximate bore and stroke dimensions that the capacity of the engine must be approximately 3 litres, so a power output of at least 100bhp was expected. They were in for a big disappointment: after several runs with ignition timing adjusted for each run, maximum power reading was only a dismal 45bhp. It was typical of Sydney, however, not to accept defeat that easily. If he was to have a championship-winning race car he needed to coax more than 150bhp out of it. Removing one cylinder revealed a hemispherical-shaped combustion chamber, so there was one good reason for the potential of more power.

Further measurements revealed that the engine had the very low 5.0:1 compression ratio and a cylinder capacity of 3.69 litres. Over the next few weeks the engine underwent a complete rebuild with extensive Allard modifications. The build of the race car was already well underway in the hands of Bob Arthur, Gil Jepson and Jim McCallan.

The engine modifications included raising the compression ratio to 12.0:1 by fitting dome-headed Martlet racing pistons that required a small increase in cylinder bore, with cut-out valve pockets to give valve clearance. The valve opening arrangement was altered with the inlet valve becoming the exhaust and larger inlet valves from an Ariel 500cc motorcycle fitted. The 12.0:1 ratio allowed the engine to run on methanol and to handle maximum fuel and air flow. In the valley between the cylinders, eight separate Amal motorcycle-design carburettors with typical slide throttle system were installed. Free-flow four-branch exhaust manifolds were routed for the pipes to run outside the chassis rails, combining into a single unsilenced exhaust pipe on each side, exiting behind the rear axle.

A Vertex magneto mounted horizontally and driven from the gear on the nose of the camshaft replaced the original distributor and ignition coil arrangements. A 'soft' grade of racing spark plugs was to be used when starting and warming up the engine and Lodge 'hard' R49 grade when racing. By the middle of the year the engine would be producing around 200bhp at 5,500rpm, exposing a design weakness, leading to expensive engine failure later in the year that was believed to be due to over-revving.

Original Steyr Allard issues would be addressed in further Allard additions to the engine: the cylinder heads were modified in 1949 and Al-Fin cylinder heads increased the capacity to 4479cc in 1951. As late as 1953 more tweaks centred on the thin con rods and the original use of bolt-on crankshaft weights: these issues were modified by the use of Dural con rods and heavier high tensile bolts, which also featured in the later Butterworth Steyr that campaigned in 1953–4.

Running the Steyr Allard

Work on bulding the Steyr continued through the winter from October 1946 to April 1947. Standard-type Allard pressed channel section chassis side members were shortened and a narrow frame built just wide enough to fit the engine between the rails and Sydney in his seat. In fact he sat high, slightly above the chassis rails, to get a better view of the position of the car on the course. Any thought of roll angles or the centre of gravity was considered relatively unimportant in 1947.

Many of the components fitted were standard or modified Allard/Ford parts. In the first build the car had a live rear axle, soon changed to a de Dion system. A Ford three-speed gearbox with close ratio gears from the J2 and a Ford clutch handled the torque with ease; a torque tube enclosed the propshaft coupling the gearbox to the rear axle. An Allard-style split-front axle assembly, narrowed by 4in, together with transverse leaf spring and Hartford friction-type shock absorbers were all installed at the front end.

At that time only a limited range of wide racing tyres was available, so Sydney copied the twin-rear-wheel set-up seen on some ERA and other hill climb racers: four wheels and tyres at the rear in pairs. He welded two standard Ford steel wheels together for maximum traction with Dunlop racing rubber. Coil springs were mounted with Girling hydraulic shock absorbers at the rear. The rear axle, a narrowed Ford type, was located by twin torque arms and housing an Allard limited slip differential.

Over the next three seasons of racing (1947–9) the Steyr was further developed by a number of changes to the original set-up, principally the installation of a de Dion type rear-axle arrangement with inboard 12in drum brakes. In an unusual design aspect, the Marles steering box, which is geared to give 1¾ turns of the steering wheel from lock-to-lock, was mounted centrally and high, with the steering column passing over the engine to the U-section front cross member. The steering box was supported on a vertically mounted steel post, housing a steering shaft that passed down the central steering arm and which in turn actuated the divided unequal-length steering arms onto the stub axles.

The Steyr, with Tom Lush and Jim Mac in attendance, made its first appearance on 25 April 1947 at the Prescott hill climb for a test run intended as a shake-down test day for members of the Bugatti Owners Club after the winter break. Sydney was very pleased with the performance, but the test showed up faults in the flimsy steering column-mounted gear change. This was replaced before the next meeting with a linkage that placed the short gear-change lever in a much better position outside the body, close to the driver's right-hand side. The normal handbrake, a long lever with fly-off action, was also placed outside of the body. It was supplemented by a separate 'hill start' foot brake with a pedal mounted to the left of the clutch pedal.

The 11 May 1947 Prescott hill climb was a major event and season opener with more than 100 entries and all the current top-line race cars and drivers. This was the first public appearance for the new Steyr Allard and it attracted great interest. Practice times on the hill course in the morning were very encouraging, but the afternoon runs were the ones that really counted. After warming the engine on 'soft' plugs, the 'hard' Lodge-type plugs were fitted. When called to the start, the Steyr was push started, and then driven up to the start line, Sydney using short blips on the throttle to keep the plugs clean. At the start signal, Sydney rocketed away from the line. The Steyr snaked as the twin tyres scrabbled for grip as it shot under the footbridge and round the first long fast bend. Sydney held second gear all the way from the start line to the first hairpin bend, at which point he had already reached 80mph. Then a short straight to a left hairpin bend, with the adverse camber causing more wheelspin, followed by the only straight, and then through a series of bends sharply uphill to the last long, fast right-hand bend to the finish line.

Sydney's name was to become synonymous with this bend, because he went off the road on several occasions making a permanent hole in the low hedge. To this day race commentators often refer to this as 'Allard's Gap'. He also once hit the bridge on the start straight at Prescott and was lucky to escape alive after the steering failed.

Sydney's first run looked fast and there was a brief hush while the time was recorded. Applause broke out when the loudspeakers announced a new hill record with a time of 47.25 seconds. Later in the paddock many of the competitors came over to the Allard service coach to congratulate him on his record-breaking run first time out.

In typical Sydney style, he tried to go even faster on the second run, but overdid it and slid wide, tail out, clipping a marshal's post and spoiling the run. Even so, his first run remained Fastest Time of the Day (FTD).

The Steyr was featured in the August edition of *Autosport*. William (Bill) Boddy described the Steyr as one of the sensations of that year's sprint events. The Steyr Allard was also on the front cover of the September edition. The Steyr was still under development during the 1947 championship and Sydney retained his championship hopes, despite the crash at Prescott caused by steering failure.

The Steyr was second at the next Prescott meeting, behind Raymond Mays in an ERA, and followed this with the fastest time on the Craigantlet course, indicating that Sydney really had created something unique.

According to David Hooper, Sydney's original 1947–9 Steyr development had led to a car with optimum gear ratios and a quick-change axle for all the championship courses that enabled it to win or be placed on most courses. It did not take the fastest time at Shelsley Walsh, however, due to a lack of horsepower and gear ratio choices.[15] Yet the Steyr went on to take trophy after trophy and was seen airborne at speed on more than one occasion.

The Steyr had poor runs at Shelsley, again due to the choice of unsuitable gear ratios. At Bouley Bay in the Channel Islands Sydney had to run on single rear wheels (producing more wheelspin), after damage sustained in a crash left no time for repair. Despite this the car was placed third in the RAC's 1947 British Hill Climb Championship.

In 1948 the Steyr appeared at the first meeting of the year at Shelsley with the new de Dion rear suspension and gear change linkage. Both these modifications improved the Steyr's performance on the hills. The Steyr ran well until the gear selectors jammed. This was soon sorted out and Sydney still came close to the FTD, just being beaten by the supercharged ERA of Bob Gerard at the Prescott meeting the next day.

The following week Tom Lush received a telephone call from a Mr Ward, who had been a spectator at the weekend event and had seen the air-cooled Steyr engine in Sydney's car. Ward ran a scrapyard handling the disposal of war surplus materials and he thought he had seen a similar engine on a pile of scrap.

Another classic view of Sydney, all arms and elbows, making a rapid climb in his championship-winning Steyr Allard at Prescott.

Next day Tom visited the yard and fought his way through piles of scrap metal and engines until the partially exposed engine assembly could be seen sitting on top of a huge heap, about 30 feet high. A travelling crane with a magnetic pick-up was brought in and the engine was soon deposited at the yard entrance. It was a V8 Steyr engine complete with all the enveloping air ducting.

Tom glanced around at other piles and was amazed to see another Steyr – just the engine this time. The front cylinders were smashed and sticking up on end from a mass of twisted girders, making it difficult to remove it quickly. Arrangements were made for both engines to be dispatched to London as soon as possible and Ward's own transporter delivered both engines to London. Ward presented his invoice and was duly paid. It was invoiced as 'mixed iron and aluminium scrap', at such a ridiculous price per pound that both engines cost less than £5 – including delivery! It turned out to be massively beneficial. Ward would take no further payment and insisted that seeing Sydney do well in the championship would be sufficient reward. He would not be disappointed the next year.

Sydney came close to winning the championship in 1948, eventually finishing third, the same position as the previous year. He was always at a power disadvantage, sometimes of more than 100bhp, when compared to the ERA and Alfa-Romeo supercharged ex-Formula One racing cars.

It was at this time that Sydney was introduced to Robert Clerk, who had some potentially great ideas. However, as Sydney was to learn in later years, great ideas can be very

expensive and do not always having a practical application, as the account below of the Clerk project will demonstrate.

After missing out in the first two years, Sydney finally won the championship in 1949 with 39 points, ahead of Dennis Poore with 35 points and Stirling Moss in third position with 29 points: 11 September 1949 must have been one of the high points in Sydney's motor sport career.

The Steyr also set new hill records at Prescott and Craigantlet, and two new class records for unsupercharged cars at Prescott and Bo'ness. At the Rest and Be Thankful hill climb in Scotland, however, he had to compete with just six cylinders after putting a rod through the side of the block and following an all-night rebuild session in a storage shed with no electricity – such was the determination of Sydney, Jim Mac and Tom Lush.

Larger-bore Al-Fin cylinder barrels and new JAP type motorcycle cylinder heads and valves had been built into the engine during the continuing engine development process.

The Clerk electrically controlled gearbox that Sydney had decided to fit had proved temperamental. As they could not risk any further problems, the Ford three-speed gearbox was refitted using a set of close-ratio gears. Sydney used only second gear from start to finish on hills such as Prescott, Craigantlet and Bo'ness. He also utilized the quick-change differential he had devised for the axle.

In 1950 Sydney had his eye on the Le Mans 24 Hour race, even though this would mean missing Hill Climb Championship runs at Prescott and Shelsley. This decision was to prove costly since, despite setting fastest times at Prescott and Craigantlet, he was just pushed down into second position in the Championship, alongside Ken Wharton's ERA.

For 1951 the Steyr had been converted to four-wheel drive. Sydney had always made traction of prime importance, so he thought that four-wheel drive might be the key to winning performances. The potential problem was that the extra weight might offset any performance gains, at least in dry conditions.

The Steyr's performance in 1951 seemed to confirm this. A Jeep front axle had been fitted with modified Rover free-wheeling hubs, designed to free-wheel under trailing throttle. It was mounted together with coil springs and the whole assembly added 200lb to the front end of the Steyr. The Steyr performed well in the first May meeting at Prescott, but was beaten into second by Peter Stubberfield's Bugatti; Archie Butterworth was third in his four-wheel drive AJB Special.

At the next meeting, at the Craigantlet Hill Climb in Ireland, Sydney made FTD and broke his own hill record. In September it was back to Prescott, where once again the Steyr was beaten by Dennis Poore, who made the FTD in his supercharged Alfa-Romeo. At Shelsley, the last meeting of the hill climb season, Sydney came third, beaten by Wharton in his Cooper and Poore in his Alfa. On that occasion, the Steyr Allard had front-wheel-drive, not four-wheel drive.

By 1952 Sydney was racing the Steyr only occasionally as he needed time to work on the Clerk project lightweight race car, as well as running his business with Adlards, his Ford dealership and an Allard race programme including the Le Mans 24 Hours. There was just not enough time to prepare and race the Steyr. Sydney wanted to concentrate more on international events, so the Steyr was sold at the end of the year.

The Steyr Allard was advertised for sale in *Motor Sport*

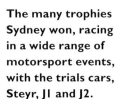

The many trophies Sydney won, racing in a wide range of motorsport events, with the trials cars, Steyr, J1 and J2.

Unusual rear view showing the twin rear wheels. Sydney sliding the Steyr around the top bend at the Shelsley Walsh Hillclimb on his way to winning the Hillclimb Championship.

in September 1952. The vendor was listed as Chiltern Cars of 11a Water Lane, Leighton Buzzard, Bedfordshire, and the Steyr was pictured fully painted in a darker hue. It was offered for sale with its own specially adapted 1947 Fordson van, complete with winch and built-in ramp, and bearing the Chiltern Cars name, livery and paint scheme.

Reincarnation

It is believed the Steyr had several owners after it was sold in 1952, but the Allards lost track of its whereabouts until it appeared in the hands of Doug Wilcock, who made FTD at the July 1955 meeting at Prescott. It also competed at other hill climbs driven by Dr G.E. Pinkerton. During its time away from Allard ownership, some modifications were made to the nose and the centre section of the body, and an air duct fitted above the engine. There were also alterations to the exhaust system and rear suspension.

Sydney repurchased the Steyr in 1962 and gave Dave Hooper the job of removing the front-wheel unit of the four-wheel-drive system and converting it back to the rear-wheel drive of its original 1947 specification. He also replaced the later added nose-cone for one more faithful to the original, as raced when Sydney won the 1949 Hill Climb Champion-

ship. During this work the car remained operational, with the Steyr appearing once more on the British 'speed' scene, notably at drag racing festivals and hill climbs, being driven by Hooper at the Valence Hill Climb, near Westerham, Kent, and the Blackbushe Drag Festival in September 1964. He recalls those events:

> The Steyr sported a new nose-cone complete with a modified M Type grille and a bonnet air scoop. The centre body section was not the correct shape, and on the top of the cockpit shroud was an external rev counter. When Sydney was competing with the car, he never bothered with a rev counter, arguing he would not have time to look at it, plus it was an unnecessary weight penalty!

The tail section was as original, still bearing the 'scars' of previous off-course excursions. The original 15in Palm Beach wire wheels were also still fitted to the correct axle beams, leaf springs, stub axles and friction-type shock absorbers. The stub exhausts had been replaced with the original type exhaust system, which had flex pipes to each cylinder head, with a long tail pipe finishing at the rear. Finally twin rear radius rods had been replaced with the original single radius rod each side. The original de Dion axle had square-section coil springs, mounted as per the J2, along with Armstrong lever arm shock absorbers. At this time suspension units were still fitted, but it was Hooper's plan to make a new dead axle tube of original design along with coil springs and lever-type shock absorbers.

On starting the Steyr it was necessary to ensure that the high-level carburettor float chambers did not flood by turning the engine over with the plugs removed and the pressurized fuel system turned off. Once any surplus fuel had been expelled, platinum-tipped plugs were fitted, then the magneto and fuel pump switched on. The Steyr would then fire up without any trouble. It was, however, very important to turn the fuel off a few seconds before stopping the engine.

After Sydney's death in 1966 the Steyr was put back into storage. It remained there until Alan Tiley, who had worked on several of Sydney's cars

Sydney at full speed climbing Prescott Hill on his way to clinching the UK Hillclimb Championship, setting new hill record of 44.26 sec and just beating Stirling Moss and Dennis Poore, 11 September 1949.

including the Steyr, said he would like to see the car running again. He purchased the Steyr in 1969. Although the Steyr appeared at a number of events, it never ran in competition again and was put on display at the Filching Manor Museum in Sussex. It was eventually sold to Kerry Horan in 1994.

Horan was determined to restore the Allard Steyr to its former glory, regardless of the cost. For this book he has kindly supplied detailed information on every part of the nut and bolt restoration. This included the discovery that one chassis tube was kinked upwards and inwards, probably the result of damage when the steering failed at Prescott in 1947 and Sydney slid into the footbridge over the track.

Horan decided to restore the Allard Steyr to its 1949 Hill Climb Championship-winning specification with two-wheel drive, de Dion layout at the rear and quick-ratio change type axle. The Al-Fin brake drums were renewed and stub axles replaced, together with new steering components, springs and shock absorbers. John and Ian Pitney (of Pitney Restorations) completely restored the body, putting it back to its 1949 condition, even down to the correct shape of the louvres in the bonnet.

DG Motorsports did much of the engine work for Horan, which presented the greatest problems. In particular the cast iron crankcase was in very poor condition, still bearing the damage caused when a con rod punched a hole in the block during the 1940s. The eight separate cylinder head assemblies similarly needed extensive restoration, along with the barrels.

It was decided that a new aluminium crankcase was required to replace the unusable original cast iron one, together with crankshaft, con rods, pistons, camshaft, flywheel and clutch. It was almost a new engine built from scratch. A new crankcase alone would require drawings, blueprints, wooden casting patterns, writing CNC machining programs, and heat treating and machining a sample casting.

More than 800 hours were spent on restoring the cylinder heads, which included machining to make the compression ratio match exactly on each cylinder. Head ports were flowed, polished and checked on a flow bench to check that each head flowed the same. A similar flow check process was required for the eight Amal carburettors. Finally a new exhaust system was fabricated and fitted to the rebuilt engine, which was then run in. It should be noted that a further huge list of new parts were fitted and other detailed work carried out. Kerry Horan describes what happened next:

The restoration of the car was finished in 2001 after six years of effort. Its first outing was in August 2001 where it completed some demonstration runs at the

Shelsley Walsh hill climb. The event was to celebrate the Midlands Auto Club's 100th year at this historic venue. It was significant that the Steyr competed at the 50th anniversary event in 1951 with Sydney driving.

In 2003 Horan took the car to the Goodwood Festival of Speed, making a rapid climb of the hill, but spectacularly blowing a hole in a cylinder head in a cloud of smoke, as he crossed the finish line:

Having run at Shelsley Walsh, Prescott and the Brighton Speed trials, we managed to win our class in timed runs at Goodwood's 10th Festival of Speed. It was pretty exciting as the previous weekend before Goodwood, we were competing at Shelsley Walsh and one of the cylinder heads blew a hole in itself, so there was a mad scramble to get the engine together for Goodwood just four days later. All of the first three runs at Goodwood went well, but on the fourth and last run another cylinder head grenaded itself in spectacular fashion as we crossed the finishing line – a true 'Hollywood' finish.

During the Festival Sir Stirling Moss came by and we shared anecdotes of how he had pitted next to Sydney on his very first hill climb – at Prescott in 1948. Stirling described with considerable emotion Sydney's advice and tactics on negotiating the challenging Prescott course.

When Kerry decided to sell the car it was featured in the catalogue for an auction held by Barrett-Jackson at Scottsdale, Arizona, in January 2009. The purchaser was Bruce MaCaw, whose collection of historic vehicles includes several significant Allards, including the Steyr, Sydney's 1953 Le Mans JR, Walt Grey's J2X Le Mans and Erwin Goldschmidt's Watkins Glen-winning J2. The Steyr Allard is taken out occasionally to prestigious events, such as the Amelia Island Concours d'Elégance in 2011, but now rests quietly and is unlikely to ever be raced again.

THE CLERK PROJECT, THE ALLARD RACING CAR THAT NEVER WAS

The Clerk Project was a concept for a lightweight all-alloy, electrically controlled, four-wheel-drive sprint car, which later became known as the Clerk Project.

In 1948 Robert Clerk, an engineer and inventor, came to meet Sydney. He had been experimenting principally with electrically controlled automatic transmissions and the use of lightweight alloys, and Sydney was persuaded to incorporate Clerk's ideas into a lightweight sprint car. The combination of light weight and four-wheel drive had always attracted Sydney, so it was not long before an agreement was reached to carry out a design exercise and build the car. All the components for the rolling chassis, right down to the nuts and bolts, were to be machined from expensive special alloys. New tooling had to be made to produce the oval-section lightweight alloy chassis tubes specified by Clerk.

All the wheel hubs were a fully floating design for maximum safety and connected to the specially made drive shaft by layrub-type couplings and joints, using aircraft quality materials.

The car was to have all four wheels electrically driven, with each wheel individually controlled by a switch box mounted on the steering column. The idea was that, as the steering wheel was turned, the power was transferred from side to side by varying the electrical current for optimum traction. Many drawings were produced for the hundreds of specially designed components and the cost of the machining of these components was considerable. Work on the components continued until 1950, when an attempt was made to start assembling the chassis. At this point a major problem arose when it was found that the material specified by Clerk for the specially produced chassis tubes could not be welded successfully, using the welding materials and processes that were then available, without hairline cracks appearing in the weld and tube material.

From this point on Clerk appears to have started to lose interest in the project and Sydney, already a very busy man, was left with a pile of bits. The car was never built, even

though half-hearted attempts were made to revive the project for several years.

THE ALLARD STEYR SPORTS CAR

After a couple of years without a competition car of his own, Sydney, at the age of 48, was still motivated to do some motor sport, in addition to his yearly entry to the 'Monte' and one or two local rallies.

He had not disposed of the remaining Steyr engines after the sale of the Steyr single-seater, so they were lying around somewhere in the workshop. Sydney's 'Clerk project' car had by now been abandoned, the final straw being the discovery that the very expensive oval aluminium alloy chassis tubes could not be successfully welded without hairline cracks developing in the welds. The ex-Archie Butterworth engine had been acquired and this engine, together with components such as the de Dion axle assembly with fully floating hubs and a quic-change differential incorporating a purpose-built ZF-type limited-slip system – one of a run of only six that Sydney had commissioned for competition use. Other items from the Clerk project included the aircraft-quality driveshaft assemblies with 'Layrub'-type couplings and, to further save weight, smaller 9in diameter inboard rear drum brakes. All these parts were assembled and built into a Steyr-engined sprint car with sportscar-style body.

Rear suspension was handled by quarter-elliptic leaf springs and hydraulic dampers, with 'Lotus'-type lightweight magnesium wheels fitted front and rear, with Dunlop racing tyres. At the front was a cut-down Ford Consul MacPherson front suspension system with lower wishbone, coil springs and disc brakes, from an Allardette Ford 105E Anglia conversion kit.

The chassis-had two straight 3.5in diameter steel main side-members, braced by tubular cross members and front and rear bulkhead 'hoops'. The aerodynamic 'minimalist' lightweight 18 SWG aluminium body was manufactured by Jack Jackman at the Southside Adlards bodyshop, resembling sketches from Sydney's notebook, and was just sufficient to cover all the essentials. It left Sydney sitting with his helmet well above the fairing behind the driver, but this suited Sydney. Aerodynamic drag from the high seat position would be insignificant on a short hill course, but could have been more significant on a straight kilometre, as at the Brighton Speed Trials, where Sydney was narrowly beaten into fourth place in the sports car class, the first three positions being taken by a 'C' Type Jaguar, Hinton-Allard and Allard J2X Le Mans.

To run in the sports car class, the Steyr had to be con-

The aerodynamically faired-in bodywork of the one-off lightweight Steyr, VUL 534, did not extend to Sydney in the open cockpit.

verted to run on petrol rather than methanol, so the compression ratio needed to be reduced from 12.5:1 to 9.0:1. This was achieved by inserting a spacer plate between the cylinder barrel and each cylinder head. The Butterworth engine already had had its capacity raised to 4525cc and ran with high performance duralumin con rods with heavy-duty big-end bolts, to guard against the previous con-rod failures and big-end bolt failures.

The gearbox, a Ford 3-speed with Lincoln Zephyr close ratio gears and Ford 9" single plate clutch, was mated with an adaptor plate to the Steyr engine.

The car performed well for a couple of race seasons during 1957 and 1958. Sydney competing at events such as the Brighton Speed Trials and also at Shelsley Walsh and Prescott Hill Climbs. It never quite had the outright performance to break records, or dominate the class, so at the end of the racing season the car was dismantled and some components, including the engine, used in the twin engined monster which followed.

TWIN ENGINED STEYR

After racing the 'sports car' Steyr, Sydney with his active mind, was looking to improve the straight line performance and I think he had seen twin and even four engined monster drag race cars featured in the US Hot Rod magazine. This had sown a seed in his mind.

The single engined sports car was abandoned and Sydney designed a new car with two Steyr engines. The idea being that two engines must give better power to weight ratio than one.

Sydney had by this time finally given up on ever building the 'Clerk' car after years of effort and at considerable expense.

One Steyr engine was lifted out of the Steyr 'sports' car – the other engine had been stored at the back of the works and was one of the original batch purchased in 1946.

The two engines were mounted side by side in a wide ladder like chassis frame, built from box section steel tube, with two chassis hoops.

The two engines each with eight Amal carburettors were converted to dry sump lubrication arrangement, allowing the engines to be mounted lower in the chassis. The 'monster' had four wheel drive, with an Allard quick (gear ratio change) differential assembly with inboard Alfin drum brakes and de-Dion suspension layout with coil springs at the rear.

TWIN-ENGINED SPRINT CAR

Sydney had by this time finally given up on ever building the 'Clerk' car after years of effort and at considerable expense. Instead he had been rather taken by the emerging 1950s American Hot Rod scene. Reading the related magazines gave him ideas about using twin-engined power. It was not long before he gathered up some parts, including two Steyr engines, and drawn up plans for a twin-engined Steyr Allard. One engine was lifted out of the Steyr 'sports' car, while the other, part of the original batch purchased in 1946, had been stored at the back of the works.

The two engines were mounted side by side in a wide ladder-like chassis frame, built from box section steel tube, with two chassis hoops. The 'monster' had four-wheel drive, with an Allard quick (gear ratio change) differential assembly with inboard Al-Fin drum brakes and de Dion suspension layout with coil springs at the rear.

The engines were to be converted to dry sump lubrication in order to reduce the sump depth and engine height in relation to the centre of gravity. A tubular steel 'frame', to which the bodywork would be clad, mounted and enveloped the engines. The front wheels would be driven part-time by a freewheel unit that would engage when slip was detected at the rear (driven) wheels. This was effectively a 'strip' or drag racer for straight-line timed racing. Front brakes were to be avoided in order to save weight. The regulations, however, insisted on some form of front braking action, so this was covered by fitting one front disc-brake assembly.

Shelsley Walsh Hill Climb, 1967. Sydney at high speed in his Steyr-engined sports car..

The twin-engined machine, with nose-cone fitted, ready for a push start, 1959.

Sydney, John Hume, Jim Mac and Alan Tiley working on the monster.

The engines' drivetrains were positively mated with synchronized clutch actuation, not some form of special device to operate clutches and gears at will.

Sydney's idea had been to try the car out at the 1960 Brighton Speed Trials, but it was not ready in time, although the car was displayed there. A run at the Goodwood circuit allowed much fettling and tuning. Those who were there say that the sound of all sixteen Steyr-Daimler cylinders singing in unison was something unique, perhaps closer to a light bomber on a take-off run than a car.

Ultimately the car was not as powerful or as fast as Sydney had hoped. It could not match the current US dragster speeds. The twin-engined Steyr Allard was a glorious failure, yet in a way it taught Allard much and opened the door to the true thoughts of dragsters – specifically the Chrysler-powered Allard dragster and all that followed.

MONTE CARLO RALLY, 1949–63

The Monte Carlo Rally became a must-do annual competition event for Sydney. From 1949 to 1954 he competed in Allard cars: first in an M Type in 1949, then from 1950 in a P1 saloon. Revised regulations, however, prevented Allard cars from running in 1951, when it was stipulated that all cars had to use engines made by the same manufacturer, and again in 1954, when rules said at least 500 examples of the car had to have been made in twelve consecutive months.

In 1955 Sydney was asked by Ford's Competition Manager

'Edgy' Fabris to drive a works Ford, so that year he drove a Ford Zephyr prepared by Ford. In 1956 he drove an Allard P1 saloon again, starting from Glasgow, but various minor problems on the route caused sufficient delays for them to fall outside the top 100 entries and so left the car unable to take part in the final tests. This was the last year in which an Allard car would compete in the Monte Carlo Rally.

In preparation for the 1956 event Sydney had spent more than two weeks practising in the south of France. Now that he had been forced out by car trouble, Sydney handed over all his vital, local navigation and driving notes to his rival Ronnie Adams, who was driving the works Mk7 Jaguar. This truly was the sporting gesture of a kind man: Adams won the rally for Jaguar and Britain.

In 1957 the Monte was cancelled due to the shortage of fuel caused by the Suez crisis. Thereafter, from 1958 to 1965, Sydney drove Fords: Zephyrs in 1958, 1959 and 1960; modified Anglias in 1961, 1962, 1963 and 1965; and a Ford Mk 1 Cortina in 1964.

1949

The first year that any Allards were entered was 1949, when Sydney drove an M Type, number 56, with co-drivers Alan May and Tom Lush, starting from Blythswood Square, Glasgow, one of six European starting points. That year in fact seven M Type Allards were entered, with drivers Jim

Tom Lush admits in his book that they were very inexperienced in this type of regularity event. Tom's attempts at regularity timing were overruled by Sydney's conviction that they were running too slowly – as he roared past the startled timing point officials. As a result they were placed 24th overall. On their return, they prepared a list of things to remember and equipment that could be needed for next year's Monte.

The Monte Carlo Rally 1949. Sydney, Tom Lush and Alan May co-driver (Sydney's brother in law) driving an Allard 'M' Type finishing in 24th position.

1950

As in 1949 Sydney entered a 4.3-litre V8 Allard M Type, registration number KLO 130 and competition number 74. He had once again chosen to start from Glasgow, with co-driver Guy Warburton and Tom Lush as navigator and time-keeper.

Sydney had also arranged for his wife Eleanor to compete in another M Type, running just behind him in number 75. Eleanor had persuaded her sisters Hilda and Edna to accompany her. This was the first time that they had driven competitively in such a high-profile event, and it must have presented quite a challenge handling a big heavy car in such treacherous conditions, particularly on the ice-bound road sections that year in the mountains south of Lyon.

They both made the traditional UK start from Blythswood Square in Glasgow on 22 January as some four hundred other competitors started from points all across Europe, converging via mostly separate routes on the finish in Monte Carlo three days and nights later.

After fog in the Rhône Valley, conditions became really bad on the stage between Lyon and Valance. During the night the windscreen de-icing panel could not cope with the very low temperatures and sheet ice was encountered on the twisty mountainous route. Driving on the limit, with many wild sideways moments, Sydney, Guy and Tom onboard Allard number 74 made it to the finish in Valance with just 7 minutes in hand.[16]

Appleton, Ken Hutchinson, Godfrey Imhof, Len Potter, Cyril Wick, Alan Godsal (with co-driver Hugo Money-Coutts) and Sydney. In 1949 the regularity test was the main feature that governed the results, rather than the severity of the route, the driver skills and the weather.

The highest placed Allard, driven by Len Potter, finished fourth overall in general classification, being only one second out in regularity; the first three competitors were faster over the whole regularity test.

Allards performed well that year considering that more than 250 cars finished, finishing in 4th, 8th, 11th, 24th and 42nd positions.

The winning Allard on the Col de Braus climb.

Using the notes of the route from the previous year, they knew they needed time in hand to allow for the slower road down into Monte Carlo, with heavy traffic on the coast. After some hard driving they dived into a petrol station and had 36 litres of fuel put in while they opened the bonnet to check oil and water. Tom counted down the time left. The stop took just three minutes and they now had twenty-two minutes to reach the finish 17km away. This meant more fast driving and it was going to be very tight.

As Sydney roared away, the car bumped over the small ramp leading onto the main road. Instantly the engine cut and stopped dead. Sydney and Guy jumped out immediately and began a frantic search to find the problem, as Tom counted down the time remaining. It took 6½ minutes to detect and cure the fault, which turned out to be as simple as the high tension lead detaching itself from the distributor cap. They now had only 15½ minutes to cover the 17km to the finish, an impossible task, but Sydney was not one to give up. With Tom bracing himself across the back seat with the watches, counting down each minute, they tore through the traffic on the twists and turns of the coast road, headlamps on and horn blaring, drifting through the many corners as they went. It was one of Sydney's wildest drives and that is a feat in itself.

Squeezing through any gaps in the local traffic, they reached the final control and slid to a tyre-smoking stop with all four wheels locked. They were only 2 minutes 23 seconds late, which counted as 30 marks lost. Ahead of them there were just five cars with no loss and two others with less than 2 minutes lost. Sydney finished in eighth position.

In the final acceleration and braking test on the sea front, Sydney was fastest of all 136 finishers, but this performance was not enough to gain the time lost.

Eleanor, Hilda and Edna in the other Allard had run out of time during the night on the icy section over the mountains.

They met up with Sydney, Guy and Tom at the finish, no doubt with some interesting stories to tell.

1951

The 1951 racing year started with new regulations for the Monte Carlo Rally entrants, stipulating that all cars must use an engine made by the car's manufacturer. This, of course, ruled out any entry by an Allard car. Despite protests, Sydney's entry of an Allard was not accepted.

1952

The 1952 Monte Carlo Rally was probably the high point of Sydney's career and a huge publicity event for Allard cars. However, the victory and the subsequent publicity was somewhat overshadowed with the announcement of the death of King George VI a week after the win.

Tom Lush, as usual, had sent in the entry form stating that the car would be an Allard P Type saloon, with Ford 3.9-litre V8 engine. While the car was being prepared in the Clapham S1 workshop in the first week of January, Sydney and Eleanor took another P Type down to Monte Carlo to check over the route that had been published in the regulations. On his return to the UK, he took his rally car to MIRA (Motor Industry Research Association) to use the equipment there to calibrate the car's distance-recording instruments.

Sydney again chose to start from Glasgow. He had also entered a P Type for Eleanor, Hilda and Edna, which would

Eleanor Allard and her sisters Hilda and Edna are greeted on arrival in France for the 1952 Monte Carlo Rally.

The 1952 Monte Carlo route map, showing how more than 300 competitors from numerous starting points would converge on the finish in Monte Carlo.

clearly be a challenge again, handling such a big vehicle over sheet ice in the days before studded tyres.

There were 73 starters from Glasgow in a total entry of some 340 cars. The cars left Blythswood Square at one-minute intervals: Eleanor's car, number 131, was flagged away at 2.07pm, while Sydney started a few minutes later in car number 146.

The road conditions south of Glasgow were quite bad after a recent snowfall. The next control was 320 miles south at Llandrindod Wells in Wales. Although the roads were icy, both cars made it in time to have a quick meal before carrying on across country to Folkestone on the Channel coast to board the Channel ferry.

After leaving the ferry, time was tight and not helped by the icy roads. The route went from Lille in France to Liège in Belgium, where more competitors joined up from other starting points, and then on to Amsterdam and Brussels and back into France. On the way to Paris the road surface was like an ice rink and many cars were late and lost marks.

There was great interest in the rally and the competitors during the stop in Paris, where the female competitors in particular received souvenirs, perfume and flowers.

The winning Allard P Type in the typically snowy conditions in 1952.

The wintry conditions in Paris indicated that it was going to get much more severe on the maze of narrow, tortuous roads over the Massif Central and then on to even more mountainous conditions further south. Sydney prepared for some very concentrated driving over the next night and day.

In 1952 the Monte Carlo Rally was one of the top motor sport events in the calendar, attracting widespread coverage in the UK and European press and among the general public. Even though it was one of the coldest winters for several years, the long train of rally cars that had now converged onto the same route from all over Europe raced south over the mountains through the snowy night, waved on by enthusiastic spectators at each village, often standing round hastily lit bonfires to ward off the worst of the cold.

By the time the cars reached Bourges, the flurries of snow had turned into a blizzard, with poor visibility from the blinding snow and treacherous road conditions. Many competitors were unable to maintain the speed required and arrived late at the Clermont-Ferrand control.

Sydney and his crew in Allard number 146 reached the control with twenty minutes in hand. Eleanor, Edna and Hilda in Allard number 131 had also made it on time, with just three minutes to spare – a great effort considering the atrocious road conditions, with many cars late or abandoned.

Soon after the control Eleanor was involved in a collision with another competitor and both cars slid off the road into a deep ditch. Luckily no one was hurt, but both cars were out of the rally, in common with more than half the other entries.

Sydney arrived on the scene just a few minutes later and saw Eleanor's car in the ditch. Knowing that he would need all the available time to reach the next control on time, he slid to a stop, saw that they were unhurt, and then drove on at high speed before they had a chance to say anything. It may have seemed harsh at the time, but not stopping and losing time was to prove vital at the next control at Le Puy, where Tom rushed into the control office to have the road book stamped with only one minute in hand. The excited officials announced that they were the only car so far to book in on time and still retain a clean sheet, but they reported that conditions were even worse ahead.

Sydney now took over from Guy, removing his duffel coat and jacket to get down to some strenuous driving in his shirt sleeves. He proceeded to hurl the big and heavy Allard over the narrow, twisty, mountainous road in appalling conditions, managing to cover the 126km in 2½ hours, arriving with just 1½ minutes in hand.

Conditions eased a little with the arrival of dawn, but the mountain roads were still difficult and many cars lost marks on this section down into Monte Carlo. Only 167 entries had reached the finish and of these only fifteen were still without penalties.

Two days later the fifteen cars with 'clean sheets' competed in a regularity test on a circuit round the twisty mountainous roads inland from Monte Carlo. The snowy conditions over much of the route covered most of the recognition points previously noted during the recce, but despite this they were able to maintain the highest average speed with the most accurate time regularity between control points on the route. The results were based on this formula and a few hours later a great cheer went up in the rally headquarters in Monte Carlo when it was announced that Sydney Allard, Guy Warburton and Tom Lush had won in their P Type Allard.

It was by all accounts a very popular win, just beating into second place none other than Stirling Moss in a works Sunbeam Talbot. It was the first win by a British car and driver for twenty-one years. Sydney Allard remains the only driver to win in a car of his own make. This achievement was all the more amazing as it took place in the worst weather conditions for many years.

The team returned to London to a rapturous welcome. The rally car was in great demand for display in various events, culminating in a Winners Cavalcade around the Sil-verstone circuit in May. He also raced the Monte Carlo car in the production saloon car race, finishing third behind Moss's Jaguar and Ken Wharton's Healey.

As a final footnote to the historic Monte Carlo car, if you look inside one of the remaining P Type saloons you cannot but be amazed as to how three big, tall men fitted inside with all their maps and rally gear, working together so effectively over three days and two nights in such a cramped space and in such treacherous road conditions.

The car was sold to Frank Curtis, the Allard J2X driver at Le Mans in 1951, but it seems to have lost its identity and disappeared. If anyone could trace Sydney's Monte car, it would be a valuable find.

1953

In contrast to the 1952 event, the 1953 Monte was run in mild weather. As a consequence, 253 of the 404 entries were without penalties at the finish in Monte Carlo. Since only one hundred cars could take part in the final mountain circuit test, a braking and acceleration test was run: Sydney, driving the Allard P Type, was fastest of all.

The regulations for the mountain speed and regularity test were the same as in 1952, but there was no ice and the target speeds were achieved by many competitors. The finishing positions were determined by judging when a certain position was passed at six points on the course at a certain average speed – a hit-and-miss approach that nearly all the competitors disagreed with. Sydney had an error of only 4 seconds over the entire 76km course, but still finished only in ninth position. The rally was won by the Dutch driver Maurice Gatsonides, who would later invent the Gatso speed camera, in a Ford Zephyr starting from Monte Carlo.

1954

The regulations for 1954 changed to require at least 500 examples of the car to have been made over twelve consecutive months. This of course eliminated any possibility of entering an Allard. The entry of a Ford was considered, but not taken up.

1955

After Sydney's win in 1952 and the ninth place finish in 1953 with his Ford-powered Allard, Edgy Fabris, the Ford Motor

Company competitions manager, had invited him to become a works driver for them in the 1955 event. They would provide a fully prepared Ford Zephyr for the event. This was a substantial change, as throughout most of his competition driving he had driven cars of his own manufacture. Sydney was pleased to accept the invitation as all expenses would be paid by Ford. The Ford starting point chosen was Lisbon and the team would be as in 1953: Sydney, Leslie Allard and Tom Lush.

All the Ford rally cars were prepared at Lincoln Cars on the Great West Road, London, under competitions manager John Welch. Alan Allard was part of the preparatory team:

This year my father decided that I should get a taste of continental rallying and took me as the third member of the team, on a pre-event recce. Even though at the age of fifteen he had to get permission for me to leave College during term time! Leslie was not with us for the recce. We checked out the worst parts of the route where time might be lost if the weather was bad. Much time was spent with experimental snow chains, particularly on the front wheels. In fact, the chains worked particularly well on ice, but not so effective on soft snow. This was just a year or two before studded tyres became widely available.

The Rally brought in a great deal of income for Monte Carlo town, so this year's regulations seemed to be set so that as many cars as possible reached the finish. Instead of timed stages over mountain roads, the rally was more of a regularity run over main roads.

The route in other respects followed the normal pattern with some 400 cars starting from seven starting points spread across Europe. Sydney at number 377 reached the finish after an uneventful run. Then the top 100 cars were selected after a timed acceleration and braking test. Despite what Sydney considered to be an underpowered and overladen car, they were in the top 100 cars. The next day these 100 cars were sent off on a 375km mountain course, from which the top eighty cars did a final five-lap race around the Grand Prix Circuit. In the circumstances, Sydney did well to finish in fourteenth position overall, driving for the Ford Motor Company.

1956

Sydney entered an Allard once again, his faithful P Type saloon, but it was to be the final year that any Allard car

would be seen in the Monte Carlo Rally, an event that featured so highly in Sydney's motor sport calendar.

More nimble cars were now coming to the fore. The Allard team had some minor delays on the way into Monte and, with insufficient time in hand, they lost marks and were not in the top 100 competitors, so could not compete in the final selective test.

1957

Having put an entry in for the Monte every year since 1949, it had become by now a traditional feature in Sydney's racing calendar. So he was very disappointed when, after entering the Allard once again, the event was cancelled due to the Suez fuel crisis.

1958

For this year Sydney's well-used 'recce' Zephyr was pressed into service. It was a Glasgow start again with team members Leslie Allard and Tom Lush back in place. Sydney had spent a week in France in December driving and making notes on the most difficult sections of the route. To make it more difficult, the route had been made much longer with a new loop in the mountains and a longer final test circuit, much of it driven at night, after only six hours' rest in Monte Carlo.

Once again the weather was bad with snow and ice on much of the route. Most competitors had already lost time by the time they reached Chambery: Sydney made it with just three minutes in hand. The next control was 160km away in Gap and they had only 2 hours and 25 minutes to cover the distance. It was early morning (5.24am), dark with ice-covered roads and freezing hard, when Sydney climbed out of Chambery on the tortuous mountain road, where the bends of all angles seem to go on for ever. Not far from Gap, as they hurtled into yet another difficult icy bend, Sydney was caught out and slid wide harmlessly into a ditch. Although it was relatively shallow, they could not move the car without assistance.

It was not until the break of dawn that a passing milk delivery lorry managed to pull them out, but by then they were well outside the rally time limit, so they continued on down to Monte Carlo at a less frantic pace.

Among the usual rally modifications and fittings, the Zephyr had an additional hand brake, a long lever with fly-off action that could be removed quickly if required, leaving the standard official dash-mounted 'umbrella' type in opera-

XXIXᵉ RALLYE AUTOMOBILE MONTE-CARLO
JANVIER 1960

In the 1955 Monte, Sydney drove as a works driver for Ford Motor Company in the Ford Zephyr. From 1957 to 1966 Sydney drove various Fords – Zephyrs, Zodiacs, Anglias and Cortinas – prepared by Adlards Motors or the Allard Motor Company.

tion. When used in an emergency braking situation it would instantly lock the rear wheels and flick the tail out – very useful on an icy downhill hairpin bend when the front end is heading for the trees!

1959

For this year, the new Mk II Ford Zephyr was entered and prepared for Sydney and his team at Adlards Motors. New to the team was Bob Holmes, an experienced driver but somewhat out of his depth when it came to working alongside Sydney, which led to some amusing incidents according to Tom Lush, who was there and recorded it all in his book.

1960

Adlards Motors, Sydney's associated Ford main dealership run by Reg Canham, had dealings with the finance company Yeoman Credit. They were interested in sponsoring Sydney in a motor sport event and it was suggested that the Monte would have the most publicity value for a company such as theirs. Accordingly Yeoman Credit agreed to sponsor two rally-equipped Zephyrs, displaying in their colours (red and green).

One car was crewed by Sydney, Bob Holmes and Tom Lush; in the other car were Eric Brinkman and Dennis Silverthorne, old hands at the Monte, with Tom Fisk as the third crew member. The chosen starting point was Oslo.

In anticipation of icy conditions from the start, for the first time both cars were fitted with studded tyres, but unfortunately this year it was mild and damp throughout the week of the rally. The heavy Zephyrs with all their rally gear were underpowered and not competitive on the vital mountain test sections, both finishing well down the order.

1961

Sydney chose Stockholm as his starting point with new co-driver Tom Fisk. Rally regulations were changing, allowing more support along the route for repairs or a change of tyres to suit the conditions. The main competitive sections of the route were now over closely timed closed roads in the mountains. Needing publicity for Allard Motor Company's growing Ford special tuning equipment business, Sydney entered a mildly modified 997cc Ford Anglia. He enjoyed the event, but with a relatively low-powered car he finished down in fortieth position.

1962 and 1963

This was my first year of entry into the International Monte Carlo Rally, alongside my father driving a similar car. My co-driver was Rob Mackie, a close friend from my schooldays at Ardingley College, and my father's co-driver was once again Tom Fisk, a rally driver himself and a British Automobile Racing Club (BARC) Committee Chairman. We both entered mildly modified Ford 105E Anglias. We had not yet obtained the necessary homologation papers to run supercharged and larger-engined 'Allardette' Anglias.

Weather-wise it was a mild year with little snow, so the small-engined, relatively low-powered Anglias were not fast enough on the mountain stages. In fact, we spent a few days before the event checking the difficult parts of the route, in particular I recall practising on the Mont Ventoux mountain climb and being very frustrated with lack of power. Taking extra runs up the climb, trying to improve our time – the little engine screaming in every gear. It was a fairly uneventful rally according to my notes and we were placed 74th out of nearly 200 finishers, with Sydney a little further down. Maybe Sydney's extra weight just made the difference in such a small underpowered car!

'In 1963 both my father and I entered Shorrock Supercharged Allardettes (modified Ford Anglias). Once again, my co-driver was Rob Mackie. We had

managed to get the Allardette 997cc supercharged Anglia FIA homologated in time for the rally. What this means is that we had sold a sufficient number of these 'Allardette' converted cars (100 examples at that time) in a twelve-month period – the same specification to be accepted under the FIA rules then applying in 1963.

The little 997cc engine only produced 39bhp in standard form, but with a Shorrock supercharger installed, power was boosted to around 75bhp at the same maximum rpm as the standard engine – so on the road performance was transformed. The torque increase was even more noticeable in the Monte on the hilly or mountainous road sections and we were able to catch and pass many larger, more powerfully engined cars. I can recall competing in the final test round the streets on the F1 race circuit in Monte Carlo. This was a regular event for many years at the end of the Rally.

In our race we were up against, amongst others, Vic Elford and Raymond Baxter in works Sunbeam Talbots and a German-crewed Mercedes 220. We could not quite match the acceleration of the Mercedes out of the bends, but when it came to the hill, climbing up past the Beau Rivage Hotel and up towards the Casino, the blower started its characteristic whine and the little Anglia accelerated past the big Merc uphill, not only to our surprise but to the amazement of the cheering spectators, such was the torque of the 997cc engine.

Both cars finished the rally, on this occasion Sydney finishing in 32nd position and Rob and I were in 49th place out of some 160 finishers.

1964 and 1965

This was the first time that the Soviet Union decided to allow a starting point in their country – at Minsk, about 100 miles inside the border.

Typically, Sydney, undaunted by the possible extra difficulties, decided that both cars should start from Minsk. What a prospect in January with temperatures down to minus 40 degrees Fahrenheit.

This year Rob Mackie and I had a standard Cortina GT, as did my father, alongside his co-driver of the past three years Tom Fisk. Just getting to the start and passing through the border was something to behold with some apprehension. I remember it was fully manned with uniformed soldiers in posi-

tion, pointing machine guns directly at the cars. The passport and document stamping was very laboured. Officials eyed us up and down like terrorists – at any point I thought that we might be searched.

We spent the first night after leaving the UK in what can best be described as a building with one room on the third floor for the four of us, with a stove in the middle. I think we slept with our clothes on as, true to form, it was perhaps minus 25 degrees outside. In the morning we could see huge ice floes, which had built up against the bridge over the frozen river. Neither car would start due to the cold, even with a fully charged heavy-duty battery. On checking the water in the radiator, fully dosed with anti-freeze, it was just starting to turn to ice with crystals forming. Eventually we had to be towed to get started. While

Sydney decided that we should start the Monte from the new starting point in Minsk in Russia (1964).

HUGH BRAITHWAITE

A little-known name of Allard rallying was Hugh Braithwaite, who would stand in as navigator between about 1955 and 1960 when Tom Fisk was unavailable. Sydney and Hugh drove in several rallies, notably in Sydney's Zephyr, a truly battered battleship that Sydney subjected to handbrake-inspired, opposite-lock slides and throttle-steered fun. By the 1960 Circuit of Ireland, Sydney's eyesight must have been troubling him, as he used Hugh as his 'eyes', demanding a constant verbal narrative of what lay ahead.

preparing for the start, shortly before being flagged away, for some reason we had our photos taken and we took the time to walk over to what appeared to be a shoe shop. Inside it looked like we had stepped back in time about 200 years, with old shoes laid on wooden racks. I noticed the windows had triple glazing and the moisture had frozen on the inside second layer. Nothing much was moving in the town, no life anywhere – just amazing that the locals were able to put up with these winter conditions every year – I guess choice didn't come into it!

After the experience of the Minsk start the previous year, [in 1965] we played safe with a rally start close to home, from the King's Road, Chelsea. Rob and I were in our Cortina GT again, but Sydney chose to take the little Shorrock Supercharged 'Allardette' Anglia with Tom.

There were no problems down through France, until we ran into a monster snowstorm in the Massif Central mountains. The snow was so heavy that it was almost impossible to see the road signs or the correct route. We made a mistake and became stuck in the deep snow when trying to turn the car round. The fall was so heavy that three inches had piled up on the car in a few minutes and the wipers could hardly cope with the weight of snow.

Under these conditions, there was no chance of maintaining the average speed required to reach the next control on time. We both retired later, before the finish, after running over the one hour lateness limit. Many cars from other starting points had missed the worst of the weather and reached Monte with time to spare.

This was sadly going to be Sydney's last Monte. Later in the year he became ill and was diagnosed with stomach cancer.

ALLARD AT LE MANS, 1950–53

1950

The lure of the Sarthe race circuit, which many cite as the greatest motor race in the world, was an established rite of passage for any race driver or aspiring performance-oriented car manufacturer even in the 1950s.

Today many of the biggest names of the automotive world throw millions of pounds into their annual Le Mans race and the supporting race teams, vying for a win at this prestigious event, with its worldwide marketing spin-off.

Even back in 1950 the well-resourced manufacturers' teams were the headline acts, but smaller manufacturers

Le Mans 1950. The happy team at Le Mans after Sydney and Tom Cole finished in third position in their J2. From left: Dennis Allard, Tom Lush, Tom Cole, Sydney, David Reece and Jim Mac.

Tom Cole rounding the Tertre Rouge bend at Le Mans in 1950. Sydney and Tom went on to finish third.

Sydney on his way to finishing third at Le Mans in 'Caddy' Allard J2.

such as Allard, and even individuals with money, could still be competitive at Le Mans against the big names. At the front in 1950 one might expect to see the like of Jaguar, Ferrari, Mercedes, Aston Martin, Talbot-Lago, Lancia, Simca and Alfa Romeo. The Briggs Cunningham team from the USA, well financed by the wealthy entrepreneur, were newcomers to the event, as were the Allard team, although considerably underfinanced by comparison. Both the Allard and Cunningham teams were running Cadillac V8 engines. Cunningham were competitive and highly placed on several occasions in the following years, although they never actually won at Le Mans. Neither Sydney Allard nor Briggs Cunningham was expected to be a front runner at the end of 24 hours of racing in 1950, but Sydney proved the pundits wrong, despite running on a financial shoestring.

Taking on such a major 24-hour endurance race was a

Sydney during Friday evening practice, at Le Mans 1950.

big gamble for such a small manufacturer at a time when the Allard Motor Company was attempting to establish its sales in the UK and the USA. Sydney, however, was a racer at heart and would have taken the gamble even if the profile and sales benefits might not justify the trip to the Normandy countryside.

For several years Sydney had been attracted to the idea of racing at Le Mans. He had been looking for a suitable V8 engine to replace the overweight and underpowered Ford flat-head V8. He had already carried out extensive testing and racing with the Ardun overhead valve conversion on this engine, but it had not proved particularly reliable, at least under racing conditions, nor had it given the expected power gains claimed by the manufacturers.

Late in 1949 the Anglo-American driver Tom Cole, who had been racing a Jaguar XK120 in Europe, spotted the then new Allard J2 and contacted Sydney about purchasing one to race at Le Mans. They had both read magazine reports about the recently announced new Cadillac 331cu in (5.4 litre) V8, already producing 150bhp in standard form. Importantly, this engine was comparatively compact and had the potential to give more than 250bhp, according to engine tuners at that time.

Tom Cole wanted to race in the USA and made arrangements with Sydney to purchase the first production J2, so in August 1949 it was shipped to the USA, less engine. He installed one of the new Cadillac 331cu in engines and said he would obtain one for Sydney to install in the J2 that he was to co-drive with Sydney in the 1950 Le Mans 24 Hour race.

Cole had great success in the USA in the J2 with the new Cadillac engine, winning in such major events as at Westhampton and Bridgehampton, where he set a new lap record and gained valuable publicity for Allard.

Le Mans 1951. Peter Reece in the number two J2 team car. This car completed the twenty-four hours, completing 215 laps.

There was a serious problem, however, with importing such an engine into the UK. Luxuries such as this were severely limited by government import restrictions then in place as a result of Britain's post-war state of austerity, when even buying steel was difficult.

Cole was able to purchase a Cadillac engine in the USA and with Sydney's support the engine was imported into the UK on condition that it was to be used for experimental and development purposes, which was permitted under UK regulations at that time.

Since the entry for the 1950 Le Mans had already been accepted and the actual race was only eight weeks away, Sydney decided to take up the offer of an entry in the Targa Florio rally in the mountains of Sicily in April, more than 2,000 miles away from London. Getting it there would be another job for Tom Lush.

The story of the race is short but dramatic. Three hours into the Sicilian event, in pouring rain in the middle of the night, Sydney misjudged a bend while trying to keep up with Italian ace driver Alberto Ascari. He slid off the road and over a railway line, damaging the underside of the car and the fuel tank. A few miles further on the car scraped a bridge parapet and burst into flames. Most of the car was burnt out, but they managed to save the precious Cadillac engine for the Le Mans race in June by smothering it in roadside gravel scooped up in their crash helmets.

The remains of the car were loaded onto the transporter for the long journey back to London. The car and engine were rebuilt and within a week was being raced by Sydney at Silverstone. It was then on to Prescott hill climb, where he was racing his Steyr Allard in the Hill Climb Championship. Eleanor drove the Cadillac J2 in the sports car class to third place, behind two other Allards driven by Guy Warburton and G.N. Mansell. Sydney's frantic efforts to get the car ready for Le Mans continued at the same time as he was running the Allard Motor Company and keeping an eye on his growing Adlards Ford main dealership.

With more than a hundred applications for the sixty entries allowed, the 'vingt quatre heures du Mans' was becoming ever more professional; even in 1950 to win or even finish such a gruelling event would require a fully financed team, with spares and equipment to back it up. It is hardly surprising, therefore, that the Allards, with their hand-to-mouth existence, were not among the fancied front runners for the 1950 event.

As an example of the shoestring budget, Tom Cole arrived on a transatlantic flight just days before the cars left for Le Mans, carrying a new twin-carb inlet manifold in his hand luggage, no doubt to avoid any possibility of import restrictions and duties.

Within hours, the new twin carburettor manifold replaced the standard single carburettor manifold and two Carter 2661 four barrels were mounted on it. With hindsight, the lack of testing and setting the correct full throttle air fuel ratio, combined with the low-octane fuel then available, quite likely led to the pre-race piston failure and the subsequent frantic efforts to repair the engine in time for the race.

In those days the Le Mans race track was all on public roads, which were only closed to normal road users for three evenings from Wednesday to Friday, between 9.00pm and 1.00am, for official practice and for the race. There was inevitably much high-speed 'practice' at other times on the long straight, which formed part of the N158 road to Tours.

On Wednesday morning, with the car transporter parked on the verge halfway along the straight, Sydney and Tom Cole took turns in doing some unofficial high-speed testing in the midst of any local traffic that happened to be around. After many laps, Tom came into report a tapping noise from the engine. An inspection revealed nothing, so Sydney took the car out again, but was soon back with a very sick-sounding engine. Removing the cylinder heads revealed three badly damaged pistons, one with the crown burnt right through and a scored cylinder bore. A major engine rebuild was obviously required. It was already late on Wednesday and with the race on Saturday, with no suitable spares and no knowledge of where to find Cadillac pistons deep in rural France, or a garage to carry out this major rebuild, they were in real trouble. Most teams faced with this situation might have given up and gone home, but not Sydney and his small team.

A helpful bystander from the crowd that had gathered around the stricken car said he knew a 'good' garage and guided Sydney and Tom there in their Allard coupé. Not only was it a 'good' garage with facilities to do the job, but the owner spoke English and there was an engineering work-

Le Mans 1951. The two Allard J2X cars, No. 1 driven by Sydney and Tom Cole and No. 2 by Alfred Hitchings and Peter Reece, make a rapid start at the head of the field.

shop nearby with all the equipment to re-bore the engine block. That, however, was only half the problem sorted, for they had to find a Cadillac piston and ring set for the 331cu in V8, which was then rare in Europe. So began one of the most amazing tales in Allard competition history.

Somewhat incredibly, it transpired that the main agent for General Motors in France had one set of oversized pistons in stock and it should be possible to re-bore the engine block to the correct dimensions to accept these new pistons. The two Toms, Cole and Lush, rushed at high speed to Paris with just had enough cash to buy the pistons by pooling their traveller's cheques. After a brief stop for lunch, the return journey was accomplished at even higher speed. The pair reached home base with the precious pistons on Thursday afternoon, with only twenty-eight hours before the last practice session on Friday evening. Tom Lush and Jim Mac, supported by Sydney, Alan May and Dennis Allard, commenced the epic task.

The engine cylinder block had to be rebored for the new oversize pistons, before the team set to work right through the night to rebuild the engine and then reinstall it. The car was running again by midday Friday, just in time to run the car round the circuit to 'run it in' for a few laps during the afternoon, before the final evening practice session when

the roads were closed for four hours. Most of the competitors had already completed their practice, so the session was comparatively quiet and Sydney was able to use the services of a well-known tuning expert to check and make adjustments to fuel mixtures.

The two drivers took turns to practise and learn the course in the dark. Towards the end of the session Sydney reported a strange feeling in the handling, but an examination revealed nothing. The team returned to the hotel full of boisterous race followers for a meal and finally to bed at 2.00am.

Sydney still thought there was a real, rather than an imagined, problem with the car. He woke Tom Lush at 6.30am and together they crept out of the hotel without disturbing the rest of the crew. A short test run on the comparatively rough local roads, compared to the smooth circuit, soon showed up a suspension fault. The front mounting eye of one of the rear de Dion axle locating radius arms had split, allowing the de Dion tube to move, seriously affecting the handling. Their local garage was already open when they drove up at 7.00am, so maybe they expected that their services would be required once again on race day. While the radius rods were being repaired, Sydney walked back to the hotel to join the others for a quick breakfast.

Time was fast running out, as all competitors and the cars had to be in their allotted pit by 1.00pm, together with all their spares and equipment. After fighting their way through the heavy race traffic, the car and support team were in place with a few minutes to spare.

As was traditional, the cars all lined up alongside the pits, with the largest capacity engined cars first in line: in 1950 the J2 Allard, with its 5.4-litre V8 Cadillac, was number four, fourth in line of the sixty competitors, going right down the line to the 600cc Panhard or Simca.

That year's number one was the supercharged M.A.P. 4.4-litre diesel, and then the two Cunninghams, both with 5.4-litre Cadillac V8 engines. One Cunningham car was dubbed 'Le Monstre' by the French on account of its huge slab-sided, supposedly streamlined body; the other was a mildly modified Cadillac saloon that might be seen anywhere in a New York street. In the next few years the V8 Cunninghams were to prove highly competitive, although never winning outright.

Being the younger man, Sydney asked Tom to take the traditional running start with each driver running across the track. With just a minute to the 4.00pm start time, there was a hush as the huge crowd fell silent with anticipation. Counting down the last few seconds before the drop of the flag, each driver stood motionless opposite his car on the far side of the track, poised ready to sprint across: the flag dropped and sixty pairs of feet sprinted across the track and the drivers leapt into their cars. With a thunderous roar the multitude of different engines burst into life from flat twin-cylinder two strokes and supercharged diesels, to the V12 Ferraris, 4.5-litre Talbot-Lagos, and the Cadillac V8-powered Cunninghams and the lone J2 Allard.

Tom in the J2 Allard was first away and was soon holding a slender lead over Raymond Somner in a Ferrari 1955 2.4-litre V12.

It had been decided, in view of the unknown race reliability of the rebuilt engine, to limit rpm to 4,000 and restrict the top speed on the long straight to about 128mph, whereas the fast cars would be reaching 140mph or more. Despite this restriction, Sydney and Tom were circulating in the top six for the first eight hours. After twelve hours of racing through the night they climbed up into second position, behind the Rosier Talbot-Lago.

The race had been going so well for the Allard team, but just after 3.00am there was a problem. The J2 had gearbox trouble and Tom Cole limped into the pits with a jammed gearshift with only top gear being usable. The rules stated that repairs could only be carried out with tools carried on the race car, so the only option was to lock the transmission into top gear and trust to good fortune that the clutch could stand the inevitable extra strain for the next ten hours of racing.

The stop took forty minutes and dropped the J2 down the order, but Sydney was soon thundering around, lapping almost as fast with only top gear. The engine showed remarkable torque to pull with such a high 'Le Mans' gearing and lapping at an average speed of more than 92mph.

With ten hours of racing ahead more than forty cars were still running, but as dawn broke Sydney was climbing up the order once again, now in sixth place.

When Tom took his stint, the two rear wheels were changed. Lapping consistently in top gear only, he had moved into fifth position, when he handed over to Sydney for the final two and a half hours.

With an hour to go, Sydney caught and passed the Aston Martin DB2 of George Abercasis and Lance Macklin. Now he had Tony Rolt and Duncan Hamilton's Nash-Healey in sight, which was also stuck in top gear. With half an hour to go Sydney clawed his way past and crossed the finishing line at the drop of the flag at the traditional 4.00pm in a magnificent third place. This was an outstanding achievement, considering the pre-race engine problems and having to nurse the car through the last ten hours of racing with top gear only. The Cadillac Allard J2 also set a new distance record for the class.

It is interesting to note that after twenty-four hours of racing, the J2 was only five laps behind the winning Talbot-Lago at the finish – or approximately 26 minutes, less than the time lost in the pit stop for the gear selector problem.

1951

The J2 and J2X were the cars to beat in many motor racing events between 1950 and 1952, particularly in the USA, where there were wins at the Watkins Glen Grand Prix and many other races.

Sydney's racing schedule was hectic in 1951, even before the Le Mans race in June. He competed in the Mille Miglia on a mountainous circuit around Italy, then went on to races at Goodwood, Silverstone and to the British Empire Trophy race on the Isle of Man. He then dashed across the Channel to race two Allard J2s in the gruelling Le Mans 24 Hours.

Once again, there were vehicles competing in a huge range of classes, from the 5.5-litre heavyweight Cunninghams down to the tiny Panhard 600cc flat twins. A total of nine Ferraris were present, alongside strong teams from Aston Martin (all of their five cars finished, taking third, fifth and seventh positions). Talbot-Lago would take second and fourth positions. The Jaguar 3.4-litre C-Type proved fast and reliable and went on to win in the hands of Peter Walker and Peter Whitehead. The two J2 Allards were driven by Sydney, Tom Cole, Alf Hitchins and Peter Reece.

As 4.00pm approached, all the cars were lined up in the traditional manner. Once again Sydney had asked Tom to do the sprint across the track and take the first stint. Drivers crouched on their marks ready to dart across the track when the flag swept down. As each one leapt into their seat there was a momentary pause before a wall of sound erupted as sixty racing cars burst into life.

Stirling Moss was away quickly, but so was Tom in the Allard. He held third position at the end of lap one and remained in a front running position for the first few laps, but the damp track caused him to slide off the road into a sandbank, bending a wing onto the tyre.

The damage was more severe than expected and two further visits to the pits were made before the problem of the wing rubbing the tyre was cured. It was going to be a wet race and on lap 22 Peter Reece, in car number two, damaged the steering after sliding off the track. A seven-minute pit stop was needed to check and adjust the track. The number one car was running well up to lap 38, when Cole came in for refuelling and to hand over to Sydney after lapping consistently with a time of 5 minutes 12 seconds, despite maintaining a maximum rpm limit of 4,000rpm. Six competitors had already retired. The rain started to fall more heavily and Sydney's lap times increased to 5 minutes 30 seconds, while Hitchins in car number two increased his laps to 6 minutes.

Around lap 50 a noise started to develop in the back axle of the number two car. Hitchins made a lengthy pit stop of 12½ minutes, but as nothing could be done to repair the potentially terminal problem, the car was sent out to lap at a speed sufficient to cover the minimum distance over the next eighteen hours to be classified as a finisher.

The transmission in car number one was starting to give trouble, making gear changes difficult, so when Sydney came in on lap 80 and handed over to Tom he gave instructions to nurse the transmission.

A further eight cars had dropped out. This year the regulations stipulated a minimum of twenty-five laps between refuelling or filling with any liquids. So Tom came in on his twenty-sixth lap, reporting the engine overheating, the clutch slipping and the gears almost impossible to select. Tom went out again and the Allard continued to lap comfortably, but on lap 120 he was back in the pits to report that only top gear remained, which was further damaging the slipping clutch. Sydney took the car out again in a vain attempt to nurse it through the next ten hours of racing. The inevitable end came on lap 134, when Sydney came into the pits to retire, trailing clouds of smoke from the burnt-out clutch. This made the J2 the twenty-fifth competitor to retire, having covered 1,120 miles in 13 hours at an average speed of 86mph (by comparison, the 1950 J2 averaged 82mph and finished third).

The number two J2 of Hitchins and Reece was still thundering round, nursing the ever-noisier back axle. Amazingly it was still going at lap 213, with just an hour to go to the end of the race. To be confirmed as a finisher it was necessary to cover the last lap in less than 30 minutes, so Hitchins drove away from the pits just after 3.30pm, intending to crawl round to the finish as the flag fell at 4.00pm. Unfortunately the officials' decision was that Hitchins had taken just over the 30-minute time limit to complete the lap, so was not classified as a finisher, even though the J2 had covered more laps than the twentieth place works Porsche 356. This was a huge disappointment for all in the Allard team.

1952

Mercedes returned to Le Mans in 1952 for the first time since the 1930s with a strong team of three 3-litre 300SLs. (The road model was later called the Gullwing, because the doors opened upwards like bird wings.)

Jaguar, Ferrari and Cunningham also had strong teams. The Jaguars featured streamlined, low-drag bodies designed by Malcolm Sayer and disc brakes, but unfortunately this body shape caused unexpected overheating problems and they were all out within a couple of hours.

Ferrari set off fast and early on Alberto Ascari led the race in a 250S, with a new lap record of more than 107mph.

As for Allard, Sydney entered two of his new J2X Le Mans models, the Le Mans name denoting the new fully enveloping aerodynamic body designed for the 1952 Le Mans race to comply with the new race regulations. These aluminium bodies were largely hand-formed by a small team of skilled craftsmen led by Jimmy Ingram and Jack Jackman at Encon Motors. Both race cars were registered for the road and driven to the race.

This year the Cadillac 331cu in had been replaced by the recently announced and more powerful Hemi-headed 5.7-litre V8 produced by Chrysler, with up to 295bhp. Most of the improved performance, however, was offset by the 160lb extra weight of the new engine and the specially prepared Ford four-speed gearbox. Sydney had modified and installed a Ford four-speed commercial box, with new gears, but it was heavy and it was not possible to get optimum ratios fitted due to the positioning of the gears. In pre-race testing the changing of the quick change gears at the rear of the differential, combined with a high 3.24:1 final drive

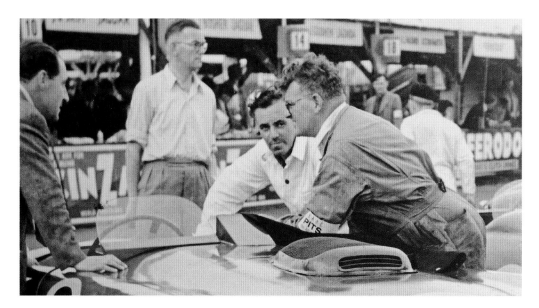

The J2X Le Mans that Sydney and Jack Fairman had driven at Le Mans in 1952 is here seen at the TT (Tourist Trophy) race at Goodwood, with Jack Fairman (left) and its owner Frank Curtis driving. The car was later rebuilt as the Hinton Special.

gear, gave the car longer legs with a top speed of more than 150mph and acceleration of 0–60mph in well under 6.0 seconds.

Sydney, in car number 4, had invited experienced race driver 'Jolly' Jack Fairman to be his co-driver, since Tom Cole had moved over to race for Ferrari. In the number 5 Allard were its owner, Frank Curtis, and Zora Arkus-Duntov, who would later become famous as the father of the Chevrolet Corvette, but was then in Europe working at Allards to gain experience with building cars and motor sport in general.

After a wet morning, the track was dry by the time of the traditional run across the track start. Fairman and Duntov took the first driving stints in the two Allards. The cars were lapping consistently around 5 minutes 5 seconds to 5 minutes 10 seconds until lap thirty, when Duntov became overdue, but rolled into the pits after a few anxious minutes with a terrifying story to tell.

On lap thirty he went for the brakes at the end of the Mulsanne straight at around 150mph and his foot went straight to the floor. Luckily there was an escape road with a long run-off, but even so he had to crash through the final barrier and duck under a wire to avoid injury.

The diagnosis was swift – a lower damper mount had broken, severing a brake pipe. The team resorted to drastic action, blanking off the broken pipe and setting off into the race, still with eighteen hours of racing to go, with only three wheel brakes. The whole episode took 56 minutes and they dropped down to thirty-fifth position.

Car number 4, driven by Sydney and Fairman, was always in the top ten and by midnight, after eight hours of racing, it was in eighth position. By the break of a misty dawn they were in sixth position.

The eventual winners, Mercedes, were consistent and fast, but not in the lead. In the early stages one or other of the seven Ferraris was ahead, but they dropped out one by one. At one point a Gordini was leading, but by mid-race Pierre Levegh, driving a 4.5-litre Talbot, had taken control: his decision to drive the remaining twelve hours was to prove over-ambitious later in the race.

Curtis had taken over the driving after the brake failure incident. Although he was lapping at only around the 6 minute mark, due to the damp track and poor brakes, he was still creeping up the placing as so many retired: of the fifty-seven starters, only seventeen cars reached the finish line.

In the early morning the drivers' lap times were being hampered by the misty conditions. Sydney, with his knowledge of the track, was able to lap at the 5 minutes 30 seconds mark and held sixth position at 4.00am when he came into the pits to refuel and hand over to Fairman. By 5.00am Fairman had moved up to fifth position. Levegh was leading in the Talbot, followed by the two remaining Mercedes, then Lance Macklin and Peter Collins's Aston Martin in fourth position.

Hopes were still running high that the small Allard team might finish with a place in the top five, as the Allard thundered past the pits every five minutes. Tearing down the long, long straight (there were no extra chicanes in those days) in a very exposed seating position at more than 140mph for hour after hour, hanging onto the steering wheel with all the wind pressure, noise and buffeting, would have been a severe test of man and machine.

Unfortunately the test proved too much for the machine. Shortly after 5.00am Fairman came into the pits to report a problem with a rough running engine. Sydney took over, but when he failed to reappear at the expected time, the pit crew knew there was trouble. Eventually, when the car arrived slowly back at the pits, it was obvious that the engine would go no further with the big-end bearings clattering like hammers. The J2X Le Mans had averaged 92mph for thirteen hours and completed 129 laps.

Meanwhile, Duntov in the other car continued to lap steadily around the six-minute mark, but not for much longer: after covering 134 laps it stopped out on the track with a broken axle shaft.

Briggs Cunningham, in his C4-R with a similar Chrysler V8, finished in fourth position, completing 252 laps, only one more lap than Sydney in his J2 in 1950.

1953

Two new JRs, registered NLN 650 and NLN 652, were built and prepared for Le Mans 1953. They carried Pye R/T radios for contact with the pits and both were painted red with chrome wire mesh guards over the vulnerable headlamps. A third car was then committed.

Briggs Cunningham had competed at Le Mans since 1950 and his success in finishing fourth in the 1952 race, driving his own Cunningham C4-R with a Chrysler V8, generated further American interest in the race.

One of those leading the way in their enthusiasm for motor sport was General Francis Griswold, at that time Commander of the US Third Airborne Division and based in the UK. He was a friend of an Allard enthusiast, General Curtis LeMay, who already drove and raced a K2, although it was considered too dangerous for a man in his position of responsibility as a General in the USAF to race himself, so he normally had an appointed driver take his place.

After the Le Mans race a meeting was arranged in the summer of 1952 between Sydney, General LeMay and General Griswold. It was agreed that three new Allard sports racing cars would be purchased by General LeMay, Colonel Dave Schilling and Colonel Reade Tilley, to be entered for Le Mans 1953 and raced as an Allard team.

The new car was to be known as the JR and Sydney commissioned Dudley Hume, who had previously designed the tubular chassis for the Allard P2 saloon, K3 and

Palm Beach, to design and draw up a tubular chassis and a new body shape for the JR.

Sydney's fundamental design philosophy for a racing machine revolved around maximum power with minimum weight. He wanted the JR to be more compact than the previous J2, J2X and J2X Le Mans models, so the front track was reduced from 'railway gauge' 4ft 8½in to 4ft 4in, while the rear was reduced by 1in to 4ft 3in. The wheelbase was reduced from 100in to 96in. By designing a 'kick out' in the chassis side rails, Dudley was able to build in more cockpit space in an overall smaller car.

Erwin Goldschmidt was one of the most prominent Allard race drivers in the USA and had just won the Watkins Glen Grand Prix in his J2X. As soon as he heard about the new JR he ordered one for the forthcoming 1953 race season.

In a few hectic months the first JR for Goldschmidt was completed in March 1953. After a short shakedown test in the UK with a Ford Mercury V8 fitted to get the basic handling sorted, it was quickly shipped to New York, less engine and transmission. Such was the pressure to get the car to the USA that in hindsight there was insufficient time to evaluate the handling effectively. Goldschmidt was never able to achieve the success he had with his previous J2X, although the lack of wins could also be put down to the increased competition from manufacturers such as Jaguar, Ferrari and Aston Martin.

The 1952 Le Mans Allard J2X LM cars were fitted with a 5.4 litre Chrysler Firepower V8 with 295 bhp.

By the cut-off time for entrants in the June race, only two JR team cars had been completed, so components for the third car were to be taken to Le Mans as spares for the other two.

Courtesy of Sydney's high-ranking American military customers – a General and the members of his 'Colonels Club' – two 331cu in engines, specially prepared by Cadillac, were flown to the UK on a USAF plane, which landed at the USAF base at Heyford. The engines were installed in the two Le Mans race JRs, chassis numbers 3402 and 3403. The USAF connection also saw the ultra-long runway (more than 10,000ft) at RAF Fairford, a designated USAF base, being made available to Allard for testing.

Sydney took one car to a club race meeting at the Ibsley airfield circuit for testing under race conditions. The engines were supplied with two Rochester four-barrel carburettors, but unfortunately these immediately developed the same problem that had been experienced on previous engines, with fuel starvation on fast bends causing the engine to cut out.

For the next event, three weeks later, the Rochesters had been replaced by two Carter carburettors. Both JR Le Mans cars were entered for the two-hour International Sports Car Race at Silverstone. This would be a further substantial test prior to the Le Mans 24 Hour race in June and would leave just enough time to rebuild and renew components as necessary before the race.

Sydney had invited Philip Fotheringham-Parker to be his co-driver. This race was to be a practice for Philip to get to know the JR, which he had not driven previously. Unfortunately he lost two laps at the start of the Silverstone race, when the starter button fell apart.

Sydney made a good start and held third place for most of the race, until he spun into a sandbank, crumpling the bodywork at the rear corner, but still managed to finish in eleventh place.

Following this, both cars were entered for a further test in two races at Thruxton. Ray Merrick would be co-driving with Zora Arkus-Duntov at Le Mans and, as Ray had not yet driven the JR, this was his opportunity to get the feel of the car. In the first race Sydney retired on lap seven when the gear selector jammed. He took over Merrick's car for the second race. When the starter's flag dropped there was a backfire when Sydney opened the throttle, causing a fire under the engine cover. Despite losing around thirty seconds, he was able to climb back up to sixth position.

Much time was spent changing the quick change gears inside the cover at the rear of the differential (both cars were fitted with this system) and comparing the acceleration with both cars running side by side. At one point Sydney was at near maximum speed, with Tom Lush at his side clinging onto his stopwatches and clipboard, when they found themselves rapidly approaching some heavy earth-moving equipment spread across the runway that the officials had failed to warn them about. At the last moment, braking very hard from 130mph, they managed to slither through a narrow gap. Typically Sydney's only concern was about the time and his question to Tom was, 'Did you get the time before I had to brake?'

This year they were going to use a radio telephone (RT) system in the cars, so before leaving for France the Pye Depot fitted a set to each car, but typically there was no time left to fully test the system.

Sydney drove his race car (chassis number 3402, race number 4) over to Le Mans. The other car was taken by

Zora Duntov drove the second Allard JR team car at Le Mans in 1953. A couple of years later he joined General Motors Competition Department in the USA and became known as the father of the Corvette.

Jim Mac and Dennis Allard in the works lorry. This year there was quite a gathering of Allard owners and drivers with their wives, who filled the small hotel booked by the team in the village of Loue. The two JR Allards drew crowds of interested spectators whenever they appeared.

Unofficial practice started on the Wednesday. The cars were parked on the verge halfway along the Mulsanne straight. The road was actually still open to the normal road traffic, so the cars mingled with the general public, travelling round the track not far short of racing speeds.

The RT system worked well during the testing and in the afternoon Philip Fotheringham-Parker, driving car 3402, came through with the bad news that he was coming round slowly with the engine sounding very rough. A compression check showed two cylinders were way down on compression. Immediate removal of the cylinder head revealed the story of broken bits of piston scattered around the cylinder. From this point, the removal and path to repair was to be a remarkable story itself.

Although Generals LeMay or Griswold could not attend the race, they had authorized a team of Air Force officers and mechanics to be there. The Cadillac division of General Motors also had two senior engineers over from the USA. Having this degree of back up, things really started to happen, even though workshop facilities at the circuit were non-existent. Within two hours Jim Mac and the Americans had removed the engine, lifted by an improvized block and tackle arrangement slung between two trees, with the engine resting precariously on the flat bonnet of a jeep with mechanics supporting it.

The engine was taken to a nearby USAF base where a transport aircraft just happened to be about to take off for a base in the USA, near where the engines had been prepared. To cap this, by some miraculous arrangement a replacement engine was bound for the USAF base near Le Mans. It's amazing what you can arrange when you are a USAF general and interested in motor sport.

Within twenty-four hours of the engine failure, a new engine had arrived from halfway round the world and was installed and running ready for the Thursday evening official practice. Practice was spent checking and bedding in the engine.

Night-time testing had shown that the headlight beams

Le Mans 1953 – Sydney makes a fast start in JR number 4, Duntov is in JR number 5.

could not be adjusted downwards sufficiently. This had happened because, during final track testing in the UK, it had been demonstrated that the cars performed better and had the power to pull larger 650 as opposed to 600 × 16 tyres. The fitting of the larger tyres raised the rear of the car, together with the longer rear coil springs that were needed to give extra wheel arch clearance. The local garage that had been so helpful the previous year came to the rescue once again and made tapered rings to be fitted behind the headlights, which corrected the alignment.

During the final couple of laps of testing Sydney reported a loose feeling at the rear of the car, but an inspection spotted nothing. Was history about to be repeated? Tom Lush had his misgivings. Once again, in hindsight, could the differential mount failure have been caused by spinning into a sandbank at Silverstone a few weeks earlier?

In 1953 the cars were still making the traditional Le Mans start, with the cars in one line along the front of the pits. Cars with the largest capacity engines were positioned: this year that meant the Talbot-Lagos and the Cunninghams, with their 5.5-litre V8 Chryslers. The Allard JRs with Cadillac 5.4-litre V8 were next in line.

At 4.00pm on Saturday 13 June the drivers ran across the track to their cars at the drop of the flag. Sydney made a brilliant start and shot away, leading under the Dunlop Bridge. Duntov in the second JR was a little slower and was surrounded by a group of cars jockeying for position.

Le Mans 1953. Sydney leading Alberto Ascari in the 4.0 litre
Ferrari and Stirling Moss in the 'C' Type Jaguar.

After the mad rush and roar of sixty accelerating engines, and after the last stragglers had hurtled under the bridge and disappeared, the track fell strangely silent. Four and a half minutes seems a long time to wait. Then a murmur of anticipation arose from the crowd in the stands opposite the pits as the last few seconds counted down and they turned to look as far as possible down the track. The leader on the first lap was always greeted by the crowds at Le Mans.

Suddenly there was a cry of 'Allard, Allard' as the pack approached in a rising crescendo. Out in front was Sydney in Allard number 4, trailing a cloud of swirling dust, followed closely be Ascari in a 4.1-litre V12 Ferrari and Moss in his 3.4-litre C-Type Jaguar. An Allard led at Le Mans lap one!

Alberto Ascari and Luigi Villoresi went on to record the fastest lap of the race at 4 minutes 27 seconds. Theirs was one of the last cars to retire, on lap 229. The Allard JRs' best lap time by comparison was 4 minutes 36 seconds.

The race, however, was a triumph for the Jaguar C-Types, with Tony Rolt and Duncan Hamilton coming in first, Stirling Moss and Peter Walker in second place, and Peter White-head and Ian Stewart in fourth. They were denied a clean sweep by a third place for Phil Walters and John Fitch in a Cunningham C-5R; Briggs Cunningham himself, with Bill Spear, finished seventh. The Cunninghams also recorded the highest top speed of 154.81mph (this being the first year that a speed trap was installed on the Mulsanne straight).

On lap two Sydney was starting to experience problems at the rear of the car. On lap four he found that he had no rear brakes at the end of the Mulsanne straight and

had to take the escape road. He reported over the RT that he had brake problems and was coming in slowly. In the pits, inspection quickly revealed that one of the differential housing mounting brackets had broken, allowing the diff assembly to twist and turn, severing a rear brake pipe. So Sydney in car number 4 was forced to retire on lap four, after such a promising start.

The car had covered 560 miles at an average speed of 98mph, but the failure was a great disappointment for the team, with both cars having to retire so early in the race after such a promising start. What this demonstrated was that the Cadillac 331cu in V8 was fine for a mass-produced V8 for everyday use and short races, but was not designed for a high-speed endurance race at the sustained speeds the cars were now capable of achieving and needed further serious modification to make it reliable.

Highlighting the point about the speeds now being reached was the news of the very sad death of Tom Cole, Sydney's co-driver in the 1950 and 1951 races, who crashed his Ferrari late in the race at the notorious high-speed Maison Blanche bend.

Duntov soldiered on in car number 5, lapping steadily at around 4 minutes 40 seconds or an average of more than 108mph. On lap fifteen he reported in on the RT that the engine was starting to overheat and on lap seventeen he arrived at the pits with a cloud of steam coming from the car. Unfortunately the rule that year was that no water could be added until lap twenty-eight had been completed, so Duntov cruised around, making several stops, until the water could be replenished on lap twenty-nine.

It was now 7.00pm and Ray Merrick took over the driving duties. He continued until lap sixty-one, when Duntov took over again. Then on lap sixty-five his voice came through on the RT to report that the engine had seized on the Mulsanne straight.

After their return to London the Le Mans JRs were displayed at Goodwood, where they were inspected by HRH the Duke of Edinburgh and Goodwood's owner, the Duke of Richmond and Gordon. Then they were despatched to their 'Colonels Club' owners in America. In more recent years Allards have made appearances at the Le Mans Classic races.

RAC RALLY

Sydney had been competing in the Monte Carlo rally since 1949, but his hectic competition programme of events did not allow him time to enter other longer distance rallies.

After driving for the Ford Motor Company as a works driver in a Ford Zephyr and finishing in a creditable 14th position in the Monte Carlo Rally of 1955, he entered his own Zephyr in the following RAC International Rally held in March 1955. The 2.5 litre engine was largely standard, apart from a Raymond May's high compression cylinder head and triple Solex carburettor.

The RAC was a tough event covering four days of rallying, with only one night rest. There were eleven special timed tests around the country. Many of these were on hill climb or race circuits. In 1955 it was particularly tough due to the snow and ice conditions. Sydney's co-driver for this event was his brother Leslie.

On the second day when Leslie had taken over the driving, allowing Sydney to rest in the reclining passenger seat, Leslie lost control on an icy narrow road bridge. The car crashed heavily into the railings, one piece of the railing piercing right through the inside of the car, narrowly missing Sydney. Once again Sydney had experienced a lucky escape from serious injury. The whole side of the car was completely wrecked and the windows missing. Despite this serious damage, after straightening the steering, they pressed on undaunted, win-

RAC Rally 1955. Sydney with co-driver Leslie Allard. Leslie slid on ice on a bridge, badly damaging the Zephyr, but typically they soldiered on to finish the event in 14th position.

ning four of the special stages and at the end still finishing 14th overall.

The Monte Carlo rules were changed again in 1956 and Sydney was able to enter an Allard P1 saloon. Soon after the Monte in March, he entered his Allard P1 into the RAC Rally and was one of only eight competitors with no loss of marks, but the final tests did not suit the big, heavy car and he dropped down the leader board. Sydney also found time to do the International Tulip Rally, based in the Netherlands, in his Zephyr, but this would be the last year in which any Allard car featured highly in the finishers list on an international rally.

In the Monte Carlo Sydney competed in Fords from 1957 to 1960 in a Zephyr and then from 1961–64 in 'Allardette' modified Anglias. His competition interests turned to sprint cars and finally the Allard Dragsters from 1960.

SILVERSTONE CIRCUIT

Sydney raced at Silverstone at many occasion in the Allard J2 and JR in the production sports cars race, and even in the Monte Carlo-winning P-type saloon, finishing third behind Tommy Wisdom and Sir Stirling Moss in the saloon car race.

On several occasions Sydney's brother Lesley raced a J2 at Silverstone and Goodwood alongside Sydney; he competed in sprints and hill climbs too.

Goff Imhof wins the 1950 RAC Rally.

THE CLASSIC ANNUAL BRIGHTON SPEED TRIALS

This standing-start motor sport sprint event is believed to be the oldest competitive event in the world, running since 1905. It is staged every year, normally in the first week in September, on the sea front esplanade in Brighton, running down the Madeira Drive. For most of the ninety-plus years it has been run over a kilometre, but was shorted to a ¼ mile sprint in 2004. It is a somewhat rough course for high-speed motor sport, particularly for the dragsters.

This was an important event for Sydney and he made a point of competing there almost every year from 1935, when he drove his stripped-out TT (Tourist Trophy) Ford, to claim a class record, right up to 1963 when he drove the Allard dragster.

The Brighton & Hove Motor Club ran the event and Sydney's brother, Leslie, was an important member of the committee and was Chief Marshall or Clerk of the Course in overall control of the event for a number of years. He patrolled the paddock and start-line area, often wearing a yellow waistcoat under his sports jacket. We (the young-sters in the family) secretly gave him the nickname of Mr Toad of Toad Hall, from the famous children's book *Wind in*

Leslie Allard racing at Silverstone in his Allard J2 during the 1950 Production Sports Car Race.

The Brighton Speed Trials, held every year in September over a kilometre with a standing start, is one of the oldest motor sport competitions on the calendar. On 3rd September 1955 Sydney broke the sports car record in Rupert de Larrinaga's Allard JR with a time of 26.47sec.

the *Willows*. Like Sydney, there was an air of authority about him in such situations.

In 1960, Leslie with Sydney, Bob Field and Neville Heath, took part in the annual veteran car run from London to Brighton driving a 1903 Napier.

Sydney usually took part in one of his own Allard cars at the speed trials, starting with the early Allard Specials, then the 'J' Types, setting class records. Then the hill climb race Steyr, then the Allard JR, when he set a new sports car record, followed by the Steyr Sports car, then onto the monster twin-engined Steyr – which failed to start on the day – and finally to the dragster.

The big dragster was not suited to the rough course and was never in top form at this venue. In 1963 he set a time of 22.04sec, not quite fast enough to claim the fastest time of the day (FTD) that day. He lost time when a hose from the front mounted supercharger burst before the finish line. This was a great disappointment to all those involved, after the huge press build-up prior to the event, with talk of a possible new course record.

Many Allards have competed at the speed trials over the years, perhaps one of the most memorable being Eric Alexander in his J2X Le Mans who, under fierce acceleration from the start line, slid sideways into a classic street lamp post, bringing it crashing to the ground. Luckily without serious damage to driver or car, but much to the dismay of Brighton Council!

In 1964, Dante Duce came over from the USA, driving Dean Moon's 'Moonbeam' supercharged Chevy sports car, leaving a trail of smoking rubber and claiming FTD. Mickey Thompson and Duce have also give wild and smoky demonstration runs over a ¼ mile.

In more recent years, Clive Skilton and Denis Priddle have done ¼-mile timed runs in their dragsters. Priddle recorded fastest time ever in 8.12sec with a very brave run, much to the amazement of the crowds watching from the terraces above. For most years since 2004, Jim Tiller in his 65-year old 750bhp J2 Allard has often beaten all comers, waving the flag for Allard ad setting several FTDs with a best time of 9.98 seconds for the ¼ mile!

THE 34TH TOUR OF SICILY – 2–3 APRIL 1950

This event may have been a tour of the island of Sicily, when the event was staged way back in 1916, and developed as an event with which to promote the island's tourist industry. By 1950, when Sydney was invited to enter the event by the Sicilian Automobile Club, it was very much a full-on race

around the island. The club's invitation to Sydney said that for the added publicity it would give to the event they would give a free entry to Sydney Allard in one of his famous cars – of course, Sydney accepted the invitation, not being likely to turn down such a racing challenge.

Tom Lush, always Sydney's right-hand man when it came to a new competition, was put in charge of preparations, together with his friend and Italian speaker Holland Birkett and in the workshop two Jims – Jim Mac and Jimmy Ingram.

This was a long-distance event, around 900 miles, driven at high speed day and night over twisty, hilly roads. The Allard coach and mobile workshop carrying the spares, tools and the J2 was prepared for the long journey through France and Italy to the start in Palermo, with a frenzy of activity during the days prior to the event. The prototype J2, not yet in full production, was fitted with the first Cadillac V8 imported into the UK – thanks to the help of Tom Cole. This J2 with its precious engine(chassis number 888 and registered KXC 170) was just two months later the one to carry Sydney to third place overall in the Le Mans 24-hour race. In the words of Tom Lush:

We moved up in turn to the starting area in the glare of the arc lights and, as the flag dropped, we screamed away with spinning wheels, snaking wildly on the wet road. The crowds were uncontrolled and they left only just enough room for the car to pass between them, so that they seemed to us like a long corridor of white faces.

As our speed built up I began to wonder if Sydney had remembered the right turn soon coming up. It was still raining heavily, making the street lamps ineffective and our headlamps only showed the people in front parting as we approached. Suddenly it became apparent that what lay ahead was not people, but the solid mass of a statue, but with masterful control Sydney put the car into a slide – the crowd had already scattered – and we passed the masonry sideways. Then, quickly straightening out, Sydney made a snap change into second gear and we accelerated hard towards the city outskirts.

We were driving so hard that in the first half hour we had caught up and passed the two cars that started just ahead of us, but Sydney was complaining of our poor headlights, shouting to me over the roar of the car that they were limiting his speed...!

After running for about 45 minutes I noticed headlamp beams behind and obviously catching up fast. I passed the information to Sydney and he replied that he would let them pass, then follow their lights.

We knew that starting behind us, apart from Tommy Wisdom, were several well-known Italian drivers including the renowned Ascari, and we were not surprised when his Ferrari hurtled past. An even more hectic drive began as we tried to follow him, but although we held him on the corners we began to drop back on the straights and eventually he drew too far ahead for his lights to be of any use. The headlights could just not cope with the speed that Sydney was driving. The road turned sharp left over a level rail crossing; he was unable to make the turn and with a tremendous crash bounced along the line.

Cramming it into reverse, Sydney accelerated hard to the accompaniment of the most horrifying lurches and crashing from underneath the car and he shot backwards over the rails. He would not stop to check for damage, saying he'd already lost too much time and he continued as before, rarely dropping below 80mph. Dawn came shortly afterwards and in the grey half light they came to a downhill stretch with a corner at the bottom, bordered by a low stone wall.

We didn't quite make the bend and the car slid heavily into the wall and scraped along it with a shower of sparks. The incident hardly slowed us down, but very shortly afterwards, a long tongue of flame stretching back in the slipstream from beneath the car was noticed in the mirror. Tom gave emergency signs to Sydney and, braking heavily, we stopped on a narrow bridge crossing a stream. As we scrambled out, the whole back of the car went up in a sheet of flame. Almost immediately flames appeared on the other side of the bridge and we realized that the flaming petrol was running down under the bridge and out the other side. With road-side gravel we managed to control the fire, but that was the end of the event for us.

1951 TOUR OF SICILY

Again, in 1951, Sydney was offered a free entry into the event, but this time he would have to use the Ford Ardun V8, which was acceptable under the Sicilian Auto Club rules, unlike the Cadillac engine the previous year. Sydney's entry for the Mille Miglia had also been accepted and so, as the Sicilian event was at the start of April and Mille Miglia at the end of the month, he would combine arrangements and cover both events.

A new J2, painted British racing green with chassis number 1971 and registered LXR 949 was allocated and prepared.

For these two long-distance road races, the seats were improved with more padding and back support. The brakes had dual master cylinders and outside brake adjusters, and on the dash there were buttons for horn and headlamp flashers, and a grab handle in front of the navigator.

The weather was much better this year and scrutineering went smoothly, as did the start in Palermo city centre, but after only a hundred miles the Ardun engine had a piston break up. A very unusual occurrence, which resulted in retirement, it was a great disappointment.

THE 1951 MILLE MIGLIA

This was an ambitious event for Sydney to tackle. The Mille Miglia was a road race of approximately 970 miles, which took place in Italy on closed public roads, Starting in Bresica and finishing in Florence. There was a huge range and number of cars competing from under 1000cc upwards. The smaller capacity cars started first at minute intervals – many hours before the last car started, due to the large number of competitors. The first cars started in the evening and the following cars started at minute intervals through the night. Each competitor's start number corresponded to the start time.

When their turn came, Sydney and Tom were handed a time card for stamping at each control and a book of coupons for purchasing fuel on route. As car number 433, they were given a corresponding start time of 4.33am. It would be dark at that hour and, with rain forecast, it would be dark, wet and cold – and true to form it was! The flag dropped and they roared off away from the glare of the arc lights and the crowded square, racing into pitch darkness, although crowds still lined the city streets.

Sydney was driving fast – very fast for the conditions on a twisty road. They covered the first hour and half at an average speed of over 80mph and, just as dawn was breaking, Sydney slid wide on a tricky corner and spu,n striking a solid kilometre marker stone with the offside front wheel in the process. The nose of the car and the front wheels were hanging precariously over an embankment, but as soon as they stopped a crowd of enthusiastic spectators appeared, as if from nowhere and lifted the car back onto the road. Unfortunately, the damage was serious. The front axle was bent and the steering box had been lifted from its mounts. Temporary repairs to secure the box took too much time, and although they got going again, they were not able to drive the car with sufficient speed to continue in the race, arriving at the next control just as it closed. Once again a very disappointing end, but as Sydney would have said 'That's motorsport, you have to accept that there are good days and bad days.'

Sydney and Eleanor drove the long journey back in the coupé, arriving just in time for Sydney to jump into his TT J2 and race at Silverstone in a formula libre race with mostly single-seat racing cars. When he finished third, afterwards he remarked 'one has to keep one's hand in'! Such was Sydney's energy and enthusiasm for racing.

THE LIÈGE–SOFIA–LIÈGE 1963

Sydney was always attracted to a motorsport challenge and this annual event, effectively a ninety-hour race across Europe, although not advertised as such, was a real challenge. Just to finish needed determination, stamina, a well-prepared car and a slice of luck.

We entered two Allardettes. Rob Mackie and I drove a Shorrock supercharged Allard-modified 997cc 105E Ford Anglia; Sydney and Tom Fisk had a 1500cc Shorrock supercharged model. Below is an account written by Tom in 1963. It paints a true picture of this dramatic event. Ninety hours of continuous hard driving with only one hour stop for rest! It was abandoned a few years later for being too much of a danger to the public on increasingly busy roads, following a number of deaths of competitors and members of the public.

For our parts, Rob and I got as far as Northern Yugoslavia before running out of time, after various problems including a wheel vibrating loose, due to the terrible road conditions. Extracts from the story of the 1963 'Liège', as written by Sydney's co-driver Tom Fisk, paints a vivid account of the event.

To my mind, now – even more than ever – this is THE RALLY. The recipe is simple – the crew and the car versus the clock – rough roads and fatigue. The crews must be in good condition to combat the inevitable fatigue that comes from such a long period of relentlessly hard driving. The car must be a tough car basically and very well prepared, with only a minimum of carefully thought-out accessories and spares.

The cars start three abreast at three-minute intervals from 10pm, setting off at high speed up the main street of Spa and out into the night. We now faced four days and four nights of practically non-stop motoring before we returned to Spa on Saturday evening, the first car being due at 5pm.

There is just one hour compulsory stop at Sofia, but as speed schedules are high one cannot get much time in hand at any controls, except enough to refuel

and perhaps a hasty meal or snack. Once Sofia is left behind there are no stops and no respite as you can gain only a very small amount of time in hand or more probably you are late and there is no let-up in this until Austria is reached some forty-four hours further on.

Unfortunately we had no up to date recce notes, only the ones from last year, only a portion of which were common to this year's route. The maps of Yugoslavia are only a rough indication of the route at their best, so we were guided also by various other means, such as tyre tracks, other competitors (these of course got less and less) and intuition. This method of navigation suffered rather a setback when we encountered the second of the protracted torrential downpours we had in Yugoslavia, this turned the road into lakes. It also obliterated all the wheel tracks of early competitors. However, we pressed on, we still had our intuition!

After leaving Yugoslavia things got a little easier as we made our way into Italy and we felt the worst was over. It was, too, up to a point, but we were still to lose many minutes in crossing the Passes of Gavia, Vivione and Stelvio on the last night. Then came the long haul back through Austria and Germany to Spa and finally, the convoy so much smaller now, back to Liège.

Some Highlights

The large rock, which had been washed down from the hillside and lay in the road, that Paddy Hopkirk missed at high speed and we didn't (same speed) when following him in torrential rain. Very bent wheel, very quick wheel change, very wet crew – and Paddy got away, which was a pity, as we weren't sure of the route directions on that bit and it was night-time too!

The leaping flames we saw ahead, which proved to be Vic Elford's special Vitesse fiercely burning, following an electrical mishap. A sad end to a promising car that had been doing so well.

The slowness of pumping petrol by hand at the rate of one gallon per minute, when you know that you need eighteen gallons and have only time for seven.

The cruel grandeur of the mountains of Albania and striking canyon-like gorge on the way into Titograd.

After Stelvio, the realization that we looked like making it and with every kilometre this became more certain, until – yes – our ambition to be a finisher in

'The Liège' was realized. The sixteenth car out of the twenty who finished from an entry of nearly 130 who set out from Spa four days before'.

Tom Fisk

THE LIÈGE–SOFIA–LIÈGE 1964

This year we both entered Allard Company-prepared Cortina GTs. These had largely standard, unmodified engines, but with all the usual rally gear for long-distance endurance events, including uprated suspension with heavy-duty sump shield and a long-range fuel tank. Once again it was a ninety-hour high-speed drive across Europe with only one hour of rest in Sofia, the capital of Bulgaria, making it an extremely tough event to finish.

Sydney ran out of time with engine problems and retired on the return leg. However, Rob and I made it, after an extremely adventurous experience culminating in hitting a rock wall in the middle of the night, on the 9,000ft Garvia Mountain Pass, rolling the car onto its side – with the steering damaged and the front wheels pointing at odd angles. I can remember the car lying on its side with the headlights shining into a starlit sky!

We made it over the pass with great difficulty with the damaged steering. Luckily, as most of the Ford works cars had already retired, the Ford mechanics treated us as part of their team, swiftly fitting new parts, and we were on our way again, continuing our hectic race across Austria and Germany.

As a result of the Ford service, we were one of only twenty-one finishers out of a hundred cars that had started the marathon event, ending up in nineteenth position with 4 hours 30 minutes lost.

TOM LUSH

Tom Lush stands head and shoulders above anyone else who worked for Sydney and supported his wide-ranging motorsport activities. Tom truly was Sydney's right-hand man in the Allard Motor Company, particularly when it came to motorsport.

Tom joined Sydney's fledgling business building the first Allard Specials sometime in 1937 – long before the Allard Motor Company was formed in 1946. It is difficult to define Tom's job at Allard: his versatility and the jobs he handled were so wide-ranging, from parts collection and car delivery to being co-driver in the Mille Miglia, and everything in between. The following account of his activities, working with and for Sydney over a period of over thirty years, demonstrates this.

Tom was responsible, following Sydney's lead, for forming the Allard Owners Register and for the Allard newsletter, which eventually became the AOC magazine. Occasionally he acted as trials 'bouncing' passenger, for both Sydney and Imhof. He was with Sydney as navigator in all the Monte Carlo rallies Sydney did from 1949 right through to 1965. No mean feat, when he was usually in the back seat, being thrown from side to side for hours on end and the being grilled when they made a wrong turn or any mistake with timings or the paperwork, entry forms and organizational matters for the many competition events Sydney entered, including FIA entries for Le Mans. Tom was also part of the pit crew at Le Mans, the Mille Miglia and the Targa Florio, and navigator and co-driver if required. He spent many hours with Sydney testing and tuning at MIRA and other tracks.

Tom helped organize the Motor Show exhibits, doing all the background paperwork, and then manned the stand throughout the various shows and events, as representative and salesman for the Allard Motor Company.

During his many years at Allard, he made detailed notes of dates and events, which enabled him to compile and write an excellent book, *Allard – the inside story*, in the form of a diary of events. He was on hand to help, advise and discuss with Sydney many aspects of the company, the cars and events, right up to the Drag Festivals in 1965.

His loyalty and work for the company are to be highly commended.

Tom Lush with the 1952 Monte Carlo winners trophies, which he won as navigator for Sydney.

ALLARD AND DRAGSTERS

Sydney preparing to start the Allard dragster at the Brighton Speed Trials, run over a kilometre on the sea front promenade. Dean Moon, over from the USA (wearing the stetson) was there to see Dante Duce, his driver, make a smokey run in 'Moon Eyes' later in the day.

CHAPTER 6

ALLARD AND DRAGSTERS

SYDNEY WAS ALWAYS ON THE LOOK OUT for new areas of interest. Those who were close to him say that this largely explains why and how it was that Sydney created Britain's first dragster. He was also behind the arrival of the first American drag racing team, and the first and second annual drag racing festivals that followed. That these were successfully managed and run by a group of inexperienced British enthusiasts is down to Sydney's people skills and his ability to make things happen. He decided that he would have an Allard dragster – and to introduce the sport to the UK.

Sydney Allard was a competition driver at heart, with the ability to compete in almost any form of motor sporting event. He had raced and rallied every model of his Allard V8-engined cars over many years, including in straight-line 'sprint' events such as the Brighton Speed Trials, before deciding to build a pure sprint car.

In 1957, using one of the spare Steyr V8 engines left behind after the sale of his Steyr hill climb car, he had a lightweight sports car built at the S1 workshop in Clapham High Street. He raced this at various hill climb and sprint events, but he never found enough performance from this engine, so this car was dismantled and replaced by a twin-engined Steyr V8

monster machine with four-wheel drive. This device was built and taken for track tests, and even appeared at the Brighton Speed Trials, but it never ran successfully and it was soon realized that the whole concept was too complicated to be easily sorted out and made effective in terms of development costs, man-hours and the eventual power-to-weight ratio.

After the 1960 racing season and the frustrating attempt to build a Steyr twin V8-engined sprint car had been abandoned, Sydney was looking for another race vehicle. Earlier in the year he had read an American publication containing details of a single-seat, exposed-chassis, high-speed, straight-track racer named the 'The Chizler' built and raced by Chris Karamesines. At this time his machine was called a 'Rail', a dragster with two chassis rails fitted with an engine, suspension and wheels, and mounted in exposed style without any bodywork. 'Rail' and dragster racing were gaining ground as a new sport in America and Sydney could see the possibilities of extending interest in the sport to Britain.

At the time no special regulations and classes existed to allow dragsters to race competitively, so the first dragster would have to run and be built as a racing car. Also it would require four wheel brakes, so a heavier, stronger chassis

The first dragster in the world, outside the USA and Canada, being built in the Allard S1 Clapham workshop in 1961. Sydney with John Hume (the man who built all the dragsters) and David Hooper, Allard draughtsman and engineer.

frame was needed, along with a fully enveloping body. Certainly building what was the first true dragster would be something of a leap in the dark. Sydney worked out the general layout and running gear needed after studying the American magazine *Hot Rod* and seeing Dean Moon's advert for supercharger and dragster components. He was not without influence and at this time was talking to the RAC about its competition and construction rules.

John Hume, who had previously worked as a race engineer for John Cooper's racing team, joined Allard to help Sydney and David Hooper in the design and actual building of the first dragster, the Allard Chrysler Mk I, which was built between October 1960 and April 1961. Hume was also responsible for the build of the small Dragon dragsters and the second (Mk II) version of the Allard dragster in 1965.

While Hume worked on the dragster during the winter and spring of 1960–61, Gerry Belton, who had recently joined Allard as sales and publicity manager, ordered components such as a crank-driven GMC blower set up with twin-port fuel injection from Dean Moon, who used a similar system on his 'Mooneyes' dragster. A 5.7-litre Chrysler Hemi V8 was acquired from a Dodge truck, stripped and rebuilt with a high-performance camshaft and solid lifter kit – big valve heads

TOP: **Spring 1961: the new Allard appeared ready for the motorsport press to inspect and report, as yet without its racing slicks.**

MIDDLE: **Russell Brockbank's cartoon of Sydney and his dragster, from his book *Move Over!* (Temple Press, 1962).**

BOTTOM: **Dragster demonstration day at Silverstone, 1963. Sydney with Dante Duce – the Mooneyes driver. Dean Moon can be seen with his Mooneyes dragster in the background.**

and high-performance ignition system with magneto. The GMC 671 blower, driven by gears from the 'nose' of the crankshaft, delivered a maximum boost pressure of 17.0psi. The Hilborn fuel injection was calibrated to run on straight methanol fuel. Although never actually run on a dyno, calculation predicted a power output of 650–700bhp.

The one-off Allard dragster chassis was ready for testing by the spring of 1961. Soon the dragster was running quarter-mile times approaching 10 seconds, including one of 10.8 seconds. At a subsequent event at Wellesbourne, Sydney ran 10.4 seconds with a top speed of 170mph. The car would also appear at a new drag racing sprint event run by the BARC at Riccall in Yorkshire.

As the coverage and profile of drag racing grew, British motor sport had a new theme. In March 1962 *Hot Rod* ran a big feature on Sydney and his car by UK motorsport journalist John Blunsden. The Allard dragster made its first outing of the year in the following month when the National Speed trials event was held on the old runway at RAF Debden. A second British sprinter also appeared at that year's Brighton Speed Trials in the form of a modified Formula 1 Cooper fitted with a Chevrolet Corvette engine. Despite the competition, Sydney was the 1962 Autosport National Sprint Champion. That year both Sydney and Alan competed in Allardette Anglias and again entered the 1963 Monte Carlo Rally with supercharged Allardettes.

No one had any experience of driving the monster in the UK. The only race cars that had approached this sort of power to weight ratio would have been the pre-1939 Auto

Union and Mercedes Grand Prix cars, but their acceleration was limited by lack of grip. The dragster, with no rear suspension, crude steering, massively heavy clutch, ineffective brakes and a parachute that often failed to open, made for a wild, rough and exhilarating ride.

Accelerating from zero to around 170mph in 10.0 seconds on an old airfield runway scattered with landing lights, with a surface that varied between rough and dangerous, could be described as a tad more than exhilarating. The seating position was also hazardous, as you sat just to the rear and astride the differential transfer gears, with eight exhaust pipes exiting on either side, only inches away, creating a massive blast of heat, exhaust gas and noise, so you could be burned, gassed and deafened all at the same time.

Its first showing to the public was in May 1961 at the Allard 'Shorrock Supercharger' day at Brands Hatch, where it appeared without the bodywork: it did an engine start-up 'noise' demonstration, but was not actually driven. A few test runs at North Weald Airfield in Essex were enough to damage the clutch.

The first proper showing in front of the motor sport press was on the Club straight at Silverstone. The fuel used was methanol with a small percentage of acetone. The theoretical maximum supercharger boost was 17lb. The dragster weighed 1,460lb (60 per cent distributed to the rear wheels) and produced 480bhp at 5,000rpm with a compression ratio of 8:1. The maximum torque was 550lb/ft at 3,000rpm.

A temporary clutch had been fitted due to the damage caused at the previous test, so a standing start could not

Sydney seen early in 1961 testing the still unpainted dragster, with triple parachutes, at Northfield Airfield, just north of London.

Alan Allard in fireproof suit speaking to one of the time keepers, just before making his World Record ¼-mile run.

be attempted, but hand timing with a rolling start indicated around 9.5 seconds, with an estimated top speed of 160mph for the quarter mile on the Club straight.

The machine looked and sounded very much the part and, still running without its distinctive streamlined blue and white bodywork, prompted many enthusiastic remarks in the press.

ENTER THE AMERICANS

Early in 1963 Dante Duce, a speed shop owner and occasional dragster driver, called Sydney from California after reading John Blunsden's article in *Hot Rod* magazine. Duce suggested coming to the UK to challenge Sydney to a drag race. Sydney told him that he had purchased the Potvin supercharger and other components for his new dragster from Dean Moon in Los Angeles. Duce knew Moon well and gave him a call. Moon, always on the look out for maximum publicity for his business, arranged to get the 'Mooneyes' dragster out of retirement for Duce to drive and ship it over to the UK with a team of mechanics.

At a regular meeting of the Speed Equipment Manufacturers Committee (SEMA), Dean Moon told Wally Parks, President of the National Hot Rod Association (NHRA), about the match race in the UK. Mickey Thompson, another speed equipment manufacturer, also heard the conversation and decided he wanted to be in on the action with his blown, Ford V8 'Harvey Aluminum Special'. Parks decided that SEMA would present a trophy to the winner of the challenge.

Dante Duce, Dean Moon and his team, sponsored by the model makers Revell and Mobil Oil, arrived in the UK with the Mooneyes dragster on 10 September 1963.

The Club straight on the Silverstone circuit was chosen as the venue for the first match, a side-by-side race between a US and a British dragster. The motor sport journalists were invited to the demonstration, but the spectacle was not quite what was expected. It was decided that there were too many unknown factors to perform side-by-side runs, and the RAC authorities decided that there should be single demonstration runs only.

Sydney made his solo run from a rolling start, covering the quarter mile in approximately 9.5 seconds. Then Duce smoked his tyres for almost all the distance, leaving snaking black lines and clouds of white smoke while clocking 9.48 seconds ET and 166mph. Both machines deployed braking parachutes at the end of the run. The assembled journalists were mightily impressed, both by the acceleration and the shattering noise. The American team were resplendent in

The dragster line up for the match races. In the foreground Mickey Thompson with his Harvey aluminium nitro-fuelled dragster; beyond him Dante Duce with Mooneyes and Sydney with the Chrysler supercharged dragster.

their white jackets with yellow Mooneyes, and white stetsons! This was a complete contrast to the Brits with their shirts and ties, and hardly a T-shirt in sight.

Both dragsters were push started. The Allard team had their Thames van with a block of wood strapped onto the front bumper. At this point the American team needed a push vehicle and up stepped Roy Phelps with his Chevy pickup. This was the starting point for Phelps, who later became a leading light in the development of the UK drag racing scene, establishing the Santa Pod Raceway in 1966.

The second event was at the famous Brighton Speed Trials along the seafront esplanade. Mickey Thompson joined the party unannounced, just in time to run, although he had a prior agreement with the Brighton & Hove Motor Club that it should only be a *mild* demonstration run.

The dragster solo demo runs were held over a quarter of a mile at the end of the day. Due to the roughness of the course, both Thompson and Duce performed some wild and smoky runs, the machines leaving the ground at times, much to the amazement and appreciation of the large crowd, who had waited patiently all day to see and hear the spectacle. They were not disappointed.

The Allard dragster had an engine backfire, which damaged the magneto drive gear, and it was not able to compete with the US dragsters that day.

The final demonstration on Sunday 22 September was at RAF Debden in Essex. The weather was good and thousands of spectators had managed to find their way into the invited guests-only event. Word had spread after the spectacular show at Brighton two weeks earlier.

This time the supercharger drive sheered on Sydney's dragster after putting down one reasonably fast run that had been spoiled by having to lift off before the end of the quarter mile. The American dragsters, however, put on a show that is still remembered by spectators who were to become avid drag racing fans. The track was smooth enough for some fast runs, but the level of grip was low and led to some very smoky runs that were perfect for the spectators, if not for the drivers.

The final run, side-by-side, between Dante Duce in 'Mooneyes' and Mickey Thompson in the Harvey aluminium dragster proved to be a key moment in the history of UK drag racing. Dean Moon dropped the starter's flag. The earth shook from the noise and power released, while smoke from the burning rubber filled the air to such an extent that neither driver could see the track! Duce had to lift off as Thompson's nitro-burning dragster pulled ahead. (Nowadays, of course, a nitro-burning dragster would not compete with one running on methanol-only fuel.)

Duce's best time was 9.98 seconds and Thompson's, despite the lack of grip, was down to 8.84 seconds, equivalent to 179mph. This run set the scene for what was to come in future years.

THE DRAGON

Club drag racing, which the British Drag Racing Association (BDRA) was intended to promote, was a potentially less costly class of racing. Gerry Belton was well aware that Allards was ideally placed to capitalize on the demand for a smaller-engined dragster:

At the time we were selling a range of Shorrock superchargers and Ford engine tuning equipment. One or two of our supercharger kits used an outrigger assembly to allow the supercharger to be mounted further back or over the engine. From my years of experience in rallying and racing Allardette Anglias, I suggested we should build a Shorrock supercharged mini-dragster, using the 1500cc Ford Cortina 4-cylinder engine.

John Hume, who had already made the big dragster, set to work constructing the small dragster, which we decided to call the Dragon. My idea was to race the Dragon and then to build and sell other complete machines, or as a kit of parts for DIY builders. However, we were ahead of the market, but we had misjudged the fact that many potential drivers wanting to compete were themselves entrepreneurial

engineering types, who wanted to design and build their own machines. So ultimately we only built two complete Dragon dragsters and a third updated chassis with slightly smaller diameter tubing was proposed with a kit of components for display on the Allard Motor company stand at the 1968 Motor Show, and offered as a kit for £600.

The Shorrock C142B supercharged Ford 1500cc engine ran on methanol and produced 175bhp at 7,500rpm. The kit, however, was never built up and was not sold as a complete dragster at that time. In 2013 Roger Hayes located the chassis and obtained most of the original components, resulting in a successful restoration.

Dragon No. 1 first appeared at Silverstone on 8 April 1964 and, with John Hume driving, was test-run to 12.4 seconds for the standing-start quarter-mile sprint. Top speed was 105mph. A time of less than 12.00 seconds was achieved on a second test run at Duxford in May.

DRIVING THE DRAGON

As well as racing there were records to break, as Alan Allard recalls:

In May we took the Dragon to Duxford Airfield for the first 'big go' event, organized by the recently formed BDRA (British Drag Racing Association). With John Hume driving, the Dragon took low ET of the meet with a time of 11.92 seconds.

In June, after further adjustments and testing on the dynometer, we took the Dragon to Chelveston Airfield in Northamptonshire for a records day event, where I was going to see if I could break the Class 'F' standing-start one-kilometre record, then held by Mickey Thompson in the USA. This was somewhat ambitious as the Dragon was only really geared for a quarter-mile run, limiting maximum speed to around 145mph at 7,500rpm.

Driving the Dragon dragster took some practice to get the best out of it, with the gear change between your knees! Starting in second gear the machine accelerates so rapidly you have to keep your hand on the gear lever for the change up to third gear, keeping straight with the other hand on the wheel.

In 1964–5 suitable slicks for 13in rims were not readily available, so we ran on Dunlop racing tyres. My best run ET of 11.11 seconds, with a top speed of 131mph, was achieved with some practice.

1964 Press Release picture of the new 'Dragon' dragster. Alan Allard with John Hume and Tom McGlone.

I can remember doing some warm-ups and test starts inside the simply huge hangar. The noise echoing around inside the building was incredible. Out on the rather rough airfield runway I had to complete two runs, one each direction within one hour, under the watch of FIA Officials.

I reached 145mph and 7,500rpm about two-thirds of the way down the course, then held the engine at valve bounce for the remainder of the run, without the engine disintegrating! A new record of 21.08 seconds for the standing-start kilometre was set. I also established a new UK record for the standing-start quarter-mile of 11.54 seconds, which no one had recorded before, but it was soon to be broken by the big-engined dragsters.

Alan Allard and Ian Smith demonstrated the two dragsters

at a press day at Silverstone in April. A second such Dragon Mk II (with large overhead roll bar) was purchased by Ian Smith, Chairman of the British Racing & Sports Car Club. Colin Glass and Dennis Jenkinson ('Jenks') were involved with this car in 1966, which may at one stage have had a Bristol engine. The third chassis has been restored by Roger Hayes, who found the car as a box of bits, with a Ford engine, in 2013. The restored Dragon made its debut at the NEC Classic Car Show in late 2017.

These were still early days for the new sport and conditions were rarely ideal:

I was given the job of driving the second Allard dragster, now that my father was fully involved with his business and planning the forthcoming Drag Festivals. It was ready for me to test a couple of months earlier, but as there were still very few dragster meet-

Build yourself a dragster from a kit of parts! An interesting idea, but very limited market in the UK in 1963, as most wanted to build their own machine.

Mini dragsters of Alan Allard in Allard Dragon and Doug Church in his Porsche-powered dragster from the USA – made for some very close racing with ETs of 11.2sec for the ¼ mile.

ings and no established drag strips, we had to test on a very rough course, with landing lights on some sections.

I hit one of these lights at high speed. The jolt was so violent (remember no rear suspension!) and with wind pressure so great that it ripped my helmet and goggles completely off, leaving me almost blind from the wind pressure at that speed.

DRAGFESTS

Sydney and Wally Parks then started discussing arranging for a full team of American dragsters and bikes to come over to the UK the following year to put on a show for the growing number of drag racing fans. This small personal moment between the two men largely explains why the arrival of the American drag racing team and how the subsequent drag festivals came to be run by a relatively inexperienced group of enthusiasts. At this time Sydney thought that he could build a new niche market for building dragsters and drag racing equipment, producing business for the company, but this never materialized.

Gerry Belton, Allard's marketing manager, was given the task of organizing the show. The most influential individuals in the British Drag Racing Association (BDRA), which was formed to run a series of drag races, were Sydney Allard, Wally Parks, Alan Allard, Len Cole and Tony Bayley. The collaboration with Wally Parks of the NHRA made the 1964 International Drag Festival series a reality and the Allard Owners Club lent a hand. Six meetings were held over three consecutive weekends in different parts of the country: Blackbushe, RAF Chelveston, RAF Woodvale, RAF Church Fenton and RAF Kemble. The BDRA served as the umbrella organizing body. The American team included such top drivers as Don Garlits, Tommy Ivo, Bob Keith, Tony Nancy, George Montgomery, Keith Pittman, Ronnie Sox and Buddy Martin, Dave Strickler and Grumpy Jenkins, Dante Duce, Doug Church, Bill Woods and Don Hyland.

Some degree of organizational and PR confusion arose in 1963–4 as the BDRA vied with the new British Hot Rod Association (BHRA) to promote British drag racing events. This was eventually resolved by creating a new British overseeing body, the British Drag Racing & Hot Rod Association (BDR&HA). An important development during these early years was the establishment of the Santa Pod Raceway.

A few days before the arrival of the American Drag Racing Team it was realized that their large and heavy dragster trailers, packed with spares, would need a substantial towing vehicle. Eventually several ex-military Humber 4 × 4 vehicles

were found. The ball hitch size was changed to match the American trailers and they were pressed into service towing trailers to each event all over the country. On 1 September 1964 the American team arrived at Southampton Docks aboard the SS *United States*. I recall how the small British team had to be adaptable:

We were performing very different tasks that day – tow driver and fitter, and dragster pilot. When the Americans arrived in Britain for the first big international drag festival, like most others I was somewhat overawed at that time by the equipment, standard of preparation, presentation and performance of the American team. At one moment I was one of a band of workers ferrying equipment around and helping to set it up at the various venues around the country and towing a trailer at night to and from events. I was one of the towing team, so I'd find myself arriving at an event delivering an American dragster and then jumping into my Dragon dragster for a run alongside the American team, then transferring into the big Allard Chrysler dragster and racing an hour or so later!

The first Drag Festival meeting at the Blackbushe Airfield strip, 50 miles west of London, drew a crowd of more than 20,000 jostling to see the first runs by the nitro-dragsters of Don Garlits and Tommy Ivo, both of whom put on an awe-inspiring show, filling the track with burning rubber smoke and earth-shattering noise. The spectators were initially stunned into silence by the experience and then a wave of excited applause spread down the strip. Don Garlits ran a best of 8.09 seconds and 195mph, to Ivo's 8.46 seconds and 184mph.

The Allard dragster was still not achieving its potential, this time having trouble with the rear axle. Alan in the Dragon put down 11.42 seconds and 125mph, but the fastest run by a UK driver was hill climb champion Peter Westbury with 11.02 seconds and 127mph in his four-wheel drive Ferguson.

The big Allard Chrysler dragster was still giving trouble at the second event at RAF Chelveston. Alan in the Ford-powered Allard Dragon was in a side-by-side race with American Doug Church in his Porsche-engined dragster and just won with a time of 11.26 seconds to Doug's time of 11.36 seconds ET. Again the American team put on a great show. A bump in the track at RAF Woodvale, where round three was held, caused some wild and out-of-shape runs, but Alan managed 12.15 seconds and 141.0mph in the big dragster, although this was still some way off its potential.

The American team put in many high-speed runs during round four at RAF Church Fenton, and both American and British bike riders scored times in the mid-ten seconds.

In the Allard Dragon, I was just beaten in an unusual side-by-side race, during round five at RAF Kemble, by Alf Hagon on his supercharged 1150cc Jap V-twin bike. I managed a better run in the Allard dragster, however, achieving 11.14 seconds and 141mph.

For the final round of 1964 everyone returned to Black-bushe, where a large crowd once again gathered to the spectacle of these most powerful machines. I finally made a perfect start in a race against some real competition in the form of Dante Duce driving the 'Moonbeam', both cars having a similar supercharged Chrysler V8. My time of 10.28 seconds, beating Duce in the process, was probably the best ever achieved in the first big dragster.

The 1964 Dragfest was considered a success by the organizers and enjoyed by the American competitors, even though it needed considerable effort to pull it off behind the scenes. Sydney, Gerry Belton and the BDRA committee were already thinking about running a similar event in 1965.

A few months later, in March 1965, with sponsorship from Ford, the Allard Dragon was flown to California and put on show, also giving a demonstration run at the Pomona Dragstrip. This was the first time a British dragster had run in the USA.

Alan Allard lifts the front wheels as he sets an International record for a kilometer, with a time of 21.08 secs.

From the USA it was flown to the Swedish Auto Show in Stockholm, before returning to Clapham. Publicity for the Allard Dragon even saw it appearing in a photo shoot with the Beach Boys, dressed in shiny blue-grey suits, with Al Jardine squeezed into the cockpit, during their November 1964 promotional tour for the album *Beach Boys Concert*.

Second Drag Festival in 1965. The first and last dragsters to be run in the wet. Alan Allard (on far side) staged against Norman Barclay in the ex-American Los Palmos dragster.

BREAKING 10 SECONDS

With a best standing start quarter-mile time of 9.98 seconds, achieved at the Chelveston Airfield Drag Festival meeting in September 1964, the Allard dragster driven by Alan Allard became the first car or motorcycle in the UK to break the 10-second mark over a quarter of a mile:

You have to understand how different things were back around 1960. At that time without the internet and computers, America and the drag racing scene seemed far away – almost another planet! So there was no one to follow or learn from and to gain experience in piloting a dragster. Only now, apart from the big dragsters, are Formula 1 cars or some supercars getting into the same acceleration performance bracket.

To accelerate from a standstill to 170mph in around 10 seconds over a quarter mile with a comparatively heavy (for a dragster) 1,550lb machine requires 650–700bhp. Remember, we never had the starts really sorted, so it probably took 6.5 seconds to reach 100mph and then only a further 4.0 seconds to accelerate from 100 to 170mph, whereas current top fuel (nitro-burning) dragsters with their maximum grip off the line must have almost linear acceleration over the full quarter mile, now reaching speeds of over 300mph.

When I first drove the big Allard Chrysler dragster in 1963, no one apart from my father had driven a dragster outside of the USA – nor seen one in the UK or Europe. The dragster was a machine built for maximum acceleration with a huge

supercharged engine and braking mostly by parachute at the end of a run, with assistance from just a large handbrake lever in the cockpit. Hauling on the handbrake could cause some interesting effects!

It now seems relatively tame, though, in comparison with achievements a few years later. Even in the USA at that time it was something special to get below 8.0 seconds ET [elapsed time] for the standing-start quarter mile. So when my father said, looking my way, 'you can drive the dragster now, I will be too busy organizing the drag festivals', I felt somewhat dropped in the deep end to say the least!

This was something very different. But once you were rolling you could trundle around – rather like a big-engined sports car of the day; something like a J2 Allard but with 750bhp!

We installed a small radiator for cooling, which meant we could run the engine for longer. From trundling along from say 20mph in top gear, one prod of the accelerator shot the machine forward with neck-snapping force. Full throttle held for a couple of seconds seemed to fire the machine to the horizon with an ever-increasing acceleration curve. The vibration caused vision to blur. The only braking was by a large handbrake lever – no foot-operated brake pedal. The real braking was by parachute. At the early testing, this was with a triple canopy and a small trailing drag 'chute, but this could only be deployed successfully at relatively high speed at the end of a run.

The British International Drag Festival in 1965 season did not follow the previous year's six-round affair, but was an important series of three meetings with two held at Blackbushe (Saturday and Sunday) and one at Woodvale, near Southport, for more northerly based fans. It also received wider recognition, not least because that year Sydney just happened to be chairman of the Society of Motor Manufacturers and Traders' motor sport committee. This official status crucially meant that, under RAC rules, it was a 'trade' supported event and advertising sponsorship was therefore allowed, which would benefit the event's viability and attendance fees paid to competitors. The Americans turned out en masse, bringing over a team of eight dragsters and six bikes, and put on a great show when the weather allowed.

This year I drove the new Allard Chrysler Mk II (with red bodywork) that John Hume, with support from Dave Hoop-

er, had developed from the original Allard Chrysler dragster. This was along the lines of an American-style machine, with extended stainless steel tubular chassis, and was front-engined (with no cover) and without any front brakes.

The engine and supercharger assembly was transferred from the original Mk 1, which had now been 'retired' and put into storage. I reached 150mph in a 10.45 second run on the damp Blackbushe runway. At the next meeting, at Woodvale, the weather was better and a crowd of more than 30,000 spectators watched the spectacular show until dusk. It was here that I achieved the first-ever sub-10 second run by a British car or motorcycle:

At Blackbushe the track was still damp with puddles in places, when I was called up to do my run in the Allard Dragster – staged alongside Norman Barclay in the Dos Palmos dragster. The water thrown up by the exposed front wheels onto my goggles made it difficult to see the track and the huge slick tyres spun violently with every attempt to open the throttle. Amazingly, we both made it. I was concentrating so hard keeping on my side of the track that I don't recall if I won or not. When the track had dried a little, one or two of the Americans made wild weaving runs. Since that experience I believe, dragsters were never allowed to run on a drag strip in the wet. Apart from the danger, lifting on and off the throttle on a run can cause a damaging backfire on these engines fitted with a radical camshaft and running heavy nitro-fuel loads.

My best run at this meeting, around 9.7, made it the first time that a UK dragster had got below 9.98 seconds for the standing-start quarter-mile. My smaller Allard Dragon dragster had been won in a publicity competition, but Chris Pattison, the winner, was too young to drive it, so Rob Mackie, my long time rally co-driver, drove it making a best run time of 11.54.

The Mk II was subjected to typical Allard publicity and was photographed at the family's Adlards dealership showroom in the company of British tennis ace Roger Taylor. The Mk II also appeared in publicity shoots for Castrol.

Some 43 years from its inception, the original Allard Chrysler dragster was taken from storage in the Beaulieu Motor Museum and fully restored (see page 159).

THE ALLARD DRAGSTERS

Allard Chrysler Mk I	1961
Allard Chrysler Mk II	1964
Allard Dragon Dragsters	1964
Allard Anglia Dragon	1966

I, constrained by work and business demands after my father's death in 1966, put the Allard Chrysler dragster up for sale and it was purchased by Clive Skilton in early 1969. Part of the deal saw the car become the 'Allard Skilton Dragster', retaining the link to Sydney. John Hume would continue to oversee its mechanical status. The Allard Skilton moved the supercharger to the less-aerodynamic top of the engine, yet it still ran in the low 9.0 seconds range and took the 1969 Grand Final at the BDRC championships.

ALLARD DRAGSTER WORLD RECORD, 15–16 OCTOBER 1966

John Hume and Tom McGlone trailered the Allard Chrysler Mk II dragster up to RAF Elvington in Yorkshire behind the trusty Ford Thames van. The van was later used to push-start the dragster, with just a block of wood strapped to the front bumper. Hume had been responsible for the design of

Getting ready for the quarter-mile World Record attempt.

the second dragster, as well as the other Allard dragsters, and came along as the third member of the team together with Tom McGlone and John Calori, who worked at the Adlards Ford dealership.

I cannot remember if we made the record attempt runs on the Saturday or Sunday. However, luckily even though it was late in the year the weather was dry, with not too much wind considering it was such an open airfield. The wide runway stretched out disappearing over the horizon, being I believe, over 2½ miles long.

The FIA International rules for record attempts state that FIA approval officials must be observing and that a two-way average time, covering one run in each direction, must be completed within one hour. I was attempting to break the absolute world record for the standing-start quarter mile, held in 1966 by a BMW car in 11.264 seconds and to establish a record for 5,000–8,000cc cars.

With the officials and timing gear all set up, I was push-started and John was leaning over the engine checking that we were running on eight cylinders and letting it warm up a little, before rolling the machine up to the start line, manoeuvring to the optimum position without breaking the timing light beam.

The grip was good at Elvington and I made a good start with very little wheelspin. As always with the wind buffeting and vibration through the chassis, the finishing line marker boards were a blur. I did not release the parachute as there was still plenty of stopping room and my team were worried that they might not have time to repack it within the one-hour time limit.

The first run time of 9.035 seconds for the quarter mile

was my best run to date. No car or bike had ever gone under 9.5 for this distance in the UK in 1966.

John checked things over and had a look at the plugs. Tom filled the tank with methanol (no nitro was used). We turned the dragster round for the second run in the opposite direction and were ready well within the hour. Unfortunately on start up, and when rolling forward to the line, the engine had a misfire and was running on only seven cylinders. As there was insufficient time left to investigate the misfire and complete the second run within the hour, we decided to go for the run anyway.

I made another good start with very little wheelspin, but the uneven engine beat made the noise even more ear-shattering. The result was a time in the 9.5 seconds bracket, producing a two-way average of 9.335, still good enough to set a new world record for the standing-start quarter mile distance. Had the engine been running on all cylinders for the second run, I might just have got under 9.0. It should be mentioned that Clive Skilton, whom I handed the dragster over to, never got below 9.04 in his first racing season with the same engine set-up, so perhaps 9.0 was the best that could be achieved with this power-to-weight ratio.

It seemed somewhat surreal at the time that I was the official world record holder, when the top dragsters in the USA were around 2.0 seconds quicker in 1966, with Don Garlits winning the US National Championship with a time of 7.14 seconds.

The 1964 and 1965 British drag racing events laid the groundwork for the sport in the UK, but there were massive behind-the-scenes issues of organizational and financial implications. The poor weather of 1965 and the resultant

Getting in position for a record attempt. One run in each direction to be completed within one hour, with International time keepers in attendance – a new world record was established (9.335sec).

The beautifully restored Allard Chrysler Dragster and the restoration team led by Brian Taylor, at the Beaulieu Motor Museum presentation. Dave Hooper on left with Alan Allard, Brian Taylor and Nick Mason (Patron).

limitations on competitive timings and crowd numbers was a big financial issue for the organizing bodies.

Sydney had been fully involved, along with Gerry Belton, in the highly complicated organizational side of the 1964 and 1965 Drag Festival events, and was under pressure for the drag racing venture to succeed and cover its costs. Unfortunately it failed to do so in 1965, which led to the reorganization of the sports bodies overseeing British drag racing. Some feel that the added stress may have contributed towards Sydney's illness.

There was a cruel irony in the timing of Sydney's death just as the first major drag racing events were introduced at the Santa Pod Raceway drag strip in 1966, establishing its place in British drag racing history. Without Sydney there may not have been a British drag racing scene until

years later. While others were to develop the movement, Sydney Allard can truly be described as the 'Father' of British and indeed European drag racing. It is fitting then that he has been inducted into the British Drag Racing Hall of Fame.

DRAGSTER RESTORATION

The first Allard dragster, with a supercharged Chrysler 'Hemi' V8, was retired at the end of 1964, when the new Mk 2 dragster was built. The original engine, supercharger and gearbox were transferred to the new machine and the old dragster was put into storage.

The restoration story began in 1982, when Allard owner

Brian Golder came to visit me. He said that he would like to see the dragster restored and running again. I handed the dragster over to Brian on condition that it would eventually be passed to the National Motor Museum at Beaulieu, once completed. Sadly Brian died a few years later, before he could complete the restoration.

Subsequently, I agreed with Brian's widow, Diane, that the dragster should go to Beaulieu. The museum gladly accepted the machine and it was displayed mounted on a wall in the museum, until eventually it was moved into storage with the idea of restoring it at some point when funds are available.

In 2006 Brian Taylor discovered the Allard Chrysler residing in deep storage at Beaulieu while researching the history of British drag racing for his book *Crazy Horses*. From there stemmed his idea to bring the Allard Chrysler dragster back to life. With American support from the SFI Foundation and Carl Olson, members of the Allard family and the Allard Owners Club, David Hooper and many others, Taylor set up the Allard Chrysler Action Group (ACAG). Taylor also secured the support of the Pink Floyd drummer Nick Mason as the project's patron in 2008. Mason, a leading collector of classic cars, once owned an Allard J2 and has described Sydney as 'a legend in British motor sport's history'.

With the help of the sponsors and the National Motor Museum's Advisory Council, work started on the long road back to restoration and securing the engine and drivetrain, and finding ways to raise the funding of about £50,000 that would be needed to complete the project. This was promoted by a very successful weblog and a great deal of work devoted to securing the correct parts. The Allard Chrysler Dragster story has come full circle in today's realization of the dream, in which the dragster has been wonderfully restored and is up and running in all its glory.

DRAGSTER RESTORATION TIMELINE

2008	Initial assessment and planning
2009	Dragster chassis on display at Silverstone and Press Day at Beaulieu
2010	Autosport Show. Restoration project started. Engine and supercharger secured. Race Retro Show. Santa Pod appearance. Haynes Extreme Wheels Show
2011	Engine build in USA. Body painted. Lloyd Allard works on the project (exhaust pipes)
2012	Engine and drivetrain completed and fired up. Engine run at Beaulieu. Engine problems
2014	Further fundraising and work. Official handover to Beaulieu as an exhibit
2016	Successful completion and running of the Allard Chrysler dragster

Alan Allard's 'Dragon' 220bhp supercharged metal flake blue Drag Racing Anglia set a new Class D competition altered record for the quarter mile at the only permanent drag strip in the UK on 14 August 1966, with a time of 105.93mph. With slick racing tyres, which were not available at the time, times would have been in the 12-second bracket. The Anglia was built to promote the sale of Allard (Ford) motor accessories and performance products. it was purchased by *Cars & Car Conversions* magazine for magazine promotions in 1968.

Allard gathering – the greatest number of Allard cars ever seen at one event, on the track at Monterey. Some owners travelled over 1,000 miles to attend.

CHAPTER 7

ALLARD IN THE USA

ALTHOUGH A SINGLE CHAPTER does not do justice to Allard's American record, we must here give credit to the key names and events that influenced the Allard brand in the Unites States of America. This will not be just a record of competitive driving, podium places and enthusiastic owners, however, because as early as 1951 the thoughts and reactions of American customers were relayed back to Allard's London base and acted upon.

Sydney Allard's J2s, especially when modified for the US market, were fast, brutish, pugnacious race winners ('Anglo-American Bastards') and utterly dominated a brief but glorious and dusty period between about 1950 and 1954. This made Sydney the most influential figure in the growth of sports car racing in the USA after the Second World War. Sydney visited America and experienced at first hand the enthusiasm for Allards that Dave Davis, his lead export manager and salesman, was eager to promote. This was especially notable on the West Coast, where Alan Moss was crucially pivotal in building the Allard legend.

We can safely assert that Carroll Shelby, who raced J2s at the start of his career, gained much of the inspiration for the Shelby Cobra from his early Allard experiences. Would Shelby have come to Sydney Allard in 1960 for a car on which to base his own ideas if Sydney had still been making cars? Would the Palm Beach Mk 3 have been the basis of Shelby's car instead of the AC Ace, at a time when AC was almost unknown and had no experience of fitting V8 engines?

And what if Allard had had the resources and been in a position to take advice from America to regroup, reframe and continue to series production of the Dodge-powered V8 Allard 'Red Ram'?

There may be several reasons why Allard and specifically the J2 series were so popular in America, but one factor should not be overlooked. From the 1920s onwards American car fanatics built 'Specials' – hot-rod, tuned-up, re-engined versions of standard models, notably Model A Fords. Some were very crude, some were excellent hybrids, others were unique iterations of 'ideas' that ran through to the 1970s race cars. From California to Connecticut, enterprising Americans made hot rods and specials. One even fitted a Ford Mercury V8 flat-head to a 1929 Riley Brooklands, while Briggs Cunningham fitted a 1939 Buick chassis and a high-powered motor into the remains of a Mercedes SSK wreck.

Given that Sydney Allard's marque stemmed from his own 1930s Specials, we can perhaps draw a link between his deeds and the fashions of the American specials movement and the reverse-effect of the Allard J2 upon American enthusiasts. As the American Allard enthusiast E. Dean Butler recently said to the authors: 'Sydney Allard was a Californian hot-rodder who happened to be English.' Although certainly an American perspective, this is an intriguing external view of Sydney.

The Allard J2 and J2X faced little home-grown competition in the USA, although Briggs Cunningham designed a roadster of somewhat Allardesque feel. From a racing standpoint, it was the Jaguar XK120, Ferraris, the works Aston Martin DB2, the occasional Frazer Nash, Austin Healey 100, MG TD and later the MGAs that tried to snap at Allard's heels. True, there were various hot rods, tuned Fords, uprated Oldsmobiles and Stutz specials, but in the main the local car-mad fraternity simply adopted the American-engined J-series cars as their own.

According to the records, only nine Allards were exported to Canada, of which only one was a J2X (chassis 320). The first 'American' market Allard, with L Type chassis number 105, was actually sent to Argentina on 29 November 1946. As early as 2 March 1947, however, Allard sent an early K Type (chassis 108) to North America, and on 8 August an L Type (chassis number 130) and two K Types (chassis numbers 158 and 165) were also delivered. K1 chassis 165, now fitted with a Cadillac 390 engine, was for sale in 2017 for $110,000, which is not bad for a mainstream Allard. Interestingly, two cars were sent to Argentina and five to Brazil in 1947.

In 1948 Sydney's close associate, Reg Canham, took an Allard M Type to America and went on a cross-country tour towing a caravan to promote the Allard Motor Company. One of the hot-rodders Canham met in Los Angeles was Eddie Meyer, who operated a tune-up garage dedicated to teasing more power out of the flat-head Ford V8. Eddie Meyer Engineering made arguably one of the 'hottest' dual carburettor manifolds on the market. Several cars using his

FIRST THOUGHTS

'I have seen those cars in New York and I would like one, but they are too expensive for me.'

Henry Ford II talking about the Allard to H.J.A. 'Dave' Davis, Brussels, 1948

'Three big machines passed me – almost blowing me off the course. Those cars were J2 Allards and from that moment on I fell in love, totally and completely. I knew then that somehow, someway, someday I would own an Allard.'

Bill Bauder, writing in the *Allard Register*, 2009

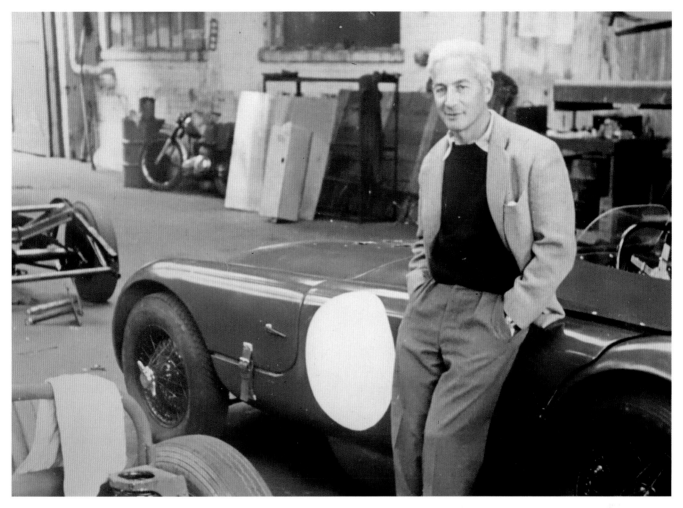

Zora Duntov in the Allard workshop in 1952, with the Allard J2X Le Mans he was to co-drive with Frank Curtis in the forthcoming race in June that year. He also raced in a JR in 1953 at Le Mans, in the Allard team car number 5.

equipment achieved records, notably at the Bonneville salt flats.

Canham brought one of these devices back to London and the performance gain from the revised manifold soon became apparent: a version was made for use on Allard's imported performance Mercury 24-stud Ford V8s. This was a somewhat contentious move by Allards as it in some sense 'copied' Meyer's design, yet carried no apparent credit to him. Meyer took no legal action but he did get a letter published in the motoring press claiming authorship of Allard's modified device.

While in the USA Canham gathered opinion about sports car design and future trends from car fanatics, hot-rodders and potential dealers. He went to several races, including the Indianapolis circuit, and questioned leading drivers. He came home armed with many ideas about what the massive, emerging American sports car market was looking

for. Canham sketched out a potential car design and, costly though Canham's trip might have been, it crucially informed Sydney about the huge opportunity that lay across the Atlantic. Once the British market for Allards had been satisfied, 'export or die' might have been a very real truism. Soon the 'new' definitive, US-oriented J2 production Allard was born with two chassis being constructed at Encon Motors. J2 chassis number 888 became Sydney's development prototype and personal car – with many additions. It was sold to an American customer in the 1950s.

H.J.A. DAVIS AND AMERICA

The man who initially framed Allard's American era was H.J.A. 'Dave' Davis. As Allard sales and export manager, he was an interesting character. An Anglo-Swiss, his full name

ALLARDS IN AMERICA: A PERSPECTIVE BY COLIN WARNES OF THE *ALLARD REGISTER*

Once the war ended, Sydney's thoughts turned to manufacturing cars for a living. However, steel was only available to companies exporting at least 75 per cent of their product, so Sydney was forced to look for customers outside of the UK. Continental Europe was also in shambles, recovering from the Allied assault. Sydney looked west to America, a land that was left largely unscathed during the Second World War but was struggling to retool to civilian production. Many veterans were returning home telling stories of the little sports cars buzzing around England.

In March 1946 Sydney Allard exported his first completed car, a K1, chassis 108 to the United States. This car was the first of almost 300 to be exported to North America in the next few years. Although that was a small percentage of the 1,900-plus cars built by the Allard Motor Company, the bulk of these cars were sports models.

Allards sold outside of America were primarily fitted with Ford V8 flat-heads for power. For America, though, the majority of cars were shipped without an engine. This allowed buyers to fit the engine of their choice including the more modern and much more potent V8s from Chrysler, Oldsmobile and the most popular choice – Cadillac (Allards in America are often called 'Cad-Allards'). These engines transformed Allards into production hot-rods that would dominate Europe's finest in sports car races throughout America in the early 1950s (it could be argued that Allards were directly responsible for the large displacement high-power Ferraris that American distributors pleaded with Enzo for more power to push back against the Allards).

Sydney realized that he needed to establish a dealer network that could promote, sell and service his cars. In 1948, following Reg Canham's cross-country caravan tour with an M Type pulling a Berkeley caravan, Sydney exhibited at the New York Auto Show, which allowed him to sign up many new dealers eager to make a buck off the emerging sports car market. It should be noted that some of Sydney's early dealers went on to become major names in the automotive world, including Andy Granatelli (STP), Roy Richter (Bell Helmets), Al Moss (Moss Motors) and Kjell Qvale (Jensen-Healy & Qvale Motors). Allard's two biggest dealers in terms of sales were R/P Motors (Perry Fina & Major Seddon) in New York, and Noel Kirk in Los Angeles.

Although exports to America were respectable for a small builder, they were never quite up to Sydney's expectations. In 1952–3 Sydney dissolved the distribution agreements with his major dealers and decided to set up company-owned distributorships in New York (Allard Motor Company) and Los Angeles (House of Allard): neither effort provided the expected turnaround in sales and both operations were closed in 1954.

Allard's sales success in American was closely linked with its successes, both good and bad on the track. As news of Allard's early racing and rally achievements in the UK and Europe filtered over to the USA, interest in their cars grew. With the J2 coupled to a Cadillac V8, Allard had built a car that could compete with Europe's finest. Allard's first US victory came at the hands of Tom Cole at Bridgehampton on 10 June 1950. Several other victories proceeded throughout 1950 into 1952 at the hands of Erwin Goldschmidt, Bill Pollack, Fred Wacker, Preston and Walt Gray, John Fitch, John Negley, Stu Rutherford, Jack Armstrong, Bob Bucher, Fred Warner and Carroll Shelby. By 1953, however, Allard J2s, J2Xs and JRs were struggling to keep up with the new models from Europe. As Allard's racing success began to wane, so did the sales of Sydney's cars. Interestingly, a few Allards remained competitive up through the early 1960s in Sports Car Club of America (SCCA) races.

In 1974 Steve Earle held a gathering for his friends at Laguna Seca, a race that would later become known as the Monterey Historics. Bill Harlan brought his white J2X to this event and the duo proved to be quite competitive. Interest in vintage racing grew and Allards, once discarded, became highly sought after by the kids that once saw them dominate tracks throughout America in the early 1950s. In 1990 the largest reunion of Allards was held at the Monterey Historics, where Allard was the featured marque. More than 100 Allards of all types came together on track for the display. With Allard prices increasing along with the age of their owners, the cars were harder to find on track. As the cars change hands, however, the new owners are finding that the cars are relatively affordable to operate and gather a lot of attention wherever they go, which has led to many cars getting back on the track.

With the rise of the Internet, the condition of the cars has improved as well. Throughout the 1970s and 1980s the condition of car restorations was very inconsistent as it was difficult to source the correct parts, even if one knew what they were. As the Internet began to link owners from around the world, however, advice from marque experts became more available. Today owners can get information online from sources like the AllardRegister.org and the Allard Yahoo Group, along with YouTube and other hot-rod and engine-specific websites. Owners are also served with newsletters by the Allard Owners Club and the *Allard Register*.

A rare view of the glassfibre Palm Beach body prototype seen outside the proposed manufacturer's offices on the occasion of Sydney's visit to New York.

was Herbert Joseph Angelo Davis and he had been a wartime RAF Vickers Wellington bomber pilot. He is said to have taken his pet spaniel into the cockpit on bombing raids (the dog had its own flight logbook). Davis used his contacts within the RAF and USAAF to sell early products of the post-1946 Allard Motor Company to many British and American pilots. Davis had joined Allard via the Adlards Ford dealership showroom in December 1945 and never looked back, becoming Allard's top salesman and export manager soon after 1950: he even sold an Allard K2 with a Chrysler 331 Hemi to Paul Tibbets, who was pilot of the B-29 *Enola Gay* when it dropped the first atomic bomb on Hiroshima; the K2 was later fitted with a Chevy 283. Like Sydney Allard, Davis kept everything and his personal 'Allard' files are now in the possession of the Allard Owners Club. The relationship between Sydney and Dave Davis was not easy, as Sydney struggled to adapt to Davis's somewhat convoluted verbal style and 'Continental' manners. Davis kept in regular written contact with all his customers, especially the Americans. Links to members of the American United States Army Air

Forces – soon to be reorganized as the United States Air Force (USAF) – based in Great Britain would soon deliver a rather incredible story via the staff who worked for General Francis Griswold and General Curtis LeMay.

Well-known and well-off Americans in corporate and society circles took an early interest in Allards, including a member of the Whitney family, and Phillip Schwartz, Vice President of the Colt Firearms Company, was an early customer. Rupert de Larrinaga followed suit with a JR. Sydney's visits to America also saw him considering the US development of a glassfibre-bodied Palm Beach.

The first few Allards that made it across the Atlantic before 1949 were handled by Major Richard Seddon through his R/P Imported Motor Car Company in New York. Seddon wrote an angry letter to Allards on 18 September 1950 about the state of the early cars he received, citing poor fittings, finish and wiring, tight brakes and the apparent 'contempt' for their American customers shown by Allards. Yet Allard and Davis built up a personal relationship with American customers and received regular correspondence and gifts from them, which did not go unappreciated in a Britain still subject to rationing. Davis also received gifts from his European distributors, notably Mr Hietanen of Kuovolan Keskus-Auto Oy in Helsinki after two J2s were delivered for competitive use in 1951.

In 1948 Allards built 401 cars, of which thirty-six were exported. In 1953 the total had dropped to just 123 cars, of which 119 would be exported, but it was not known how long this dominance of export sales would continue.

An early Allard seller in California was Oxford Motors, who sold one of the first J2Xs to Sam Weiss: despite his name, the car was painted black.

Contact between Allard in London and its potentially massive US market was often by telegram, such as an example dated 7 February 1950, when H.J.A. Davis cabled Alan Moss:

TO SHIP IMMEDIATELY THE FOLLOWING: ONE J-TYPE LESS ENGINE GEAR BOX OTHERWISE FULLY EQUIPPED COLOR BLACK LEATHER GREEN OR AVAILABLE AT 2297 DOLLARS CIF LOS ANGELES HARBOUR ALSO ONE TOURER FULLY EQUIPPED COLOR SILVER GREY LEATHER LIGHT BLUE HOOD MAROON AT 2478 DOLLARS.

E. ALAN MOSS – ALLARD'S MAN ON THE WEST COAST

Alan Moss did not just sell Allards in America, he raced them too. His first Allard in 1949 was a K Type, which was raced at Palm Springs in 1950, driven by Moss's sales manager Tom Frisbey. The K Type was the fastest car at the event and, even though it overheated and blew a head gasket, Allards received superb publicity when *Motor Trend* put the car on the front cover of its June 1950 issue. In February 1950 Moss had ordered a J Type for delivery to Los Angeles and was soon in direct communication with Sydney Allard. By 16 March 1950 Moss had informed Allard that he would be holding an Allard promotional competitive event in April, and could he have a Cotal gearbox shipped over?

Soon after Tom Frisbey purchased the Allard K2 off the 1951 New York Motor Show stand, intending to install an Edelbrock-built Mercury engine. Moss invited Sydney Allard over to Los Angeles, but Sydney had to decline in a letter on 12 April 1950:

Regarding the race at Palm Springs, I am sorry that I am unable to come over but it is entirely due to one of two factors that I cannot alter.

Firstly, I already have prior engagements to meet people in New York this weekend. Secondly, I am the only representative from our firm in New York, and it is imperative that I should be there, to see that the cars are all ready, and the third reason, which may not seem very important to you, is the fact that should I compete in any event that is not of international status, I should most certainly be barred for any future racing in this country.

I hope you will appreciate therefore the fact that it is not through lack of interest that I am unable to accept your generous invitation, but I shall do my best later on in the year to come and see you.

This provides a detailed vignette of Allard's early American history. By October 1950 Moss was fitting a Cadillac engine into the J2 and tweaking it with a Zenith carburettor (x2), a Mallory dual-point distributor and a specially ground camshaft, complemented by revised tappets and rocker arms. Just weeks later, at a *Motor Trend* 'Motorama' in Los Angeles in November, Moss exhibited Allards to Californians at the largest motor show yet seen on the West Coast – 'Spreading the Allard literature and goodwill', according to Moss's correspondence with Davis back in London. At the same time the Moss Cadillac-engined J2, driven by Michael Graham, won its class heat against a Jaguar and, despite suffering a fan belt failure, recovered to fourth place in the results. The J2 lapped ten seconds faster than any other competitor.

Moss wrote to Davis suggesting that expanding the US Allard dealership to cover Texas would be a good idea, and described how his Cadillac-powered J2 was being received: 'My Cad J2 is meeting with approval wherever it was seen. I drive it to work every day and go for a ride almost every night. Yesterday I did a standing start quarter mile in 15.21 seconds. The car was in standard trim and un-tuned.'

But not everything was sweetness and light. Moss kept Allard informed about his customers' observations, and his own, regarding the numerous issues concerning the cars' design and build. Sydney was notoriously parsimonious and his early cars had less than showroom standards of finish. American buyers, weaned on 'shine' and glossy paint, complained that the Allards had poor paintwork, with bare metal showing, and observed that the seats didn't adjust, ventilation was poor and heat-soak was problematic in everyday use. Many of the 'nuts and bolts' parts of the cars were rough and seemingly very basic, leading to references to 'blacksmiths' and 'angle iron'. A few customers even looked underneath and found chassis that differed between cars and with differing types of construction materials.

ABOVE: **Martin Stickley's beautiful K2 at Pebble Beach 2008. Men in blazers looking for restoration perfection might not have been in Sydney's plans, but here is one of his cars preserved many decades later.**

Allard Americana – the Picariello stable of contrasting Allards.

The years from about 1950 to 1954 were marked by a series of uniquely personalized Allards registered in America. In 1999 Alan Allard and his son Gavin visited Lime Rock and Watkins Glen to meet up with the American Allard 'family' to celebrate fifty years of road racing at the 'Glen'. Many Allards turned out, even if was 'only' forty-nine years since an Allard first competed at the circuit. Alan was rather taken with a J2X with an external, side-slung supercharger, whereas Gavin had his eye on a china blue J2. Organized by Jim Donick, Andy Picariello and Syd Silverman, who had long been Allard Americana luminaries, the 'Allard-Fest' was a memorable moment with Sydney's son and grandson in attendance.

A GENERAL AND THE 'COLONELS CLUB'

A number of the great names of American automobilia feature in the history of Allard during the 1950s, such as Corvette's later chief engineer Zora Arkus-Duntov (of mixed Russian, Belgian and American ancestry), who appeared as early as 1948 with the Ford-Ardun engine modifications. Vic Edelbrock built Tom Carsten's 6-litre Cadillac V8 for the J2 'Number 14' that won so many events in the 1950s. The car was then driven by Bill Pollack, a young law student with a talent for driving who went on to win the 100-mile road race at Pebble Beach in 1951.

The Allard-America affiliation really began with a number of USAAF (and later USAF) officers stationed in Britain after the war, who got the Allard 'bug' and played a pivotal role in Sydney's move from trials to race tracks. The 'Colonels' were to be great Allard supporters.

General Curtis E. LeMay was introduced to Sydney by General Francis Griswold and bought his first Allard, a Cadillac-powered K2 that was raced by his driver Roy Scott. Several of LeMay's senior staff also became Allard enthusiasts, often visiting Sydney's London factory. LeMay sold his K2 to Colonel David Schilling, a wartime fighter ace

Monterey Car Week 2017 with the two red K2s of Doug Klink (K2 ex-George Myers) and Jon LeCarner (K2 ex-Jim Degnan), seen beside Augie Grasis' ex-Shelby J2X and the blue K2 (Buick-engined) of John Moke. Vince Vento's J2X (Hydramatic) was also present. C. WARNES

**Watkins Glen seen during Allard's heyday: Allards lead assorted cars including a
Bugatti T55, a Jaguar XK140 and a mix of British and American marques.**

who was also stationed in England in the immediate post-war period. Schilling was killed instantly when racing with another car from the Officers' Mess at RAF Mildenhall to RAF Lakenheath. He lost control and slid off the road into a drainage ditch as the Allard was torn into two.

LeMay also purchased an 'aerodynamic' Allard JR, which he allowed Sydney to race at Le Mans for 1953. When the engine blew up in practice, LeMay arranged for the overnight delivery of a new engine on a USAF transport flight from America to France (for the full story, *see* Chapter 5).

For his efforts in supporting the development of American sports car racing, which included allowing the use of military airfield runways as racing circuits during closed periods, LeMay was awarded the Woolf Barnato Award.

One member of the Allard 'Colonels Club' was LeMay's aide-de-camp Lt Colonel Reade Tilley, who took third place in a J2 at the MacDill Air Force Base races in May 1954, beaten by two Ferraris driven by Jim Kimberly and Phil Walters. At the same event Gray and Hall drove an Oldsmobile-engined J2X to sixteenth place and a class win.

Colonel Reade Tilley began his military career in the Royal Canadian Air Force. After joining the American Eagle Squadron of the RAF he flew in combat during 1941 and then transferred to the USAAF after the USA declared war. Credited with seven kills, he also was one of the first men to fly a Spitfire off an aircraft carrier during the defence of Malta. His claim to have shot down a low-flying German Stuka with his Smith and Wesson .38 at close range during ground attack at Malta was later fully verified and credited.

The American Allard chapter really begins in 1949. Americans had shown early post-war interest and Sydney booked an expensive stand at the 1950 New York Motor Show. In the same year Sydney and his Anglo-American co-driver Tom Cole made an impact at Le Mans, and Zora Arkus-Duntov was also on the scene. Orders poured in after Cole's win at Bridgehampton in 1950 in a Cadillac-engined J2. Six Cadillac-Allards were ordered in New York State alone; the engines were fitted by two early Allard collaborators, Perry and Joe Fina of New York.

FRANK BURRELL AND AN ALLARD ASSOCIATION

Frank Burrell was a mechanical engineer who 'built' his first car when he was just thirteen and went on to race modified Model T Fords. After graduating from the University of Wisconsin, he was found employment at Cadillac in 1942 working with Harry Barr and Ed Cole, who developed the Cadillac ohv and Chevrolet's small block V8 engine designs, on military tank engine development. Frank was tasked with getting more horsepower out of the Cadillac engine, which he did by tweaking the intake manifold and compression head designs. By 1946 such performance 'tweaking' had led to the idea of a sports performance engine option at Cadillac. Frank also worked on performance enhancements for the engine in Briggs Cunningham's 1950 Le Mans car and a five-carburettor intake for Cunningham's 1951 Le Mans entry.

When Frank Burrell met Sydney Allard and Zora Arkus-Duntov he was running Cadillac's experimental garage and was the point of contact for any customer wanting to use a 'developed' Cadillac engine and anything like special cams, multi-carb intakes or tuned exhausts. Not surprisingly Sydney was soon in correspondence with Frank Burrell.

Cadillac's ohv V8 was the leading 'new' engine design of the early 1950s and Burrell, by now an organizing member of the SCCA, was approached by Fred Wacker who had just purchased an Allard J2 (the '8-Ball') and wanted the new engine fitted to it for the 1950 Watkins Glen race. So Frank Burrell modified an engine, not least by using the manifold of that year's new Le Mans Cadillac engine. A strengthened transmission, using military-spec, tank engine components, was also fitted. This was a Hydramatic design, essentially 'automatic' yet modified for a manual gear change function. This very unusual car, capable of 0–60mph in 4.5 seconds, came third at Watkins Glen and was then entered into the six-hour Sam Collier Memorial Grand Prix (Endurance) at Sebring. At that event, Wacker (with co-driver Burrell) finished two laps ahead of the rest of the field, but came eighth overall on handicapped aggregate scoring.

Frank Burrell also worked at this time on Fred Warner's J2X. Warner worked for General Motors as a pilot and it is suggested that the Allard he owned was being used as some form of private test bed for the Cadillac engine modifications. These two Cadillac-powered Allards were seen at major US races between 1950 and 1953. This was the era when General Curtis LeMay and his associates ordered new Allards, had American engines fitted and assisted with Sydney's Le Mans entries using these cars. LeMay used his position as Commanding General of the US Strategic Air Command to reward Frank Burrell for all his engine work, not least in assisting Sydney with his JRs at Le Mans, by

Erwin Goldschmidt's Allard J2, which won the 1950 Watkins Glen Sports Car Grand Prix, on display at the New York Motor Show.

J2X under cornering load at speed at Laguna Seca. C. WARNES

inviting him to France. Burrell travelled free courtesy of an official letter from Strategic Air Command, Omaha, Nebraska, inviting him to 'Travel from Detroit to Paris for 21 days for the purpose of giving technical assistance to this Command'. Issued on 6 May 1953, the letter gave Frank free return travel on any US military transport aircraft. Never was the US taxpayers' dollar put to better use! 'Government facilities and subsistence' (free board and lodging) were included. Apparently all this was 'necessary in the public service'. Quite what the Cold War had to do with Le Mans, we do not know.

Frank Burrell must have got on well with Zora Arkus-Duntov, who had actually worked for Sydney Allard in London and been with him at Le Mans, because in 1955 Frank left the secure employment of GM's Cadillac division to go and work with Arkus-Duntov at GM's sportier Chevrolet marque; he stayed for the rest of his career. Arkus-Duntov, of course, had a major hand in the Chevrolet Corvette story, but Fred Burrell was the 'other' Allard fanatic behind its development. Burrell oversaw the 1957 Corvette RPO/684 and /579D optioned Corvettes, and he designed the improved steering modifications and managed much of the factory support for Corvette at places like Sebring.

Frank Burrell was a significant figure in the development of Cadillac-engined Allards and their Le Mans appearances. Although he died in 1985, his son Barry recorded his father's exploits for the *Allard Register*, commenting that his own earliest childhood memory of an Allard was of sitting in the cockpit of Fred Warner's J2X, chassis number 2191, as it was loaded onto a trailer en route to a race in 1954.

ZORA ARKUS-DUNTOV AND ENGINE DESIGN

Numerous small tuning companies in America devised new heads, revised inlet ports and valve designs, overhead valve gear, and numerous water pump and oil pump tweaks to improve the Ford flat-head V8 in the period after the war. Those whose work would be relevant to Allards included Vic Edelbrock, Chet Herbert and George Riley. Zora Arkus-Duntov had the most direct influence through the Ardun hemi-head and valve gear that were fitted to Ardun (Ford/Mercury) V8s in certain J2 and J2X production series Allards about 1950. The mechanism had been designed by George Kudasch while working with Zora and Yura

Arkus-Duntov, both of whom had known Kudasch in pre-war Berlin. Kudasch and Duntov fitted the 24-stud (Ford Mercury specification) V8 with a revised overhead valve gear and an alloy hemispherical cylinder head design that boosted power to 140bhp at 4,000rpm. Kudasch worked on the revised cylinder heads that converted the flat-head to ohv configuration. Later developments would take the power to 275bhp, and even more with forced induction. No engine mounting or clutch housing modifications were needed to fit an Ardun to a J2X, which may have been why Sydney selected this method. In the early 1950s Sydney also sold kits for this Ardun modification to convert any Ford flat-head for the not inconsiderable sum of £160. The Ardun unit is 30in wide and was a tight squeeze in the J2, but could be fitted.

Zora and his brother Yura founded the Duntov Mechanical Corporation engineering firm in post-war America, but it did not last long and was soon wound up. Duntov had been in contact with Sydney during this period, however, and, with no other immediate opportunities, relocated to London to work with Allard at Sydney's invitation. This culminated in the Le Mans drive. Back in America, George Kudasch moved on to work for Sikorsky helicopters and perhaps failed to receive sufficient credit for his input on the Ardun head development with Duntov. Approximately 300 Ardun kits were sold. The first open, four-wheeled car to exceed 200mph at Bonneville was Ardun-powered. Later hot-rod developments took the Ardun head to the level that Duntov and Kudasch had considered but never achieved. There may be some Duntov Ardun 'design' influence in the later Chrysler 331 hemi engine. Today reproductions of the design are in demand and expensive, while original Ardun heads sell for many thousands of dollars.

Arkus-Duntov was to some extent embedded in the Allard experience during those years, spending many hours in Sydney's office and on the factory floor in London. Driving at Le Mans for Allard taught him much and he went on to drive a privately entered early Porsche there in 1954 and 1955.

After Arkus-Duntov joined Chevrolet the General Motors brand started to show an interest in Allard cars that extended beyond Fred Warner's J2X. An Allard K3 (chassis 3171) was bought via the curiously named 'Vauxhall Motors USA'. GM had owned the once upper-crust British brand of Vauxhall since the mid-1920s and would also absorb Germany's Opel. Buying the car through 'Vauxhall' was a nice ruse.

The first Corvette, a modified saloon chassis with a sportster body, was launched in June 1953. By August, however, Arkus-Duntov had issued an internal GM report on the key aspects of the the J2X Cadillac-Allard chassis 952 (later

owned by Vince Vento). It would not be long before subsequent Corvettes became more directly 'sporting' in their design and execution. This is further evidence that Arkus-Duntov created an 'Allard effect' within Chevrolet, as he built himself an 'empire' within GM and never looked back.

In 1959, not long after the launch of the Corvette C1, Arkus-Duntov pulled off what some might consider a massive blag by getting GM to pay for him to design and build a racer-cum-hill climb 'Special' as a concept car. Indeed GM's Ed Cole was of the opinion that Arkus-Duntov had 'bootlegged' more useful parts through Chevrolet than any other engineer. This Special was the Chevrolet Engineering Research Vehicle 'CERV 1' prototype, the Allard roots of which could not have been more obvious.

The CERV had an airflowed front end, transverse leaf-springing to its independently mounted rear and a glass-fibre body. It provided a test bed for numerous GM engines, notably alloy units and Corvette development powerplants, which were hoisted in and out across the early to mid-1960s. Indeed by 1965 CERV was powered by a 377cu in small-block alloy V8 that took the car to 200mph. In its first year (1960) CERV had achieved some very fast times in pre-practice 'test' laps at the US Grand Prix and it had been driven not just by Arkus-Duntov and Dan Gurney, but also by Stirling Moss.

Given just how much time Zora Arkus-Duntov had spent with Sydney in the factory and drawing office, at Le Mans and behind the wheel of various Allards, we can only wonder if everything that Arkus-Duntov had learned at Allard in the 1950s culminated in the realization of his own concept as the CERV.

CERV went on to be owned by Briggs Cunningham, Miles Collier and Mike Yager. We might say that Allard influenced

BRIGGS CUNNINGHAM

Allard's great competitor Briggs Cunningham deserves a mention in the Allard story. Although he was quite unlike Sydney Allard in character, there was some similarity in his output. As many, including David Kinsella, have suggested, there are obvious links in the use of V8 engines, chassis design and the de Dion rear suspension. Cunningham was also an active competitive driver at tracks such as Le Mans and Watkins Glen. He was wealthy, an America's Cup sailor and yacht designer, and a real driver. Some Allard mechanical men even went to work for Cunningham.

Zora Arkus-Duntov, that Zora influenced the Corvette, and that the Allard-inspired CERV was one of the most important pieces in American automotive history because it was a GM and Chevrolet test bed for the future at a time of massive development when money was of little concern, engineering really counted and the accountants could go hang.

A particularly touching moment in American Allard history was when Zora Arkus-Duntov, accompanied by his wife Elfi, was reunited with the original 1940s Ardun conversion Allard test car, a prototype J2, which he had raced at Watkins Glen in 1949. This took place in September 1992 at the Watkins Glen Vintage Grand Prix. The car was then owned by Dr Tom Turner, who was there with Dean Butler and George Chilberg, all of them with Allards and including Jimmy Dobb's ex-Australia J2 Ardun.

SHELBY AND ALLARD

Allard and Carroll Shelby were closely linked, too, often through the circuit at Elkhart Lake, Wisconsin, which was a major home to sports car racing in the American Midwest. The circuit was originally laid out on the open roads around Elkhart Lake from 1950 to 1952, and then moved to a purpose-built circuit in 1955. The track, situated in the hills between Milwaukee and Green Bay, was known as one of the most challenging and scenic circuits in North America.

Carroll Shelby started his career in a Cadillac-powered Allard J2X (3146). His early results in an Allard J2 shared with Fred Cook in 1953, entering ten races and winning nine, were the basis of his success. On 12 June 1953 he was second overall in a Cadillac-engined J2X and first overall on 23 August 1953, both at Fort Worth, Texas. Wins at Omaha and Eagle Mountain showed the way ahead. Shelby won the 1953 Floyd Bennett race in New York State on 28 August at a local track temperature of 120°F driving a two-tone J2X owned by Roy Cherryhomes. In January 1954 Shelby raced in the 1,000km event in Argentina, where his tenth place performance (with co-driver Dale Duncan) earned him the attention of Aston Martin. Shelby would later dominate at Elkhart Lake with his Allard-inspired Shelby-Cobras. Carroll Shelby's original 1952 J2 was later owned by Dana Mecum.

The idea of an Allard influence on Arkus-Duntov, the Corvette and then the CERV seems all the more obvious when you consider how Ferrari produced larger-engined cars to compete with the J2s that were wiping the Italian marque off the podiums at American races, that Ford, Cadillac, GM and Chevrolet all learned from Allard, and how Carroll Shelby went from his J2X to creating an AC Cobra with similar driving qualities.

MR FORSYTH, THE 'ALLARD-FRAZER' AND THE 'ALLARD DODGE'

The importance of the American market to Allard was increasingly obvious by late 1952. Allard's official American distributors had employed the engineer, designer and salesman Robert W. Forsyth, who wanted to modernize the somewhat dated Allard image for the rapidly evolving and developing 1950s American market. Forsyth was aware of the faults in the Allard range and was not bothered about having to tell Sydney.

The previous year Forsyth had been talking to Larry Richards, a salesman with the Horgan Ford dealership in New York, about Ford of Britain's new 4-cylinder 1508cc Consul engine, which had just debuted in America. Sydney and Forsyth both thought that the tough little 1508cc engine could be down-tuned to below 1500cc, using cylinder liners to reduce the excess capacity, and become an excellent competition engine in that class. But where was the chassis or car to take it? They believed the answer was to design one. Richards knew that Sydney was keen on utilizing the new engine to revamp his car's appeal to a wider market, and within days Richards had put Forsyth in contact with Allards in London.

Forsyth, recalling the story, says that he was as inspired by the 1.5-litre Jowett Javelin that ERA had modified. A 95in wheelbase was selected.[17] Forsyth drew up the plans but was called up to do his US military service. Sydney, however, did not use Forsyth's designs and instead turned out the Palm Beach Mk 1, based on existing Allard parts and looking like a brick with the corners rounded off. Richards suggested to Forsyth that a light restyle or facelift of the car's body and nose details might help its US sales prospects.

Quite how closely Sydney was involved is hard to decipher, but Forsyth stated that he drew up the revised styling and that Richards helped organize a 'one-off' body proposal to be built by the De Guia brothers' coachbuilding outfit in Connecticut. The story goes that Joseph Frazer of the Kaiser-Frazer marque was interested in the rights to the car via his interests in the Graham-Paige company, which had promoted advanced design since its association with Norman Bel Geddes in the 1930s. Frazer had thought about using the new-fangled glassfibre body construction process for an American market version of the Allard car.

Frazer had extensive business interests including an involvement with a company called Anchorage Incorporated in Warren, Rhode Island. Owned by W. 'Bill' Dyer, the Anchorage shipyard was a pioneer in making glass-fibre-hulled boats ranging from dinghies to larger hulls for military

Allard on the fly – the ex-Carroll Shelby car seen at speed.

Bill Pollock was a key figure in the American Allard movement.

use, which were then the largest 'plastic' boats constructed anywhere. The fashionable yachting centre at Newport, Rhode Island, supplied many opportunities for innovative uses of the new glassfibre technology and a subsidiary company, Anchorage Plastics Corporation, was investigating the material's wider potential. The reality of a prototype 'plastic' Allard, using a Ford engine, was planned by Bill Dyer and his son, Larry Richards and Joseph Frazer. The straightforward plan was to get Allard to ship over the basic chassis of an early Palm Beach Mk I and then Anchorage Plastics would fit a locally made, lightweight body. Costs, import taxes, overheads would all go down, with the further benefit of a great improvement in fuel consumption. This could perhaps be viewed as an early 'kit car', except that it would be finished off by the importing agency rather than the customer.

Unfortunately constraints of time and money meant that Forsyth's design work did not make it into the moulds and the 'one-off' glassfibre Allard more closely resembled the existing, production Palm Beach Mk I. Forsyth's design, however, would later re-emerge as the elegant Palm Beach Mk II.

But how far did the 'fiberglass' American Allard go or was it just a single prototype example? The company records of what is now Anchorage Incorporated-Dyer Boats show that seven glassfibre bodies were taken from the master moulds.[18] The Dyer family retain the main cited example of the completed running 'plastic' Allard to this day – chassis number 21Z5000 – as the developed Palm Beach Mk I 6-cylinder prototype, fully road-registered as 7Z80 55.

The seven glassfibre Palm Beach Mk I bodies, constructed from late 1951 through to early 1952, are sometimes confused with the production, steel-built Allard Palm Beach Mk IIs. The build team included Manny Cardosa as lead pattern maker/mould shop manager, assisted by his brother Tony. Another brother, Joe, worked in the shipping department. The workshop foreman was Luiz de Barros. Luiz and Manny had been employed by Bill Dyer in the boatyard at Warren since the 1920s. The current location or fate of the other six glassfibre bodies is unclear.

The discovery of a car of unknown provenance in Germany has recently led to speculation that it was an Allard derivative. Perceived wisdom, however, so often a powerful blinker, decided that the car was some form of BMW-Glas Company prototype. That may be true, but there have sometimes been whispers that H.J.A. Davis might have been involved in some kind of external private deal to sell such cars in Germany about 1950. Is it possible that the discovery might provide some evidence? The Davis paperwork, now within the Allard records, needs forensic examination to reveal its details, yet as long ago as 1983 Tony Dron noted in print that the file contained letters about a 'private' deal involving Davis and the supply to Germany of some form of Allard 'copy', possibly in glass reinforced plastic. These letters were dated 1950 and were addressed to Davis's home. They also mentioned R.M. Overseas Motors Sales of Düsseldorf (perhaps Ronnie Myhill[19]), someone just named as Fritz and a Mr Hurley, who also had Davis's address. (Hurley, perhaps coincidentally, was Mrs Davis's maiden name.) It appears that some kind of deal had been done and that the coachbuilders Abbott of Farnham had been consulted about the external supply of a body to fit an Allard-derived chassis. But what of the glassfibre bodies that were to be created by Anchorage Plastics in Rhode Island so soon after the letters sent to Davis's home?

The only 'Fritz' known at Allard was engineer, toolmaker, welder and machinist Fritz Skatula, but this does not mean that he was implicated. Is it possible that subterfuge was involved? The story suggested by the Davis paperwork and by Tony Dron's 1982 discussions with Davis's widow, who knew nothing of the 'Hurley' mention, might indicate the possibility of intrigue behind the scenes – but nothing seems to have actually resulted.

The Allard-Frazer-Anchorage Plastics project, however, was indeed very real. The first finished car was photographed in New York outside the head offices of Owens Corning Fiberglass with Sydney Allard himself at the wheel.

Meanwhile, Frazer and Dyer created a new company, Glass Plastics International, in conjunction with the Graham-Paige concern. This company would assist Simca in Paris with its 1950s plastics body technology projects. Sadly, for all sorts of business reasons, not least the apparent conservatism of those backing the ideas, the glassfibre (or 'fiberglass') Allard-Frazer idea of 1951–2 for the American market came to nothing.

Larry Richards would leave the Ford dealership and became the first general manager of the New York-based Allard Motor Company Inc. This would be directed by Edgar De Meyer as President, with co-directors Max Krumpholz, who had helpful links to Chrysler, and Henryk Szamota. By July 1953 Robert Forsyth had left the army and joined Allard's American outpost. This led to the design of the Palm Beach Mk II, which itself reflected the design of the American glassfibre prototype and the little-known Dodge-Allard design proposal.

The Allard Motor Company Inc. of America began to express frustration at the poor fit and finish of some of the cars, and that too many models were derived from another. Allard was losing ground on the American car market to MG and Jaguar, so Allard Motors Inc. looked around for a major motor manufacturer to assist with creating a revised Allard solely for the US market. Joseph Frazer introduced them Allard Motors Inc. to Studebaker's H.S. Vance, who was apparently keen to agree a tie up with Allard, but nothing came of this.

Allard Motors Inc. then turned to A.G. Cunnings at Chrysler, who guided the agreement that could lead to an Allard-Dodge. Forsyth drew up plans for a cheaper body, a simpler, licensed Frank Kurtis design suspension, abandoning the de Dion, and a Dodge powerplant.

By late 1953 Forsyth had drawn up a design for Sydney's overview. This was for a smart, stylish roadster that looked like a precursor of the later Palm Beach model that he so influenced. An earlier idea had been for a more modern Allard powered by a Dodge engine with 140bhp from a V8 block and a centre-mounted proper gearstick, rather than a ponderous column change. It needed to be decided whether the cars could be built in London and shipped to the USA, where the engines could perhaps be installed at a lower cost. The standard Allard-fit divided front axle was to be retained – rather unwisely, although this again may have been down to costs – even though J2 owners intent on racing would often discard such axles. The steering rack was 'fast' at 2.25 turns from lock to lock.

A very rigid steel-tube underframe, which was much stiffer than channels and a stiffened bearer chassis construction, would support a sleek, elegant (steel?) body, one that had a continuous line from the front wing (fender) through the cabin, and up across a swept rear wing line. Forsyth achieved a blend of modernism and traditional British styling. The use of curves in the side panels avoided Allard's previous slab-sided appearance and there was a touch of 'tumblehome' to the sculpting. In the American tradition, a bench seat would allow roomy accommodation for two occupants or slightly cosier perches for three.

The Dodge-engined Allard came to nothing, not least because Allard were unable to resolve contractual issues with their American distributor. The car was to be priced at $2,995 and the distributor would have had to purchase the cars from Allard prior to the engines being fitted on arrival in America and then the cars being sent across the country to dealers or customers for sale. It seemed a rather tight piece of accounting and the American distributor would need to carry costs and stock for some time after paying out to Allard for the cars ex-works. Such a framework would also apply to the sale of other Allards in America by the Allard Motor Company Inc. of New York. There was a question whether the American distributor could sell 500 of the Palm Beach Mk1 and 250 of the K and J series in 1953. On On the same terms, would the distributor be prepared to take 1,000 of the entirely new, 1956 model year Palm Beach Mk II?

With hindsight, we can see that the future of Allard was hanging by a potential lifeline, but that was probably not entirely clear at the time, at least on one side of the Atlantic.

The 'one off' Dodge 4.5-litre V8 'Red Ram'-engined Allard Palm Beach Mk I was not related to the proposed Allard-Dodge. This single car resided in Argentina for some years, before going to the Atwell Wilson Motor Museum at Calne, Wiltshire. It is now owned by the German collector Hans-Jörg Hübner.

Forsyth's styling ideas of 1953 for the Allard Dodge were in fact several years ahead of the game and we might suggest that later Jaguars, Healeys and Triumphs followed its lead after the exact styling appeared in the form of the Palm Beach Mk II. This was a more economical and tamer Allard with new suspension and body engineering that threw off the Mk I's typical old Allard construction, derived from the K Type, and made more defined use of the Allard's intended

Andy Picariello seen enjoying himself on the back roads.

engine, the 2.2-litre Ford Zephyr (1.5-litre Consul engines were also available). The Jaguar engine option was to be a final hope for Allard in the late 1950s.

All these plans, however, were frustrated by Allard's lack of money, so Forsyth had to abandon the completely new car design for an Allard Dodge and a re-engined Palm Beach Mk I with the Chrysler-Dodge motor. Larry Richards left Allard's employ and Forsyth was appointed General Manager of the American concern.

Allard Motors Inc. was losing money, new 'old' Allards remained unsold across America and the Allard Dodge, even in its simpler, re-engined form, failed to achieve a launch as a production model. By September 1954 Allard Motors Inc. had been dissolved and a critical chapter in Allard's history, and its viability, was over. Yet, via Joseph Frazer, the Henry J. Kaiser Company was in the loop, so what about their attempt to licence build K2s in America? Things went ahead to the point of the Allard directors meeting to vote on the Allard-Kaiser deal, but one of the directors refused the deal, so it died, just like that.

In 1954 Kaiser quickly produced its own 'fiberglass' bodied car, a sleek two-seat roadster that looked like Forsyth's design suitably stretched, swept and launched as the 1954 Kaiser DKF 161.

For the 1956–57 model year Allard suddenly announced the new Palm Beach Mk II with its Ford engine options. Its advanced styling was taken almost directly from Robert Forsyth's original drawings for the earlier Palm Beach Mk I glassfibre proposal and the Allard Dodge prototype.

It was at this point that Sydney somehow missed out on an opportunity to produce a smaller-engined car and a variant for the American market. Forsyth was just one of those who felt that it could have been the stepping-stone to survival via the American market, the circumstances seem to have been against it. Forsyth joined the Lockheed concern and went on to work on several clever engineering projects. For many years he owned a Palm Beach Mk II, which was sold by his

widow Connie to Dean Butler. Larry Richards ended up with Mercedes-Benz USA.[20]

ALLARD'S AMERICAN YEARS

- Allard's appointed dealers included R/P Imported Motor Car Company (New York), Fergus Motors, Grancor Automotive Specialists (Chicago), British Motor Company (San Francisco), Noel Kirk Motors (Hollywood), Speedcraft Enterprises, Sports Cars Incorporated, and the bizarrely named 'House of Allard'. Moss Motors (Los Angeles) would soon dominate West Coast Allard profile and sales.

- The J2, powered by Ford, Cadillac or Chrysler V8s, was a huge statement that created the Allard movement in America and contributed to the development of motor sport in the USA. The first J2 exhibited in America was at the New York Motor Show in April 1950.

- The Allard J2 race drivers who competed and won against assorted Ferraris, Healeys, Jaguars and MGs in the early 1950s included Fred Wacker, Tom Cole, Frank Burrell, Jean Davidson, Bob Greer, Michael Graham, Fred Cook, Preston Gray and George Weaver. By 1954 Allards were losing to V12 Ferraris, but it could be argued that it was their earlier successes that persuaded Enzo Ferrari to create faster, larger-engined cars with which to beat Allard at its own game. Famous racing drivers who cut their teeth driving Cadillac and Chrysler Allards from 1950 to 1954 included Erwin Goldschmidt, Peter Collins, Carroll Shelby, John Fitch and Masten Gregory, who owned and raced from new the 1952 J2X, chassis number 3065.

- Hot-rod tuning and the development of V8 engines, their carburation and injection, soon became of interest as customers had a choice of American-designed engines that could be fitted to imported Allards. Edelbrock, Offenshauser, Grancor and Ardun variations could all be bolted to the J2. One of the earliest Allard tuners on the East Coast was Frick-Tappet Motors of Long Island, which was bought by Briggs Cunningham. Perry and Joe Fina of New York installed the Cadillac engine in J2s and at least one K2. In Detroit, Foster and Boyer fitted the 5.4-litre Chrysler engine bored and stroked to 290bhp to a later J2X.

- American J2 tweaks and modifications also included front axle changes, the fitment of lightweight Italian Borani wire wheels, the use of the Halibrand quick-change rear axle, brake drums, a Cunningham inlet manifold, Siata gears, Herbert camshafts and the fitting of side exhausts. Owners often modified the cooling system on the nose. Edelbrock manifolds and Stromberg carburettors were

PUBLICITY – LOS ANGELES STYLE

In 1952 Noel Kirk Motors in Los Angeles chose to promote Allard cars in rhyme, or at least in doggerel:

Allard's scat
Beats scalded cat,
Rivaling that of the
Proverbial bat.

popular, and it was not uncommon for the butterfly chokes to be removed.

- Changes to the Allard front suspension design were also made by adding transverse leaf springs and multi-linked radius rods. Lincoln brakes and ball joints and spindles were also fitted. Clutch failure at high speed could cause serious damage, so tougher clutches, notably Schiefer 11in alloy types, were used. Ram-air cooling under the bonnet and to the brakes was designed in to the J2s.
- Detroit Racing Equipment supplied Cadillac V8s for J2s, including Erwin Goldschmidt's car, which was tuned up by Calvin Connell and Alfred Momo; Goldschmidt would win in an Allard at Pebble Beach in 1950.
- The first American J2 to carry the Chrysler 'Firepower' 5.4-litre 180bhp (later 290bhp), multi-carburettor Hemi-head engine was built by John Perona, owner of the El Morocco nightclub in New York. The car was driven competitively by Tom Cole. Despite being 120lb heavier than the Cadillac V8, the Chrysler engine had excellent torque characteristics that made it competitive. When Sydney Allard visited New York, this was the car he drove.
- Tom Cole won at Bridgehampton in 1950, getting to 130mph in his J2. Cole reckoned that the Cadillac-engined J2 would run to 60mph via the Lincoln Zephyr gearbox in first gear, to 100mph in second gear and to more than 130mph in third gear; 0–60mph took about eight seconds. According to Cole the J2 was faster and handled better than the Maseratis, Alfas, ERAs and even the Ferraris he had driven.
- Hubert Route, a one-time dirt track star driver and Ford's chief mechanic in Washington, DC, prepared a 5.4-litre J2 for Jean Davidson. Like most J2s, whatever the chosen engine, the car had a heavy-duty Ford gearbox. The engine could rev to 5,500rpm and 130mph. It was damaged at Watkins Glen in 1950 and later sported a Maserati-style nose-cone.
- Tom Carstens, based in Seattle, ordered a J2 in 1950 and enlarged the Cadillac V8 that he fitted to 6 litres. He went on to many wins and class rankings across the West Coast and Midwest, sharing the driving with Bill Pollack: they both won a race in the same meeting at Reno in 1951.
- J.C. Armstrong owned a J2 and used it on his daily commute to work as a test pilot for the Douglas Aircraft Company in Long Beach, California. At weekends, however, he

The ex-George Myers K2, owned by Doug Klink in 2015, powers along at Laguna Seca. C. WARNES

raced the car, carrying his personal weekend kit in it and driving hundred of miles on public roads to compete at circuits and then drive home. He should not be confused with another test pilot named Jack Armstrong, who was killed in 1954 when trying to break his own world speed record.

- Alexis Dupont owned a J Type and a J2X that was fitted with an early Chevrolet V8 and a McCulloch supercharger. Harry Steele of Arizona prepared his own unique J2 in 1952 with a new, highly tuned 5765cc Lincoln V8 with eight carburettors.

'8-BALL' – WACKER'S ENIGMA

Perceived wisdoms in classic car history mean that errors, as well as correct facts, can become current 'certainties' that are very difficult to challenge. Such issues may be relevant to '8-Ball'.

The name '8-Ball', a term for a winning ball in a game of pool, was applied to the red J2 raced by Fred Wacker, a Chicago socialite. The car was modified and prepared by Frank Burrell at GM and featured heavy-duty components and a uniquely modified Hydramatic transmission. '8-Ball' was bright red and had a white number '8' in a black circle painted on its nose. It had twin, free-flowing exhausts running down under the car, exhausting from a state-of-the-art, works-developed twin-carb V8 engine from Burrell's own Cadillac engine shop, racing spec wire wheels and a speedometer calibrated to 140mph. '8-Ball' was a mighty beast that could hit 60mph in less than five seconds. Perhaps only Tom Carsten's J2 with a similar engine and Edelbrock tuning could be said to rival '8-Ball' for audacity and style at this time.

The '8-Ball' pit crew included Les Baldwin, Ted Boynton, George Lamberson, Jim Lee, Bayard Sheldon and Bud Stevens. Fred Wacker took '8-Ball' to many podiums, notably beating the Ferraris at Sebring on 31 December 1950. The red car was famous and successful, but there has long been a mystery regarding what happened to '8-Ball'.

A fanciful story, written under the pseudonym 'Rudyard Quisling', about the discovery of a 'barn find' Allard J2 somewhere north of Chicago appeared in the *Allard Register* in 2009. Clem, 'the old geezer who was manning the fuel pumps', met the author in a bar and told him about working for Fred Wacker and how Wacker had a black J2 (perhaps even labelled '8-Ball') before the famous red J2 '8-Ball'. Wacker had sold the black car after a race in Argentina, and then came back and secured the Burrell-modified red '8-Ball'. The bartender, who'd heard Clem's stories develop

PRESTON GRAY

Preston Gray raced K2, J2 and J2X Allards in the early 1950s and remained an Allard luminary for decades, as Andy Picariello has testified: 'In my years of Allard ownership, I have had the opportunity to meet many interesting people because of this association. One of those was Preston Gray … Preston was one of the last of a breed of noted 1950s auto racers.'

It was to Picariello that Gray told the story of meeting Sydney Allard at the New York Motor Show. When Preston complained that the brakes on the J2X were not up to the potential of the rest of the car, Allard replied, 'Well sir, if you rely on brakes to win races, you're not driving the car properly.' Allard added that he thought his cars were designed to go, not stop. Preston Gray's belated response was that he sold the Allard and bought (and raced) a Ferrari. Gray also said that the Allard K2 he owned was one of the worst cars he had ever raced.

The J2X was sold to Harry Payne Whitney, who replaced the Cadillac engine with a Bill Frick supercharged Corvette engine. The Gray/Whitney 1952 J2X was more recently owned by Bill and Annabelle Wilmer, who had no idea that it had been Gray's car until they recognized 'their' car while looking through Picariello's album of Gray-Allard photographs. Gray was a leading light of the Vintage Sports Car Club of America and died in 2008, aged 91.

over the years, offered to show 'Rudyard Quisling' the red car for $100. Next morning, after a ride on the back of a vintage Norton motorcycle wearing a blacked-out helmet, he was shown a battered red J2 in a garage. The photographs he was able to take show that it had body modifications, changes to petrol and oil filler locations (as per racing regulations?), air scoops for the brake drums and a turned alloy dash.

The article's title lays out the options: 'Fantasy, Hoax, or Fact?' If it was a fake or copy the modifications were remarkably accurate. If this was indeed the real '8-Ball', it is known that at a later stage it did wear non-standard number decals: instead of a black number on a white background, it wore a white number painted on a black background, which itself was painted over the original white circle. The 'barn find' car possessed exactly this feature – and it was old and patinated.

Throw in the other changes, notably the bodywork and front wing (fender) support plates, and we can have some confidence that this was the original '8-Ball' that had been involved in an accident at the 1952 Watkins Glen Grand Prix in which one boy died and ten spectators were injured. At some time in the mid-1950s the car was sold to a member of the SCCA in Chicago and it continued to be raced by a series of owners until it 'disappeared'. Barry Burrell, whose father Frank had been co-driver of the red '8-Ball' at the Collier Memorial Race at Sebring in 1950, followed the car's trail and revealed his findings in the Allard Owners Club magazine in 2004. Paul R. Brownell of Milwaukee bought '8-Ball' in 1986 and stored it in a garage for several years before starting work on a mechanical restoration. '8-Ball' then passed to his nephew, Paul V. Brownell of Houston, Texas, who had joined the Allard Owners Club by 2016. So '8-Ball' was alive.

But this is not the only thread of the '8-Ball' story, because

there was another. The story was complex. Allard J2 chassis number 1575, with Mercury engine number 5343/31, was built on 10 June 1950 and started out with the registration number BJV 365. Its owner, a Mr Hyde, bought the car from H.E. Nunn & Co. of Manchester and took the car to America when he moved to Atlanta, Georgia. The car then found its way into the hands of Dr Tom Turner of Fort Worth, Texas, who wanted to call the car '8-Ball' but could not as Fred Wacker's had come first. As far as anyone knew, the original '8-Ball' had been damaged in an accident and the remains were 'unknown'. Turner failed to secure the original car from Wacker, but made an agreement to use the '8-Ball' name and logo on Turner's chassis number 1575. So '8-Ball' Mk II came into being, fettled by Turner's personal mechanic Dewayne Grammer. It even found itself

The famous 14B Carstens Allard J2 of Bill Pollock, more recently owned by Bill Marriott.

fitted with Tom Lush's own personal Allard 'spare' steering wheel, which he took with him when collecting customers' Allards, as it was the practice for the owner to remove the steering wheel and keep it before the car was taken away: no spare steering wheel meant no car to be driven.

After Dr Turner died in 1994, his widow Yvonne took a race driving course and entered '8-Ball' in competitive events requiring a race licence. Mrs Turner sold the car in 1999 to Rock Wilson, a Ford enthusiast from Billings, Montana, and the grandson of Henry Sprague, Henry Ford's first mechanic, who went on to own the the Lincoln-Ford dealership in New York City. Wilson's '8-Ball' (also known as 'Marny') remained as part of the competitive Allard scene. Yvonne Turner later sold Wilson the original 'matching numbers' Mercury V8 engine that been fitted to the car. Wilson's car became the visible embodiment of the original, but 'missing', '8-Ball' and made high-profile TV appearances. Allard J2 chassis number 1575, still in the same condition as when it was raced by Tom Turner, is now resident in Switzerland.

To compound the confusion, a British J2X registered as BJV 365 won a major event at Goodwood in 1954 and was later purchased for £395 from Chequered Flag Motors in 1957 by John Tinsley, an AOC member. He sold the car back to the garage in 1958 for £275. The car was subsequently owned by AOC members Jim Tiller and Peter Moore in the 1980s. The problem was that this registration was also supposed to have gone to America with Dr Hyde and later belonged to Dr Turner and Rock Wilson. Is it possible that the registration number BJV 365 had been applied to more than one J2?

Meanwhile the remains of the original red '8-Ball' languished in a barn somewhere near Chicago unless, of course, Wacker's first J2 – the black car – should be cited as the original?

The story of the J2 BJV 365, as originally told in the *Allard Register*, and its double life as two or perhaps even three '8-Balls' is typical of the difficulties inherent in researching Allards.

ALLARD'S AMERICAN YEARS: PART 2

- Roy Richter won the 1950 Santa Ana Road Race in his J2, beating Phil Hill's Jaguar. This required 5,500rpm in second gear at a sustained 80mph, using 4,000rpm at 90mph on the main straight.
- John Fitch was an undoubted American automotive legend. Born in 1907, he grew up surrounded by the early develop-

ment American automotive culture. He was a mechanic, designer, inventor and thinker, and raced all sorts of cars: Specials, MGs, Maseratis, Jaguars, Cunninghams, Corvettes and an Allard J2. In 1951 he was given an entry card for the fifth Gran Premio Eva Perón, but Fitch did not have a car. Tom Cole sold Fitch his damaged J2, chassis 1514. Quickly straightened and fettled, Fitch headed off to Buenos Aires to find that Cole and Fred Wacker were also present in their Allards – and it was Fitch's J2 that won overall. Briggs Cunningham subsequently offered John Fitch a drive at Le Mans for the 1952 race.

- Stu Rutherford was an early SCCA racer in north-east America as well as a hot-rod and drag-race enthusiast. It was natural then that he should turn to Allards, racing a Cadillac-powered K2 in 1951 and trading it for a more nimble J2 at a hill climb. After fitting a larger engine he 'broke' the J2's chassis during drag racing and the car was effectively scrapped. Rutherford built a 'Special' and sold on the remains of the Allard to Don Milligan of Andover, Massachusetts. He kept the parts in a barn for forty years until the car took to the road again in unrestored but working condition in 2004 at the Mt Washington Hill Climb centennial meeting.
- American K1 owner Jerry Besinger purchased chassis number 595 with an original registration number of JYK 438. Research by Mel Herman, the Allard Owners Club K1 registrar, revealed that not only was this car one of the rare alloy-bodied 'sport-spec' K Types, the first owner was none other than Len Potter and it was delivered to him on 10 July 1948. This is the car that Len Potter and C.A.N. May entered in the Alpine Rally three days later. Competition brake pads were thrown on the K1, as were heavy-duty shock absorbers. Extra cooling vents were rather quickly cut in the bonnet sides. After the Alpine Rally, Allards used the car as a works demonstrator. It was re-entered in the next Alpine Rally and driven by Potter and Peter Smith, who won their class and five stage awards. *Autocar* tested the car in October 1948. In 1949 Potter competed against Sydney and Leslie Allard in their J2s at Silverstone. All three finished in the top ten, despite the onslaught from more modern cars. In 1953 the Potter Alpine Rally K1 was sold to A.F.M. Luscombe and moved to Los Angeles. It was later sold to Lee Neighbours of Rancho Cordova and then on to Bill Harrah's Motor Museum in Reno, Nevada. In 1971 the car was sold to Pete McManus. It was acquired in 2003 by the classic and vintage racer Victor Pastore of Chester, New Jersey, who asked Hoffman Vintage Racing of Bangor, Pennsylvania, to restore it.
- George Putnam was one of the earliest TV news anchors, based in Los Angeles, and he also had a radio talk show in

the 1950s. His J2X was driven by Robert Stack in Douglas Sirk's movie *Written on the Wind* (1956). The car was originally black but had to be resprayed a lighter colour (yellow) to make more impact in Technicolor.

- Emile Loeffler's silver J2 with a 392cu in Chrysler engine was bought new by him in 1950. It was a star of the Allard gathering at the 2008 New Jersey Thunderbolt Historic Races at Melville Park, attended by David Hooper. Others taking part included Pete McManus in his K1 and John Maiuccuro's highly modified Cadillac-powered K1. Roger Allard provided the event's pace car in his J2X Mk II replica. Andy Picariello, the organizer, showed his K2, an award-winning 3,000-hour restoration. Victor Pastore's alloy-winged K1, Bill and Annabelle Wilmer's 1952 J2X (ex-Preston Gray), Terrel Underwood's LType (rare in the USA) and David Watson's 1951 J2X were all on show at the event's Concours.

- Vintage racer and Elva Mk 7 driver Wayne Adams found a J2 in a barn in the Midwest and began a lengthy restoration process. The car had been abandoned for years, but investigations showed that it was chassis 1971, the actual car that Sydney Allard had specially built to run in the Targa Florio in 1950 and the Mille Miglia of 1951. Apparently it was set up with dual function engine mounts so that an Ardun or a Cadillac engine could be fitted. The Targa Florio had specific regulations that meant the Cadillac engine could not be used. Having been raced and used as Sydney's own car, it was rebuilt and sold to Dr Warren Sites of Columbia, Missouri, as a 'new' car in the mid-1950s. This practice was not unusual among car makers at the time – even Bugatti had done it. The car was part-exchanged in 1961 for a Jaguar E-Type and was then owned by Jim Williamson. The car then entered storage, unused, until being found by Wayne Adams in 1989. He raced the restored car at Watkins Glen in 1998, coming fourth overall. The car was sold in 2003 to Don Shead in the UK.

- Harold Haase bought his Cadillac-powered J2X (number 3147) from a New York dealer in 1955. He converted the car to Ford-Ardun power in the 1960s and has owned the car ever since, driving it at the 2011 Watkins Glen Allard gathering.

- John Negley Jr was an Allard enthusiast who purchased a J2 (2020) in 1951 and started racing in the summer of 1952, scoring a win and three third places. Spurred on by hearing about the J2X at Le Mans, Negley simply went out an ordered a new one from Otto Linton of SpeedCraft (chassis 3140). Linton expressed concerns about such a powerful car being in the hands of a relatively inexperienced driver, yet Negley and his J2X achieved two wins and numerous placings on and off the podium during the

1953 season – and he was gaining experience. Sadly, during practising for the South West Georgia Sports Car Race at Turner Air Force Base on 25 October, Negley lost control when cornering and the car rolled over. His death was one of the very few recorded in an Allard. The cause is unknown, but some feel that aerodynamic modifications to the car's body design and inlet cooling may have affected the car's centre of pressure and lift behaviours, leading to handling troubles.

- Duncan Emmons was a long-time Allard owner and a leading figure in vintage racing in America. Emmons started his own body repair shop in Rancho Mirage, California, in 1955 when he was just nineteen and he was to become a major automotive restorer: his Kurtis 500 resembled an Allard with over-large dentures fitted! Emmon bought and restored several Allards (his J2 is still racing) and was a stalwart at American Allard events up to his death in 2005. His skills kept many Allards on the road, including Bernard Dervieux and George Myers, who was honoured with the Spirit of Vintage Racing Award in 2006. Myers purchased his first Allard, a K2, in 1961 and was a vintage racing stalwart for four decades to come.

- Al Reynolds was an Allard fan from about 1950 when he first saw a J2 race in California. On US military service in Europe some years later, he secured an Allard – it was not the J2 he wanted but a tuned-up, L Type Special with bodywork modified following an accident in the previous owner's hands in 1955. Reynolds would use the car's 21-stud Canadian-Ford engine but also prepare a full-house 24-stud Ford engine for the car, which he owned for more than forty years.

- J2 chassis number 2123, ordered through Wood Motors of Detroit, was delivered to Delvan Lee on 31 August 1951. As it happened, the new owner worked for Connell Cadillac of Detroit, who supplied tuned high-performance

John Moke's blue K2 dives through the Corkscrew at Laguna Seca.

engines to the marine industry, and it was Connell's who dropped a Cadillac engine into the Lee J2. The car was entered into local races, including ice racing in winter, and events at Watkins Glen and Bridgehampton in 1953 and 1954, respectively. Lee won the Giants Despair hill climb with the fastest time of the day in 1953. In 1954, however, the car was sold to Fred Lavell, who took the J2 to Bonneville and achieved a top speed of 127mph. The car was later re-bodied with a Sorrell fibreglass body designed to 'streamliner' ideas. A De Soto engine is said to have been installed and the car topped 150mph. Today this car had been restored to original specification and has been a regular sight on the vintage racing scene on the Eastern seaboard. In 2018 it was up for sale at $350,000.

ALLARD REGISTER

The *Allard Register* remains at the heart of American interest in Allards as an enthusiasts' club and much more. The Register is separate from the American branch of the original Allard Owners Club, but the two organizations are friendly and cooperative. (The American owners club used to maintain its own news magazine, but more recently the American and British club magazines have been amalgamated into a single edition.)

The *Allard Register* was originally conceived by Ray May and Tom Lush to have a worldwide function, which it retains, but it is also an essential American-based publication that is now particularly valuable as a superb on-line resource. It supports serious competitive use of Allards and the maintenance of the marque's image.

The *Allard Register* was founded in 1971. Its officers included Tom Lush as President and Fred Wacker as Vice-President, but it was Ray May, an important early influence on the original Allard Owners Club, who initially promoted the *Register*'s output. May served as Hon. Secretary until his death in November 2005.

Syd Silverman was to become the publisher and sponsor, while Jim Donick, at that time deputy editor of the Vintage Sports Car Club of America magazine, although based overseas, notably in Finland and Moscow, would provide the second term of editorial leadership from mid-1988 after Ray May retired from the role. The *Register* produced a basic but informative publication that became a quarterly *Bulletin* from spring 1971 onwards. The managing committee comprised Allard owners such as Dr Tom Turner, Cyril Wick and Bob Lytle, and later John Harden and Yvonne Turner.

The years 1986 and 1987 were eventful for the *Register* and its *Bulletin* because its members were busy competing in events. The 1986 Tacoma Grand Prix saw John Wallerich enter an Allard J2 in the vintage race and finish seventh in his class. Bob Lytle finished fourth in the Monterey Historic Races in his black J2X. Lytle, Dean Butler, Alan Patterson,

Bob Lytle was a major figure as a racer, historian and enthusiast for Allards in America.

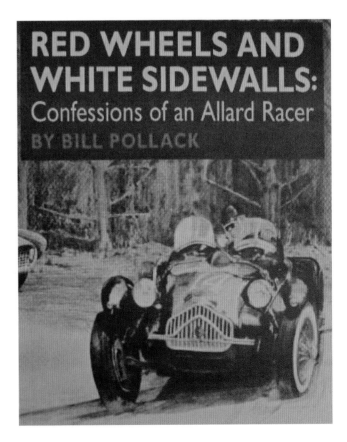

The cover of Bill Pollack's superb book about his life with Allard, *Red Wheels and White Sidewalls*.

Tom Turner and Silverman gathered at Watkins Glen for the Seregenti Cup and all were highly placed. The same names, joined by Bob Girvin (GT), Fred Aibal (J2X), Les Newell (J2) and Jim Donick (K2) all turned out a week later at the Lime Rock Vintage Festival on 12 September. On this occasion, however, a rash of mechanical failures marred things somewhat. Syd Silverman had fixed his J2X's gearbox in time to get on the grid at the Atlanta Vintage Grand Prix a month later and finished third. Dean Butler was to break his gearbox in his car.

A highlight of 1987 was the turn-out of Allards at the Mid-Ohio Vintage Sports event, which was particularly memorable after the pits were struck by lightning. Tom and Yvonne Turner, Bob Lytle, Al Long and Alan Patterson entered their cars, with support from Ted Bernstein, Charlie Bang, Dean Butler, Bob Girvin, Jack MacGregor, Don Marsh, and Syd and Jan Silverman. The main (Sunday) Allard group race results revealed Bob Lytle in the lead, Tom Turner second, Al Long fourth and Alan Patterson at the back of the grid. Gordon Keller, special assignments manager of *Victory Lane*, introduced himself as an Allard owner, which explained why Allards featured regularly in the magazine and helped emphasize that the Allard marque was still revered across America.

In 1988 the informal 'America Newsletter' created for Allardistes became effectively incorporated into the new *Register Bulletin*. Allard's ex-engineer Dudley Hume became President of the group in 1999. Jim Donick edited the *Allard Register*. Drew Lucurell and members of the Warnes family – Chuck, Colin and grandson Jacob – have been closely involved in the sponsorship, publishing and content, respectively, of this particular aspect of Allard history. The *Register* looks forward but never forgets the early 1950s foundations of Allard's contributions to American motoring, while maintaining the archives that make research possible.

MORE AMERICAN ALLARD PERSONALITIES

Syd Silverman

Syd Silverman, the one-time owner and restorer of the Le Mans JR chassis number 33403, was a linchpin of Allard's more recent era. When he passed away in 2017 he left a huge legacy devoted to Allard restoration and racing, which his son Michael continues through the publication of classic car media, notably *Vintage Motorsport*. It was Syd Silver-

It's large, red and powerful – an Allard in America. Note the non-standard aero-screens.

man, magazine publisher and sponsor of the *Allard Register*, who presented Tony Dron with a cast metal 'Allard' belt buckle, inscribed on the back, at the second Allard reunion at Atlanta in 1984.

Syd was owner and chairman of *Vintage Motorsport* magazine from 1990 to 2012. He was also a staunch supporter and participant in the preservation and celebration of motor sports and its history for nearly four decades. His sponsorship of the *Allard Register* allowed the group not to charge any fees for joining the *Register*.

Syd became hooked on British sports cars after seeing a yellow and black J2X when a young man, but it would be 1978 before he purchased his first Allard, a Hemi-powered J2X. As publisher of the *Allard Register*, the organizer of the 1982 and 1985 Allard reunions and an important part of the great 1990 Allard gathering at Laguna Seca in 1990, Syd Silverman was an Allardiste to the core.

Bob Lytle

Bob Lytle of Cottonwood, Arizona, who died in December 2009, was a leading American-based Allard enthusiast, exponent and driver, described by the owners club as a 'bright star in the US Allard firmament'. From 1982, when he purchased his J2X (chassis 3162), until his last years, Lytle and his black 'nailhead' Buick-powered J2X, race numbered 65, went everywhere together. He fettled the car himself and raced at many circuits, becoming a Laguna Seca fixture as part of the Monterey Historic Races. Lytle bought his well-worn, ex-racing Allard sight unseen and then drove it home more than 1,000 miles across America. He is said to have clocked up 10,000 race miles on his Allard.

Lytle had served in the US Navy and learned about engineering by tinkering with engines as a Motor Machinist's Mate. Having a father who owned a garage in Hollywood must also have helped in the 1950s. Andy Picariello, Vice President North America of the Allard Owners Club, knew him well:

Bob was an ardent Allard enthusiast, archivist, historian, ambassador and accomplished racer – and my good friend. More than his cars or his racing accomplishments, Bob will be remembered for his vast knowledge of Allards and his records of virtually every Allard in North America. Bob served as the technical advisor to the Allard Register. Whenever I had a question about, or where, an Allard was, or its history, I asked Bob. It was very seldom that the answer was not forthcoming, and most from his memory.

Bill Pollack

Bill Pollack had been a bomber pilot with the United States Army Air Corps and started competitive driving in an MG in 1949. He later teamed up with Tom Carstens to drive the Ed Iskenderian-tuned, Cadillac-engined Allard J2. Carstens had in fact purchased two J2s from Alan Moss after being ignored by a snooty Jaguar salesman in their Los Angeles showroom – Carstens walked off, keeping $10,000 cash in his pocket.

Bill Pollack, born in 1925, was the son of the songwriter Lew Pollack, whose works include the standard 'Charmaine'. Throughout Bob's long life – he died in July 2017 – he epitomized the guts and enthusiasm of the American Allard scene, which he recalled in his 2004 book *Red Wheels and White Sidewalls: Confessions of an Allard Racer*.

Pollack drove Tom Carstens's black Allard J2 (chassis 1850) as car '14', run by West Coast Racing. He entered the Pebble Beach Road Races in 1951 having only driven the car for the first time the day before – and nearly crashing, being unused to the power. But he won the subsequent race. Among the many races he won in this J2 was a novice race at Reno and he beat Phil Hill's Ferrari at Madera Races in 1952.

He was set to win at the 1953 Pebble Beach race when the car suffered brake failure in the race's dying moments: Phil Hill's Ferrari took top place on the podium, Bill Spear (Ferrari) was second and Pollack managed third. When the race was over he set off on a post-race 'demonstration' lap to diagnose the brake problems. The car was nearly destroyed when an axle snapped and it hit a tree; both occupants somehow survived.

Car 14's sister car, J2 (chassis 1851), was raced as car '15' and owned by Carstens's racing partner Dave Fogg. We might say that Carstens drove for Fogg and Pollack drove for Carstens. Car 15 dominated the club racetracks and hill climbs in the Pacific Northwest until 1958, after which the car was sold. Car 14 was found by David Brodsky in the 1980s and later owned and restored in the 1990s by Bill Marriott of the famous hotel group.

Pollack's brilliant book also reveals that American racers preferred 'white wall' tyres, not least on Allard J2s, because white wall tyres were made from natural rubber and not the synthetic blend of later 'black' coloured tyres. Natural rubber offered more grip and better qualities of rubber hysteresis, although this was at the expense of increased wear.

Alan Patterson

Alan was one of those rare Allard owners who could say that they were an original owner. Alan purchased his first Allard J2X, chassis number 3072, from Motorsport, Inc. in Pittsburgh in 1952. He raced this car from new at many locations, including overseas, and entered at Watkins Glen from 1954. Although Alan has owned and raced several other cars over the years, Allard was always his first choice. In addition to 3072, he has also owned another J2X, a J2X Le Mans and, most recently the bizarre Clipper and Sydney Allard's GT Coupé, which he raced at Monterey. One of Alan's greatest achievements was co-founding the Pittsburgh Vintage Grand Prix in 1983. Sadly, Alan Patterson, a true Allard enthusiast, died in 2017.

ALLARD'S AMERICAN YEARS: PART 3

- *Automobile Quarterly* published an early feature on Allard (vol. 8, issue 4) and included a road test of a red J2X. Thirty years later the same magazine featured a fourteen-page article on Carstens's J2, known as 14B, as driven by Bill Pollock (vol. 44, issue 1). This is the car that was in the care of Bill Marriott by 1995, after years of hibernation.
- In July 1956 the *Bulletin* of the International Association of Automotive Modelers (IAAM), which was edited by the evocatively named Phil Jensen and based in New York, devoted its entire issue to the Allard marque. The IAAM's artist Hugh McCall provided superb drawings of all the vital Allard cars and additional sketches were supplied by Marshall Johnson. The whole issue may be viewed online via the *Allard Register*.

American Allards gathering under the sun: K3, J2X, GT and K2.

- A model of the Allard J2X was manufactured by Berkeley Models of New York at the height of the Allard fame in 1950s America. It was based on drawings by Don McGovern and built by Bill Effinger. At just over 6in long and painted bright red, it featured a wooden body buck with add-on moulded plastic parts, as well as some die-cast detailing.
- David Watson rescued a J2X from a storage container in New Jersey. The car chassis number 2222 had been delivered to the United States in January 1952. It was raced competitively and modified to side-exhaust specification. Widely featured in the press, this car had at some stage been temporarily fitted with the Hydramatic transmission. Despite its racing provenance, the J2X spent more than 30 years stored in a trailer and suffered serious body damage when a racing car was slung above it. Suitably restored by the owner and Barry Parker, the 'wreck' was awarded the

Lazurus Trophy by the owners club for raising the J2X from its terminal condition.
- A low-profile, Hemi-powered J2X LM, belonging to John Reeves of Tulsa, Oklahoma, was beautifully restored and then showed at the November 2005 Allard 'Clan Gathering' at the Texas World Speedway.
- In 2015 Wayne Carini of Chasing Classic Cars purchased Bill Bauder's J2X, chassis 3059, known as 'The Bitch', for his personal collection. An example of why Allard retains a special place in the hearts of American classic car enthusiasts may be found in Sydney's response when Bauder had difficulty finding parts to restore 'The Bitch'. Bauder first wrote to the Allard Company during the first restoration of the car in the 1960s asking for help finding spares for the Marles steering gearbox worm gear, which was worn and cracked. He needed a left-hand-drive unit, but none

MARYHILL

Watkins Glen, Monterey, Lime Rock and Sebring might be the famous circuit names, but Allards also raced at the lesser-known Maryhill hill climb between 1955 and 1963. Maryhill, and its 'Loops', was a private road 'circuit' or track near Goldendale in Washington State, built by railway magnate Sam Hill as early as 1909, which would make it the oldest paved roadway in the Pacific Northwest. It was just over 3 miles long, with 27 turns and a 1,000ft climb. The original Maryhill track was replaced in the 1950s by a new track.

Between 1955 and 1958 Tom Carstens drove David Fogg's '15' Allard J2 to repeated wins against all-comers for four years running. An Allard J2X also competed at Maryhill.

In October 1999 four Allards, including two original Maryhill competitors, returned to re-enact the hill climb. The drivers were John Allard (Chevrolet-engined Palm Beach), Bernie Allard (1948 L-Type), David Cammarano (ex-Fogg J2) and John Hunholz (Chrysler Allard J2X). David Cammarano managed a time of 2 minutes 40.82 seconds against very powerful competition, including a Sunbeam Tiger and a Chevron B2.

John Hunholz owned a 1951 K2 since the mid-1970s, a 1952 Chrysler Hemi-powered J2X and a 'Hunholz Special', which was an Allard J2-shaped one-off that he built as a penniless university student about the beginning of the hot-rod era somewhere in the 1950s. Hunholz was inspired by the Allard run by his neighbours: Dale Duncan and Masten Gregory.

The revival of the Maryhill hill climb, organized by the Society of Vintage Racing Enthusiasts, became a regular event in which Allards continued to shine.

was available. Bauder then wrote directly to Sydney, who replied that he was about to have lunch with the chairman of Marles and would ask about the parts. Bauder received a telegram soon after stating that Marles would be making a special one-off replacement unit in their workshop and that this would be delivered free of any charge. Sydney was that kind of man.

- The 1953 K3 'Beowulf', chassis number 3166, which belonged to Janet Kinsinger of Milford, Michigan, may be the prototype build car that was built before General LeMay's car. It had a race-built 324 Oldsmobile Rocket V8 with a Cadillac La Salle three-speed transmission, and the original de Dion rear end and centre-pivot front axle.
- Bob Valpey, a stalwart Allard enthusiast for many years, won the 1991 Allard Transatlantic Trophy at the Lime Rock BMW Vintage Festival in his J2X. He rescued the J2 in which Tom Cole won at Bridgehampton in 1950 from a chicken coop yard and spent years sympathetically restoring it.
- Gary Peacock was an American Allard admirer who owned two Palm Beaches and a K3. He set up an Allard-related website and also collected Allard memorabilia.
- Paul Schoonmaker realized a dream in later life by purchasing the very Allard J2X he had seen racing about the streets of his home town when he was a young man. It now looks amazing in Bugatti Blue.
- Doug Klink is a recent K2 racer who took to the track at the 2017 Coronado Speed Fest in San Diego, chasing but not catching Bernard Dervieux's J2 at high speeds.

THE GATHERINGS

One of the most vivid aspects of Allard enthusiasm in America has been the annual 'Gatherings', at which more than 100 Allards have sometimes congregated in one go. As recently as 2017 a 'Gathering of the Clan' event at the Keeneland Concours, Lexington, Kentucky, saw twelve Allards, corralled by Allard organizer Jere Krieg, arriving from all over the United States and being hosted locally by Tom and Connie Jones. Ted and Luzia Bernstein's stunning, bright blue J2X won the main 'British' class, Tom and Terri Shelton were in second place with their J2. David and Carole Grant took a Judges' Award in their J2X.

During the 1990s, the first period of great Allard gatherings, large numbers of Allards and their owners would turn out at various American circuits, starting with the eighty Allards at the 1990 Watkins Glen reunion; another reunion at the Glen in 1998 aimed to top that.

Also in 1990 thirty-nine Allards raced in four classes at the Monterey Historic Automobile Races and a further forty road-going Allards also attended. Syd Silverman said at the time: 'Monterey promises to be the all-time best Allard reunion. Almost 40 Allards are expected and enthusiasts from both coasts, plus half-dozen from Britain, will make this a super gala. The factory never had so many cars in one place at one time!'

In 1992 Jack McGregor was awarded the Allard Owners Club Transatlantic Trophy for his work in restoring the ex-Bob Wilder J2X and a J2 and K1. McGregor also assisted many Allard owners with data, information and reworked brake drums, which have long been fitted to concurrent racing Allards.

Also in 1992, Syd Silverman gathered together at Lime Rock, Connecticut, the biggest group of Listers seen in the USA for years. These were joined by eight Allards, seven of which raced.

The season of 1992–3 saw Allard Gatherings at Mid-Ohio, Monterey and Lime Rock. At the 1993 Mid-Ohio Historic

events Alan Patterson turned up with his owned-from-new 1954 J2X, which had finished third in the 1954 Seneca Cup at Watkins Glen. Jack McGregor, Tom Turner, Bob Girvin, Syd Silverman, John Harden and others helped to create a memorable piece of Allard history. At Lime Rock John Harden's JR lapped in 1 minute 8 seconds and Jim Donick ran 1 minute 20 seconds in his K2.

Eleven Allards were gathered at Lime Rock in 1999, with nine competing in the Dodge Vintage Festival. One of these

The restored Steyr Allard.

was the Allard GT coupé then owned by Bob Girvin, which was raced even though there are only two of them. Kerry Horan's K2 went really well and Bob Lucurell's Hemi-powered K1 proved to be a real stormer. Jerry Lettieri of Automobilia Auctions, Connecticut, brought the ex-Duntov, ex-Tom Turner J2-Ardun.

Lime Rock Park Dodge Vintage Festival, September 1999

Group A	Jerry Lettieri	J2
	Marc Perlman	K1
	Jim Donick	K2
Group E	Bon Girvin	GT
	Mike Stott	J2X
	Randy Riggs	J2X
	Jim Donick Jr	
	Kerry Horan	K2
	Bob Lucurell	K1
Non-competing Allards	Rich Taylor	P Type
	Dan Rapley	J2X

RACING ALLARDS IN THE NEW MILLENNIUM

A later resurgence of Allard gatherings was marked by events such as a Texas-based 'Gathering of the Clan' in November 2003, attended by such Allard stalwarts as Andy Picariello (a one-time J2 and K2 owner), Pete McManus and Jon Lee. Chuck Warnes played a large role too, and J2X owner Lindsay Parsons drove across the country from New Jersey to be there and compete in the Texas 1000 Vintage Rally. The previous year Parsons had driven his J2X to Amelia Island, Florida, from his New Jersey home. The first Allard that Parsons owned was a J2 Cadillac (chassis 31358) ordered in 1953 from Major Seddon, the New York representative. He used the car, painted red and trimmed in brown leather, competitively in the 1953 Giants Despair hill climb and put 15,000 miles on the Allard in one year, which was perhaps a record for the annual mileage in a J2 at that time. Parsons had to sell the car in 1954 upon entering USAF flight training. His next purchase would be a J2X that had belonged to Dr Morris Gardner. This car had originally entered the USA in October 1952 via an order from Noel Kirk, the Hollywood Allard dealer, and passed through Alan Moss's garage.

The grand total of seventeen Allards turned out in Texas, several for competitive use on the circuit, others just to gather. Jim Tiller of the British owners club, whose exploits included the Brighton Speed Trial and a 200mph Allard

attempt at Bonneville, attended and had a superb time. Others who turned out included John Allard (no relation), Gary Peacock, John Harden, Bob Lytle, Bob Girvin, Bob Lucurell, Axel Rosenblad, Larry Marriott, Tom Kayuha and Bill Bauder, who had first raced his Allard at Texas Speedway in 1969 and was timed on the oval at 148mph. The event was hosted by Texas World Speedway's owner Richard Conole, who brought two Allard Palm Beach variants from his collection. Herman Groezinger brought his newly restored Lincoln-powered K3, a car with forty-seven years of continuous family ownership.

Chuck Warnes was also present. He secured his first Allard in 1984 when he saw an advert for a 1953 Chrysler Hemi-headed Allard K3 that was described as a 'basket case' – and Chuck spent the next twenty-two years restoring the car. He then swapped it for another restoration project, this time a J2X LM, in expectation of another marathon rebuild.

Twenty-five Allards gathered in 2006 for the Northwest Tour, culminating in Seattle, where Allard was the featured marque for that year's Pacific Northwest Historics Vintage Races. Eleven of the cars also took part in circuit racing at the event, which was run by the Lucurell and Peden families, and some Allardistes even came from Australia and New Zealand. David Hooper turned up too. A notable attendee was Steven Schuler, who brought his restored 1950 Le Mans specification J2, which had previously been resident in Australia and had appeared at the 2005 Phillip Island Allard gathering (the largest grouping of Allards seen in Australia in the modern era). Schuler served a 'cocktail' in the pits that was blended using a two-stroke powered drinks maker! Lindsey Parsons trailered his red J2X across from New Jersey, but after the tow-car expired in North Dakota, he drove the J2X 1,400 miles across Montana, the Rockies, the Cascades and into Seattle.

In 2008 Allard made it onto the revered grass at Pebble Beach with Martin Stickley's K2 wowing fans on the lawn in the 'Open Wheeler Racer' class and on the roads during the event's tour section. Stickley described his experience of getting an Allard into Pebble Beach in 'The Road to Pebble Beach', an article for the *Allard Register* (summer 2008). On the first day Martin's K2 disgraced itself with a broken Bendix unit, but a local spares shop procured an original replacement off the shelf early the next morning, just in time for the 60-mile Pebble Beach Tour. The judges made the mistake of penalizing the Allard for not being in its original colour or having its original engine, but what did they expect from an Allard? Since when did new paint, albeit in an original colour, imply the kind of 'originality' Pebble Beach's judges claim to seek, since over-restoration destroys the patina and story of a car.

K3s on the Californian coast. C. WARNES

A tribute to the great American 'Special' movement was held at the Monterey Historic Automobile Races meet in 2005 and foreign examples were permitted to take part. Theer were five Allards in the Group 3A races running amid Jaguar C-Types, two Mercedes 300SLs and numerous 'Specials'. Three of the Allard squadron were in J2Xs: Bob Lytle, Alan Patterson and Peter Booth, the owner of the ex-Carroll Shelby J2X. Bernard Dervieux drove his J1 and Jim Degan ran his K2. All five Allards finished the eleven-lap race. 2007 saw another 'gathering' at the Virginia International Raceway Gold cup races where Bob Girvin was fifth in his Group D just ahead of Micheal Silverman's (Syd's son) Jaguar Lister 'Knobbly'. Other Allard attendees include Connie Nyholm in a J2X. The usual 'Allard suspects' of Kuyaha, Krieg, Pastore, Terrel, Underwood, all kept the Allard legend alive.

The assorted Allards at Amelia Island in 2007 included Jim Taylor's Le Mans-bodied J2X (restored but not over-done). The ex-Jim Dobbs K2, customized by George Barris in the 1960s with a unique Von Dutch livery, then owned by owned by Dennis Machul, was also on the Concours lawn; this car was sold for $242,000 by Gooding & Company at Pebble Beach in 2017. Jim Donick and his son Mike sold the fabulous, Donick family K3 at this 2007 auction. Looking far more regal than any K3 had a right to, the rich, dark Delft blue paintwork and claret maroon leather interior, and superb restoration by Mike DiCola, created an Allard with an aura.

That same year, Allard's gathered at the Virginia Interna-

tional Raceway for the Gold Cup races. Bob Girvin's 1958 Chrysler-engined Allard GT coupé (one of the pair) saw action amid the heat, finishing fifth in Group D ahead of the Lister 'Knobbly' Jaguar.

Another resurgence of Allard attendees in American events in 2015 and 2106, notably at Monterey, added impetus to the brand's profile. Three generations of the Warnes family, Chuck, Colin and Jacob, completed the Allard tribal gathering.

The Donick family also have a J2 that they race together, calling themselves the 'Whimsey Racing Team'; there is no connection to Lord Peter Wimsey, so perhaps they are just being whimsical. In 2015 the Whimsey Racing J2, maintained by Mike DiCola (with a K2 in reserve), was seen at Lime Rock with Jim Donick at the helm. He scored a win and several places until an engine 'event' ruled out any further action. Jim's son Mike drives for a Toyota team in the national endurance racing formula, but sometimes gets to drive for his father's Allard-based team. Whimsey Racing finished second and third behind a Lotus 18 Formula Junior, The Donicks' J2 and K2 proved to be the fastest two-seat sports cars in August 2014 at the Mount Equinox races, a meet where Allards have excelled since 1951.

Six Allards were seen gathered on the grid of the 2016 Monterey Historics Motorsports Reunion, proving that the appetite for Allard, remains a remarkable American addiction.

American Allard owners also returned to the scene of

1950s success at Elkhart Lake, Wisconsin. In 2015 Andy Picariello organized the appearance of fifteen Allards, including two J2X cars that would race on the old road circuit. Picariello had his J2 and K1 transported 1,200 miles from home to the event. A display at the circuit's Road America Center framed Allard as a featured marque alongside Jaguar. A memorable event for Allard at Elkhart Lake on 18–20 September culminated with the ex-Carroll Shelby J2X, owned by August 'Augie' Grasis, heading a squadron of Allards on the lawn of the Osthoff Hotel after a Road Course Re-enactment following the course where the Road America event took place six decades before.

In 2015 the California coastal classic car events scene saw Steve Schuler on the track at Monterey in his J2 (the car that finished third at Le Mans in 1950). A week earlier he had been at Laguna Seca with his J2, finishing seventh in the Rolex Monterey Motorsports Reunion. David Rossiter showed his red K2 at Concours on the Avenue in Carmel, and Martin Allard's cream K3 won the British Car Award at the Carmel Mission Classic. Jim Taylor's red and white J2X made it into the posh environs of the Quail Motorsports Gathering. The Warnes family's former K3 was auctioned by its then owners, Jim and Lisa Stec. All of this happened in California in the course of one week. Allard Owners Club President Josh Sadler also turned up in California to race, but driving his 1972 Porsche 911ST in the RennSport Reunion at Laguna Seca's Mazda Raceway.

In 2017 Doug Klink, owner of the ex-George Myers K2, made his Allard debut at the Rolex Monterey Motorsports Reunion with his car, having driven it 1,300 miles to the event from Colorado. Also present in the Allard line-up were Augie Grasis (J2X), Vince Vento (J2X), John Moke (K2) and John LeCarner (K2). Three red Allards, one black Allard and one blue Allard looked amazing in a Californian setting. When owned by Myers the Klink K2 had previously raced against LeCarner's K2 (then owned by Jim Degnan): 2017 was the first time the two cars had met in years. All the cars attended the Quail gathering.

In America today, the Allard Owners Club and the *Allard Register* play an essential role in preserving and promoting the Allard legacy and its 'live' existence, which can hardly be described as a reincarnation as Allard has never really gone away. Allards remain everywhere – even entering the hallowed turf of Sir Michael Kadoorie's extremely well-heeled Quail event, which would surely have made Sydney smile.

Allard was a 'showcase marque' at the Amelia Island Concours d'Elégance in 2011. The event's founder, Bill Warner, stressed the enduring affection for the Allard marque in America when welcoming the participants:

Andy Picariello and I have been working in concert for the past few years to assemble a definitive display of Allards to put on the fairways … We look forward to working with you to ensure an outstanding display of significant Allards and tell the story of Sydney Allard and his accomplishments.

Darell Allard and David Hooper served as Amelia Island judges (along with Brian Redman): Bruce McCaw took an award with the Steyr Allard, and Pete McManus and his K1 took the trophy for 'Best Historic Race Car Still Actively Raced'. McManus also owned a Ford-Mercury flat-head V8 engine 1929 Riley Brooklands, which its original owner, Miles Collier, called the 'Ardent Alligator'. Bob Hartson's Palm Beach Mk II won first in its Class, with Don Marsh's J2 second. Steve Schuler's J2 was first in Class, with Alan Rosenblum's J2 second. Axel and Hanko Rosenblad's Palm Beach was second in Class and Bill Wilmer's J2X gained the 'Spirit of Mille Miglia' Trophy.

In 2016 a new format was introduced for the North American edition of the Allard Owners Club magazine, produced by Andy Picariello. The British-produced club magazine, itself now under the editorship of Chris Pring after many years with Mike Knapman at the helm, became the sole monthly publication for the club. No longer was there a notably different American edition. Whatever the past events of the 1970s 'split' between the formally constituted British Allard Owners Club and the American Allard owners that grouped around the *Allard Register*, today they all share their fundamental love of everything related to Allards and have fostered great personal friendships over the decades.

A subject that is much discussed in an American context is the issue of restoration, over-restoration and the great 'preservation' debate. The views of Andy Picariello on the subject of 'real' cars and real Allards are pertinent to the discussion. When he heard about how 'matching numbers' were being interpreted in the concours judging criteria for another car make, taking into consideration not just the condition of the paint on the chassis, but whether the chassis paint had been applied in the factory way by dipping the chassis rear-first into the paint pit, Picariello asserted in the AOC Newsletter that:

With Allards we do not have to deal with such minutiae as most of them, at least those delivered abroad, were built to order. One could then say that it has to be as it left the factory. That in itself presents a problem. My 1950 J2 Allard was built to order. That order stated: without engine but mounts for Ford engine;

no wheels; tyres; transmission; electrics; instruments and lights. The car was shipped in a crate. When it arrived at Moss Motors, in California, a Canadian Mercury engine with transmission was installed, and a hodge-podge of lights, wheels etc, were provided.

This was the way it raced at Pebble Beach the next year (1951). After that it was sold. The second owner replaced the Mercury flat-head engine with a Chrysler Hemi engine, and raced it for several years that way. That was the way I bought it in 1963 (for $500!). Was it 'original'? Certainly not. Was it authentic? Yes it was, as that was the way it was last raced. Did I like it that way? No way! I replaced the cracked disc wheels with wire wheels. The race-worn bias-ply tyres were replaced with radials. I purchased the vintage-appropriate Lucas lights.

An Allard is original if it is the way it was when it was first driven. Today, this is a very rare Allard indeed. It is authentic if today it is, as it should or would have been equipped when it was first driven or last raced.

Allards have always been appreciated in America through a unique Allardism that really does signify a major mark on automotive history. Of the 507 Allards known to exist worldwide, 244 are resident in America. There must surely be others resting unseen, waiting to be rediscovered in yards and barns.

Zora Arkus Duntov at the wheel of a famous Allard.

THE ALLARD OWNERS CLUB (AOC)

In 2001 Jim and Sheila Tiller took their 1950 J2 Allard to the Bonneville Salt Flats. After a monumental spin at 175mph (282km/h), Jim reached 197mph (317km/h) on the next run!

CHAPTER 8

THE ALLARD OWNERS CLUB (AOC)

Allards and a lovely sunny day at Prescott; it doesn't get much better.

John Peskett

BY THE END OF THE 1940s there were nearly one thousand Allard cars on the road and many more Allard 'enthusiasts'. Sydney asked Tom Lush to produce an Allard newsletter from early 1948 to be circulated to Allard staff members and a selected band of Allard car owners. Tom, with the support of Pat Kierny (years later to become his wife), edited and produced the newsletter, which was just two or three Gestetnered printed sheets. There were different editions for motor trade people and Allard enthusiasts.

Sydney also decided that there should be an Allard Owners Club (AOC). The first meeting to discuss this took place in November 1950. Sydney chaired the meeting, which took place in Sydney's office at 24–28 Clapham High Street, and those present were Jim Appleton (Secretary), F.L. Cyprien, F.D. Dent, B.D. Skelton, F. Rogers and A. Rumfit; all were Allard owners. Sydney became President of the club and held this position until his death in 1966. So was born the Allard Owners Club.

A book of 'Allard Owners Motor Club' or AOC rules was subsequently printed. The club was not officially incorporated as a limited liability company until much later in 1964, when Sydney asked the club to help with the responsibility of organizing the Drag Festival Meetings. A few years later the club was de-registered.

The AOC was officially formed at the Club AGM on 1 March 1951 at the Red Cow pub in Hammersmith, West London, when four additional members were elected to the committee: A.G. Imhof, J. Lockyer, T. Lush and D. Price (about whom little is known). Tom Lush carried on producing the club newsletter on a monthly basis until Sydney decided that this should be added to Ray May's duties as Club Secretary.

COMMITTEE AND NEWSLETTER

Ray became the first co-ordinator and 'editor' of the AOC's newsletter. Sydney had, in typical Sydney manner, handed Ray a typewriter and said. 'We ought to have an owners club and you'd better run it.'

Ray regularly attended Allard events wearing his French style beret and ready with his catchphrase, 'Care for a boiled sweet, old boy?' He was a charming old-world character who did so much to hold the club together at a time when Allard's profile in motor sport was low. He was deeply involved in

AOC stalwart Jim Tiller with the world's fastest Allard, 'Old Fella'.

everything to do with Allards: after their wedding Ray and his wife Win were driven away in an Allard. Ray was a Francophile and took to driving long distances on their annual trip to France.

Ray corresponded with Allard owners in many countries, particularly the USA, where many of the cars were exported, and he built up a register of Allard cars and owners that would become the basis of the *Allard Register*. When relations between certain AOC committee members became acrimonious, Ray decided that he had had enough and resigned as Club Secretary in 1970. Ray and Win moved from London to Sussex, where their home became a regular haunt for Allardistes. He was an avid motorcycle man, in addition to owning an Allard P Type and then the last Palm Beach Mk II (with the Jaguar engine).

Pat Hulse stepped in after Ray's departure and did an excellent job for nearly thirty years. Ray continued to correspond with Allard owners in the USA through the *Allard Register*, which was then based in California. Michelle Wilson took over from Pat Hulse and held this position until 2005, when Jim Tiller became the Club Secretary.

Jim Tiller first met Ray in 1958 when he joined the AOC and the pair became friends. He took on the job of producing the club's magazine from 1980 and improved its style with the assistance of his wife Sheila. Between 1983 and 2009 he served as Club Chairman and Captain, also becoming Club Secretary in 2005. Jim stepped down from the committee in 2009, after ably managing club activities for more than twenty-five years.

A new committee was formed in 2009 with Mike Knapman (a club member since 1961) stepping into Jim's shoes as Vice President UK, Andy Picariello Vice President for the club members in the USA and David Moseley offering his services as the Hon. Secretary.

Alan Allard agreed to be Patron in 2010. The committee were very pleased when Josh Sadler, a long-time Allard owner and racing driver, accepted the invitation to become the new President of the Club.

Mike Knapman, who has a special place maintaining the recent Allard archives, took on the production of the news magazine, which became *The Tailwagger*, a title taken from the name used by the Allard hill climb and trials car team

Jim Tiller is also famous for his Allard artworks, which AOC members often receive as Christmas cards.

back in the early years. In addition to the club members in the UK and USA, there are now members in Australia, New Zealand, Germany, the Netherlands, Sweden, France, Belgium, Italy, Switzerland, Ireland, Brazil, Malta and Monaco. Among the club members in Canada has been Tony Cove of Oshawa, Ontario, who rescued and fully restored a 'barn find' J2 (chassis 1717), which was the only J2 exported directly to Canada by Allard in London.

Trials, speed tests, rallies, hill climbs and circuit races, remain the core activities of the AOC, just as they were at its inception when enthusiastic Allard owners included the likes of Eric Alexander from Sussex, who in 1955 owned a P2 Monte Carlo saloon, an M Type and a Cadillac-engined J2X LM. He had previously purchased an ex-works J2. Eric's J2X LM hit a lamp post at the Thorney Island race and he was presented with a bill for £275.

Jim Tiller has contributed so much to the affairs of Allard ownership, and Sheila's skills, both organizational and driving her L Type, also deserve special mention.

More evocative Allard imagery from Jim's pen.

AOC OFFICERS

President	1951–66	Sydney Allard
	1966–2010	Alan Allard
	2010–	Josh Sadler
Vice President	1951–65	Lt Gen. Francis Griswold USAF
	1964–9	Reg Leather
	1969–73	Reg Canham
	1974–91	Gordon Viola & Harry Moore
	1991–2009	Peter Moore
	2009–	Mike Knapman
(North America)	2009–	Andy Picariello
Chairman/Captain	1964–70	Gordon Viola
	1971–83	Alan Tiley
	1983–2009	Jim Tiller
	2009–	Dave Loveys
Hon. Secretary	1951–4	Jim Appleton
	1954–70	Ray May
	1970–98	Pat Hulse
	1998–2005	Michelle Wilson
	2005–9	Jim Tiller
	2009–	David Moseley
Patron	2010–	Alan Allard

2019 club officials:

Darell Allard	Treasurer/membership
Chris Pring	Editor AOC News
Ron Dowle	Competitions Secretary
Mel Herman	Exhibitions Manager
James Smith	Social Secretary
Gavin Allard	Historian
Sam Sammels	Publicity
Peter Wright	Midlands Rep.
Chris Lowth	Pacific Region Rep.
Rick Newman	AOC Rep

In recent years Allan Cameron, Competitions Secretary of the Bugatti Owners Club at Prescott, always looked after AOC members and their cars during events at Prescott events, a place of special importance in the forging of Allard's early reputation. Sadly Allan died in 2016.

During the 1950s the club held annual 'Allard Owners Gymkhana' events, at which private owners could join an organized motor test and 'trial'. In 1952, when Jim Appleton was the club's Honorary Secretary, a brand new K1 (chassis No 533), registered as KTA 309, was purchased by Jim

Lockyer and entered in several such events. The car is still known to the club. Today, awards are bestowed across various ownership categories at the club's annual Allard 'Concours'.

Allard owners are true enthusiasts. It woud not be possible to mention every member who has contributed to the club's activities, and some may feel it unfair to name some but not others, but it is important to attempt to encapsulate all that they have done for the marque.

Across the decades the owners club has established numerous regular events for its members, ranging from the 'classic' rallies to the annual French trip, the 'Trois Vallées', which still sees up to a dozen entrants. The club members take part in Motor Sports Association (MSA) events, numerous Vintage Sports Car Club (VSCC) races and Bugatti Owners Club events, as well as regular AOC meetings such as the Pickering rally and West Country meetings. The Berwick Rally always sees Allard entries, and Allards appear at the Monaco Historic Grand Prix, the Goodwood Revival and Members Day, and the Silverstone Classic. Glorious Prescott and the essential Shelsley Walsh hill climb remain at the core of the club's meetings. The club makes a regular appearance at the *Practical Classics* Classic Car & Restoration Show at the NEC in Birmingham. K1 and M Type owner Mel Herman and his sons design and build the stand to display a plethora of Allard cars and memorabilia with a skill that wins *Classic and Sports Car* magazine awards in the process.

The various Silverstone races, including the Bentley Drivers club series, often see Allards on the grid. Tim Llewellyn's J2, co-driven by his son Oliver, is a regular sight and took pole position at the 2015 race. Mark Butterworth also takes a lead role.

Jim Tiller rarely misses a Silverstone outing with his J2. Allard owners also get to Spa-Francorchamps for the RAC Woodcote Trophy and to Goodwood for various races, including the 'Freddie March' Trophy. Among the regulars at these events are Bob Francis, Till Bechtolsheimer and Hans-Jörg Hübner. The AOC's Competition Secretary, J2 Special-owner Ron Dowle, took over after Gerry Auger's many years of dedication and his followers are assured of some great days out.

At Goodwood's 2016 Revival Meeting the Canadian Allard owner and racer Bob Francis drove his ex-works Mille Miglia J2 at the meeting's test day. The British Regis Classic Tour also sees regular Allard outings, and Sheila Tiller took part in her L Type named 'Eleanor' (MWL 380) as early as 2008.

The club has visited the Nürburgring since 2015. The first of these 'AOC Continental' trips involved Darell and Jenny Allard's P Type, Dave Loveys' K Type, and James and Bridget Smith's L Type. Sheila Tiller and David Wixon rode 'shotgun' in a Jaguar XJS. Ivo and Lillian Nijs from Belgium supported the trip in their Cadillac-engined K2. Gerhard Ankenband from Switzerland also arrived in his L Type. Lloyd Allard turned up at the Ringhaus Hotel, run by Frank and Christine Hiersekorn, which provided a base for the AOC team – as did Sabine Schmitz, the 'Queen of the Nürburgring' and 'fastest taxi driver in the world', whose mother owns a local

James Smith goes up Prescott's main straight in his early short-wheelbase, Special-bodied J Type, as originally favoured by Len Potter to great competitive effect.

AOC Captain Dave Loveys in his K1. They are a highly competitive Prescott fixture.

restaurant. Sydney would have loved the idea of Allards at speed on the 'Ring'.

In an attempt to reach out to a younger audience, the club appointed Sam Sammels to engage a wider demographic – so Allard now Tweets @AllardOC.

JIM AND SHEILA TILLER: 'OLD FELLA' AND 197MPH IN AN ALLARD

Jim Tiller is the man who beat five Ferrari Daytonas at the Brighton Speed Trials in his ancient 6.4-litre Allard J2 with a time of 25.1 seconds. He also reached 197mph in his Allard on the Bonneville Salt Flats. Imagine, nearly 200mph in an Allard! In his orange J2 big block Chevy V8 Jim Tiller also made 9.98 seconds on the quarter-mile sprint at a terminal velocity of 145mph.

Jim and Sheila Tiller have been two of the most influential members of the Allard Owners Club and were responsible for holding the club together during those low points when interest in Allard and its cars was waning and relations within the committee were troubled. Jim is not just a fast driver (even at 83 years old) and mechanical fettler, he is a skilled

artist and taught art for twenty-five years. His annual Christmas cards, which he draws and paints, show Allard cars in all sorts of action, along with handwritten notations, and are truly cherished by all fortunate enough to receive one.

Jim became Club Chairman in 1983 and Sheila took control of publishing the monthly 'Allard Newsletter', which became a proper club magazine.

He became interested in Allard cars when he purchased his first Allard, a J2, back in 1958, the same year that he married. This car is the 1950 J2 that he still races in 2017. In 1958 the J2 was powered by the standard flat-head, side-valve Ford V8, producing only 85bhp. 'Old Fella', as this J2 is now affectionately known, progressed to Mercury and Ardun versions, then to 390cu in and 500cu in Cadillacs. A change to a BB Chevy of 427cu in was not potent enough, so today it is powered by a 540cu in (8.9 litre) Chevy V8, producing more than 800bhp, and accelerates from 0–100mph in around 5 seconds.

At one stage Jim owned four Allards. He inherited the two Tiller Allards in 2004 from his rally co-driver Mike Wharton. After gender reassignment Mike Wharton later selected to become Michelle Wilson, but still owned an Allard Palm Beach.

Jim's J2 was featured on the front cover of *Autosport* in October 1962, shown in classic Allard racing pose under

Sheila Tiller in her L Type, appropriately named 'Eleanor'.

hard acceleration out of a bend with nose up, inside wheel off the track and the outside wheel showing masses of positive camber. His driving style in the J2 was very much in the manner of Sydney: in 1970 the sight of Jim and his J2 going uphill more sideways than straight was too much for the steward of the meeting at Shelsley Walsh and Jim was given a temporary ban.

He has developed and raced his J2 for fifty-eight years. During this time he has kept the flag flying for Allard cars, competing in all manner of speed events and winning many awards. He is the only person, who Sydney allowed to drive the first big Allard dragster.

Jim has been a regular racer at the annual handicap race at Silverstone run by the Bentley Drivers Club. Starting from the back of the grid, either he passes everyone down the straight and gets to the front, or there is a major off-track excursion.

The Brighton Speed Trials is another annual event where Jim can show a clean pair of heels to all the fastest sports cars gathered on the sea front. His usual ET time for the 1.4 mile course is around 10.2 seconds (10.28 seconds in 2004, for example). His best time to date on what is normally a rather rough public road, the Esplanade, was the 9.98 seconds achieved in 2005, breaking the 10-second barrier with a terminal speed over 145mph.

Tiller has been a frequent visitor to the American Allard scene, a notable occasion being the 'Gathering of the Clan' meeting at the Texas Speedway in November 2003 (see Chapter 7). He has also admitted to being a fan of Bill Bauder: 'I admired the J2X of Bill Bauder who, though past his first flush of youth, produced a wonderful J2X with his own fair hands.'

A best-ever Shelsley Walsh time of 33.79 seconds was recorded by Simon Taylor in 2008 in his Chevy-powered HWM, the 'Stovebolt Special'. Jim Tiller did it in 36.34 seconds in the J2X 'Old Fella'.

Jim has been passionate about the Bonneville salt flats in Utah for many years and set about achieving his ambition of breaking the 200mph barrier in a fifty-year-old Allard J2. Every year in September an event called Speed Week is held on the salt flats, during which vehicles of many shapes and sizes attempt to reach the highest speed possible over a measured distance.

It was decided to take part in the 2000 Speed Week, but much work needed to be done, burning the midnight oil, before the old car would be accepted to run under the different regulations in the USA and for this particular event.

First, a specifically designed roll cage had to be installed. The front motorcycle-type wings were removed and a completely new aerodynamic front-end body made, but still retaining the classic J2 Allard grille. The body was extended downwards all round, almost down to ground level and back to the rear wheels. These modifications made it necessary to install an Allard aerodynamic windscreen, manufactured from a special polycarbonate material used in riot shields.

Many night hours were spent by Jim and Alan Hassell getting the Allard ready for their great adventure. The huge 540cu in (8.9 litre) Chevy V8 was built by Jim Reid in Whitman, Massachusetts, where it was mated to the existing Turbo Hydro 400 transmission. Jim says that, with the Salsbury 2.88:1 final drive ratio limited slip differential, the car is theoretically geared for a maximum speed of 240mph.

The skinny front wheels were only 3½in wide with purpose-designed narrow tyres. At the rear 'Old Fella' ran on 7 × 18in Compomotive wheels with huge round-profile M/T Bonneville tyres.

The J2 was shipped to the USA in September 2000. Andy Picariello acquired a massive trailer and towed the rig from Cape Cod to Utah. There were the usual hassles at scrutineering and driver briefings to attend, with strict instructions to limit the maximum speed to 150mph on the initial runs. Sheila wanted some of the action, too, and the event stewards told her to restrict her speed to 125mph on the first run. She was obviously enjoying herself and exceeded the allotted speed by reaching 152mph on her only run: the officials were not amused.

Jim's target was to break the 200mph barrier, which had never been done in an Allard – even by the Allard dragsters. Various problems troubled the first few timed runs. It was apparent that there was insufficient downforce at over 150mph to stop the machine lifting up off the salt, causing loss of traction and wheel spin at 170mph.

The AOC in action on the main straight at Silverstone with L, K, M and J Types all roaring along.

On one run at around 170mph, Jim lost traction and went into a monumental spin. He has told how he took his hands off the wheel and crouched down low as the car spun many times, miraculously without somersaulting. In fact, it spun so far that it appeared to go out of view, due to the curvature of the earth. On the next run it spun at 180mph.

Despite this, the intrepid Jim went out on the last day and reached 197.30mph – an astonishing achievement from a private unsponsored venture in a fifty-year-old Allard with, dare I say, a sixty-five-year-old 'young' driver.

Sheila Tiller is not your stereotypical 'racer's wife'. She drives her own L Type with verve, as well as the J Type with Jim, and takes an active role in their racing lives:

Jim prepares the car, except when an extra pair of hands or feet are required, and I do the rest – even so far as deciding which events we will enter.

When I am asked the question about being nervous or scared when he is racing, the answer is a very big yes, but fortunately Jim does not see this. Driving a J2 Allard is not the easiest car to race competitively, and when it is driven at ten-tenths as JT does, it is easy for the Old Fella (our car) to take over and say 'no more'. So you are lucky if you don't hit anything if she spins off the track. If that does happen, then we take her home and rebuild her once again. I worry because of the many times this has happened in the last twenty-four years.

Since 1995 Sheila, undoubtedly the club's most active female driver, has taken part in her L Type 'Eleanor' in the Randonée des Trois Vallées classic car rally, organized every June by the Association Normande de Véhicules d'Epoque. Jim Tiller has also taken part in various cars. Together with her navigator, Joan Chmura, Sheila drove in the 2012 Cape Wrath to Cape Cornwall run, straight after competing in the Regis Rally. Regular AOC members on the Randonée include the Tillers, Clive and Helen Board, and Peter and Pat Wright.

Andy Picariello recalls a visit to the Tillers that neatly sums up the fun and enthusiasm the couple have given to the club and its members over the years:

A Clipper resided in Jim and Sheila's garden many years ago. Each December Jim would revive it so it could participate in their annual Boxing Day party. After sufficient Christmas cheer was consumed, an impromptu Grand Prix was held, as each guest took turns racing the Clipper around the outside of the house. One guest could always do better on foot, due no doubt to higher octane fuel in his tank!

When Andy Picariello purchased his 1950 J2 in 1963 he contacted Ray May and was put in touch with Jim Tiller, who was of great help in getting the car back to operating condition: 'In 1968 I finally got to visit both Ray and Jim in England. A long lasting friendship developed between us. More important than the cars are the relationships that develop because of them.'

PAT HULSE

Pat Hulse had a passion for Allards. She joined the AOC in 1958 and served as the Hon. Secretary from 1970 to 1996. Pat, who died in 2015, was a qualified opthalmic optician and a competitive rower. She was equally competitive as a driver in a Ford-engined MG J2 Special, Singer Coupé and Singer Le Mans. Pat was co-driver to Fred Damodaran in his L Type (JGX 651) and Chrysler Firepower J2X (ORL 320), in which they claimed third place in the Land's End Trial.

Pat was a key organizer in 1960s Allard events at Silverstone, Brands Hatch and many other circuits, as well as at drag racing events, running the club's stands at many shows and events. She also assisted Fred Damodaran in creating the Historic Sports Car Club. Among the people Pat introduced to the AOC was Mel Herman. Current AOC Captain Dave Loveys underlines Pat's contribution as 'a significant figure in the Allard Owners Club over many years and a driving force behind so many events. She really does deserve a place in the record.'

The leading historic racer Josh Sadler has been an Allard fan for decades and President of the AOC since 2010. He drove the Allard Mercotto Special GGE 523 in the 1980s and campaigned J2X registration ORL 320, notably at the 2003 Dijon Historic Grand Prix Cars Association race weekend. Josh recalls an early encounter with an Allard:

I can clearly remember the day that David Moseley and I went down to the Classic car show in Brighton with the intention of buying a classic car and visiting the Allard stand being managed by Pat Hulse and Gerry Auger. They pointed us in the direction of Roger and Sylvia Hayes who lived near Silverstone where we saw an L Type with a tree growing up through the chassis. This car is now owned by the Tillers. We eventually found a blue L Type in Newton Abbot and it has been in my garage for most of the years since. It was built in 1948 in the year that I was born, and built in the road that we lived in, in Putney.

ABOVE: **Long time Club member Steve Taylor's lovely Palm Beach Mk.1. There are approximately 30 of these cars remaining in the world – 5 in the UK.**

Roger Hayes is a much respected Allard restorer and racer of some repute. Here his J2 (Cadillac V8) is seen at Prescott. Roger's son-in-law, Will Gilbert, was fortunate to survive when he left the track on the hill in 2018.

SOME AOC PILOTS AND THEIR CARS

- Mel Herman first joined the AOC in 1969 and restored an M Type (chassis 823), which was subsequently sold to Kate Manley-Tucker; she and her husband Richard drove it on the 9,800-mile 1990 London to Peking Motor Challenge, which they completed. Mel left the club for a while to concentrate on developing his business, but rejoined in 2005 and set about restoring a second M Type, chassis number 716, to a show-winning standard. Another project that Mel hopes to finish in the near future is an Allard K1 sports, fitted with a Cadillac engine and four-speed box and intended for competition use. Mel is a highly enthusiastic member of the AOC Committee and is responsible for shows and exhibitions. He also acts as the club's Registrar for M Type drophead coupés and the K1 sports model.

- The first Allard Tim Baker bought was a very early example of the Allard P1 saloon. This was soon joined by a remarkably authentic 'replica' J2 (FPN 300), which stands above lesser replicas. It has an accurate body by Pitney Restorations, which has had a long association with Allards, a Ford (France) 24-stud V8 with Allard heads, a dual carb Edelbrook manifold mounting a Stromberg 97, Iskenderian 88 cam with adjustable lifters and Mallory ignition, all stirred by a Rover five-speed gearbox. In this car he competed in the 1968 London-to-Sydney Rally. Until recently Tim has campaigned

the J2 at the Prescott and Shelsley Walsh hill climbs, always driving it to events. Tim has also competed with the P1 in the Randonée des Trois Vallées. He supports club events and, with the assistance of friends, takes both cars.

- Current Club Captain Dave Loveys owns a K1 that he really knows how to handle and regularly gets below 59 seconds for the Prescott hill. Dave and his brother Roger also took Dave's P Type to participate in the 2012 Monte Carlo Rally Historique event as a celebration of Sydney's 1952 Monte win. The pair started from Glasgow and had an eventful French tour.

- James Smith, a major contributor to the AOC and K2 owner, also owns the ex-Len Potter J1, KPB 242, chassis number 275, which had been specially built as a short-wheelbase trials car. The car has a freshly installed engine tuned by Jim Turnbull of the Royal Kustoms tuning company, which was responsible for a 12.8-second quarter-mile world record for a Ford flat-head engine. James previously campaigned a hot-rod 'Rellard' but wanted a competition-tuned Allard. He had a spare Ford Mercury 24-stud engine in his garage and it is this engine that Turnbull had tuned: 180bhp beckons. Clanfield Restorations restored the car's body to the original Len Potter specification.

- Roger Ugalde lives in the West Country. His main forte is classic trials and he has rigorously campaigned Robert Robinson-Collins's KLD 5 in Motor Cycling Club (MCC) events, collecting many Gold Awards. Roger currently

This famous K2 captures the essence of open-top Allard motoring, as an M Type hustles along behind it at Silverstone.

owns a K2 and for a time owned the fixed-head M Type delivered by the factory as a part-bodied chassis to Gould of Regent Street, whose coachbuilders completed it. This car is now believed to be in Germany. So successful was Roger at trialling that he was eventually appointed to be Clerk of the Course for the Exeter and Lands End Trials. Roger has several cars in his collection including an early Gordon Keeble. As well as being a staunch member of the AOC, Roger also serves as a committee member for the MCC and for the Crash Box & Classic Car Club of Devon, who run the Powderham Castle Classic Car Shows.

- Robert Robinson-Collins owns KLD 5, Godfrey 'Gof' Imhof's successor to HLP, and has campaigned it in many of the MCC's classic trials, his best result being a Silver Award. Robert is a long-time member of the AOC and has served on the committee as Competition Secretary.

- Although he would hate such a tag, most people consider John Peskett to be the 'go-to' Allard guru. He has owned an L Type, the Sydney Allard-owned J2, ORL 320 (the ex-Damodaran car), which he preserved with perfection, and Sydney's Jaguar-engined GT. Long ago he succumbed to 'the Allard disease' and he has absorbed much Allard knowledge over the decades, clocking up fifty years of membership of the AOC since he joined in 1967. Many Allards and other cars have passed through his hands over the years. He currently owns several Allards, the most notable of which is KXC 170, chassis 888, the first production J2. Many years ago John pounced when he became aware that the chassis was available after a spell in the north-east United States. Shortly after the remaining original bodywork was purchased from another source. The first step in the restoration was the painstaking removal of all old

The Allard pits at Ruapuna, New Zealand, 2008: Bill Boone's J2X, Jim Phillips's J2X replica and Rob Boult's J2.

paint and filler. After several years of hard labour the J2 is now back in first-class condition and fitted with a 330cu in Cadillac engine, the last of the three engines Sydney Allard installed when using it for competition (Mercury, Ardun and Cadillac). John still competes at the Prescott hill climb with an Allard Special he constructed himself twenty years ago. He also shares a Triumph-based Special with Peter Thurston.

- Roger and Sylvia Hayes have been Allardistes for many years. Roger owned his first Allard, a J1, at the age of seventeen. He is now a renowned Bugatti and restoration expert, and owns the Allard Dragon Mk II dragster, a J2 and J2X. He makes expert copies of unobtainable Allard J2 and J2X parts and campaigns his cars with real verve.

- Tim Wilson claims to have been 'an Allard watcher since the early Fifties, thanks to the enthusiasm of my old man'. He owns an Allard M Type 'Special', built up from the chassis of a 1949 car modified to a 100in wheelbase to create a Trials-type one-off body/chassis combination built by Roger Daniel. Known as 'Huey', the car employs an amalgam of Allard P, J and M Type parts and truly evokes the spirit of the post-war 1940s Tailwagger team cars.

- The Rt Hon. Sir Greg Knight PC MP has chaired the All Party Parliamentary Historic Vehicles Group since he returned to Parliament in 2001. His Allard is a P1 that is believed to have been owned at some point by Leslie Allard, Sydney's brother.

- Stan Knight was a member of the Allard Owners Club from November 1956 until his death in April 2015. He competed in many 1950s rallies and events, initially with the ex-Howard Roberts J1 (GAB 779) and latterly in a P1 saloon (GNT 630). Stan worked for Fairey Aviation and then the Heston Aircraft Company, producing ailerons for the Supermarine Spitfire in 1940. He enlisted in the Royal Navy and saw active wartime service. After the war Stan returned to sheet metal working. He became involved with motorcycles and then cars, starting with a Jaguar SS100. Stan became close friends with Jim and Sheila Tiller and has worked on cars belonging to several members, such as Fred Damodaran's J2X (ORL 320), which appears on the front of David Kinsella's book *Allard*. Stan crashed his P1 on the North Circular Road in the 1950s and rebuilt the car's rear body himself.

- Roger Murray-Evans is a well-known Allard collector and at various times has owned an L Type, Monte Carlo saloon, a Caddy-powered K1, K2 and an J2X (the famous MGT 850). Roger has carried out a great deal of Allard restoration work.

- Keith Baker has owned Allards since he bought a P Type in 1957. The first owner of his Allard Palm Beach Mk 1, registered 4655 H, which he purchased in July1960, was the film director John Paddy Carstairs, who did not buy it from Allard/Adlard but from Dagenham Motors. Baker had also owned a K3 (PLE 888). In the 1970s Baker refitted or upgraded his car to Palm Beach Mk 3 specification with the 2.6-litre Ford Zephyr engine with Derrington cylinder head, revisions to gearbox and transmission and wire wheels. A series of drivetrain mechanical issues, including five snapped half shafts and snapped wire wheel spokes, then followed and it was decided to fit a Jaguar 3.8 engine (as per Allard Palm Beach Mk 3 option) and gearbox with the Salisbury H4 rear axle. Keith also added a one-off, fast-backed alloy hardtop of his own design to the car. The result was an Allard with the engine of an E Type, but much lighter than the Jaguar.

- Gerry Auger joined the Allard fraternity back in 1968 and was Competitions Secretary to the AOC, as well as owning an L Type.

- Jeremy Bennett owned MLX 400, the P Type used by Eleanor Allard on the Monte Carlo events in the 1950s.

- Several AOC members have owned their Allards since the 1960s: Joe Clegg has had his K2 since 1967, Blair Shenstone his L Type since 1964, and John Aldridge an M Type since 1966.

- In 2016 Sydney's nephew Darell sold his bright blue P1, registration 454 XUP, which was fitted with an 8BA/8RT engine, a floor-change gear selector and a high ratio 'touring' final drive, and purchased M Type chassis 322. Darell and his wife Jenny are key figures on the Allard driving scene. Replacing the more normal column gear change with a floor-mounted one was a 1950s Allard modification: Sydney used a modified column change mounted on the floor with the cranks relocated in a new vertical position in order to permit acutuation of the gear change rods (the original Ford arrangement was a side-change system).

- Chris Pring's J2 (chassis 2120), registered as OZ 4444, was displayed on the Allard Motor Company's stand at the 1951 Festival of Britain and was later delivered to Belfast driver Desmond Titterington, who immediately put the J2 to good use by winning the 1952 Leinster Trophy and scoring an outright win at the 1953 Knockagh hill climb. The car was then powered by a 3917cc Ardun-converted engine on eight Amal carburettors. Titterington's success with the Allard against more 'refined' machinery helped him secure drives with Ecurie Ecosse and the works Jaguar and Mercedes Benz teams. It is wonderful to see this historically important Allard back in action. Credit must go to the dedication shown by Chris and Paul Weldon at the Leiter Motor Company during the comprehensive twelve-year restoration. This was an incredible feat, considering

MARY ELLIS, 'SPITFIRE GIRL'

Mary Ellis (née Wilkins) owned a 1947 K1 (chassis 239), registered as CUD 818, and won the Isle of Wight Car Club's Ladies Challenge in the 1956 Isle of Wight Car Rally. In 1941 Mary joined the Air Transport Auxiliary (ATA) and became one of the female pilots (168 in total throughout the war) who delivered aircraft to frontline airfields with minimal or non-existent training.

Mary was sharp, competitive, alert and a 'natural' flyer and driver. She was one of the first female pilots to fly Spitfires (logging more than 400 flights) and became the oldest woman in the world to fly one, aged 93. Mary flew more than seventy types of aircraft, including Tiger Moths, Wellingtons, Lancasters, Spitfires, Hurricanes, Mosquitoes, Ansons and many other RAF machines down to the Gloster Meteor jet fighter. Mary recounted her experiences in the book *A Spitfire Girl* (Frontline Books, 2016), written with Melody Foreman.

Her post-war car of choice was a powerful, agile and responsive V8 Allard K1, purchased by the Wilkins family on 18 November 1947. Mary's nephew Charles Wilkins took the car with him when he emigrated to Australia in the 1970s. Mary was made an Honorary AOC Member in 2017.[21] Mary died in July 2018, aged 101.

- Sam and Jane Sammells' mid-green K1, BAS 120, has been seen everywhere from Silverstone to the Beamish Run.
- Three generations of the Johnson family in Northern Ireland have owned Allards. Living close to Craigantlet hill climb, they were bound to get the Allard bug! The 1950 1,000-mile Circuit of Ireland (Ulster Automobile Club) was won by M Type, MZ 1201, with the husband, wife and son team of Dermot, Gertie and thirteen-year-old Michael Johnson as crew. Young Michael got Sydney Allard's autograph, too, and met J2 driver Peter Collins and local hero Desmond Titterington. Today Michael Johnson, who once owned a blue J2, watches as his own sons undertake vintage motor sport drives.
- The motorcycling writer Ralph Venables owned the thirteenth of Sydney's J1 special production variants, registered as MPG 250, in the 1950s, but sold it in 1961 to Joe Gardner, who blew the engine on the Land's End Trial. MPG 250 then went to Hugh Gledhill and on to Don Batchelor, who stored it outside. It was rescued by Roger and Sylvia Hayes, who had also owned the twelfth J1 special, KPB 242. They were helped by Paul Harvey, who then had a 1951 J2 Special and also swapped his K Type for Sylvia Hayes's McAlpine/Potter J1, KPB 242. Harvey later acquired MPG 250. This essential Allard raced at Prescott and Shelsley Walsh and was present at Blackbushe for the 1964 Drag Fest.
- Chris Lyons enjoyed a fifty-two year membership of the

that the car was rescued from a scrapyard and spent much of its later life in cardboard boxes.
- Les Brooks joined the AOC in the 1950s and rallied his P2 for more than five years. Les was a member of the Hertfordshire County Auto and Aero Club and a committee member of the AOC.
- Patrick Watts, the former British Touring Car driver, owns the ex-Ken Watkins J2 chassis, which is believed to be the car that Peter Collins drove at Dundrod in 1951. At events since 2014 this car has been on grid pole for the Silverstone Classic race, first in Class at the Le Mans Legends event, fifth at the Monaco Historic Grand Prix, and third at the Goodwood Revival. Prior owners include Captain David Wixon and Simon Edwards.
- Jeremy Bennett's J1 is the ex-Jim Appleton car, one of the twelve special early-build competition J1s of 1946.
- Daniel White restored the ex-David Kinsella M Type and his brother Patrick owned a J1.
- Steve Taylor completed the restoration of his Palm Beach, registration AAB 555, in 2008.

THE 'FROST' ALLARD

Edward 'Ted' Frost owned the Drift Bridge Garage in Reigate Road, Epsom, Surrey. He came to know Sydney and his brothers as a fellow pre-war member of the Streatham Motor Club. Frost went on to success as an international motocross rider and in trials as a Norton works rider. His Allard J1 (chassis 79415J), registered as MPG 250, was delivered on 23 September 1948 and is still extant. It was built with the Mercury 24-stud version of the Ford V8 and had an ohv conversion and eight Amal carburettors. Intriguingly, the car's main bodywork was not an original factory fitment and a simple alloy-over-tubular steel affair was added. As per racers of the day, it had no passenger door.

Bill Boddy of *Motor Sport* was co-driver in the car on the Gloucester Trial in 1948. The car also won the Quick Start and Acceleration test at the 1949 Lancia Motor Club Competition, which would not have gone down well.

club. From 1964 he restored a special-bodied J1, OS 7265, fitted with a 5.0-litre Oldsmobile engine, which gave him a successful motor sport year in 1966. Lyons was associated with the Allard Essex Aero Coupé and several P Type and K Type chassis restorations.

- Dr David Reid Tweedie survived internment at Changi during the Second World War and stayed on to practise in Malaya, before retiring back to Surrey. In an interview with Alan Whicker in the 1970s, he recalled owning a rare P1 Monte Carlo and driving it extensively throughout the colony. It is believed that its remains lie rusting in peace somewhere in today's Malaysia.

- Tony Bianchi's Farrallac won the 1950s Sports Cars Class at Silverstone in 2006 in a duel with the Lister Jaguar. A JR (Dean Butler) and a J2XLM (Tom Walker) were sixth and twelfth respectively. The Farrallac's fastest lap time was 1 minute 10.36 seconds at an average speed of 83.86mph. Bianchi prepares Till Bechtolsheimer's historic race entrant J2.

- The motoring writer and TV presenter Jerry Thurston has written regularly for the AOC *Newsletter* about his various Allards, notably a J2X and an L Type. His Thurston Cadillac-engiend J2X, PKGJ 412, was featured on the front cover, and in a four-page feature, of Classic Cars in July 2003. Jerry's father also owned Allards.

- David Kinsella owned the L Type HUE 574 for four dec-

Allard Owners Club award on the AOC stand at the Practical Classics Classic Car & Restoration Show, NEC Birmingham, 2018: (left to right) Dave Loveys, Charles Gough, Mel Herman, Dave Mattingley, Peter Bayliss and James Smith. R. GUNN

ades. It later resided with the late Daniel White in Brittany. David remains a stalwart supporter of all things Allard and a regular at AOC outings.

- Julian Sutton served an engineering apprenticeship at the Rolls-Royce Aero Division, so he is used to fettling things. He purchased his Palm Beach in Lisbon in 2016 and drove it, with Gary Ungless, 1,000km across Portugal and Spain to the ferry at Bilbao.

Eric Alexander on the left, Cyril Wick and Rubert de Larrinaga pose for the camera with their cars – J2X Le Mans, J2X lightweight and JR – after competing in the Brighton Speed Trials in September 1956.

The Tom Walker J2X Le Mans seen in recent years at Prescott. The car was originally raced by Eric Alexander.

- Tom Walker's ex-Roger Reece J2X Le Mans (with a 4-barrel Holley carburettor), registered as JM 7942, was about to compete in the 2017 Pomeroy Trophy, which was held on a dank February day at Silverstone Circuit, when a fuel pump float adjuster screw came loose and caused a fire in the engine bay. The car was soon back in action with just some blistered paint to show for it.
- Martin Walford drove Dean Butler's Allard in the 2002 Le Mans Classic race and came second in his class behind a factory-tuned and supported Jaguar D-Type driven by Win Percy. The Allard would touch 167mph on the Mulsanne straight. A broken differential on the last lap put paid to a podium place, but it was enough for eleventh place overall.

INTERCONTINENTAL ALLARDS

One Allard was originally exported to Madagascar, another to Malaya, several to Kenya, Nigeria and to Rhodesia. A P Type hides in Zimbabwe. One famous Allard has recently been repatriated from India where it had raced. It is possible that further Allards lurk undiscovered in obscure tropical places. Perhaps the most glamorous Allard export was the K2 that found its way to Hawaii in 1960. This ex-Seattle car had an Oldsmobile engine and was originally exported to California in 1952; it ended up in recent years in New York

State in the ownership of Otto Meijer. One Allard is known to still exist in Lebanon, of all places. At the time of writing, there is a roadworthy J2 in Japan and a K2 in Uruguay.

For reasons unknown, in 1987 the official Post Office of Tuvalu, formerly the British protectorate of the Ellice Islands, issued two stamps depicting the Allard J2 as part of its 'Auto 100' series. A member of the East African Motor Sports Club (Rift Valley Branch) named J. Roddo campaigned his Allard K1 in Kenyan hill climbs about 1950.

The AOC Continental Group allows European mainland Allard owners to gather at their own regular meets and shows. Hans-Albert Oppenborn and Hans-Jörg Hübner are the key movers in the German club and its show appearances. Hans-Albert runs the membership and has several Allards: his red M Type often arrives in the UK for the Silverstone Classic. Hans-Jörg owns Sydney's GT and the original Dodge-engined Red Ram car, as well as the ex-Merrick/Duntov 1953 JR, the car that attended Le Mans but did not compete. Horst Muller is a recent L Type Allardiste, as is Gerald Fellner of Munich with his Caddy-J2. Up in Berlin, Malte Müller-Wrede owns a J2X Le Mans.

An Allard stand appears at Techno-Classica Essen, under the stewardship of Hans-Albert Oppenborn, and AOC regulars include Victor Gonzales Nascimento, Kurt Biller, Achim Rester, Jules Tibolt and Bernd Sgraja. Rainer Herbst, another regular, collected the K1 that formerly belonged to Michelle Wilson from Jim Tiller and gave it a new home in

Germany, but had the hard task of deciding whether to keep the car red or return it to its original hue of maroon. Allards often appear in the German magazine *Motor Klassik*.

The Germans seem to have become the major Allard collectors in recent years. Dr Bernd Dannenmaier runs the ex-Frank Curtis J2, OBB 377, and travels to many events with the car, competing in three long-distance rallies in 2016, including the Sachs Franken Classic, where he took fourth in class. He won his class in the Vintage Sun Run and then entered the Paris-Vienna run. Till Bechtolsheimer, driving his J2, came third at the 2016 FIA Historic Grand Prix de Monaco for 1950s sports cars.

In 2010 the blue J2 of Patrice Cousseau and François Cointreau was placed sixtieth in the Le Mans Classic. Car number 48, the J2 of Jean-François Bardinon and Daniel Patrick Brooks, was fifty-sixth. Jean-François has owned J2 chassis 1572 for many years and intends to keep it looking as 'real' as possible. The car has a standard 3.9-litre Ford flat-head, original Ford three-speed gearbox, and sports a very rare full-width windscreen. Jean-François is perhaps France's most avid Allard owner, also part-owning a Chrysler-engined J2X, which that he co-drove at the first Le Mans Classic event. He is also responsible for the Coupe des Printemps event, held every spring at the Autodrome de Montlhéry circuit near Paris. Another Allard that has had a result in the Le Mans Classic was the Colombian J2X of the Steur family.

Two Allards were recently spotted in the paddock at the famous street race in Angoulême. They were the well-travelled black J2 of Patrick Watts, and the relatively unseen K2 of Frenchman Bruno Rigoli, which was difficult to miss given its striking green and black paint job.

Eight Allards currently reside quietly in Swiss collections, although they occasionally venture out to Essen, Silverstone or Goodwood. The Pantheon Basel project in Basel facilitates the exhibition of vintage and classic cars and was the brainchild of AOC Continental Group's Stephan Musfeld, a K1 and K2 owner. The 1930s Allard Special FGF 290 appeared there in 2009.

The Allard P1 (RF 620) of Clas Palmberg in Finland keeps the crimson enamel badge alive in northern lands. Clas's restored 'barn find' P1 competed against Sydney in the 1952 and 1953 Monte Carlo Rallies. Its original owner-drivers Vilho Hietanen and Onni Vilkas tried to sell the car to Palmberg's father Sven in the 1950s. Decades later, Clas would buy this very car – RF260. Hietanen had competed in the Midnight Sun Rally, but electrical gremlins forced him out. Yet he and RF260 won the Jyväskylän Suurajot (Jyväskylä Grand Prix). Hietanen sold the car to a local garage owned by a Mr Bomna, who sold it on in the 1960s to a farmer

The Allard dragster No. 3, newly restored by Roger Hayes, was displayed at the NEC Restoration Show in 2018.

named Mr Petrell. The car was rescued from his barn in Klaukkala and restored by Reijo Koivunen Martti, prior to its sale to Clas Palmberg.

In the Netherlands, Rob Debets is known for his restoration of the 1953 Palm Beach Mk 1. Since 1984 Dick van Dijk has owned his K2 (chassis 2029), the only one delivered new to the Netherlands. The car was restored by Rod Jolley. In Belgium, Olivier Lavédrine owns a J2 and an K1 (Ardun spec), and Ivo Nijs runs a K2, Serge Allaert runs a J2X, and Marcel Roks owns a J2.

On Malta, David and Felixa Arrigo fettle their M Type, owned and restored by David since 1970; the car competed in the 1997 London to Cape Town Rally, but unfortunately broke down in Malawi.

Another M Type quietly resides at the Museo Automovilistico in Malaga, Spain, an old tobacco warehouse that provides perfect storage conditions. The car is chassis number 806 delivered on 18 March 1949 and exported to Malaya.

Godfrey Imhof's KLD 5 from the Candidi Provocatores race team car has been campaigned to great effect by Robert Robinson-Collins.

Massimo Betati, owner of the 'most owned' J2, ORL 320 (previously owned by Josh Sadler), took the car to the 2016 Goodwood Members Day, qualified seventeenth out of thirty runners and finished the race. The Historic Grand Prix of Monaco is a regular, premier event in the classics calendar and Allards often take part. Past Monaco Historic entrants include Chris Phillips (J2), Malcolm Verey (J2), Klaus-Peter Reichle (J2X) and Albert Otten (J2). The 1952 Monaco Grand Prix was a non-championship race for sports cars and two J2X Allards were entered in the hands of Anthony Hume (Britain) and Fernando Mascarenhas (Portugal). The race hit the headlines because of a multiple pile-up at Sainte Dévote, in which Hume's J2X was involved; Mascarenhas retired with a split tank.

In 2017 the 1947 K1 registered in Italy as DX207ZJ (chassis number 242) was part of the Mille Miglia (Brescia–Roma–Brescia) event as car 234, piloted by Ettore Prandini and Ezio Maiolini. It was previously owned by Paul Harvey and Roger Hayes, and now belongs to Italian AOC member Domenico Paterlini. The only Allard to have competed in the original Mille Miglia was Sydney Allard's J2 in 1951, with dual mounts for Cadillac or Ardun engines.

An Allard L Type, chassis number 771, with an original 'LI' style body emerged in Monaco in 2008 when owner Alexander Edmonds purchased the car for restoration. This modified-body L Type was delivered new to Italy in 1948. Gabriele Fabrri, President of the Adriatic Veteran Cars Club

and until recently owner of the Hotel Promenade in Riccione, owned the 1947 K1, MBB 802.

Mauricio Marx's J2 keeps the Allard flame alive in São Paulo, Brazil. The late Tommy Steur from Bogotá owned a J2X and his sons Camillo and Thomas continue the tradition in Colombia, where three Allards are known to be 'live'. Bill Mallalieu has secured an Allard P1 for the Mallalieu Motor Collection and Car Museum in Hastings, Barbados.

ALLARDS IN AUSTRALASIA

Allards made it big in Australia from the start. Power and traction, allied to strong chassis and good ground clearance, meant that the Allard was soon a firm favourite with racer and rural farmer alike. At the time of writing, there are twenty-eight Allards known in Australia and fifteen in New Zealand.

Chris Lowth runs the Australian Allard section as Pacific region co-ordinator. An AOC Pacific Award was instigated in 2014 to better recognize the efforts of Allard owners and restorers 'down under'. The first recipient was Derek Maude, a K1 owner and P1 restorer. The famous competition Allard J1, originally HXC 578, owned by Peter Briggs, has an illustrious driver history. It was one of the three Allards in the 1946 London Cavalcade (see Chapter 3). It now forms part of the superb York Motor Museum in Western Australia, and has been celebrated in the booklet *Allard HXC 578: The White Challenger* (2016) by the museum's curator, Graeme Cocks.

Allards in Australia go way back. As early as 1953 a Ford-powered M2X owned by Ray Neely took part in the annual Redex Reliability Trial, which was a tough, long-distance 'race' around Australia sponsored by Redex, which became a major fixture in the Australian motoring calendar.

Neely's M2X drophead (chassis no. 2000), registered as ACN 408, was fitted with a micro-cell glassfibre one-piece bonnet. Near a remote town named Kingoonya, the car's torque tube broke at the weld where it joined the differential housing, but fortunately they found a local man with an arc welder. Neely's mechanic, Allen Ashcroft, welded the car up and they proceeded back onto the car-breaking corrugated ruts and stone tracks of the outback, heading south to the next stage at Adelaide. The M2X suffered several failures on the tough outback roads, but covered 6,500km on the Redex and completed the event into Sydney.

Ian McDonald's Cadillac-engined 1951 J2 (OLD 1691) was exhibited at Motorclassica 2014 in Melbourne's Royal Exhibition Building. Driven by his son Nick, the J2 achieved a 13.35 second run for the quarter-mile sprint at the 2016 Geelong Revival meeting. Graham Smith's Ardun Ford-engined J2, which MacDonald had raced in the 1960s, recorded 13.2

Stalwart AOC member Mark Butterworth races his Allards: J2, Palm Beach and K3 (shown here).

seconds. MacDonald's J2 was an original entrant in the 1956 Geelong Speed Trials and was invited to return for the sixtieth anniversary celebration.

Back in February 2005, the Australian Allardistes had a grand meeting at the Historic Race Meeting at Phillip Island, Australia's oldest racing circuit. Four Allards paraded in and were displayed in an 'Allard Corral'. Present were Steve Schuler's J2 (the 1950 Le Mans car driven by Sydney Allard

Allards gathered for the Historic Race Meeting on Phillip Island, Australia, 2005: (clockwise from left) P1X (Lowth), J2 (Sharley), PB (Lowth), K2 (Sharley), K2 (Schuler), J2 (Rodd), Special (Pearce), K3 (Calleja), J2R (Butler) and J2 (Smith). STUART GRANT

and Tom Cole), Graham Smith's J2 (raced in Australia since new), Graham Sharley's J2X and Dean Butler's JR (1953 ex-General Curtis LeMay Le Mans car), the last of which was shipped down to Australia for the event. Chris Lowth has also been giving a regular Allard 'display' at the annual Melbourne Albert Park Formula One Grand Prix meeting.

Tom Fisk, who was Sydney's navigator for six years, was based in Canberra after his return to his native Australia and supplied the local enthusiasts with many stories and old photos. Having met his wife-to-be Jean in England during his Allard days, which included driving with Sydney and then with Alan Allard, Tom was a BARC member and made a mark on British motor sport. He died in 2009, aged ninety-one, an Allard fan to the end.

J2 chassis number 1699 was built in January 1951 and delivered new to New South Wales in the rarely seen paint finish that some call 'Allard Blue', though it is more commonly known mistakenly as 'almost Bugatti Blue'. The car was restored and owned by Philip Stanton prior to new ownership in recent years.

Ian MacDonald's famed 'Aussie Allard' was a Cadillac-powered J2 owned by 'Gelignite' Jack Murray, who purchased it new in January 1951 from Gardiner's Motor Service, Sydney. Gardiner's fitted a competition Cadillac 331cu in engine. Murray was a successful rally and race driver, adventurer, sportsman and businessman. He used the car rarely and only for races in his home state of New South Wales. This Allard has been perhaps the most successful of the six J2s sold new in Australia. Murray later became involved in running the Jack Parker D-Type Jaguar, so he sold the Allard to friend and neighbour John William ('Bill') Firth in February 1957.

Firth ran the car on the street and in club events, sprints and hill climbs. In his hands the car ran 12 seconds for the quarter-mile at Castlereagh in the early 1960s. He fitted the Allard with an MG TC screen, soft top and side curtains for road use. He was interested in performance and later fitted a GMC 6-71 supercharger with two four-barrel Carter carburettors. In 1973 the car was taken off the road and stored.

Time-warp time – Prescott again sees assorted Allards line up in the paddock, keeping the cars and the legend alive.

In 1995 Bill Firth's brother Jim took over the car and commenced a restoration on the low mileage car, which was completed in 1998. The Cadillac engine is fitted with its original Edmunds custom inlet manifold with two Carter carbs and Mallory ignition. The car remained in the Firth family for fifty-four years and has travelled some 23,654 miles since new.

Other Australian Allards included a P1 in Sydney owned by Tom Morrison and Nick Bolton's K2, which has taken part in many Australian historic events including the Australian Historic Festival of Speed in 2000. Derek Maude's K1 took part in the RACV Great Australian Rally in 2006 and his P1 received an AOC Pacific Area award: Chris Lowth's P Type sadly expired in the 40°C heat. Despite this, three Allards made it to the finishing line to take the Best Post-War European Classic Trophy.

Among the leading lights of Australian Allardism we must cite Barry Ellison in Queensland, Derek Maude, David Underhill and long-time Allard owner Charles Wilkins, the nephew of 'Spitfire Girl' Mary Ellis (see above). Alan Naber from Perth was a J1 owner.

Chris Lowth modified his 1954 2263cc Zephyr-powered Palm Beach CH7633 (British registration NYO 66), which was tested by *Autocar* in 1954, to improve weak points such as the three-speed gearbox (adding an overdrive) and fitting improved (gas) shock absorbers, twin SU carburettors, power-assisted drum brakes and 15in wheels. Lowth's 'improved' Palm Beach was faster, more economical and had a top speed more than 25mph faster through the gears. Lowth also discarded the 'add-on' Allard waterfall grille and chrome trim on his P1 and, in a most successful styling tweak, used a differing frontal treatment around the nose-cone aperture.

This Palm Beach may have lacked the design features of the rival 1950s MGA, but it was nearer to a final production series idea of what the Palm Beach could have become. David Hooper said in 2012 that Lowth's car was now 'the production Allard should have made'.

There are also Allard enthusiasts across the Tasman Sea in New Zealand. A notable Allard there is the late Rob Boult's J2 (088), registered as JT 7618, which has a Moss gearbox. Its logbook carries the names of several well-known New Zealand drivers. It was originally purchased by George Smith, who won the New Zealand Hill Climb Championship with the car in 1952. The next owner was Frank Shuter (third in the 1952 Ohakea Trophy race), before passing through a series of owners up to 1979, when Rob Boult purchased it in Christchurch. In 1983 this J2 won its class in the Australian Cannon Ball run from Darwin to Ayres Rock/Uluru and back, covering more than 2,000 miles. The J2 was twelfth overall and was the oldest car to take part. Marty Strain was Rob's Allard fettler-engineer.

JT 7618 was later restored and fettled by the late Brian Middlemass, curator of the Queenstown Motor Museum, with further advice from Tom Carstens and Dave Fogg, both of whom raced J2s in the USA in the 1950s. Boult's J2 competed in many of the historic events in New Zealand, up to and beyond 2000. John Fernyhough, who himself owned a J Type, accompanied Boult on Allard days in New Zealand.

In 2008 a J2 featured on the poster for the Classic and Historic Race Meeting at the Timaru International Motor Raceway. David Hooper visited the New Zealand Allardistes during that year's events, as part of an Allard tour of New Zealand organized by Rob Boult and Barry Ellison, and watched Boult's Cadillac-powered J2 and Bill Boone's J2X in action on South Island. He also saw Kath Morrow's K1. In 2007 Boone had purchased Syd Silverman's Le Mans Allard JR (see Chapter 7).

Andy Leach has created a 'K1-style' roadster out of a modified P1 saloon body that, however 'non-original', actually represents a true spirit of Allard fettling and modification. Roy Savage of Wellington now owns Palm Beach 21Z chassis 5138.

Rob Williams bought his 1953 New Zealand-registered K1 in 1974 in Auckland. He said of the car:

It was in original condition having had twenty-five owners and about twenty coats of paint and was badly in need of restoration. The first step was to get it drivable, as it had no motor. Luckily I had a Mercury side-valve Ford V8 Coupé Deluxe, so I pulled it out and used it in the Allard. I liked driving the K so much that I postponed the restoration so that I could do some gravel hill climbs and grass track events.

Rob used the Allard to pull a trailer for his car bodywork repair business, and on one memorable occasion pulled the trailers with his Arnott, JAP Formula 3 car to race meetings with the Allard. Rob's car turned out to be a K Type 1.5 – that is it had a K1 chassis but had originally been fitted with a genuine K2 body sourced directly from Allards.

An unexpected 'hot rod' at Waikanae Beach was the P Type 'Special' that David Starling created in 2007 from the ruined remains of a 1951 P Type, chassis number 71. David ripped off the rotten body and fitted numerous competition parts, Jaguar components (notably Mk 10 rear suspension), a Chevrolet small block engine with 300bhp, and a disc conversion for the pre-war Ford axle (as used by hot-rodders). The result was a trials-type Special that Sydney would surely have approved of.

AOC CONVERSATIONS

The Allard owners have had long-running conversations about many aspects of Allard ownership. Such AOC conversations help owners deal with the consistent issues that are inevitable in any old car, not just an Allard. Issues with brakes, gearboxes, wheel bearings, fuel pumps, electrics, ash frames, propshafts, radiators, and the unavoidable Ford flat-head cooling and water pump issues populate the AOC's tales of Allard challenges.

How about tweaking the Ford V8's exhausts to improve running? And don't Allards run on a relatively low oil pressure, say 25–35lb? And surely keeping your radiator unblocked and your water pump and dynamo in top fettle will make for cooler running Ford engines?

The original Allard specification was for the radius rods to provide a critical function locating the de Dion tube fore and aft in the rear suspension and transmitting the forces of acceleration and deceleration in the chassis. Given that the original tubes must now be at least sixty years old, a rash of 'rusted-from-the-inside-out' failures in club members' cars has not been a surprise. Of course they failed when new too, as any outback Aussie with an Allard could tell you.

Use of the de Dion mounted axle gave rise to an issue with the universal joints. The need to transmit power smoothly via the joint (non-Cardan type) is that it is not a constant velocity joint and both joints must be at the same angle if they are to achieve such a state, which is hardly likely. The de Dion beam imposes a degree of asymmetric strain on the axle and drive forces. Some members wonder if these characteristics lie behind the differential, half shaft and hub problems sometimes encountered on the Allard.

It is also the case that Silentbloc steering bushes used to wear. Today a more complex and longer-wearing, phosphor-bronze-based material seems to have solve the problem of the idler arm bush wearing.

Tales of the Marles steering box abound. The nuances of the Marles design have occupied many pages in the club's publications with contributions from David Hooper, Dean Butler, Andy Picariello and many other commentators. There was disagreement over whether it was the Marles design that was the issue, the adjustment of the design or its maintenance.

The headline to David Hooper's article in the AOC *Newsletter* of July 2008 referred to 'The Much Maligned Marles'. Was Sydney's early commitment to this design an error? Or was it clever because of the unique, patented mechanism by which a worm and cam action translated the steering wheel's rotation to a drop arm via a roller action that was supposed to give minimal wear?

In the context of its time, Hooper was among many to suggest the Marles design was a direct and effective steering that transferred input and 'feel' far better than contemporary mechanisms then available: the recirculating ball type, with its so-called improved characteristics, would only be accepted later in automotive use, while rack and pinion was expensive and exotic stuff for Allard, a bit like double wishbone multi-link suspension.

Yet experience over decades has proved that wear ensues if oil drains from the Marles box. Fifty years on, can synthetic or multi-formula lubrication oils or greases make matters better or worse for Marles? Maintenance was the Marles issue: unless regularly checked and serviced, it, like so many earlier mechanical aspects of engineering, suffered wear. At the time when the Marles design was being used cars still had chassis and suspension grease nipples. Adding too many 'shims', another 'old' practice, also denuded the Marles's efficiency. Some suggested machining the worm ball tracts and fitting special assemblies. Despite all these ideas, however, it appears that Lubrimatic 11302 with lithium grease is the thing to use on the Marles steering box.

During Sunday morning practice at the Angoulême street race Patrick Watts had the misfortune to be a victim of the infamous J2 'bonnet lift'. Strapped in and with his vision blocked by the piece of vertical and bent aluminium, Patrick's practice session came to an abrupt end. Across the years many new and latter AOC owners' J2s have fallen victim to this phenomenon, which is thought to be the result of high-speed airflow being unable to escape from under the bonnet.

The AOC has made many friends over the years and one such is the Early Ford V8 Club. There are many variants of flat-head Fords and the design has many followers. Neil 'Biggles' Bennett is a respected name in flat-head Ford racing and he has been one of the fastest men in hill climbing using such machinery. In the 1960s Bennett restored a P1 (chassis number P2288), registered as NLN 922. The car was damaged beyond repair of the alloy bodywork in a crash in 1964, so a Special was created. This was an open-cockpit roadster-type with two small rear seats in a 2 × 1in mahogany rear section and various additions such as a Morris windscreen frame. Bennett also purchased Ardun heads and a McCulloch supercharger for the Allard special, by then known as 'Boz'. It was impossible to fit the Ardun heads to the car, so they were swapped for a racing engine built by Tom Hutchinson. The supercharger was fitted, however, and as Neil Bennett told the AOC in 2012, 'much fun was had'. Eventually the car was abandoned after it overheated. A 'Boz 2' came along in later years.

Such was the stuff of an owners club and the many conversations it inspired.

ALLARD DIVERSIFIES

1964 and the televised event at Brands Hatch, where invited competitors from the recently completed Monte Carlo Rally battled it out in snow and slush. Sydney is seen here leading Pat Moss and Eric Carlsson in his Saab. Eric signed this photograph for Gavin Allard at the Goodwood Festival of Speed.

CHAPTER 9 | ALLARD DIVERSIFIES

AS THE DECADE OF THE 1950S PASSED its midpoint, Allard's situation began to appear uncertain. The car market – its demands, its fashions, its needs – all began to change. Add in the Suez crisis and fuel rationing, and then, after constriction, an expansion of the car market, and the question arose of how Allard and its cars would evolve into this new era.

In 1953 the Allard Motor Company manufactured 138 cars, which was down from a high of 441 cars in 1948. In 1954, however, this had fallen to only thirty-four cars. The writing was on the wall for the company: it needed to diversity and find new projects in order to keep going. The larger car manufacturers were getting their act together and productionizing the process of building cars. Donald Healey had done a deal with Austin to produce the Austin-Healey, while MG and Triumph were coming on strong with new models.

Sydney could see that he would need to raise substantial sums of money in order to manufacture a cost-effective car, and bring his scattered sites together to build cars under one roof, but he was not able or willing to do this. In addition, his Ford dealership was doing well and expanding as the Allard Motor Company declined. From 1957 onwards Sydney was looking for lines of business so that the remaining Allard workforce might make use of the works area. Some of these ventures were profitable, but others were not. They included the Clipper, the Atom dirt track car, the LCC ambulance conversion, Golde sunroofs, Shorrock superchargers, Allardette conversions and the motor accessory shop. But Sydney wanted to keep the Allard business going, so diversification was essential.

ALLARD CLIPPER, 1954

Throughout 1954 the Allard development team were struggling with ideas for a new economy car to be known as the Clipper. Testing was carried out on several different engines, but none could give the desired performance with the advertised economy.

The Clipper was a concept designed for the specific context of post-war 1950s austerity. Ideas for economy cars like the Clipper were springing up all over the place, drawing upon the pre-war German three-wheelers that were experiencing a resurgence in 1950s Germany, which was itself suffering economically.

Lightweight, two- or three-seat vehicles, many of them home-built specials, based on a three-wheel chassis with twin-pot engines, were all the rage in the mid-1950s. These were effectively motorbikes with bodies and three wheels to add to the confusion. The Bond Company was a leading purveyor of 'micro-cars', and even AC came up with the 'Petite'. Only Reliant would go on to make money from the three-wheeler austerity car concept in Britain. The Mini had given way to the 'Swinging Sixties' and the rise of chrome-embellished modernism of pressed steel, vinyl-roofed, plastic-coated and swage-lined fashion.

The Clipper's three-wheeled configuration, with a single front wheel leading, was powered by a Villiers 24B 346cc single-cylinder two-stroke and the resultant noise, vibration and smoke was entirely of its time. The gears were actuated by a right-hand side-mounted gear lever.

The concept for the car was not an Allard idea, but came to them via a pre-existing project run by David Gottlieb and the Powerdrive company, who had investigated a front-driven motorcycle concept and who had envisaged an economy car prototype design that would be sold through a

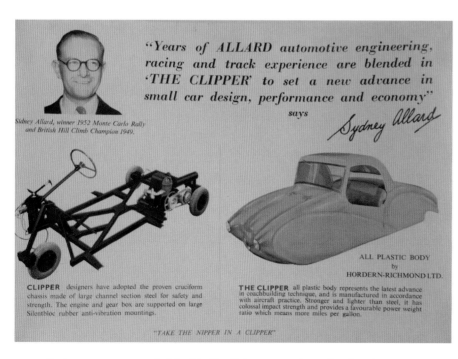

Sydney was persuaded by Mr Gotlieb to complete the development of the plans for a micro car, the Clipper. Unfortunately the project had to be cancelled due to excessive engineering costs.

north London outlet. Gottlieb is said to have 'styled' the Clipper himself.

The car was wide enough to seat two or three on a 48in front bench seat with a boot-mounted fold-out 'dickey' seat for children. It had a large windscreen and a capacious moulded hardtop-style roof that was also available in duo-colour. No rollover protection was offered and the crash-worthiness of glassfibre construction, or its lack, was unresearched and probably not considered. Aerodynamics would be a further unlikely issue at the speeds the Clipper might dizzyingly attain: 40mph.

The Clipper used as many 'off the shelf' parts as possible to save development costs. Underneath the glassfibre shell was a strong girder-frame cruciform chassis. Suspension was by independent swing arms. Allard's men, principally Gil Jepson, were tasked with turning the Clipper into a car that could be marketable in preparation for production in collaboration with Powerdrive Ltd. The glassfibre body would have the colour within the gel coat. The body was to be built by Hordern and Richmond of Haddenham, which had experience in aviation structures and the new-fangled glassfibre or plastic material. Difficulties getting the moulds to work properly were to prove financially disadvantageous to the whole project. Instead of making a dummy body buck from which to take moulds, individual panels were laid up and then joined together. Although not a convertible, the add-on roof panels looked like a *de facto* hardtop – but it was not meant to be removable.

Early Clipper prototype cars had no side doors and access was inelegant for ladies, but forwards-hinged opening doors are clearly shown in some of the sketches for the car. Clippers were one-piece shells, but at least one later built car had a completely separate front-end moulding that was a hinged front body similar in style to those used on certain Allards. Leather straps restrained at each front wing secured the front-hinged front body moulding.

The Clipper had deeply cut-down side panels, meaning that unless fitted with a side window panel the cabin was likely to be a cold, wet and draughty place in the prevailing English weather. The car was to cost just £267, so margins for design, engineering error and rectification were tight.

Unusually for vehicles of this type, the Clipper had Lockheed hydraulic brakes, Nieghart trailing-arm suspension, a 12-volt electrical system (upgraded from the 6 volts originally specified) and numerous features of 1950s modernism. The bobbin and cable-actuated steering system was an austerity step too far and a Burman-type steering box mechanism was submitted during the development of the car that Allard were contracted to undertake.

A triple V-belt drive coupled the throbbing little engine to the gearbox. Drive was to the left-hand rear wheel only, which gave rise to asymmetric traction in left-hand bends, not least when only the driver's seat was occupied.

The Clipper was first framed by a British patent application, number 654,325, registered on 22 October 1948 by David Gottlieb and filed by Cymo (Cycle Motor) Limited of 364–365 Kensington High Street, London WI. Gottlieb was not a newcomer to design and Sydney obviously took him seriously, but the Clipper was a car of its era and, in hindsight, a design that somehow Sydney was persuaded to invest in. It is not known if Sydney ever thought about how his big-car customers would react to the company producing an economy car of such a poverty-level specification, but the need for money and new projects was a more immediate priority. Maybe the mood and mindset of the era got the better of him, since the market for a successful cheap car for the masses was huge.

Issues with the Villiers engine led to testing with a revvy little 322cc Anzani twin-pot, which was much smoother in operation, but the charging rate of its 'dynastarter' mechanism was to prove inadequate for the electrical demands of the Clipper. A JAP engine option was suggested but not developed.[22]

Allard were to manufacture the car through the Encon Motors subsidiary operation in Fulham, but the reality was that the 1954 Clipper was to Allard what the 2012 Cygnet was to Aston Martin – doomed to sink. Allard's advertisements for the Clipper, however, depicted a strangely upmarket, elongated depiction of the Clipper as a sleek and curvaceous car of grand proportions in upper-class settings, including a view of the Clipper at an airport with a Lockheed Constellation, which was hardly the 'aspirant' world of the three-wheeler micro-car buyers. We can only assume that potential 'moneyed' customers were shocked when they saw the real thing in all its truncated glory. The Clipper was available in gel-coloured maroon or blue, both with white roofs, or an all-white ivory hue. Allard's advertising also talked about chassis safety and 'indestructible' glassfibre, all in a sub-400kg, three-wheeled car with one-wheel drive.

The first bodyshell was delivered to Allard on 15 March 1954, yet the project is reputed to have stalled within a year at the non-delivery of a bodyshell amid associated build-cost issues. The first Clipper was registered one month later on 15 April 1954. How many actually reached a customer is difficult to know. A run of 100 cars was originally agreed but never achieved. We know that the Clipper was developed with prototypes of varying specifications. All achieved running status, yet ultimately this bizarre micro-car project went nowhere. Only three Clippers are known to exist today.

The Allard Clipper Company commissioned a beautiful painting of a long, lithe, elegant red Clipper set amidst English 'cottage' countryside with an elegantly dressed upper middle-class mother seeing off her husband and son in their red-bodied, white-roofed Allard Clipper. A '70mpg' strapline boasted of the car's economy and that the body was modern and manufactured 'in accordance with aviation practice', which seems to be stretching the point.

The line 'Take the nipper in a Clipper' was also used in adverts that offered the car for sale at 255 guineas (£267.75).

Sydney Allard appeared in the advertisements claiming that 'Years of Allard automotive engineering, racing and track experience are blended in The Clipper to set a new advance in small car design, performance and economy'. The car in the adverts, however, was a far cry from the physical reality of the Clipper.

ALLARD ATOM, 1955

Ronnie Greene, the manager of Wimbledon Speedway, approached Sydney with the idea of building a Midget speedway race car, using the same JAP engine as used in the dirt track motorcycles. He took up the idea and agreed to build a prototype. Gil Jepson was employed to build the car, which was known as the Atom.

If the Allard Clipper was to be a strange and erroneous diversion, the Atom was surely something far more Allard. Stemming from 1955, the Atom was an idea for a motorcycle-inspired, speedway-type lightweight racer – almost a modern version of the Edwardian 'Light' car concept. Greene talked to Sydney about a small 500cc car, suggesting that it used the JAP engine. The idea was to create a four-wheeled version of the motorcycle speedway sport.

A midget car was then created at the Encon Works in Fulham, with 13in wheels, the requisite JAP 500cc motorcycle engine pushing out nearly 50bhp and inspiration from

Sydney's blue biro in a series of sketches. At this time the device had no name ('Atom' came later). The car was highly responsive, with a 54in wheelbase and 'fast' steering, as well as being 'twitchy'. The whole idea was to get the car broadsiding in oversteer – drifting in today's parlance.

No brakes were specified, just as with the speedway motorcycles, and the steering system was lifted from a small Ford. The little car's specification involved a chain drive to a solid back axle hung from the U-section steel channelled chassis, from which the engine and direct-drive clutch were directly mounted. Built by Gil Jepson, the car was fitted with pressed steel wheels from the Ford Anglia 100E (12in front, but 13in rear). The front axle was a stock Ford item using stub-axles and quarter-inch in elliptic springs with radius locating rods, somewhat akin to the early Frazer Nash style.[23]

The Atom was ready for track testing in June. All you needed to do was pour in fuel and light the blue touchpaper. The 1954 world speedway champion Ronnie Moore did just that and completed several very competitive laps. Unfortunately the four-wheeled Midget car, unlike the two-wheeled bikes, dug into the cinder track, making it unbalanced and liable to turn over. Moore rolled the Atom over and broke his collar bone. The car had a 'dummy' headrest-fairing, but there was no roll bar. The car was repaired and testing at the speedway circuit continued in the hands of Moore and other speedway riders, but in the end the Atom did not explode into a dominant device or a single-series formula. Further tests were abandoned and another loss-making venture went no further. 'Midget' car racing of this type took off in America, though not in Britain, but somehow Allard's little device was not involved and only two Atoms (or perhaps three) were constructed at Fulham (the first chassis being damaged during the demonstration at Wimbledon).

John Pitney, who had worked at Allards in Estcourt Road, rebuilt an Allard Atom for a customer in 1999–2000. Ronnie Moore came back from New Zealand to drive the car at the Wembley speedway event in September 2000.

ALLARD AMBULANCE CONVERSION, 1957–60

During the fuel shortages caused by the Suez crisis the Allard company's prospects were at a low point, but in early 1957 an enquiry was received from the London County Council (LCC), which was in the process of designing a more comfortable and manageable ambulance to replace the fleet of 200 or so heavy old Daimlers. The engineer in charge at the LCC workshops, which were only a couple of miles from the Allard works at Putney, had seen the Allard de Dion axle and

Ronnie Moore, world speedway champion testing the Allard Atom Midget on the cinder track at Wimbledon.

218

suspension arrangement and thought it could give the ambulance a lower floor because the differential was bolted to the chassis, so additional clearance was not needed between floor and axle to allow for axle movement. The independent rear suspension with coil springs could also give patients a softer, more comfortable ride.

The Morris light commercial 2LD 1½ ton chassis was chosen and the de Dion axle conversion was similar in many ways to the Allard P2 layout. The first few conversions were carried out at Southside, then delivered to the LCC workshops to have the glassfibre body fitted and integrated behind the standard steel cab. Once the conversion had been fully tested on the road in service as an ambulance, Allard received confirmation of the order to convert all 200 vehicles. To avoid the cost of stripping and cutting standard vehicles before conversion, and due to the size of the order, the LCC was able to persuade the vehicle's manufacturer to deliver the parts in CKD kit form.

The conversion proved very successful and further orders were received from other municipal authority ambulance departments around the country. Orders for kits also came from the Crown Agents in Hong Kong.

Once the large order to convert the complete fleet had been confirmed, space was made to install the conversions at the Upper Richmond Road works, transferring the remaining Allard service and parts sales to Keswick Road and merging this into the Adlards business. Bill Tylee was then put in charge as manager of all LCC conversion work at Upper Richmond Road from late 1957 until completion of the work towards the end of 1960.

SUNROOF CONVERSIONS

As the 1960s dawned and the fuel rationing crisis came to end, the motor trade suddenly woke up. Car sales were soon booming and a market for sunroof conversions started to grow. Allards were looking for work to keep loyal car trimmers employed, so Allards became a fitting agent for Webasto sunroofs. Business soon became brisk, but Webasto were dropped when there were supply shortages from the company and Allard became a fitting agent for the Golde Sunroof Company. The kits were imported from Germany, but the wooden ash frames were machined at Hiltons by men who previously made ash frames for Allard car bodies.

When the LCC ambulance contract had come to an end, and with car accessory sales increasing, the Golde sunroof department moved over to the workshop at the rear of Upper Richmond Road, Putney. Percy Barwood took over from Bill Tylee as workshop manager when Bill, after many

years of service to the company, retired. Bob Day was sales manager for the sunroof section. The Allard/Golde sunroof business expanded to fill most of the works and the fitters

Golde sliding sun roofs were very popular. These were fitted by some of the original Allard Motor Company employees, who stayed with the company after car manufacture had finished.

Sydney with Alan and Rob Mackie ready for the 1964 Monte at the Allard Performance Centre and sun roof fitting workshops.

were very busy for years, right up to the time after Sydney's death, when the family decided to sell Adlards Motors as a going concern.

ALLARDETTE FORD ANGLIAS

The idea for the name 'Allardette' came from James Watt, a motor enthusiast who had previously been a sales manager for Aston Martin. He approached Sydney back in 1958, at a time when the company was looking for new business and car manufacturing had come to an end. Watt thought that there was a market for what we would now call 'customizing' a small Ford saloon. He chose an Anglia 100E: the new Anglia 105E was not announced until towards the end of 1959. Adlards Motors lent him a car for a few weeks to see what he could do with it.

When it was returned with Allardette badges and bodywork modifications, it can only be described as bizarre. At the rear it had tail fins with orange plastic windows set into them, and at the front it had large hoods above the headlamps, which added more drag to an already slow car. Perspex covers were later added in an attempt to reduce the drag, but it was still a struggle to reach a top speed of 72mph. Finally it had two-tone paintwork with a black roof and salmon pink body. Needless to say, James Watt's services were not sought again.

The idea for the name had been sown, however, and a couple of years later, after the launch of the Anglia 105E, it was decided to market a modified Anglia as an Allardette.

In September 1960 the Allard Motor Company issued a press release revealing the sad news that the company had ceased car manufacturing and would no longer be taking orders for new cars. In fact, the last car had left the works in 1958.

The Allardette modifications applied to the Ford Anglia comprised a C75B Shorrock supercharger, front wheel disc brakes, an additional anti-roll bar and anti-tramp bars. There was also a long list of optional extra tuning parts.

From 1961 the Allardette components and conversions based on the Ford 105E Anglia were developed. In 1962 the 997cc Shorrock supercharged Allardette was FIA homologated, shortly followed by the 1198cc naturally aspirated version.

The Allardettes were sold as either complete converted cars from Adlards Motors, or as a conversion kit from Allard. More cars and conversions were sold when the 1340cc engine became available with the announcement of the new Ford Classic, followed by the 1500 GT engine when the Cortina GT appeared in 1962.

The very first Allardette, based on a side-valve 1172cc Ford 100E, at the start of the Pilgrim Rally, 1958. Note the rallying dress code of the time, with Alan Allard (then 18 years old), Mike Thomas and Rob Mackie all wearing ties.

Sydney, with co-driver Tom Fisk, drove a group one 105E Anglia in both the 1961 and 1962 Monte Carlo rallies, although the modified Allardette Anglias were not yet homologated and so approved for this event. Alan also entered the Monte Carlo in 1962 with co-driver Rob Mackie in an almost standard 105E Anglia.

My old friend Rob Mackie and I both drove Allardettes in a muddy rallycross at Brands Hatch in February 1963 alongside famous names like Carlsson, Moss, Makinen and Hopkirk, in the first ever televised rallycross event.

In 1963 we started fitting the 1498cc Cortina GT engine, together with the larger C142B Shorrock supercharger, raising power output to 128bhp at 6,000rpm. I spent the 1963 season racing at various circuits around the country in a modified Allardette setup with this engine. It proved quite competitive. John Young, one of the most successful Anglia racers, bored and stroked the engine and managed to increase capacity to 1720cc, I believe. We went on to develop the supercharged engine for my Dragon Dragster, which delivered 175bhp running on methanol. With further development, it could have produced much more power, as I did with the Allard drag racing Anglia (Dragoon) a couple of years later.

The Allardette Anglias were driven in the 1964 Liège–Sofia rally. At that time this event was the longest, roughest and toughest rally in Europe and possibly in the world, with ninety hours of almost continuous driving, there being only a one-hour rest stop in Sofia, the capital city of Bulgaria. In fact, the rally regulations said we had ninety-six hours to complete the race (rally?), but when you

Alan Allard in supercharged Allardette Anglia – chases 'Doc' Merfield in the Lotus Cortina Twin Cam through the chicane at Goodwood in 1963.

The Monte, 1963. Alan and Rob Mackie slide their way down the notorious Col de Turini with its many lacets (hairpin bends) in a 997cc Shorrock-supercharged Allardette Anglia. Studded tyres were an essential fitting.

1964 Racing Car Show.

added up all the times for the rally stages, total time allowed was only ninety hours, which turned the return leg into a race across Europe, where anything went if you wanted to finish within the time limit getting back to Liège.

SHORROCK SUPERCHARGERS

Shorrock superchargers entered the Allard story in 1959 when one or two Shorrock superchargers were fitted to diesel engines to improve performance and fuel consumption. This led to Sydney holding a meeting with Chris Shorrock and the Rubery Owen Company, who had recently acquired Shorrock Superchargers Ltd. In September 1960 it was announced that Allard would become the sole marketing agent for Shorrock superchargers worldwide.

Although Allard had previously marketed a few engine tuning parts for Ford cars, this marked the start of a new venture for the much-reduced Allard Company, marketing motor accessories and tuning equipment for Ford cars and Shorrock supercharger kits for a whole range of vehicles.

Allard Motor Accessory Catalogue first edition was produced in 1963

**Alan's book 'Turbocharging & Supercharging'
first published in 1982.**

The showroom at the front of the workshops became the Allard Performance Centre, mainly for Ford cars, supplying and fitting the conversion kits for the Allardette Anglia, Shorrock supercharger conversion kits and a wide range of motor accessories. Supercharger kits were sold for a range of popular saloons and sports cars from 1960 through to 1976.

Gerry Belton joined Allards in 1961 as marketing and publicity manager and instituted widespread advertising and special events, such as hiring Brands Hatch circuit for a day for journalists and others to test a range of supercharged cars. Supercharger kit sales grew, even reaching seventy-five kits in one month, which was surprising for such a specialist and comparatively expensive conversion kit.

The supercharged 997cc Allardette Anglia was FIA homologated in 1962 in time for Sydney and me to each enter a supercharged Allardette in the 1963 Monte. Both cars completed the course, Sydney finishing in thirty-third place and me in fifty-first out of some 350 starters and 200 finishers.

With any other engine modifications the Shorrock supercharger installation increased engine torque considerably on an engine that had very little torque in its standard form. Power was increased from only 39bhp to around 72bhp at the same maximum rpm with the supercharger.

1967–2008

By 1967, the Allard Motor Company had shrunk to a skeleton of its former size and was effectively partly absorbed into the growing Ford Dealership, Adlards Motors Ltd.

By 1969, the decision was made to sell Adlards Motors. When the sale was completed I managed to hold onto the Allard Motor Company business and continued trading, marketing supercharger conversions and Ford Motor accessories, from the Performance Centre, 1 Upper Richmond Road, Putney, until we moved away from London in 1976.

The Allard business continued trading from various locations, turning its attention away from superchargers to the rapidly developing turbocharging market, becoming a specialist in aftermarket turbo conversions over the following years. My book *Turbocharging & Supercharging* was first published in 1982. I continued the motor accessory and special tuning conversion business, being joined by my son Lloyd in 1993, until I took a back seat in 2008 and handed the reins over to Lloyd.

Like myself and his grandfather, Lloyd has competed in many national and international motor sports events. Competing many times in an Allard turbocharged diesel VW, in the UK and Germany, on the famous Nürburgring circuit. This included a 24-hour race ending in a spectacular crash, when he lost a front wheel and brake assembly, which disappeared into the woods, setting fire to the surrounding forest.

SPORTS CARS – RESTORATION AND REVIVAL

New JR chassis 3408

CHAPTER 10

ALLARD SPORTS CARS – RESTORATION AND REVIVAL

THE ORIGINAL ALLARD MOTOR COMPANY LIM-ITED was struck off the limited companies register in 1985 through non-use, because the Allard business had been carried on as a sole trader since 1975.

In 1987, however, the engineer Christopher Humberstone put forward a proposal to start building new Allard cars and came to the Allard office in Coleford, together with Peter Goodwin, to discuss reviving the once-famous Allard brand.

In August 1988 the Allard Motor Company Limted was re-registered for the purpose of manufacture of motor cars: the four directors were Alan Allard, Christopher Humberstone (Secretary), Peter Goodwin and Leslie Thacker.

The plan laid out by Chris was for the manufacture of several new models of Allard cars, including a new P Type and a J92, closely related in style to the 1952 J2X.

The cars were to be built in substantial numbers – 500 units per year was proposed – which was very ambitious indeed. There were doubts about the project's viability, a few months later, when Chris announced that they would need several million pounds of investment to get everything up and running.

After a further two years and many meetings trying to raise funds, without success, Chris came up with the idea of getting Toyota interested by building an Allard-modified 'Allard-Lexus', rather in the way that Lotus had done with Ford when the Lotus-Cortina was produced.

By 1991 Chris's attention had shifted towards building an Allard World Sports Car Championship racing car. This escapade rather diverted attention away from the Allard cars project, which in itself was overambitious and not sufficiently realistic.

By 1995 I had decided that the Allard business was not developing or going the way he would have liked, so I resigned from the company; Chris followed a few months later.

A signed agreement states that the Company 'Allard' and its directors would have to manufacture a minimum of three new Allard cars within three years. If this was not achieved, the Allard trade mark would automatically return solely to me. The attempt to get Toyota interested also fizzled out. After I resigned two or three Lexus LS200 cars were cosmetically modified, but nothing was changed mechanically.

An attempt was made to publicize and pass off the three Toyotas as new P3 Allards, but they were obviously not new Allard cars by any stretch of the imagination. All the cars were DVLA registered as Toyota LS200 cars and bore no resemblance to the completely new Allards planned by Humberstone. Some years later Lloyd Allard purchased one

of these cars and inspected it thoroughly. Nothing mechanically had been changed from the original Toyota specification.

After years of expensive legal haggling, the question of who owned the Allard trade mark has finally been resolved and the mark is now securely in the hands of the Allard family.

ALLARD GROUP 'C' SPORTS RACING CAR (J92)

In 1990 Chris Humberstone met Costas Los and Jean-Louis Ricci, two racing drivers with considerable financial backing from their families. It was at this time he decided, independently with Los and Ricci, to form Allard Motorsport in order to build a racing Group C sports car to compete in the World Sports Car Championship. More than £375,000 is believed to have been spent in setting up a new factory and building this one racing car. After nearly two years of work, a spectacular racing car appeared.

Against my wishes, Chris wanted to call it the new Allard J2X early in its development.

I made many visits to the factory in Basingstoke during the course of the build, where some dozen people were involved in the work. The car's autoclaved carbon fibre monocoque assembly was a work of art. An innovative feature at that time for a 'sports car' was the suspension mountings being directly built into the monocoque.

An F1 3.5-litre DFV engine was installed, but it was designed to take other high performance engines if required.

I watched the car performing in the wind tunnel, complete with moving floor, to simulate airflow underneath the car, which is extremely important in such a high-performance machine. In fact the downforce figures generated were so 'good' that Chris quoted, 'We think we have designed one of the most efficient race car chassis ever built. We should have so much downforce that spectators should not be too surprised to see Allard drivers wearing G-suits.'

The new 'Allard' was certainly at the leading edge of body and chassis design at that time, but the results of track testing at various circuits, Le Mans in particular, were disappointing. Maybe there was just too much downforce. Then to cap it all, the class regulations changed and the sponsors lost interest, so the project came to an abrupt end – the car eventually being sold without ever achieving any significant results.

The Allard J92 race car, powered by a Ford DFV V8, was built by Chris Humberstone and his team in 1992 for the World Sports Car Championship. The futuristic body was designed in a wind tunnel.

CONTINUATION

After discussion and co-promotion with several Allard business ventures over a period of thirty-five years, some of which have resulted in manufacture of a few modern J2X 'lookalike' cars, the Allard family formed a new company, Allard Sports Cars, to revive the Allard car marque and manufacture authentic Allard cars.

The last Allard car to be manufactured, a Palm Beach Mk II, was produced in the Allard Motor Company's works at Clapham Common. One of only two believed to be extant in the UK, this Palm Beach Mk II was registered as 545 EXR, chassis number 72/7000Z and built on 15 October 1956. It was that year's Earl's Court Motor Show display car, and the following year it was used as a works demonstrator by Brian Howard, a manager at the Allard Motor Company. From 1969 it was in the ownership of the Hemsworth family.

John Peskett heard about the car and it was acquired in 2012 for restoration by Alan and Lloyd, with the assistance of former staff from the Allard factory and several very committed AOC members. The eighteen-month process saw a massive restoration of its chassis and body for what had been an open-stored car. The 2553cc Ford Zodiac-engined car, authentically rebuilt, was snapped up at auction for just under £100,000.

It was not until the 1980s that more interest in Allard, as a marque and its cars, began to push up residual values of the cars, with the J2 and J2X series heading the investment potential. This trend was assisted by active club members in the UK and the USA, where the Allard profile remained high. Recent J2 series prices hover around half a million dollars, and nearly three-quarters of a million was asked for an original one-off J2 development car. A, P, M or L Type with no particular history, however, can still be purchased for less than £30,000. K Types can reach £80,000, so breaking the magic $100,000 barrier.

Road test reports, reprints and magazine articles continued across the major motoring media titles throughout the 1980s and 1990s and into the new millennium.

Since about 2000 the collectability of original Allards, as cars worthy of expensive restoration, has gathered pace. As a consequence, very few have been lost or scrapped in this period, and those with competition history are especially prized. Interest in classic cars and the resulting rise in their value has been rapidly expanding in recent years, given added impetus by trends in the world financial markets. This particularly applies to rare and competition-related vehicles made in limited numbers.

In the current classic car world of 'matching numbers' and '100 points', many cars have been 'restored' to resemble

Allard J3 prototype rolling chassis, made by Lloyd Allard with a Jaguar 3.4-litre engine.

more-than-perfect, plastic-dipped, vinyl-trimmed 'replicas' of the original car, in which all the patination and the very soul and story of a car have been wiped away by obsessed 'restorers'. This has resulted in a huge 'restoration versus preservation' debate. Some people, especially in America, may have been far too keen to restore old cars to the point of oblivion, ending up with a pastiche of what once left the factory decades before. With Allard this does not tend to happen too often, not least because some Allards left the factory in part-completed state so that their new overseas owners could then finish off the car.

The point is that Allards differed significantly in specification, build and equipment when they were new. Some were even refurbed 'new' cars that had already competed in a major event. Others were never 'kit' cars in the latterly perceived idiom, but they were part-constructed and then delivered to a dedicated overseas original owner to fettle and tweak to their exact personal specification, often for racing and rallying. This means that a definitive modern 'show standard' consistent factory-spec never really existed for some Allards, which seems very liberating and typically Allard!

ALLARD CAR COPIES

Replica, continuation, evocation, reincarnation, lookalike cars – many names have been used to describe examples of cars built by individuals or companies that copy the original body profile of the authentic car. A true replica would be built in every detail to the designed specification of the original car model.

Over the years since the Allard Motor Company ceased manufacturing cars in 1959, there have been six or more attempts to build copies of Allards. Apart from one or two specials, all focussed on the iconic J2/J2X, but only one of those behind these ventures negotiated with the Allard family, with a view to manufacturing an exact copy – a true replica of a J2X. This was John Ould, based in Victoria, Australia, back in 1991.

All the others made no attempt at copying the J2X chassis, so they are not true replicas. They have just copied the iconic J2 or J2X body profile and, in addition, the body is formed in composite plastic-type materials, not aluminium as all original 'J' types were.

We should separate the building an Allard J2 or J2X to the original specification and clothed in a correctly built aluminium body, from all the other 'copy' cars. The Allard family and the Allard Company are prepared to consider authenticating these cars

All other copy cars, however well presented, are not authentic Allard cars. They are plastic-bodied kit type cars, that under the skin, are largely constructed from off the shelf, widely available car components. The chassis is usually built from box-section steel and is similar to what can be seen on other hot rods and unlike any authentic Allard chassis. The Allard family, the Allard Company, the Allard Owners Club and the Allard Register will not authenticate, sanction or recognize any of these copies.

REVIVAL OF THE ALLARD MARQUE

As the classic car market became a multi-billion pound global movement, it seemed only right for the Allard name to be carefully revived via a series of authentic continuation cars in a strictly controlled scenario. After discussion and negotiations with a number of potential Allard car building ventures over a period of some thirty years, the Allard family decided that the growing interest worldwide in continuation classic cars meant that the time was right to revive Allard as a sports car manufacturer.

The new Allard cars are true, authentic Allard cars, actually built by the family. The cars are being built almost exactly to the original specification of Allards from the 1950–60 period and to similar but updated specifications which were discussed and planned by the Allard Company at that time – but never actually produced by the time manufacture ceased in late 1958. Some way further down the line are plans to build completely new models.

It was not until the 1980s that more interest in Allard as

a marque and its cars began to push up residual values of the cars, with the JR and J2X series heading the investment potential. This trend was assisted by active Allard Owner Clubs and club members in the UK and in the USA, where the Allard profile remained so high.

Road test reports, reprints and magazine articles continued across the major motoring media titles throughout the 1980s and the 1990s, and beyond the Millennium.

In the last 15–20 years, the collectability of original Allards, as cars worthy of expensive restoration, has gathered pace. As a consequence, very few have been lost or scrapped in this period and those with competition history are especially prized. Interest and consequent rise in the value of classic cars has been rapidly expanding in recent years and has now been given impetus by the trends in world markets and the move towards electric cars.

The first car, an Allard JR with continuation chassis number 3408, has been hand-built by Lloyd and Alan Allard (grandson and son of Sydney) and their team, with support from Dudley Hume, the original designer, and David Hooper, chief engineer at Allards, and many knowledgable Allard owners and club members worldwide.

This sports racing car is a copy of the Cadillac V8-engined JR that was built for Sydney Allard to race in the 1953 Le Mans 24 Hours. Only seven JR cars were manufactured between 1953 and 1955 (chassis numbers 3401–3407). All seven cars were still in existence in 2017 and those with a significant racing history are especially prized and valued at more than £500,000.

The Allard Sports Car Company was formed with plans to revive the manufacture of authentic classic Allard cars, bridging the sixty years since the last Allard car was pro-

The new, authentic Allard JR – chassis number 3408 – follows on from JR chassis number 3407, built in 1955. This is the chassis frame.

duced by the Allard Motor Company in 1958. Plans are underway also for new models.

The J2 and J2X 'Caddy' Allards were race-winning cars, ahead of the field between 1950 and 1952. Carroll Shelby, later famous for his AC Cobra cars, gained most of his early racing experience in an Allard J2. It is not surprising that the J Type Allards were a benchmark for the Cobra, which came to prominence a few years later.

An Allard J3 was proposed in 1954 by the Allard Motor Company and a tubular chassis was designed and drawn, but production did not take place before the Allard Company ceased car manufacture in 1958. The proposed new J3 has a redesigned tubular chassis and front suspension, but the car retains the de Dion arrangement at the rear. Inboard discs replace the Al-Fin drums and there are also discs at the front. A new emission-compliant 6.2-litre GMC V8, producing over 400bhp, is installed, together with a six-speed manual transmission.

Rack and pinion steering replaces the old Marles box. The front and rear suspension employ coil spring-over-damper, with top wishbone and a lower link, an anti-roll bar and, at the rear, twin parallel radius rods and a Watts linkage type arrangement.

Two body styles can be mounted on this chassis. The first body (all aluminium) is an updated development retaining much of the original iconic J2X body profile but with distinctive features, in particular the twin 'fairings' behind both driver and passenger seats.

The second model with this same base chassis is the Allard Palm Beach Mk 3. This has an aluminium body that is essentially the same as the 1956 Palm Beach Mk II, but with updated features.

The Allard continuation cars, unlike the 'lookalike' Allards built by other business ventures since 1985, are true authentic Allard cars actually built by the Allard family. The cars are being built to almost exactly the original specification of factory Allards from

JR assembly in works.

JR bodyshell.

the 1950 to 1960 period, with the exception of similar but updated specifications that were discussed and planned by the Allard Company but not incorporated by the time manufacture ceased in late 1958.

Allard as a company never really died. It was dormant for a while, but today it is revived and carefully stepping into a new future producing Allard cars – at the hand of Sydney's family. The Allard brand is being carefully rebuilt and new Allards are being created from original plans.

As this Allard narrative ends, a new era begins. Influencing it all was Sydney, his personality, his deeds and his wonderful achievements. The Allard family, the Allard Owners Club, its members, and the *Allard Register* all deserve their place in the record beside the deeds of the man they salute and whose cars they revere and drive.

The man whose efforts and feats that created the Allard story felt unwell in October 1965 at the end of the Allard Drag Festival events. Diagnosed with stomach cancer in November, Sydney was gone within a few short months, dying at his home in Surrey. He left many ideas unrealized and some have been revealed earlier. From major headlines and a conspicuous PR presence, notably in America, to being largely forgotten by the public seems a tragic journey. Sydney's was a truly great story of British automotive endeavour and he left a significant legacy.

To those who know something of the history of Sydney Allard and his cars, and to many motor sport fans worldwide, he remains a hero who played a significant role in both British and early American sports car racing history. Yet beyond these arenas, Sydney and his Allard cars have sadly become somewhat lost in the archives of the automobile world.

Sydney Herbert Allard died on 12 April 1966 at just fifty-six years of age. A few hours earlier, a fire that may have been smouldering from the previous day erupted during the early hours at the Allard premises in Clapham High Street. A sharp-eyed patrolling policeman saw an orange light flickering behind a third-floor window. The fire brigade arrived promptly and halted the spread of the flames, but sadly many drawings and records were destroyed. By a coincidence or chance, the strange synergy of Sydney's death and the fire framed the end of an Allard era.

A very specific narrative of a very special character in British motor sport closed with the death of its creator. Sydney Allard and his cars must rank among the most interesting chapters in motor sport. If ever there was a motor racing

Allard family members at the Open Day; from left, Lloyd, Lynda, Jenny and Alan; behind them Darell and Gavin.

classic amid the story of iconic cars, Allard – as a man and a marque – must surely qualify as one of the defining chapters.

We might wonder what more Sydney might have achieved if his life had lasted another twenty-five years. An Allard car revival is currently underway. So as Sydney's story ends, a new era begins.

Sydney H. Allard

REFERENCES

1 Allard Owners Club (AOC) *Newsletter*, no. 6 (2017).
2 Hogg, T., *Road and Track* (May 1980).
3 Lush, T., *Allard: The Inside Story*, p. 32.
4 Statement to Marshall Thursby-Pelham, *Auto* (June 1952).
5 Allard, S.H., Allard family archives.
6 Biggs, H.L., 'Detroit Magic', *Motor Sport* (April 1944).
7 Pring, C., 'Wanderings', AOC *Newsletter* (January–February 2015), pp. 23–7.
8 Knapman, M. and D. Hooper, AOC *Newsletter* (February 2005).
9 Hume, D., personal communications to Allard family, and *The Tailwagger*, no. 9 (July 2010) and 4 May 2016.
10 AOC *Newsletter* (March 2008), pp. 4–5.
11 Lush, *Allard: The Inside Story*, p. 86.
12 Potter, L., personal communications to Lance Cole.
13 Hume to AOC.
14 Hume to AOC.
15 Hume, D., AOC *Newsletter* (September 2004), pp. 6–7.
16 Lush, *Allard: The Inside Story*.
17 *Allard Register Bulletin* (September 1973).
18 *Allard Register Bulletin* (Winter 2013).
19 Dron, P., *Thoroughbred & Classic Cars* (March 1983).
20 AOC, *The Tailwagger* (May 2016).
21 AOC, *The Tailwagger*, no. 46 (September 2013) and Wilkins family.
22 Hooper, D., communications to AOC, cited by G. Hacker, *Forgotten Fiberglass*, www.forgottenfiberglass.com.
23 Hooper, D., AOC *Newsletter* (November 2003), pp. 6–7.

BIBLIOGRAPHY

Kinsella, D., *Allard* (Haynes Publishing Group, 1977)
Lush, T., *Allard: The Inside Story* (Motor Racing Publications, 1977)
May, C.A.N., *More Wheelspin* (G.T. Foulis, 1948)
Pollack, B., *Red Wheels and White Sidewalls: Confessions of an Allard Racer* (Brown Fox Books, 2004)

Allard Owners Club, *Newsletter/The Tailwagger*: archive, publications, and members' communications
Allard Register: archive, Bulletin, volumes and members' communications

Allard, Darell, AOC published communications
Allard, Gavin, AOC archivist and communications
Allard, Lloyd, communications

Allard, Sydney, archives, personal notes, diaries, archives and family communications
Hooper, David, communications and AOC output
Hume, Dudley, communications with Alan Allard and AOC output
Kinsella, David, communications with Alan Allard and AOC output
Knapman, Mike, AOC and personal communications
Loveys, David, AOC and personal communications
Picariello, Andy, AOC output and personal communications
Pring, Chris, AOC output and personal communications
Shenstone, Blair, personal communications
Smith, James, AOC output and personal communications
Warnes, Colin, *Allard Register* and personal communications

Twelve pre-war Allard Specials were built between 1936 and 1946 at Adlards Motors, in Keswick Road, Putney, south west London (before the Allard Motor Company existed). The last car, LMG 192, was completed in 1946, when hostilities ceased.

The Specials were road-going vehicles, all but three having relatively light-weight bodies and specifically designed for off-road trialling, in which they proved highly successful.

Reg.	Date	Type	Original	Information	Owner 2019
CLK5	1936	V8/2-seat	S.H. Allard	Sold 1957	Disappeared 1960
AUK59	1937	V8/4-seat	D. Gilson	Found 2017	Marc Mears, UK
ELL300	1937	V8/4-seat	S.H. Allard	J. Guest, 1938	Disappeared 1951
ELX50	1937	V12/4-seat	K. Hutchison	–	Scrapped 1950
EXH455	1938	V8/4-seat	Mr. Allard (Snr)	Restored 1992	Tony Piper, UK
EYO750	1938	V8/4-seat	Unknown	–	Josh Sadler, UK
FGF290	1938	V12/2-seat	K. Hutchison	Restored & re-registered	Nicolas Joeron, Switzerland
FGP750	1938	V8/2-seat	S.H. Allard	K. Hutchison, 1942	Des Sowerby, UK
FLX650	1939	V12/3-seat	D. Silcock	Alpine Rally	Destroyed 1950
FXP469	1939	V8/2-seat	Unknown	Rebuilt 1972	Peter Bland, USA
FXP470	1939	V8/4-seat	V.S.A. Biggs	–	Disappeared 1946
LMG192	1946	V8/4-seat	M. Wick	–	Disappeared 1965

ALLARD J1 (COMPETITION) RACING CAR SPECIALS 1946–1948

The J1 model was, in effect, a dual-purpose vehicle, as it could relatively easily be converted into a mug-plugging trials car, with the removal of the front wings and windscreen.

Fourteen vehicles were built and principally used for trials, hill climbs and sprints with considerable success. They were powered by a Ford 3.9 or 4.3 V8 (side valve).

Chassis number	Reg number	Original owner	Owner 2019
103	HLB430	S.H. Allard	Unknown
106	HLP5	G. Imhof	Robert Robinson-Collins
109	JHW100	K. Burgess	Unknown
110	HXC578	J. Appleton	Peter Briggs (Australia)
111	GOM2	G. Marshall	Unknown
112	KPB242	K. McAlpine	Unknown
114	HLF601	S.H. Allard	Unknown
117	HYW331	M. Wick	Unknown
148	JYH613	J. Appleton	Unknown
152	MPO640	L. Potter	Unknown
273	–	L. Potter	Unknown
274	–	L. Potter	Unknown
275	–	L. Potter	James Smith
415	NPG250	R. Frost	Paul Harvey

Len Potter in the J1 Allard.

ALLARD JR SPORTS RACING CAR CHASSIS NUMBERS 3401–3408

The cars were built by the Allard team at Encon Motors, a subsidiary business of the Allard Motor Company. Seven cars were produced between 1953 and 1955. The first car was supplied less engine and transmission, and car number 5 was fitted with an Armstrong Siddeley Sapphire engine. The other five cars originally had Cadillac 331cu in V8 engines with a LaSalle three-speed gearbox.

All seven had aluminium bodies with divided front axle, de-Dion arrangement at the rear with quick ratio change differential assembly, Al-Fin drum brakes all round and Marles steering box – only one car was built with left-hand drive. *(information correct at time of writing in 2019)*

Chassis Number JR-3401
30 March 1953 – purchased by A.E. Goldschmidt, 102 Maiden Lane, New York 38 USA.
Red body, red leather upholstery, supplied less-engine, wire wheels, Oldsmobile g/box.
1976 – purchased by Peter Bland, Londonderry, USA for restoration.
In 2017 believed to be with Peter Bland in unrestored condition.

Chassis Number JR-3402
Colonel Dave Schilling, USAF, 25 July 1953 Turner AFB, Turner, Georgia, USA (ordered by General LeMay)
Blue body, blue leather, Cadillac 331 V8, engine no. 25-316

Driven by Sydney Allard and Fotheringham Parker in 1953 Le Mans 24 Hour Race. Exported to the USA after race. Involved in fatal crash on public road in the UK after being brought back to the UK. The remains were purchased by Paul Emery, who rebuilt it using a new Allard JR chassis. He modified the chassis and installed a Jaguar 3.4 engine in place of the Cadillac. The car was fitted with a glass fibre body. In 1976 the car was found in Brussels by Dr Pierre Haveland. After a repair and racing for one season it was sold to a UK dealer in 1977.

In 1984 it was purchased by Cyril Wick on behalf of Allard owner Don Marsh, in Ohio, USA. He gave Dudley Hume the job of restoring the car to its original specification. The car was rebuilt with new aluminium body and a Cadillac 331cu in V8 installed when the car went back to the USA. In 2016 has a new owner and is being cared for by Vintage Racing Motors in Redmond, WA, USA.

Chassis number JR-3403
Colonel Reade-Tilley, USAF, 4 July 1953, Headquarters, Strategic Air Command, Offutt AFB, Omaha, Nebraska, USA.
AF Blue body, blue leather, wire wheels, Cadillac 331 V8. Engine No. 25-433

Raced by Zora Duntov and Ray Merick in 1953 Le Mans 24 Hour race. Held in General Griswold collection, then imported to the UK and passed through various dealers. Purchased by Syd Silverman in 1982 and exported to the USA. Purchased by Hans Hubner (Germany) in 2013. Competed in the 2015 Classic Le Mans race, which it completed. From 2016 in the UK for major rebuild to make the vehicle FIA HTP compliant. At Valley Motors, Wrexham, UK.

Chassis Number: JR-3404 (R.H.D.)
General Curtis LeMay USAF Commander Strategic Air Command, Offutt AFB, Omaha, Nebraska, USA.
Blue body, blue leather, wire wheels, Cadillac 331 V8, engine no. 25439

Exported to the USA. Raced by Roy Scott as driver for General Curtis LeMay. Found by Dean Butler in the USA, purchased by him in 1988. Various modifications carried out, including race prepared 390cu in Cadillac V8 and rack and pinion steering. Imported into the UK 2006 and raced for several seasons. In 2011 the car was purchased by Julian Mazjub. In 2017 the car is in the UK undergoing an extensive build, back to its original FIA-approved specification.

Chassis Number 3405
Purchased by Tommy Sopwith (Armstrong Siddeley Company) in 1954 as a rolling chassis only. Sopwith then supplied the Allard Company with an Armstrong Siddeley 'Sapphire' engine, which Allard fitted. The car was subsequently named the 'Sphinx', registered OLT 101 and raced by Sopwith with a new Sopwith-designed body. Sold to Brian Croot, who raced the car for several years. The car is believed to have gone to an owner in France. Then exported to the USA. It appeared at the Dragone Auctions in the UK in 2016 and was purchased by a new owner in the UK. In 2017 the car is in the UK at Brazenly Engineering in the Midlands for restoration. (We noted in 2017 that this car does not have the Hume-designed JR chassis, but a J3 chassis, which was drawn more along the lines of a Palm Beach chassis.)

Chassis Number JR-3406 (left-hand drive)
Norman Moffat, Canada, 3 March 1956

Built as a touring car with full width screen and tonneau cover. This was the only JR built as a left-hand-drive car. Exported to Canada. Some twenty-five years later, was found in poor condition. Stripped and rebuilt in Vermont USA by Mr Du Breil, then sold in 1987. In 2015 the new owner was James Taylor of Taylor Made Products and was in his car collection in the USA. Believed to have been purchased in 2016 by Bruce Macaw, Washington, USA and is now in his large car collection, which includes several other Allard cars.

Chassis Number 3407 – 17 September 1955

Built for Rupert de Larrinaga to replace his J2X. Appeared on the Allard Motorshow stand in 1955 as a new car, after being driven at Brighton Speed Trials and Hillclimb events, the drives being shared by Sydney Allard and de Larrinaga. Registration OVT 983. At this time the car was fitted with lightweight Borani wheels and the Cadillac engine with four twin-choke downdraught Solex carburettors. Purchased by James St Clair, 8522 Tronville Ave, Playa Del Ray, Los Angeles, California, USA. Purchased by Mr Emmons in the USA from the estate of the deceased St Clair. 1987 imported into the UK by Mr Brian Sharpe. Colour green. Returned to

the USA, when Mr Sharpe sold his collection of Allard cars. Purchased at auction in 2016 by Mr Vijay Mallya in the USA. Imported back to the UK 2016. Sent to Allard Sports Cars in 2017 for a full restoration and build, to correct specification for FIA approval.

JR: 3408

The first authentic Allard built since the factory closed in 1958, JR 3408 was built at Allard Sports Cars by Lloyd and Alan Allard and their team, with the support of David Hooper and Dudley Hume – the original engineer and designer of the JR. The car is built to the specification of JR 3407, the JR raced by Sydney Allard in the 1953 Le Mans 24-hour race, with an FIA-approved Cadillac 331cu in V8 and Lesalle transmission. It has been used as a promotional tool for the launch of the revival of Allard as a specialist car manufacturer, prior to sale.

Rupert de Larrinaga at Presceott in 1955 in JR chassis number 3407.

These were the last limited 'production' run of Allard cars produced by the Allard Motor Company between 1956 and 1958. Detailed information was not kept, owing to the running down of the company and the limited manufacturing space remaining due to the expansion of the associated Adlards Motors Ford Dealership. Manufacture was a difficult and drawn-out process.

All except the prototype cars had hand-formed aluminium bodies and the Allard-designed front suspension arrangement with laminated torsion spring and MacPherson-style pillar (except for 72/7000Z).

Chassis 72/7000Z

This car was the prototype and built for display on the Allard Stand at the 1956 London Motor Show. Painted red and powered by a 6-cylinder Ford Zodiac fitted with triple SU carburettors, this prototype, unlike all the following Palm Beach Mk 2s, still retained the divided front axle. The car was used for publicity photos/events and run by Brian Howard, Manager at Allard's sun-roof fitting works.

In 1960 it was sold to a Mr Hemsworth in Hertfordshire, UK. His son, David Hemsworth, acquired the car in 1982. In 2012 it was sold to Alan Allard, in very poor condition, not having run for many years. Alan and Lloyd Allard restored it and sold it in 2015 to Barry Adams in Worcester, UK.

Chassis 72/7101 XK

This car was also on the 1956 Motor Show stand as a rolling chassis. It had a new, Allard-developed front suspension, using the MacPherson strut principle, but with laminated torsion springs at the front; the engine and gearbox came from a Jaguar XK140.

This car, in 2018, is in Germany, owned by Mr J. Rester.

Chassis 72/7102 XK

The red car was the first Palm Beach GT Coupé, with a Jaguar XK140 212bhp engine and Moss 4-speed transmission with overdrive. It was converted to front-wheel disc brakes and de Dion rear axle layout.

This was Sydney Allard's car (registered UXB 793) until his death in 1966. It was passed to Alan Allard. The car was acquired by Brian Golder in 1983 and then passed to his family after his death, being stored until 2006 in a museum in Hertfordshire. It was then purchased by John Peskett, long-standing AOC member and Allard specialist. Following this it was sold to John Patterson in 2009 and exported to Cincinnati; since his death it is believed to have passed to his family.

Chassis 72/7103 XK

This car, a light blue right-hand drive model, was on the London Motor Show stand in 1956. It had a Jaguar XK140 engine and transmission, Salsbury live axle and drum brakes all round.

It was shipped to a customer in Houston, Texas in August 1958, and purchased by Robert Forsythe – the sales manager for Allard in the USA. Until 1954. Forsythe's design for the body was adopted by Allard for the Palm Beach Mk 2.

This car was purchased by Dean Butler in 2009, from the widow of Mr Forsythe and a process of restoration was started.

Chassis 72/7104 Z

The chassis number denotes that this car was fitted with a Ford Zephyr 6-cylinder engine and shipped to the USA in 1957. It is currently owned by Ron Sears, Marston Mills, MA, USA.

Chassis 72/7105 V8

The second GT Coupe, built for the Dupont family, was shipped to the USA in 1958. This grey left-hand-drive car was fitted with 5.4-litre Chrysler V8, coupled to a Torque-flite auto transmission, front-wheel disc brakes and de Dion axle at rear.

This car was owned and raced by Bob Girvin for many years. Modifications included fitting a 450bhp Chrysler V8 with manual transmission and suspension changes front and rear, together with roll cage and other racing equipment. It was sold to Hans-Jorg Hubner, based in Dortmund, Germany in 2015 and in 2017 was painted red.

Chassis 72/7106 XK

Pained black and fitted with a Jaguar XK 140 engine, this car was owned by Ray May, Secretary of the Allard Owners Club for many years before being sold to a new owner in the USA in 1969. It was owned by Richard M. Stilwell in German Town, MD, USA, until sold to Mark Moskowitz, of Gastonia, NC in 2019.

Chassis 72/7107

Painted white, this left-hand drive car had a Jaguar engine and front disc brakes. It won concours d'elegance at Brighton in 1959, before being shipped to the USA.

It has been owned for many years up to the present day by Robert Hartson in Stratham, New Hampshire.

APPENDIX V | ALLARD CAR PRODUCTION

According to the information currently available, a total of 1,901 Allard cars was manufactured between 1946 and 1958. In addition there were eleven Allard Specials built between 1935 and 1939, plus one post 1939, and another ten or so competition cars and dragsters up to 1965.

NOTES:
A number of J2, J2X and J2X Le Mans cars have been built by individuals. These cars are mostly based on a modified 'P'

Type Allard saloon chassis, using the original Allard saloon chassis numbers and VIN plate. The Allard Company can potentially authenticate these cars as authentic Allards, even though they may not have been built by the Allard Company.

Other cars with body profile of an Allard 'J' Type, but not with an Allard design of chassis, built by or for individuals over the years, even though they may be carrying the Allard badge, are not Allard cars and will not be recognized as such by the Allard Company or Allard family.

ALLARD CARS MANUFACTURED 1946–1958

Year	Model	Type	Body	Engine	Number produced	Number remaining
1946–47	J1	Competition	2 door 100in w/b	Ford V8 s/v	12	4
1946–48	K1	Touring	2 door 106in w/b	Ford V8 s/v	151	44
1946–48	L	Touring	4 door 112in w/b	Ford V8 s/v	191	35
1947–50	M	Drophead	2 door 112in w/b	Ford V8 s/v	500	51
1949–51	P	Saloon	2 door 112in w/b	Ford V8 s/v	559	45
1950–51	J2	Competition	2 door 100in w/b	Various V8	90	74
1950–51	K2	Touring	2 door 106in w/b	Ford V8 s/v	119	70
1951–53	J2X	Competition	2 door 100in w/b	Cadillac V8/various V8	71	57
1952–53	J2X(LM)	Competition	2 door 100in w/b	Cadillac V8	12	11
1951–53	M2X	Drophead	2 door 112in w/b	Ford V8 s/v	25	4
1952–53	K3	Touring w/b	2 door 100in w/b	Ford V8/Cadillac V8	62	36
1952–54	P2(M)	Saloon	2 door 112in w/b	Various V8	11	6
1952–54	P2 (S)	Estate	2 door 112in w/b	Various V8	10	4
1952–54	PB1(21c)	Touring	2 door 96in w/b	Ford 4 cyl.	8	2
1952–54	PB1(21Z)	Touring	2 door 96in w/b	Ford 6 cyl.	65	27
1953–55	JR	Competition	2 door 96in w/b	Cadillac V8	7	7
1956–58	PB2(72)	Touring	2 door 100in w/b	Ford 6 cyl./Jag 6 cyl.	6	6
1956–58	PB2 (GT)	Touring	2 door 100in w/b	Jag 6 cyl./Chrysler V8	2	2
	Totals:				**1901**	**485**

Additional cars – 12 Specials and 10 one-off cars.

Total Allard cars known extant: 498

INDEX

Allard Owners Club (AOC)   191, 194
  committee and newsletter   194–198
  Continental Group   208
  Continental' trips   197
  conversations   214
  events for   197
  Hulse, Pat   195, 201
  May, Ray   194–195
  officers   202
  pilots and their cars   203–208
  Tiller, Jim   198–201
  Tiller, Sheila   198–201
  'Trois Vallées,'   197
Adams, Wayne   182
Alan Moss, E.   166–168
Alfa Romeo   13
Allard   10
  in America   11, 12, 162–163
    Alan Moss, E.   166–168
    Allard Register   183–184
    American years   177–179, 181–183,
    185–187
    annual 'Gatherings'   187–189
    Association   170–171
    Burrell, Frank   170–171
    Davis, H.J.A.   163–166
    Duntov and engine design   172–173
    '8-Ball' – Wacker's enigma
    179–181
    Forsyth, Allard-Frazer and Allard
    Dodge   173–177
    General and Colonels Club   168–169
    Lytle, Bob   184–185
    Patterson, Alan   185
    Pollack, Bill   185
    racing in new millennium   189–192
    Shelby, Carroll   173
    Silverman, Syd   184
  in Australasia   210–213
  car production   236
  dragster World Record   15–16 October
  1966   157–159
  fans   17
  and GM   59
  intercontinental   208–210
  and its origins   13
  in Monte Carlo Rally. See Monte Carlo
  Rally, Allard entries in
  in motor sport. See motor sport, Allard
  in

name and its recognition   15
prices of models   15
question about   13, 15
reputation   16
sales of models   15
sales success in America   164
success   11
true Specials   40–43
wartime vehicle (1939)   46
Allard, Alan   15, 18, 99, 101, 151, 152, 195,
227
Allard ambulance conversion (1957–60)
218–219
Allard Atom (1955)   218
'Allard Blue'   212
Allard car copies   226–227
  J2 or J2X   227
Allard Chrysler dragster   154, 156, 157
Allard Chrysler Mk 1   147
Allard Clipper (1954)   216–218
Allard & Co   22
Allard Dodge   99, 173–177
Allard Dragon   154, 155
Allardette Anglias   220–221
Allard-Frazer   173–177
Allard-Frazer-Anchorage Plastics
  project   175
Allard Gatherings   187–191
Allard group 'C' sports racing car (J92)
224–225
Allard GT   53
Allard J1   68–70
  racing car specials 1946–1948   232
  technical specification   70
Allard J2   88–91, 162
Allard J3   228
Allard JR   94–97
  chassis numbers 3401–3408   233–235
  technical specification   96
Allard J2X   10, 91–92, 162, 186
  technical specification   92
Allard J2X Le Mans   92–94
Allard K1   70–73
  technical specification   71
Allard K2   85–86
  1950–51   71
Allard K3   55, 86–88
  technical specification   87
Allard, Lloyd   15, 18, 97, 99, 101, 197, 222,
227

Allard L Type   73–76
  technical specification   75
Allard marque   13, 184, 185
  revival of   227–229
Allard Motor Company   13, 16, 17, 21, 22,
44
  of America   175
  1946–66   making the cars   48–51
    coachbuild consultants   62
    design question   60–62
    engine and gearbox
    problems   63–64
    famous endorsements   57–58
    into the fifties   58–59
    further thoughts   1954–9, 64–66
    and GM   59
    GT   59–60
    J2X factor   54–57
    start up   51–52
    Tom Cole steps in   52–54
  1967–2008   222
Allard M Type   77–79
Allard M2X   81–82
'Allard Owners Gymkhana' events   196
Allard Palm Beach Mk 3   228
Allard P2 Monte Carlo   58, 83–85
Allard P1 (RF 620) of Clas Palmberg   209
Allard P2 saloon, technical specification   83
Allard P Type saloon   79–81
  technical specification   81
Allard racing car   117–118
Allard Register   17, 183–184, 191, 195, 229
  Perspective of Warnes, Colin   164
Allard Safari   82–83
  technical specification   83
'Allards Gap'   23, 113
'Allard Specials'   13, 22, 31–32, 44
  CLK 5   34–35
  1950s   102
    Essex Aero Allard   105
    Fairley   106
    Farrallac   104–105
    Hinton   94, 105–106
    Lotest   106
    LXN 5   103
    Sphinx   103–104
  1936–9   44–45
  1936–1946   231
'Allard Special V12'   40, 44, 45
Allard Steyr Sports Car   118–120

Allard, Sydney Herbert   10–11, 13, 15–18
  achievements   11–13
  Ben Nevis attempt   41
  early days   20–22
  eighteen days, winter 1936   38–40
  ethos   23
  first thoughts, 1910–30   23–25
  fourwheel-drive car and 1939   45–46
  scrapbook   30–31
Allard V8 Specials   45
aluminium grilles   65
America
Allard in. See Allard, in America
American Drag Racing Team   154
American dragsters   151
Anglia 105E   220
annual 'Gatherings'   187–189
AOC. See Aallard Owners Club
Arkus-Duntov, Zora   134, 136, 137, 138,
  171, 173
  and engine design   172–173
Armstrong, J.C.   178–179
Ascari, Alberto   138
Auger, Gerry   205
AUK 59   40–41
'Aussie Allard'   212
Austin Healey 100   54, 55, 57
Australasia, Allard in   210–213
Automobile Quarterly   185
Baker, Keith   106, 205
Baker, Tim   203
Ballamy, Leslie Mark   37, 38
Bauder, Bill   186
BDRA. See British Drag Racing Association
Belton, Gerry   151, 154, 222
Bennett, Jeremy   205, 206
Bennett, Neil 'Biggles'   214
Besinger, Jerry   181
Betati, Massimo   210
BHRA. See British Hot Rod Association
Bianchi, Tony   207
'Bill' Dyer, W.   173, 174, 175
'The Bitch'   186
Blackbushe Drag Festival   116
BMW   60
Boddy, Bill   20, 22, 40, 51, 68, 113, 206
'Bridgehampton'   98
Brighton & Hove Motor Club   140
Brighton Speed Trials   117, 140–141, 146,
  148, 150, 198, 199, 207, 234

British Drag Racing Association
  (BDRA)   154
British Hot Rod Association (BHRA)   154
British International Drag Festival   156
Brooks, Les   206
Bugatti 'bits'   30, 35–36
Bugatti, Jean   36
Bugatti Type 35   36
Bugatti Type 43   35, 36
Bugatti Type 51   35, 36
Bugatti Type 59   36
Burrell, Frank   170–171
Cad Allards   90
Cadillac engine   53, 170, 213
Cadillac's ohv V8   170
Cameron, Allan   196
Canham, Reg   23, 38, 44, 45, 48, 49, 50, 66,
  88, 97, 162–163
Carstens, Tom   178
CERV 1. See Chevrolet Engineering
  Research Vehicle
chassis number 3405   233
chassis number 7102   59
chassis number JR-3401   233
chassis number JR-3402   233
chassis number JR-3403   233
chassis number: JR-3404 (R.H.D.)   233
chassis number JR-3406 (left-hand
  drive)   233–234
chassis number 3407 – 17 September
  1955   234
chassis number 72/7107   235
chassis number 72/7105 V8   235
chassis number 72/7101 XK   235
chassis number 72/7102 XK   235
chassis number 72/7103 XK   235
chassis number 72/7106 XK   235
chassis number 72/7000Z   235
chassis number 72/7104Z   235
Chevrolet   172, 173
Chevrolet Engineering Research Vehicle
  (CERV 1)   172–173
Chris Shorrock   221
Chrysler Firepower V8   60, 135
Chrysler 'Hemi' V8   159
Classic and Sports Car magazine awards   197
classic annual Brighton speed trials
  140–141
'Clerk' car   119
Clerk Project   117–118

Clerk, Robert   65, 114
Clerk-type electromagnetic gearbox   63
CLK 5   30, 33–36, 38–40, 57
coachbuild consultants   62
Cobra-engined J2   91
Cole, Tom   52–54, 89, 90, 129–133, 178
Colonels Club   169
Cooper Cars   65
Corvette C1   172
Craigantlet Hill Climb   114–115
Cunningham, Briggs   96, 135, 138, 162,
  172
Cunningham team   129, 133
Cunnings, A.G.   175
Curtis, Frank   134
CZ 5955   33
CZ 5969   33, 34
CZ 6054   33
Daimler SP250   58
Dannenmaier, Bernd   209
Davis, H.J.A.   163–166, 175
Day, Robin   61
de Dion rear axle   88–90
de Larrinaga, Rupert   56, 97, 165, 234
design question   60–62
Dolphin, John   64
Don Farrell   104–105
Donick, Jim   190
Dragfests   154–157
Dragon   151
  driving the   151–154
Dragon Mk II   152
dragster restoration   159–160
Duce, Dante   150
Duntov Mechanical Corporation   172
Dupont, Alexis   179
'8-Ball' – Wacker's Enigma   179–181
ELL 300   41–42
Ellis, Mary   206
ELX 50   41
Emmons, Duncan   182
empty roads   26–27
engine and gearbox problems   63–64
Essex Aero Allard   105
Evans, D.   36
EXH 455   41
EYO 750   42
Fairley   106
Fairman, Jack   134
Farrallac   104–105

Fastest Time of the Day (FTD)   89, 109, 113, 114, 115, 141

Ferrari   13

Ferrari team   133

FGF 290   42

FGP 750   33, 42–44

Firth, John William ('Bill')   212–213

Fisk, Tom   143, 212, 220

Fitch, John   181

FLX 650   43, 44, 45, 61

Ford Ardun V8   142

Ford developments   32–34

Ford gearbox problems   63

Ford-Lincoln V12   40

Ford Model 48 V8   34

Ford Motor Company   66

Ford TT (CZ 5969)   33, 34

Ford V8   33, 34, 40, 69, 79, 106
    engines   27, 31, 34, 41, 46, 52, 53

Forsyth, Richard   98, 99

Forsyth, Robert W.   98, 99, 173–177

Fotheringham-Parker, Philip   136

Frazer, Joseph   173, 174, 175, 177

Frazer Nash   25–26, 40

Freikaiserwagen   31

'Frost' Allard   206

FTD. See Fastest Time of the Day

FXP 469   43

FXP 470   37, 39, 43

'Gathering of the Clan'   189, 199

General Motors (GM)   58, 59, 172, 173

Glass Plastics International   175

GM. See General Motors

Goldschmidt, Erwin   135

Goodwood Festival of Speed   117

Greene, Ronnie   218

Griswold, Francis   96, 135, 137

GT   59–60

Haase, Harold   182

Hans-Albert Oppenborn   208

Hans-Jörg Hübner   208

Hayes, Roger   205, 206

Hayes, Sylvia   205, 206

Herman, Mel   203

Hersham and Walton Motors (HWM)   65

Hill Climb Championship of 1949   116–117

Hinton   94, 105–106

Hobbs, Howard   63

'Hogan heads'   106

Hooper, David   11, 61, 62, 63, 64, 65, 66, 104, 113, 214

Horan, Kerry   117

Hulse, Pat   195, 201

Hume, Dudley   55, 61, 62, 63, 94
    J2 development process   91
    JR's development   94–95
    on working for Sydney Allard   101–102

Hume, John   147, 157

HWM. See Hersham and Walton Motors

IAAM. See International Association of Automotive Modelers

Imhof, Godfrey   49, 51, 61, 69, 88
    LXN 5   103

Ingram, Jimmy   83–84

intercontinental Allards   208–210

International Association of Automotive Modelers (IAAM)   185

J2 (088)   213

Jaguar team   133

Jaguar XK140   54
    engine   235

Jaguar XK150   58

J2 Cad Allards   90, 228

J2 copies   227

Jensen, Richard   33

Jepson, Gil   102

Johnson, Michael   206

JR   55, 56, 59

J2R   55

JR: 3408   234

J2 sports cars   52

JT 7618   213

J2X   54–57, 59

J2X 'Caddy' Allards   228

J2X copies   227

J2X Le Mans   55

K3 'Beowulf,' chassis number 3166 (1953)   187

Kinsella, David   207

KLD 5   69

Klink, Doug   187, 191

Knapman, Mike   195

Knight, Greg   205

Knight, Stan   205

LCC. See Light Car Club

Le Mans race
    1950   128–132
    1951   132–133

1952   133–135

1953   135–138

LeMay, Curtis   135, 137, 168, 169, 170

Liège–Sofia–Liège
    1963   143–144
    1964   144

Light Car Club (LCC)   39, 40

Lime Rock Park Dodge Vintage Festival, September 1999   189

LMG   192, 43

Loeffler, Emile   182

London County Council (LCC)   218–219

Lotest   106

Loveys, Dave   198, 201, 203

Lowth, Chris   212, 213

L Type JGX 651   58

Lush, Tom   110, 112, 113, 114, 121, 122, 136, 141, 144–145

LXN 5   103

Lyons, Chris   206–207

Lytle, Bob   183, 184–185

MacDonald, Ian   211, 212

Mac, Jim   110, 113

Mackie, Rob   143

Manta Jaguar   66

Maryhill hill climb   187

May, C.A.N.   181

May, Ray   194–195

McGlone, Tom   157

McGregor, Jack   187–188

Mercedes   134, 135

Mercedes-Benz SSK   39

MG   54

Mk II Ford Zephyr   126

Monaco Grand Prix (1952)   210

Monte Carlo Rally   10, 13, 23, 26, 57, 139
    Allard entries in   120
    1949   120–121
    1950   121–122
    1951   122
    1952   122–124
    1953   124
    1954   124
    1955   124–125
    1956   125
    1957   125
    1958   125–126
    1959   126
    1960   126

1961   126
1962 and 1963   126–127
1964 and 1965   127–128
Moon, Dean   150, 151
Moore, Ronnie   218
Morgan   21, 22, 25, 31
Moss, Stirling   11
motor sport, Allard in   108–109
Allard racing car   117–118
Allard Steyr sports car   118–119
classic annual Brighton speed
trials   140–141
Clerk Project   117–118
Le Mans   1950–53, 128–138
Liège–Sofia–Liège 1963 & 1964
143–144
Lush, Tom   144–145
Monte Carlo Rally   120–128
1951 Mille Miglia   142–143
1951 tour of Sicily   142
RAC Rally   139
Silverstone circuit   139
Steyr Allard   109–117
34th tour of Sicily   141–142
twin-engined sprint car   119–120
twin engined Steyr   19
Murray-Evans, Roger   205
Murray, 'Gelignite' Jack   212
MWE 254   91
Neely, Ray   211
Negley, John Jr.   182
Nellemann, Robert   89, 91
1951 Mille Miglia   142–143
1951 tour of Sicily   142
'Old Fella'   194, 198–201, 201
OXE 475   84
Palm Beach CH7633   213
Palm Beach GT   59–60
Palm Beach Mk I   55, 56, 57, 97–99, 173,
174, 175
technical specification   98
Palm Beach Mk II   56, 57, 58, 99–101, 226
chassis numbers   235
7106 and 7107   60
technical specification   100
Patterson, Alan   185
Peacock, Gary   187

Peskett, John   204–205, 226
Picariello, Andy   195, 200, 201
Pitney, John   218
P2 Monte Carlo Saloon   55, 195
Pollack, Bill   183, 185
Potter, Len   70, 181
Prescott hill climb   108, 109, 113, 114
Pring, Chris   205
P2 saloon   55, 56, 83
PI Type saloon   51–52, 54, 81, 84
Putnam, George   181–182
RAC Rally   139
radio telephone (RT) system   136–138
Ranalah   44, 49, 62
'Red Ram' V8 Palm Beach   55, 59
Reid Tweedie, David   207
reincarnation   116–117
Reynolds, Al   182
Richards, Larry   54, 98, 175
Richter, Roy   181
Rileys   60
Robinson-Collins, Robert   204
Route, Hubert   178
RT system. See radio telephone system
Rubery Owen Company   221
'Rudyard Quisling'   179
Rutherford, Stu   181
Sadler, Josh   195, 201
Safari Estate   55, 56
Sammell, Jane   206
Sammell, Sam   206
Schoonmaker, Paul   187
Sewell, Brian   62
Sheila, Jim   198–201
Shelby, Carroll   162, 173, 228
Shorrock superchargers   221–222
Silcock, Derek   44
Silverman, Syd   184, 187, 188
Silverstone circuit,   139
Skatula, Fritz   175
Smith, George   213
Smith, Ian   152
Smith, James   197, 203
Society of Motor Manufacturers and
Traders (SMMT)   74
Sopwith, Tommy   103–104
specials survivors   43

Sphinx   103–104
Steyr Allard   109–111
reincarnation   116–117
running the   112–116
Steyr engine   111–112
Steyr-Daimler engines   111
Sunroof conversions   219–220
Sutton, Julian   207
The Tailwagger   195
Talbot (BGT 407)   34
Taylor, Brian   160
Taylor, Simon   10, 11
Taylor, Steve   206
34th tour of Sicily   141–142
Thompson, Mickey   150, 151
Thurston, Jerry   207
Tiller, Jim   195, 196, 197, 198–201
Tiller, Sheila   198–201
Tilley, Reade   169
Triumph TR2   54, 55, 57
'Trois Vallées'   197
true Specials   40–43
Turner, Tom   184
twin engined sprint car   119–120
twin engined Steyr   119
Ugalde, Roger   203–204
Valpey, Bob   187
V12 ELX 50   44
Venables, Ralph   206
V8 engines   27, 31, 34, 41, 46, 52, 53
Villoresi, Luigi   138
Vintage Sports-Car Club (VSCC)   39
Voll & Ruhrbeck   62
Volvo gearbox   63
V8-powered Ford model 48 coupé   38
VSCC. See Vintage Sports-Car Club
Wacker, Fred, '8-Ball'   179–181
Walford, Martin   208
Walker, Tom   208
Wandsworth Bugatti   36–38
Warner, Fred   170
Watson, David   186
Watt, James   220
Watts, Patrick   206
Whittingham & Mitchell   44, 61, 62
Williams, Rob   213
Wilson, Tim   205